Foundations
of Brazilian
Economic Growth

AEI-Hoover Research Publications

The books and monographs in this series are issued jointly by the Hoover Institution on War, Revolution and Peace and the American Enterprise Institute for Public Policy Research. They are designed to present background information, including the findings of original research, on matters of general policy concern. The views expressed in these studies are those of the authors and do not necessary reflect the views of the staff, officers, advisory panels or members of the governing boards of AEI or the Hoover Institution.

Foundations
of Brazilian
Economic Growth

DONALD E. SYVRUD

Hoover Institution Press, Stanford University, Stanford, California

American Enterprise Institute for Public Policy Research
Washington, D.C.

Distributed by Hoover Institution Press

AEI-Hoover Research Publications 1
(Hoover Institution Publications 141)
International Standard Book Number 0-8179-1411-0
Library of Congress Catalog Card Number 74-11812
© 1974 by the Board of Trustees of the
Leland Stanford Junior University

To Amelia Lee Syvrud

TABLE OF CONTENTS

FOREWORD *Howard S. Ellis* xv

ACKNOWLEDGMENTS xvii

CHAPTER I
AN OVERVIEW 1
How Long Can the Boom Be Sustained? 2
Foundations of Economic Growth—1964 to 1972 4
Economic Issues in the Brazilian Experience 8
Scope and Structure of the Book 10

CHAPTER II
IMPORT SUBSTITUTION INDUSTRIALIZATION—
1947 to 1963 12
Industrialization Ideologies 14
Industrialization Policy Instruments 15
Economic Consequences of Industrialization 15
Growth and Stagnation—1947 to 1963 16
Sectoral Income Disparities 24
Social Imbalances 26
Causes of the Economic Crisis—
       1962 to 1964 27
Summary Assessment 29

CHAPTER III
STRATEGY FOR DEVELOPMENT,
STABILIZATION, AND REFORM 32
Political Background 33
Strategic Options 36
Development Strategy—1964 to 1967 39
Stabilization Strategy—1964 to 1967 41
The Strategy of the New Economists— 1967 to 1972 44
Consequences of the Balanced Growth Strategy 46
Savings and Investment 47
Trends of Growth 49
Corrective Inflation 51
External Equilibrium 53
Trends in Income Distribution 54
Assessment of Balance Growth Strategy 55

CHAPTER IV
MONETARY AND CREDIT POLICY 59
   The Monetary Management Apparatus 60
   Monetary Trends—1953 to 1963 65
   The Role of Monetary Policy—1964 to 1967 72
   Monetary Policy Objectives—1967 to 1972 81
   Assessment of Monetary Policy 88

CHAPTER V
THE IMPACT OF INTEREST RATE POLICY
ON STAGNATION AND INFLATION 95
   Interest Rate Policies to 1964 96
   Interest Rate Trends to 1964 97
   Distortions in the Financial Structure 100
   The Monetary Correction Approach to Interest Rates
      1964 to 1967 105
   Resolution 63 Transactions 110
   The Subsidy Approach to Interest Rates—1968 to 1970 111
   Direct Intervention in Interest Rate Market 112
   Other Developments Affecting the
      Interest Rate Structure 115
   Summary of Post-1964 Interest Rate Policies 116

CHAPTER VI
FISCAL POLICY FOR GROWTH
WITH INFLATION 118
   Fiscal Policy in the Decade Prior to 1964 119
   Salient Characteristics of the Brazilian Tax Structure 123
   Fiscal Policy since 1964 128
   Role of the Public Sector in the Brazilian Economy 139
   Assessment of Fiscal Policy 143

CHAPTER VII
WAGE POLICY 146
   Wage Policy Prior to 1964 147
   Post-1964 Wage Policy 155
   Summary of Post-1964 Wage Policy 160
   Wage Policy for a Developing Nation 162

CHAPTER VIII
FOREIGN EXCHANGE AND TRADE POLICY 167
   Pre-1964 Policies—"The Disequilibrium System" 168
   Post-1964 Policies—"The Equilibrium System" 187
   Import Liberalization 199
   Assessment of Foreign Exchange and Trade Policy 213

CHAPTER IX

THE CRISIS IN AGRICULTURE 216
    Agricultural Policies to 1964 217
    Trends in Agricultural Output and Productivity—
        1947 to 1964 220
    Agricultural Exports—1947 to 1964 223
    Diagnosis of the Agricultural Crisis 223
    Assessment of Pre-1964 Agricultural Policies and
        Performance 225
    Agricultural Policies since 1964 229
    Agricultural Trends since 1964 237
    Assessment of Post-1964 Agricultural Policies and
        Performance 238

CHAPTER X

THE CONTRIBUTION OF COFFEE
TO INFLATION 240
    Coffee Policies Prior to 1961 243
    Coffee Defense Fund—1961 to 1964 245
    Consequences of Coffee Policy—1953 to 1964 247
    Coffee Policy—1964 and 1965 249
    Coffee Eradication Program—1966 to 1967 249
    Coffee Policy—1967 to 1970—and Domestic Outlook 250
    International Outlook for Coffee 254

CHAPTER XI

MOBILIZATION OF RESOURCES FOR
INVESTMENT AND GROWTH: CAPITAL
MARKET POLICIES—1964 TO 1972 256
    National Housing Program 257
    Northeast Development Program 260
    Agricultural Investments 262
    Capital Markets Development Program 264
    Program for Social Integration 265
    Domestic Savings 268
    Investment Demand 268
    Assessment of Resource Mobilization Programs 271
    Lessons in the Brazilian Experience 273

BIBLIOGRAPHY 277

INDEX 283

LIST OF TABLES

II-1   ANNUAL RATES OF GROWTH IN GNP—
         TOTAL, PER CAPITA, AND BY SECTORS,
         1948-1964 17

II-2   ANNUAL RATES OF INCREASE IN THE
         GENERAL PRICE INDEX, 1947-1964 19

II-3   REGIONAL DISTRIBUTION OF POPULATION
         AND INCOME 1950, 1960 AND 1968 24

II-4   SECTORAL DISTRIBUTION OF WORKING
         FORCE, INCOME AND INCOME PER
         WORKER, 1950, 1960 AND 1968 26

III-1   ANNUAL RATES OF GROWTH IN GNP—
         TOTAL, PER CAPITA, AND BY SECTORS,
         1964-1972 50

III-2   ANNUAL RATES OF INCREASE IN
         GENERAL PRICE INDEX, 1964-1972 51

IV-1   GROSS DOMESTIC PRODUCT, MONEY
         SUPPLY, AND INCOME VELOCITY OF
         MONEY, 1953-1963 64

IV-2   SOURCES OF MONETARY EXPANSION,
         1953-1963 66

IV-3   FEDERAL GOVERNMENT AND PRIVATE
         SECTOR CREDIT, 1953 AND 1963 67

IV-4   COMMERCIAL BANK RESERVES AND
         DEPOSITS, 1953-1972 70

IV-5   PRIVATE SECTOR CREDIT AS PERCENT
         OF MONEY SUPPLY AND GNP, 1953-1963 71

IV-6   MONETARY BUDGETS AND SOURCES OF
         MONETARY EXPANSION, 1964-1966 77

IV-7   YEARLY CHANGE IN MAJOR
         DETERMINANTS OF MONETARY
         EXPANSION, 1967-1972 84

IV-8   INCREASE IN MONEY SUPPLY AND
         GENERAL PRICE INDEX, 1964-1972 89

IV-9   PRIVATE SECTOR CREDIT, 1964-1972   93

V-1   OUTSTANDING LOAN BALANCES OF
         MAJOR FINANCIAL INSTITUTIONS TO
         THE PRIVATE SECTOR, 1956-1972´ 98

V-2   AVERAGE NOMINAL INTEREST RATES
        ON LOAN INSTRUMENTS, 1956-1972 99
V-3   AVERAGE REAL INTEREST RATES ON
        SELECTED SAVINGS AND LOAN
        INSTRUMENTS, 1956-1970 101
V-4   VOLUME OF PRINCIPAL FINANCIAL ASSETS
        HELD BY THE PUBLIC, 1956-1972 103
VI-1   FEDERAL EXPENDITURES, REVENUES,
        AND DEFICITS, 1953, 1958 AND 1963 120
VI-2   CURRENT EXPENDITURES OF THE
        FEDERAL GOVERNMENT, 1953, 1958
        AND 1963 121
VI-3   INVESTMENT BY FEDERAL GOVERNMENT,
        FEDERAL AUTARQUIA AND SOCIAL
        SECURITY, 1953, 1958 AND 1963 122
VI-4   TAX REVENUES AND EXPENDITURES IN
        FINAL GOODS AND SERVICES, BY LEVEL
        OF GOVERNMENT, 1967 123
VI-5   DIRECT AND INDIRECT TAXES, BY
        LEVEL OF GOVERNMENT, 1967 124
VI-6   PRICE INCREASES, REAL GNP GROWTH
        AND FEDERAL REVENUE AS PERCENT
        OF GNP, 1956-1967 127
VI-7   FEDERAL GOVERNMENT EXPENDITURES,
        REVENUES AND DEFICITS, 1963-1972 130
VI-8   FEDERAL GOVERNMENT EXPENDITURES
        ON PERSONNEL AND TRANSFERS TO
        TRANSPORTATION AUTARQUIA, 1963-1971 .. 132
VI-9   FINANCING THE DEFICIT, 1963-1972 135
VI-10   PARTICIPATION FUND FOR STATES AND
        MUNICIPALITIES, 1967-1972 139
VI-11   PUBLIC SECTOR SAVINGS AND
        INVESTMENTS, 1963-1969 141
VII-1   INDEX OF AVERAGE ANNUAL REAL
        MINIMUM WAGE—RIO DE JANEIRO 149
VII-2   MINIMUM WAGE AND COST OF LIVING
        CHANGES—RIO DE JANEIRO, MAY 1943-
        FEBRUARY 1964 150
VII-3   AVERAGE SIZE OF ANNUAL WAGE
        ADJUSTMENTS UNDER OFFICIAL WAGE
        FORMULA 1964-1972 157
VII-4   WAGE FORMULA ALLOWANCES, AUGUST
        1964-AUGUST 1970 158

VII-5   FRINGE BENEFITS AND PAYROLL TAXES
           REQUIRED BY LAW AS A PERCENT OF
           WAGES PER NORMAL WORK PERIOD 160
VII-6   EARNINGS OF EMPLOYEES IN
           MANUFACTURING INDUSTRIES,
           1962-1970 161
VIII-1   BRAZILIAN IMPORTS, GROSS DOMESTIC
           PRODUCT, AND IMPORT COEFFICIENT,
           1947-1964 171
VIII-2   BRAZILIAN EXPORTS AND NON-COFFEE
           EXPORTS, 1946-1964 175
VIII-3   BRAZILIAN EXPORTS AS PERCENT
           OF EXPORTS OF LATIN AMERICA,
           DEVELOPING COUNTRIES, AND TOTAL
           WORLD—1948, 1953, 1958, AND 1963 178
VIII-4   BRAZIL'S BALANCE OF PAYMENTS,
           1955-1963 181
VIII-5   BRAZIL'S DEBT SERVICE RATIO,
           1950-1964 183
VIII-6   BRAZILIAN FOREIGN DEBT
           OUTSTANDING AT YEAR-END,
           1951-1963 186
VIII-7   OUTSTANDING VALUE OF SHORT-TERM
           FOREIGN OBLIGATIONS, 1964-1972 190
VIII-8   BRAZILIAN EXCHANGE RATES,
           PERCENTAGE DEVALUATIONS AND
           GENERAL PRICE CHANGES,
           1964-AUGUST 1972 194
VIII-9   BRAZILIAN NON-COFFEE EXPORTS,
           1964-1972 198
VIII-10   BRAZIL'S BALANCE OF PAYMENTS,
           1964-1972 202
VIII-11   NET FLOW OF PRIVATE CAPITAL FOR
           INVESTMENT AND WORKING CAPITAL,
           1956-1972 204
VIII-12   NET CAPITAL FLOWS TO BRAZIL, 1964-1971 .. 207
VIII-13   MATURITY STRUCTURE OF BRAZIL'S
           FOREIGN DEBT, DECEMBER 1963 AND
           DECEMBER 1971 208
VIII-14   BRAZIL'S DEBT SERVICE RATIO,
           1963-1972 209
VIII-15   FOREIGN EXCHANGE RESERVES
           AND IMPORT REQUIREMENT 212

IX-1   GROWTH IN AGRICULTURAL OUTPUT,
            SELECTED COUNTRIES, 1950-1968 221
IX-2   CHANGE IN GRAIN OUTPUT, AREA AND
            YIELDS, SELECTED COUNTRIES, 1950-1968 . . 222
IX-3   CHANGE IN GRAIN OUTPUT AND GRAIN
            AREA PER FARM PERSON, 1950-1968 223
IX-4   EXPORTS BY VALUE: BRAZIL AND OTHER
            COUNTRY GROUPS, 1955 AND 1963 224
X-1   COFFEE PRODUCTION, EXPORTS,
            CONSUMPTION AND STOCKS, 1946-1970 242
X-2   COFFEE GUARANTY PRICES, 1946-1970   247
X-3   COFFEE EXPORTS, 1946-1970   248
X-4   NET MONETARY IMPACT OF COFFEE
            OPERATIONS, 1961-1969 252
XI-1   NATIONAL HOUSING PROGRAM,
            1965-1972 260
XI-2   NORTHEAST DEVELOPMENT PROGRAM,
            1962-1972 262
XI-3   CAPITAL MARKET DEVELOPMENT
            PROGRAM, 1965-1972 266
XI-4   PROGRAMS TO MOBILIZE FINANCIAL
            SAVINGS, 1964-1972 269
XI-5   TREND OF INVESTMENT DEMAND,
            1964-1972 270
XI-6   DOMESTIC AND FOREIGN SAVINGS
            AS PERCENTAGE OF TOTAL
            SAVINGS, 1964-1971 273

FOREWORD

The name of Brazil is currently being emblazoned in the honor role of postwar "economic miracles," along with Germany and Japan. Belonging still to the category of less developed areas, Brazil has farther to go than these two highly industrialized countries. But if its present accomplishments afford legitimate grounds for satisfaction, the very fact of its underdevelopment opens up roseate vistas for the future of this immense country. Perhaps Brazil is succeeding to the enviable position, long enjoyed by the United States, as the "country of unlimited possibilities."

The turnabout in less than a decade from a land beset by threats of revolution, anarchy, and general civic and economic decline is indeed a miracle. But, in general, the breed of economist is inimical to the idea of miracles. The recent phenomenal progress of Brazil has occasioned a number of useful attempts to give rational explanations of what happened. To this body of analysis, the present book makes a substantial contribution for several distinctive reasons.

In the first place, the author, as the United States Treasury attaché in Rio de Janeiro from 1965 to 1969, lived through the critical years of this transformation, experiencing intimate views of the action at its very center. Almost daily contacts with the protagonists gave him a substantial advantage seldom, if ever, available to scholarly researchers, whether foreign or domestic. Furthermore, since Brazil was currently benefiting extensively from United States aid, nearly all relevant economic data passed regularly over Dr. Syvrud's desk. His participation in advising or making decisions adds to the weight of his judgments, which, however, he has not been precluded from voicing.

Perhaps equally important with these background elements is the fact that the present volume does not represent any strongly doctrinaire position in economic theory or policy, and discernible political bias, let alone any suspicion of personal axe-grinding. Thus the reader benefits from analysis which is not only well-informed, but as objective as is attainable in human affairs.

Dr. Syvrud's central message is the necessity of considering the whole social, political, and economic matrix of any set of economic policies under appraisal. Thus, concerning the problem of inflation, he would look back of the money supply to all the chief factors determining its behavior; and in appraising its effects, he would look not only to the direct effects of inflation on prices and real incomes, but also to the manifold repercussions of efforts to conceal or offset inflation without stopping it or coping with its mainsprings.

The author never sacrifices the sober truth to the dramatic phrase, nor—for the sake of easy explanation or brevity—does he omit relevant facts. He rides no hobbies nor does he strain for orignality. His readers rest in expert and honest hands.

Howard S. Ellis

ACKNOWLEDGMENTS

There are many who deserve my thanks for their guidance, persuasion, criticism and encouragement during the eight years from 1965 when my family first arrived in Brazil until 1973 when my wife delivered the manuscript of this book to the American Enterprise Institute.

From August 1965 to August 1969 I served as Treasury Department Representative at the U.S. Embassy in Rio de Janeiro, Brazil. As financial advisor to ambassadors Lincoln Gordon and John Tuthill, I had a once-in-a-lifetime opportunity to work closely with senior Brazilian officials on their economic development and stabilization program. Without this close range view of the policy issues and how they were resolved, this book could not have been written.

I am deeply indebted to my friends and colleagues who served with me on the closely knit economic team which represented the U.S. Government during this critical period of United States-Brazilian relations, Minister Stuart H. Van Dyke, director of the U.S. Agency for International Development Mission in Brazil; his assistant director for Development Planning, John H. Kaufmann; and the Embassy's economic counselor, Robert Elwood. Two officials of the U.S. Department of Agriculture, Abner E. Deatheridge and Robert Johnson, earned both my deep respect for their insights into the Brazilian agricultural economy and my thanks for taking the time to share some of them with me.

I am indebted to a dozen or more Brazilian economists for their constructive support over these several years. Many of them appear in the body of this work. But I must express my special gratitude to Alexandre Kafka, Brazilian executive director at the International Monetary Fund, and two former directors of research for the Central Bank of Brazil, Eduardo da Silveira Gomes Junior, and Basilio Martins.

Following my return to Washington in August 1969 I had the good fortune to work for John Petty, assistant secretary of the Treasury for International Affairs, who recommended me for a Federal Executive Fellowship at the Brookings Institution. This one year fellowship, from 1970 to 1971, permitted me to complete the research work and to write the first draft. But I also discovered that it's a long road from the first draft to a published work. I owe an immense debt to Professor Howard S. Ellis for his encouragement to persist in completing the manuscript for publication.

The responsibility for all views expressed in this book rests solely with the writer.

CHAPTER I

An Overview

> Happily our national economic system did not
> know that it was condemned to eternal poverty
> and, not knowing it, gathered all the strength
> of which it was capable to overcome its own
> difficulties.
>
> Antônio Delfim Netto
> *Planejamento para o*
> *Desenvolvimento Econômico*

Brazil has long been described as "the land of tomorrow" because of its vast resources of unexploited land, labor, minerals, and hydroelectric power. Yet, 400 years after its settlement by Portuguese colonists, Brazil remained among the poorest of nations. In addressing the assembled economic leaders of the western world in Rio de Janeiro in September 1967, George Woods, president of the World Bank, hinted at Brazil's great potential.

> Brazil comprises nearly half the area and population of South America. It is two and a half times as large as Western Europe, including the British Isles and Scandinavia, and has a fourth of the population. . . . It is rich in minerals and agricultural resources. It has a third of all known iron reserves and the world's fourth largest potential for hydroelectric power. In production, it ranks first in coffee, third in manganese, fourth in sugar and eighth in iron ore.[1]

Despite the development potential suggested in this brief summary, Brazil's per capita income in 1967 did not reach a quarter of the per capita incomes in Western Europe. The Brazilian economy had remained stagnant for six years, foreign investment was fleeing the

---

[1] George Woods, Presidential Statement at the Annual Meeting of The World Bank in Rio de Janeiro, September 1967.

1

country, and the economy in general seemed a long way from achieving its potential. However, in the succeeding five years, 1968 to 1972, the rate of growth of the Brazilian economy averaged only slightly under 10 percent per year. This growth record is among the best of any country, developing or developed, for any similar five-year period. Only Japan, among the major countries, experienced a faster economic growth rate during these years. In 1965 Brazil ranked fourteenth among nations in the total production of goods and services; by 1971 it ranked eleventh, close on the heels of India.

How Long Can the Boom Be Sustained?

The economic statistics for the five years 1968 to 1972 show an incredible, almost miraculous, rate of economic growth. And perhaps because it seems miraculous the question persists: how long can the Brazilian economic boom last? Brazilian economic history is replete with economic booms followed by catastrophic periods of economic depression. During the 400 years of its modern history, Brazil has experienced cyclical booms in wood, sugar, rubber, and coffee, these booms alternating with declining prices and collapse of the domestic economy. Even within the past decade it has experienced a full cycle of boom and bust.

From the end of World War II to 1961 the Brazilian economy had been growing at a rapid pace. Brazil's average annual growth rate of 7 percent was the highest in Latin America and ranked among the highest anywhere in the world. Inflation was also continuing, at an average annual rate of about 20 percent, but without any obvious adverse impact on economic growth. A shortage of foreign exchange was not creating any particular constraint on growth, owing initially to the use of foreign exchange reserves accumulated during the war and later to large annual inflows of private foreign investment and of official capital. A growth-oriented climate prevailed as a new capital city of Brasilia was being carved out on a remote interior plateau. The automobile industry, initiated only in 1957, had by 1961 already produced its first half-million automobiles.

In short, by 1961, the Brazilian economy seemed well on its way to becoming another of the postwar economic miracles in the style of Germany, Italy, and Japan. And the miracle seemed greater since this was a genuine example of development rather than reconstruction as in the case of these other countries. Then, the entire progress of the Brazilian economy seemed to collapse in a matter of months. The growth rate, which had reached 10.3 percent in 1961, declined to 5.3 percent in 1962 and to only 1.5 percent in 1963. With the population growing at an estimated 3 percent per year, the 1.5 percent growth rate meant a decline in per capita income for a population whose average annual per capita income did not exceed $300. At the same time, the steady inflation of 20 percent turned sharply upward, unemployment rose to record levels, and the heavy accumulation of foreign debts brought the country close to international backruptcy. These were only the most conspicuous of the many indications of growing imbalance, stagnation, and eventual chaos in the economy.

The political implications of these economic developments were as evident as the inability of the government to deal with the deteriorating situation. The eventual economic collapse constituted one of the underlying causes of the political revolution of April 1964—the overthrow of a democratically elected president and the establishment of a military oligarchy which has now survived three military presidents. Unlike the many previous occasions when the Brazilian army took over the reins of government for short periods of time, following the April 1964 revolution the military, although initially announcing its aim of restoring political control to the civilian politicians after a period of three years, has extended its reign indefinitely.

Given the history of boom and bust, there is a degree of urgency to the question of how long the present economic boom will continue. This question forms part of the broader question to which this study is addressed, how economic growth can be achieved and sustained in a developing country. The answers to both the more specific question and the broader question are the same. The current successful economic growth record of the Brazilian economy is based on foundations of political stability, sound economic management, the ability of the economic policy makers to diagnose accurately problems in the context of a market-oriented development strategy, and, finally, their ability to react promptly to these problems with an effective mix of policy instruments.

The economic growth of the 1950s, the ensuing collapse of the early 1960s, and the recovery and boom of the late 1960s can all be explained in terms of the effectiveness or ineffectiveness of domestic Brazilian economic policies. The import substitution industrialization policies pursued by the Brazilian governments of the 1950s were peculiarly suitable to the requirements and capabilities of the Brazilian economy at that time. The failure or inability of successive Kubitschek, Quadros and Goulart governments to adjust these policies in consonance with the changing requirements of the economy led almost inevitably to economic collapse. The current economic boom is likewise attributable to economic policies appropriate to current conditions and implemented in a pragmatic and flexible manner. But the developments, however sound, have to date laid only the foundation for continued progress; if growth is to continue, additional measures to increase the productivity and incomes of Brazilian workers in all sectors are essential. This means an intensified effort in areas of education, technical training, and extension services. It also means a greater equality in the distribution of income through increased employment opportunities and greater progressivity of taxation and expenditure policy in all echelons of government.

Foundations of Economic Growth—1964 to 1972

The answer to the question of how to sustain the Brazilian economic boom may be found in an assessment of four foundations of the current economic growth: political stability, continuity of economic management, a market-oriented development strategy, and competent economic planning. In addition, the Brazilian economic growth has benefited since mid-1970 from a developmental ideology, the challenge of the interior.

Political Stability. The keystone of the recent economic growth record has been the high degree of political and administrative stability offered by the military government. In exercising strong direct control over the political instruments and institutions, the Brazilian military offered the economic policy managers, a group of experienced and competent economic experts, a degree of freedom and continuity not available to economists in democratic countries. With delegated responsibility for economic policies and the capability of avoiding the time-consuming, cumbersome channels of democratic politics, the economic authorities were free to innovate with new approaches to old problems and, through a process of trial and error, were able eventually to stabilize and restructure the Brazilian economy.

Continuity of Economic Policy. Despite changes in government in 1967 and 1969, there has been only one significant change in the groups of economists who have managed the Brazilian economy since 1964, and both groups have pursued essentially the same economic development strategies. The first team of economists, appointed by President Castello Branco shortly after the revolution, was headed by Professor Octavio Bulhões as finance minister and Ambassador Roberto Campos as planning minister. All the members of this team of Castello Branco experts represented the liberal laissez-faire school of economics. However, their years of experience in government had led them to recognize the need to modify orthodox doctrines to meet

Brazilian realities. Their policy response to their diagnosis of the Brazilian crisis therefore, was a variation of the orthodox stabilization and reform approach to inflation and stagnation. During the three-year period from April 1964 to April 1967 this team guided the Brazilian economy through a crucial period of economic reform and restructuring. Yet by 1967, although signs of economic recovery were appearing, the economy remained, in general, stagnant and inflation-ridden. The Brazilian masses and, more importantly, the Brazilian military leaders were disenchanted by the austerity of the stabilization and reform measures.

Nevertheless, Marshall Costa e Silva, succeeding to the presidency in 1967, committed his government to continuing the general line of economic policies pursued by his predecessor, and the appointment of Professor Antônio Delfim Netto as minister of finance assured this continuity. Professor Delfim Netto was a logical choice, having served as a consultant to Finance Minister Bulhões and Planning Minister Campos during the previous three years. He had also served as consultant to the São Paulo industrial and financial community and was, for a short period, secretary of finance of the state of São Paulo, the wealthiest state in the union. To assist him in his new capacity Finance Minister Delfim Netto brought into the government a new team of young, inexperienced but outstanding economists who had been associated with him in the state government of São Paulo and at the University of São Paulo as colleagues and students. This new breed of economist, under the strong leadership of Delfim Netto, has provided the core of Brazil's economic management since 1967.

Market-Oriented Development Strategy. The liberal market-oriented economic philosophy of the Brazilian economic authorities, together with their recognition of Brazilian realities, forms the third cornerstone of the current Brazilian growth record. In determining the shape of the stabilization and development program in 1964, Planning Minister Campos, Finance Minister Bulhões, and their associates faced some fundamental philosophic choices concerning the direction of the economy for the future: the choices between a private sector market orientation or a public sector state-planning approach to domestic development, between a protectionist or export-promotion approach in foreign trade, between a nationalist or internationalist approach to foreign investment, and between a monetarist or structuralist approach to stabilization.

The choices of the Castello Branco policy makers tended to reverse the trends of the previous Brazilian government: from state planning to market orientation, from protectionism to export promotion, from nationalism to internationalism, and from structuralism to monetarism. These choices were not easy: not only did they reverse the trend of Brazilian economic policies, but also they countered the prevailing trends in academic thinking and in the international development institutions, both of which had succumbed to the trend toward centralized planning and regulation. These choices were particularly out of step with the entrenched economic ideology of the United Nations Economic Commission for Latin America.

But while the economic authorities reversed the trends in all these policy areas, they did not succumb to the temptation of moving to the opposite end of the ideological spectrum. They proved to be notably eclectic in their choice of economic ideologies, selecting and modeling them to fit the realities of Brazilian traditions, institutions, and resources. Can an economy survive, let alone thrive, with an annual rate of inflation in excess of 20 percent per year? Market-oriented ideologies answered in the negative. The Brazilian response is indicated by the fact that in 1972, eight years later, the rate of inflation had barely dropped below 16 percent. Can an underdeveloped economy move into a period of sustained economic growth through reliance on the market mechanism? Can Brazil obtain the benefits from private foreign investment without losing control over its own resources? Can exports be expanded in the face of an inelastic foreign demand for primary products? The experts responded to all these questions in the affirmative and the results of the past eight years confirm the wisdom of their choices.

Planning in a Market-Oriented Economy. Effective economic planning comprised the fourth and final cornerstone of the Brazilian economic progress since 1964: planning not in the sense that the government involved itself directly in each economic decision, but planning which was aimed primarily at improving the environment in which the private sector can effectively assist in achieving the desired objectives. In the Brazilian context, planning included (a) a diagnosis of the constraints and capabilities of the economy in terms of economic and social objectives; (b) the preparation of an expenditure and tax program for the public sector; and (c) the outline of a program to induce the private sector, through the use of the price mechanism and fiscal incentives, to allocate resources in consonance with these social and economic objectives.

The Brazilian authorities therefore combined effective economic planning with extensive use of flexible pricing policies to influence the allocation of resources and investments into priority sectors. Their aim was not a price mechanism in which autonomous supply and demand factors determine the price, but a mechanism in which the government played an important, even a determining, role. This was not a novel approach in Brazil. During the 1950s the Brazilian government had used with great success exchange, credit, and tariff policies to alter the relative prices and thereby stimulate investments in the industrial sector. In the post-1964 years, the Brazilian government extended this same approach to the agricultural, export, and housing construction sectors and to priority regions of the economy. To overcome the savings and investment constraints in each of these priority sectors and regions, the Brazilian planners innovated with new institutions and instruments to combine effectively the generation of savings with the investment decision. For example, the National Housing Program, based on workers' pension funds, monetary correction, and the National Housing Bank, provided both the source of savings and the means for channeling these savings into needed investments in housing. The Northeast Development Program, the state revenue sharing program, the agricultural credit and pricing programs, and the National Economic Development Bank all played important roles in generating additional savings and channeling these savings into priority sectors and regions. The savings generated by each of these programs financed a major part of investments in their respective sectors. And since the institutions which manage these programs are under the jurisdiction of the National Monetary Council, of which the finance minister is the chairman, the council maintained a high degree of centralized control over both the level and direction of investments in the Brazilian economy. The degree of this control over investments and its implications for the Brazilian economy are discussed in Chapter 11.

Challenge of the Interior—A Development Ideology. Although not necessarily crucial to Brazilian development, the challenge of the Brazilian interior is an important force in mobilizing the productive forces of Brazil for development. During the 1950s President Kubitschek oriented the domestic forces to industrialize and develop the interior of the country. The new capital, Brasilia, built in the previously inaccessible regions of Mato Grosso in the heart of Brazil, offered the Brazilian masses an ideology which permitted them to forego present consumption for the benefit of the future growth and power of their country. The stabilization program of the Castello Branco government, on the other hand, attracted only slight popular support. Austerity can never match imaginative goals for developing the riches of the interior, however great or little the imagined riches may be.

Several key economic leaders in and out of government, recognizing the need for an ideology to mobilize the support of the Brazilian people, fatigued by three years of austerity, attempted in 1968 to provoke a popular reaction to Herman Kahn's projections in *The Year 2000*.[2] In that book Kahn projected a Brazil in the year 2000 even further behind in the economic race than it was in 1968. The Brazilian counter-challenge, suggested by economists João Paulo Velloso, director of the Planning Institute and later planning minister, Murilo Melo Filho, and Mário Simonsen offered the choice of a Brazil which in the year 2000 either would be the world's third most powerful country or would remain far back among the list of less developed countries, depending upon the policy response to a number of crucial issues.[3]

But the Brazilian people did not react to the artificial challenge of the year 2000. In mid-1970 President Médici found a challenge closer to the Brazilian temperament. Whether planned as such or not, President Médici's Transamazonica Highway Project sparked a new development ideology in Brazil. This project, widely criticized for its marginal economic value, proved to be most effective in mobilizing the Brazilian people for a common cause, that is, the development of Brazil's interior. In this sense the Transamazonica Highway is a continuation of the challenge of the interior offered by President Kubitschek. Its importance as a development ideology for the Brazilian people is immeasurable.

Economic Issues in the Brazilian Experience

Perhaps the key issue in the Brazilian experiences of the past two decades is whether economic growth can be sustained without attention to the underlying economic and social problems. Economic growth and socioeconomic development are not necessarily synonymous. Many developing nations have experienced relatively high growth rates accompanied by unemployment and underemployment and worsening of the income distribution pattern. Brazil's experiences leading up to the 1964 revolution offer a clear example of such growth without development. Under the import substitution industrialization policies of the 1950s the Brazilian economy achieved for a time a high rate of growth combined with a neglected social development, intensified unemployment, widened disparities in income distribution, and stagnating educational opportunities.

Is the post-1964 Brazilian government pursuing a similar pattern of growth without development? Is the current Brazilian government

---

[2]Herman Kahn and Anthony J. Weiner, *The Year 2000*.
[3]Murilo Melo Filho, *O Desafio Brasileiro* and Mário Henrique Simonsen, *Brasil 2001*.

facing up to the basic economic and social problems of the country? The sceptics have tended to describe the 1964 revolution as a preventive coup aimed at averting the initiation of needed economic and social reforms. The motivating force in the revolution, according to these writers, was maintenance of the status quo with a small ruling elite benefiting from the economic gains while the majority of the population remained illiterate, unemployed, and undernourished. Those who justify the authoritarian government of Brazil, on the other hand, do so on the assumption that an authoritarian government will be more effective in achieving high rates of economic growth and that eventually a more prosperous population will evolve a more democratic political system. But the experiences of the past elicit the question as to whether even an authoritarian regime can sustain a high rate of economic growth without attention to some of the basic problems of education, income distribution, land reform, labor productivity, and health. Can economic growth be sustained without expansion of the domestic market, which requires rising productivity and incomes?

What should be the priorities, growth or social reform? Should the focus of policy makers be on income distribution, with land reform in the agricultural sector and higher wages for industrial workers? What priority should be given investments in the educational infrastructure? Can the productivity of agricultural workers be increased without the incentives of land ownership? Without basic education? Without technical advice and extension services? On the other hand, can the underlying social and economic problems of Brazil be solved without economic growth?

Another issue inherent in the Brazilian inflationary experiences is whether a country can sustain a high level of savings, investment, and economic growth in the face of continuing inflation. How can savings be encouraged for the financing of housing and of long-term investments in infrastructure, agriculture, and industry? What role does the interest rate play in generating savings and in allocating financial savings among competing investment opportunities? What is the role of institutions and other determinants in the savings process? Can a country live, let alone thrive, on inflation?[4]

The degree to which the balance of payments imposes a constraint on the development of a country is also called into question by the Brazilian experiences. Are the developing nations justified in assuming a defeatist attitude toward export expansion? Is the foreign demand for their exports as inelastic as is widely held? Is the import

---

[4]Stefan H. Robock, "We can live with inflation," pp. 20-44.

constraint the major obstacle to growth? Are protectionist or import substitution policies the only path open to developing nations?

These aspects of the Brazilian experiences raise a further question about the applicability of macroeconomic analysis and policies for solving the problems of underdevelopment. Is the level of investment the key determinant of output and employment? Or, in developing nations, is the structure of investment of equal or greater importance? What is the relative significance of foreign trade in the determination of the level of output and income? What are the implications of a relatively inelastic domestic supply for the effectiveness of macroeconomic policies? Is there a tendency, in response to macroeconomic policy stimulants, for more inflation and less growth in developing nations than in industrial nations?

Finally, the Brazilian experiences stimulate thinking about the applicability of many of the prevailing theories of economic development.[5] How important is capital accumulation in economic development? How important the allocation of resources? How important entrepreneurial innovation? How necessary an agricultural surplus, a labor surplus? How significant are educational, cultural, and institutional characteristics in the stimulation and continuation of economic development?

Hopefully this study of the political economy of Brazil will provide the reader with some answers to these many questions and issues. Undoubtedly many more will remain unanswered pending further research on the political economies of Brazil and of other nations.

Scope and Structure of the Book

The study begins with a diagnosis of the Brazilian economic crisis of 1962-1964, including a description of the economic policies and performance of the Brazilian economy in the years prior to the 1964 revolution. It then proceeds to the policies of the Castello Branco government during the years 1964 to 1967, to an assessment of the consequences of these policies, and, finally, to the policies of the new breed of economists under the leadership of Finance Minister Delfim Netto.

The study is organized in three parts. The first offers an assessment of the import subtitution strategy of the years preceding the 1964 crisis (Chapter II) and an assessment of the more balanced growth strategy in the years since 1964 (Chapter III).

---

[5] Howard S. Ellis, "The Applicability of Certain Theories of Economic Development to Brazil."

The second focuses on the instruments of economic policy available to the Brazilian authorities to achieve the several economic and social objectives. It is organized into seven chapters, each of which is devoted to a major instrument of economic policy: monetary policies (Chapter IV), interest rate policies (Chapter V), fiscal policies (Chapter VI), wage policies (Chapter VII), exchange rate and trade policies (Chapter VIII), agricultural pricing and credit policies (Chapter IX), and coffee-pricing policies (Chapter X). Each of these seven chapters compares the implementation of a major macroeconomic policy instrument under the import substitution industrialization strategy of the 1950s with its implementation under the balanced growth strategy of the later 1960s.

The compartmentalization of each policy instrument in separate chapters has a major shortcoming in that, in actual practice, no policy instrument can be considered in isolation. At any given moment the Brazilian authorities, like other economic authorities, weighed the comparative effectiveness and costs of all the available policy instruments in achieving the several, sometimes conflicting, objectives. And in practice this is the only rational approach. For purposes of exposition, however, the organization of this study has the advantage of giving the reader a concentrated study of how the Brazilian authorities implemented each instrument under varying circumstances and for different objectives.

The third part, the final chapter, summarizes the major programs and institutions developed by the Brazilian authorities to mobilize savings for investments in priority sectors and regions. Sound implementation of macroeconomic policies, described in the second part supplied a necessary condition for the upsurge in savings and investments which has occurred since 1967, but these policies in themselves did not provide a sufficient condition. The economic recovery of Brazil since 1967 cannot be explained without consideration of the key roles played by the revolutionary housing program, the expanded development program for the Northeast, the Capital Market Development Program, and the agricultural sector investment program. These four programs, in combination with the public sector savings effort and the measures to maximize foreign savings, generated the capital for an estimated 70 to 80 percent of total investments in Brazil since 1969. Given the importance of these programs in the Brazilian economy, the prospects for continuation of the successful growth record of the past few years are heavily dependent upon their continued effectiveness.

CHAPTER II

Import Substitution Industrialization, 1947-1963

For almost two decades prior to 1962 Brazil had experienced an annual increase in national product of about 7 percent, one of the highest sustained growth rates of any country during those years. The industrial sector, growing at an annual rate of about 8 percent, had given Brazil by 1962 a diversified industrial base capable of producing the most sophisticated consumer goods and capital equipment. And the continuity in these growth rates induced Brazilian economists to announce, as did Planning Minister Celso Furtado, that Brazil had come very close to the position where "development becomes a cumulative circular process creating its own expansionary momentum."[1] At the very time Furtado was writing these words, however, the Brazilian economy was already in the midst of the most critical economic crisis in its modern history, a crisis which combined stagnation in economic output with hyper-inflation, near-international bankruptcy, and an intensification of the traditional income disparities on a regional, sectoral, and personal basis.

The single-minded objective of Brazilian economic policy during the 1950s was industrialization. All the economic ideologies of the day pointed to industrialization as the solution to Brazil's economic needs. The Economic Commission for Latin America (ECLA) doctrine explained Brazil's economic backwardness in terms of the lack of an industrial base; economic theorists in all lands emphasized capital accumulation as the path to development; and the international financial institutions joined the ideological consensus by concentrating their financing on industrial and infrastructure projects. This emphasis on industrialization proved to be peculiarly appropriate for the conditions prevailing in Brazil during the 1950s and the ideological consensus provided the Brazilian government with the backstopping

---

[1]Celso Furtado, *Diagnosis of the Brazilian Crisis*, p. 108.

necessary to focus its economic policies on industrialization. Other economic objectives of price stability, balance in international accounts, and economic efficiency, as well as the social objectives of full employment, equitable income distribution, better housing, and an improvement of educational opportunities, were sacrificed on the altar of rapid industrial growth. It would have been astonishing if the resulting industrial growth had not been impressive, and it may be an ironic mark of the success of the Brazilian industrialization that in 1962, for the first time in its history, Brazil began to experience its own homemade industrial recession to add to traditional problems stemming from seasonal fluctuations and secular booms and busts in primary production.

By 1962, Brazil had advanced toward its industrialization objective and had come very close to the threshold of self-sustaining growth. But at the same time, the very successful process of industrialization had created another set of problems. Rapid growth in the import substitution industries, the primary growth industries during the 1950s had been at the cost of neglecting the export and agricultural sectors. Government subsidies, direct and indirect, to stimulate industrialization had created an unbearable burden of public sector spending, financed increasingly by the printing press. The ensuing inflationary environment killed the housing construction industry and distorted the financial structure. Moreover, the fruits of industrialization had not been equitably distributed. Brazil had become, by 1962, a prime example of a dual economy with the "prolonged coexistence and cohabitation of modern industry and of preindustrial, sometimes neolithic, techniques."[2] The accumulation over time of these distortions and structural imbalances came to haunt the Brazilian government leaders. The imbalances remained tolerable as long as the industrial sector boomed along at a 10 percent growth rate. But with the decline of opportunities for further profitable investment in the industrial sector, the appearance of idle capacity, and the lack of an alternative growth sector, the economy moved into a stagnation which lasted through 1967.

This chapter offers a summary of the ideological underpinnings of industrialization policies, the industrialization policy instruments, and the economic consequence of these policies. Subsequent chapters will describe these policy objectives, instruments, and consequences in greater detail.

---

[2] Albert O. Hirschman, *The Strategy of Economic Development*, p. 125.

Industrialization Ideologies

It is easy to conclude from a study of economic policies and trends during the early postwar period that Brazil developed in spite of itself, that the Brazilian industrialization was spontaneous, without deliberate policies directed to that end but following the line of least resistance. The Brazilians themselves seemed to recognize this in their popular adage, "Brazil grows while politicians sleep." The immediate postwar years, 1947 to 1951, in particular were years of spontaneous industrial development, stimulated primarily by foreign exchange and trade policies. Overvalued exchange rates combined with quantitative import controls served, on the one hand, to protect the balance of payments from an excessive volume of imports and, on the other, to protect the home market for domestic producers.

The first efforts at establishing a development ideology with policies and machinery to stimulate industrialization began in the early 1950s. The import substitution industrialization doctrine expounded by Raul Prebisch of ECLA proved to be perfectly suited to the conditions prevailing in Brazil. It provided the theoretical rationale for Brazilian policy makers to continue and enlarge upon existing policies. Also consistent with this development doctrine were the 1951 recommendations of the Joint Brazil-United States Commission to embark upon fourteen major development projects to stimulate industrial development and to finance the essential infrastructure. But not until the election of President Kubitschek in 1956 was the first deliberate effort made to channel public and private sector energies and resources into a concerted industrial development program. President Kubitschek's Target Program focused on industrialization through continuation of the import substitution policies and other incentives to the private sector. The Target Plan itself included a variety of public sector investments directed at removing bottlenecks to industrialization, especially in the fields of transport and power, as recommended in the report of the Joint Brazil-United States Economic Development Commission of 1953. All public sector policies were directed toward the major objectives of industrialization and, secondarily, construction of the new federal city of Brasilia.

With Brasilia, President Kubitschek struck a major latent response in the Brazilian economic and political environment. The thrust to the interior represented by Brasilia offered a development ideology with appeal to wide masses of the Brazilian population. The combination of this appealing developmental ideology and an economic doctrine which emphasized the need for industrialization provided a powerful ideological basis for governmental action. And the policy instruments, in place for several years, needed only refinement to achieve the goal of industrialization.

Industrialization Policy Instruments

Import substitution policy instruments, including overvalued exchange rates, quantitative import restrictions, and preclusive tariffs, provided the main stimulus to Brazilian industrialization during the 1950s, but the inducements to investment in the industrial sector did not end there. Tax policy offered additional indirect subsidies to industry through delayed payment of taxes at reduced real values; interest rate controls in the inflationary environment limited the cost of industrial credit to negative levels (in real terms); and government investments in key sectors of the economy, like steel, power, oil, and highway construction, helped to alleviate some of the critical bottlenecks to industrial growth.

While the emphases varied with the changes in government, the use of the major policy instruments to stimulate industrialization continued unchanged through 1961. In that year the Quadros government initiated some significant changes in economic policy, including unification of the exchange rate and an improved coffee-pricing policy, but these changes alone proved to be inadequate in the face of the existing structural and financial disequilibria.

Economic Consequences of Industrialization

The set of policy instruments pursued by successive Brazilian governments to promote rapid industrialization proved to be highly effective in expanding industrial investment and in stimulating rapid economic growth, but they proved to be effective only under specific conditions and tended to carry the seeds of their own destruction. The conditions prevailing in Brazil during the early 1950s were peculiarly suited to industrialization through import substitutions and the demands it imposed on other sectors of the economy. Brazil had already developed a large and geographically concentrated potential market for import substitution goods, and a sufficiently diversified productive capacity to react to favorable price incentives. The abundance of the unemployed and the underemployed provided a cheap and readily available labor supply which, with government control over the labor unions, kept wage increases below the increase in labor productivity and hence preserved real savings for industrial investment. The availability of frontier land meant that the food supply could continue to expand without significant investments of capital in agriculture. The combination of inflation and interest rate controls precluded investments in the capital intensive housing construction industries. The improved terms of trade during the early 1950s and the huge inflow of foreign, private, and public capital during the latter 1950s financed essential imports, with the result that investments in the export sector, again primarily agriculture, did not detract from industrial investments. This combination of factors permitted Brazil to grow during the 1950s with an unusually low capital output ratio.

However, failure of the Brazilian authorities to implement needed changes in industrialization policies as the conditions changed led inexorably to hyper-inflation, economic stagnation, and balance of payments disequilibrium. Continued reliance on forced savings measures to finance growth resulted inevitably in accelerating inflation. Excessive reliance on external savings through direct foreign investment and "the disequilibrium system" expanded the foreign debt to an unsustainable level and intensified the nationalist opposition to foreign ownership and control of Brazilian industry, while the growing distortions in the financial system hampered the mobilization of domestic savings for investment and growth. The concentration of growth, both sectorally and geographically, exaggerated the existing dualism of the economy, widened the regressivity of personal, sectoral, and regional income distribution, and limited the market for the industrial output. Finally, in requiring for its sustenance an increasingly effective and comprehensive administrative system, the industrialization exposed the inadequacies and inefficiencies of the highly centralized Brazilian governmental bureaucracy.

Growth and Stagnation—1947 to 1963

The import substitution policies pursued by the Brazilian government resulted in one of the highest growth rates of any country during the post-World War II years. During the period 1947 to 1961 the Brazilian gross domestic product grew at an average annual rate of 7.2 percent, as shown in Table II-1. The total output in 1961 exceeded by two and one-half times the total output of 1947. Industrial output expanded at an average annual rate of more than 8 percent during the entire period. Agricultural output increased at an average annual rate of about 4.2 percent, but with sharp year-to-year fluctuations, highlighting the impact of weather conditions in this sector. The service sector rose at an annual average rate of about 7.2 percent, identical with the overall GNP growth rate.

The year 1963 marked a dramatic change in this bright picture and by 1963 the economy had fallen into a major crisis. In that year agricultural output increased by only 1 percent and industrial output

Table II-1

ANNUAL RATES OF GROWTH IN GNP—TOTAL, PER CAPITA,
AND BY SECTORS, 1948–1964[a]

Year	Agriculture	Industry	Services	GNP	GNP Per Capita
1948	7.0%	11.2%	5.6%	7.4%	4.7%
1949	4.5	10.1	6.0	6.6	4.3
1950	1.5	11.3	7.1	6.5	4.0
1951	0.5	6.2	10.0	6.0	2.8
1952	9.0	5.0	11.0	8.7	5.6
1953	—	8.7	—	2.5	−0.5
1954	7.8	8.7	13.0	10.1	7.0
1955	7.7	10.6	3.2	6.9	3.7
1956	−2.0	6.7	4.5	3.2	0.2
1957	9.2	5.7	9.0	8.1	4.9
1958	2.0	16.0	5.7	7.7	4.6
1959	5.1	11.0	1.2	5.6	2.4
1960	4.7	9.3	8.9	9.7	6.6
1961	7.9	10.5	12.0	10.3	7.2
1962	5.3	7.8	3.5	5.3	2.3
1963	1.1	0.2	2.7	1.5	−1.3
1964	1.2	5.5	2.1	2.9	0.0

[a]Percentage change over prior year in constant prices.
Source: *Conjunture Econômica*, June 1970; *A Economia Brasileira e Suas Perspectivas* (Rio de Janeiro: Edicões APEC), July 1972, Table A.2.

failed to grow at all. The resulting growth of 1.5 percent in gross domestic product was only about one-half the population growth rate. After fifteen years in which per capita income grew annually by 4 percent, 1963 per capita income actually declined by over 1 percent. The 1 percent growth for agriculture was not exceptional, given the chronic instability of that sector; in fact, it was more unusual that the poor harvest of 1963 had been preceded by four years of relatively stable growth at above 5 percent. Brazilian economic authorities had always expected agriculture to have its seasonal fluctuations and its secular boom and bust cycles.

The stagnation in the industrial sector in 1963 was another matter. Industrial output had grown by a minimum of 5 percent in every year for the previous sixteen years and had averaged in excess of 10 percent during the immediately preceding five years. Now for the first time Brazil began to experience the cyclical problems of an industrial economy. The explanations of the stagnation ranged from excessive real savings (overcapacity in the industrial sector) to deficient financial savings (unavailability of long-term financial capital to finance new investments). The explanation offered by the ECLA school, which had proclaimed import substitution as the road to industrial development, focused on the exhaustion of import substitution opportunities, an explanation also offered in the Three-Year Plan, 1963-1965, by the Brazilian Planning Ministry.

Inflation—1947 to 1963. Brazil has experienced inflation every year since prior to World War II. From 1947 to 1958 the annual rate of inflation stayed generally within a range of 12 to 16 percent, with an average of 14.4 percent for these eleven years. In 1959, however, with the heavy demands of Kubitschek's Target Plan, the rate of inflation shot upwards to 39 percent and in 1961 shifted into the high gear of hyper-inflation. The accelerating price inflation after 1958 is presented in Table II-2. By the time of the April 1964 revolution, inflation had risen to an annual rate in excess of 100 percent.

Periodic attempts to control inflation by means of a conventional stabilization program along the lines recommended by the International Monetary Fund proved to be singularly unsuccessful during these years. One such effort, initiated in the latter part of 1954 when the inflation rate had reached 27 percent, was discarded in 1956 with the implementation of Kubitschek's Target Plan. The dynamism of the industrialization process during the Target Plan period, 1956 to 1961, and the gradual resort to direct price controls combined to hold the rate of inflation to an acceptable level (by Brazilian standards) with an average of about 25 percent per year. Toward the end of his presidency, as the inflation rate accelerated to above 30 percent, Kubitschek asked Roberto Campos to prepare a stabilization program, but neither this program nor the stabilization elements of the Dantas-Furtado Three-Year Plan were ever carried out.

Four factors militated against implementation of an effective stabilization program in Brazil. The first was the concern on the part of Brazilian economic and political authorities that stabilization would result in a business recession, increased unemployment, and reduced incomes. The defeatism of the ECLA doctrine, which held that monetary policy is powerless against the extremely powerful structural factors in Latin America, tended to support this view. Orthodox economic policies seemed to offer no alternative to this dismal out-

Table II-2

ANNUAL RATES OF INCREASE IN THE GENERAL PRICE INDEX, 1947–1964[a]

Year	General Price Index[b]	Year	General Price Index[b]
1947	2.7 %	1956	24.4%
1948	8.3	1957	7.0
1949	12.2	1958	24.3
1950	12.4	1959	39.5
1951	11.9	1960	30.5
1952	12.9	1961	47.7
1953	20.8	1962	51.3
1954	25.6	1963	81.3
1955	12.4	1964	91.9

[a]Percentage change over prior year.

[b]The "general price index" is a weighted average of the wholesale price index (60 percent), the cost of living index (30 percent), and the construction cost index (10 percent). The cost of living and construction cost indexes are for Rio de Janeiro, state of Guanabara.

Source: *Conjuntura Econômica*, November 1972, p. 41.

look for a stabilization program, and no politician had the courage to face his constituents with a program offering such consequences. Secondly, there was a widespread belief that inflation had contributed to the high rate of economic growth. Less orthodox economists encouraged the view that, in an economy without an adequate financial mechanism to stimulate domestic savings, inflation provided a forced savings mechanism to finance the high growth rate. Third, a policy of stabilization was usually associated in the minds of the Brazilians with foreign interference in their internal affairs. The International Monetary Fund usually bore the brunt of the accusations that the stabilization disciplines were imposed from without. Finally, many economists and economic authorities held the view that Brazil had insulated itself against inflation so that it had no damaging or distorting effects on the economy.

The original cause of the Brazilian inflation seems to have been, as most interpreters of the Brazilian inflation have indicated, the growing level of federal government expenditures financed by money creation. Support for this view is offered in Chapters IV and VI. Spending programs for both current operations and capital investments continually rose faster than the government's ability to increase tax revenues. Once the inflationary spiral got under way, however, other factors helped to perpetuate it. Coffee guaranty pricing, interest rate controls, wage policy, agricultural pricing and credit programs, and, to a limited extent, private sector credit policy all contributed in varying degrees and at different times to perpetuating the inflation. Any attempt to allocate to each of these policy instruments its relative role in the inflation would be a difficult, if not impossible, task. Complicating any analysis of the source of inflation is the fact that the inflation took on a character of its own with built-in expectations, institutions, and instruments designed to protect the income shares of each sector and with government policies combining inflation control with other policy objectives. The economic literature is replete with studies of structural imbalances and financial distortions, which are both a cause and a consequence of inflation.

My assessment of the Brazilian experience indicates that inflation was less a cause of these imbalances and distortions than it was, itself, a symptom of the structural imbalances and financial distortions in the economy. As the inflation accelerated, government efforts to repress the prices of specific goods and services served to intensify these distortions and, in the traditional vicious circle, the inflationary spiral. The distortions in the price structure created by unbalanced economic policies, not inflation, forced the transfer of savings from the wage earners and agriculture to the industrial sector in order to finance investments and growth. These same policies perpetuated the inflation and led eventually to economic stagnation. Financial inducements to industry combined with price controls on agricultural products tended to increase investment returns in industry relative to agriculture, with the result that agricultural production in critical commodities did not expand adequately to meet the growing demand. Coffee-pricing policy led to excessive profitability in the coffee sector relative to non-coffee agriculture, and to an overproduction of coffee. Rental controls reduced incentives for housing construction, except that of a luxury nature. Overvalued exchange rates restricted export growth and imposed severe limitations on the ability to import. Utility rate controls limited the ability of the utilities to finance investments. Public sector wages in excess of labor productivity set high wage standards for the private sector and added significantly to the public sector deficit. Overriding all of the other price distortions were negative interest rates, which stemmed from the usury law and inflation and which reduced the effectiveness of the interest rate as a means of stimulating savings and channeling savings to productive uses.

While Brazil was able to live with the distortions in the price structure for a time, they tended to create structural and institutional disequilibria which were not readily reversible. Structural and financial distortions in agriculture, housing, foreign trade, the financial system, and the public sector complicated the problem of stabilization and resumption of development. Thus, it was not just a matter of eliminating the price controls and the distortions in the price structure. The price mechanism required time to take effect in terms of offering incentives for expanding agricultural output, exports, and housing and for stimulating the private sector to take up the slack from a reduced public sector role. And in most cases changes in the price mechanism alone were not sufficient to bring about the desired changes in the short run. Vested interests in the institutions and instruments, developed by the various economic sectors to protect themselves against inflation, resisted change. The time and extended effort needed to bring about the development of new instruments and institutions raise questions about the capacity of an unstable democracy to implement an effective stabilization effort.

In sum, Brazilian inflation can be viewed in a clearer perspective if it is considered as one of the consequences of the entire set of economic policies and conditions prevailing in Brazil. Inflation and growth, as well as inflation and stagnation, were the result of a common cause. The same set of economic policies and conditions which provided the big push to industrial growth also created the imbalances between industrial and agricultural production, coffee and non-coffee production, imports and exports, the private and public sectors, and the other structural imbalances which contributed to the hyper-inflation and stagnation.

External Disequilibrium—1947 to 1963. The key measures in the import substitution policies, the overvalued exchange rates and the protective trading system, also contributed to moving the Brazilian economy toward international bankruptcy. Excessive reliance on foreign savings— the current account deficit averaged $250 million per year during the latter half of the 1950s and early 1960s—gradually raised the foreign debt service burden to an unsustainable level. While causing exports to stagnate, the import substitution policies had not reduced the need for imports. There was a continued requirement by the new industries for raw materials and capital goods, as well as the need of a growing population for foodstuffs and fuel not produced in adequate quantities in Brazil, that is, wheat and petroleum products.

The growing current account deficits caused no serious difficulties during the late 1950s as the inflow of private foreign investments helped to sustain the necessary level of imports. But by 1960 the neglect of Brazil's export potential, the inadequate supply of long-term capital, and the deterioration in Brazil's terms of trade added up to crisis proportions. In that year 36 percent of Brazil's export earnings were devoted to servicing existing foreign debt, and the scheduled repayments for 1961 were even higher. To maintain its debt service and to finance needed imports Brazil resorted increasingly to high-cost and short-term source of credit, such as the swap transaction (short-term credit with an exchange rate guarantee), short-term bank credits, and commercial arrears. These short-term and high-cost credits served only to postpone temporarily the need for a debt rescheduling which finally occurred in 1961 after the Goulart government had committed itself to exchange reform and a stabilization program.

Unfortunately, the needed reforms in economic objectives and policy instruments were postponed during the period of instability that followed the resignation of President Quadros and the succession of Goulart. With some minor exceptions, the economic policies continued unchanged, with the same predictable consequences, under the Goulart administration. At the time of the 1964 revolution, the Goulart government was again actively seeking a new round of debt rescheduling and refinancing. At that time, Brazil had accumulated one of the heaviest foreign debt burdens of any developing country, although only fifteen years earlier its debt had been one of the smallest. Brazil's creditors did not express much enthusiasm for another rescheduling, and the virtual exhaustion of Brazil's foreign exchange reserves, the equivalent of about ten days' import requirements, did not permit any further postponement of the necessary actions to eliminate the balance of payments disequilibrium.

Income Disparities. The import substitution policies tended to intensify the existing regressive income distribution in three different spheres: regional, sectoral, and social. While the Kubitschek government initiated important programs for the impoverished Northeast and the neglected agricultural sector, these programs served to offset only in part the adverse impact of the macroeconomic policies and programs which provided a greater stimulus to concentration of income and power in the south-central industrial region of Brazil, primarily in the state of São Paulo. This state, which contains less than 3 percent of Brazil's land area and about 18 percent of its population, accounted for 57 percent of total industrial production, 23 percent of total agricultural production, 36 percent of gross national product, and about 40 percent of total foreign trade in 1963. The concentration of trade, output, and income in São Paulo, which began with the earnings from the coffee sector, was accentuated by the external economics of scale and perpetuated by the industrialization policies.

The high level of federal expenditures and the commercial activity at the important seaports also stimulated a lesser concentration of industries around the city of Rio de Janiero, which with São Paulo formed the axis of the south-central industrial region.

The high concentration of income in the south-central industrial region is set forth in Table II-3. These two states, with less than one-fourth of Brazil's population, generated almost one-half of the total national income. This remained as true in 1963 as it had been in 1947, since the decline in the importance of Guanabara during these years was more than offset by the growth of São Paulo. The northeast region, on the other hand, with one-third of the total population, generated less than 15 percent of national income.

More significant than regional income shares are the levels and trends of per capita income in the several regions. Table II-3 reveals the acute disparities in per capita income within the major regions and states of Brazil at the time of the 1950 and 1960 censuses. In 1950, per capita incomes in the Northeast amounted to less than one-half (43 percent) of the national average, less than one-seventh of the average in the city of Rio de Janeiro, and one-fifth of the average in the state of São Paulo. Per capita income in the eastern states of Minas Gerais, Espirito Santos and Rio de Janiero, comprising 21.3 percent of the population, was also less (77 percent) than the national average and about one-fourth of the average income in the city of Rio de Janeiro (Guanabara). The remaining states received income shares greater than their population shares, the one-time federal district of Rio de Janeiro having by far the highest per capita shares, more than three times the national average and 50 percent more than the state of São Paulo.

By the time of the 1960 census, the northeast states' share of population had fallen to 31.6 percent while income shares remained at about the same level, 14.8 percent, as in 1950. Per capita incomes in the Northeast, therefore, rose slightly, yet remained less than one-half of the national average and only one-fourth or per capita incomes in São Paulo. The northern states of Amazonia and Para increased their relative income shares during the decade to about the same level as the western states; however, all of these states continued at less than two-thirds of the national average. The shares of all the other states remained relatively stable, with the single exception of Rio de Janeiro, no longer the federal district, where total and per capita income shares declined rather sharply. Despite this decline, however, per capita incomes in Rio remained in 1960 more than two and one-half times the national average.

These large income disparities between the northern and southern states and between the urban and rural areas attracted a

Table II-3
REGIONAL DISTRIBUTION OF POPULATION AND INCOME,
1950, 1960 AND 1968
(in percentage of totals)

Region[a]	Percentage of Total Population			Percentage of Total Income			Average Income Shares as Percentage of Total Income		
	1950	1960	1970	1950	1960	1968[b]	1950	1960	1968[b]
Northeast	34.6	31.6	30.3	14.7	14.8	14.4	42.5	46.8	47.5
East	21.3	20.8	19.1	16.2	16.2	16.2	76.0	77.9	84.8
Guanabara	4.6	4.7	4.6	14.6	12.0	11.5	317.4	255.3	250.0
South	15.1	16.8	17.7	16.4	17.8	17.3	108.6	106.0	97.7
São Paulo	17.6	18.3	19.0	34.7	34.7	35.2	197.2	189.6	185.3
Central West and North	6.8	7.9	9.3	3.5	4.7	5.3	51.5	59.5	57.0

[a]The regions comprise the following states:
  Northeast–Maranhao, Piaui, Ceara, Rio Grande do Norte, Paraiba, Pernambuco, Alagoas, Sergipe, and Bahia;
  East–Minas Gerais, Espirito Santos and Rio de Janeiro;
  South–Parana, Santa Catarina, Rio Grande de Sul;
  Central West–Mato Grosso, Goias and the federal District of Brasilia;
  North–Amazonas, Para, and the Northern Territories.
[b]Latest year for which regional income distribution data are available.
Source: Population figures from *Annuário Estatistico do Brasil 1971*, Ministério do Planejamento e Coordenação Geral, Table 2.1.1.1.3, p. 41; income figures from *A Economia Brasileira e Suas Perspectivas*, July 1972, Table A.10.

migratory flood southward into the cities and, despite the small income differential, into the interior. These migrations are indicated in the census data which show the relative decline in population in the low-income states and increases in the high-income regions.

Sectoral Income Disparities

As a consequence of the dynamic growth of industrial output and productivity and the relative stagnation in the agricultural sector, the sectoral disparities in income intensified during the decade of the 1950s. While the industrial output grew at an annual average rate of about 8 percent, agricultural output increased at only 4 percent or slightly higher than the population growth rate of 3 percent. Moreover, productivity in industry continued to rise while the growth in agricultural output was due almost entirely to the increase in area under cultivation, primarily in the interior states. The rapid growth of the industrial sector reversed the relative role of industry and agriculture in the Brazilian economy. In 1947, agriculture generated 27.6 percent of national income; industry, 19.9 percent. By 1963, agriculture contributed 19.8 percent and industry 26.8 percent. With almost 60 percent of the Brazilian working force estimated to be in the agricultural sector, and an estimated 13.7 percent in industry, the per capita income in agriculture in 1950 must have been no more than a quarter of the per capita incomes in the industrial and service sectors. By 1960 the income disparity between agriculture and industry had increased while the gap with the service sector narrowed significantly.

A factor contributing to the rapid decline in the role of agriculture in the Brazilian economy during the 1950s was the absence of incentives to invest in that sector, as the government controlled agricultural prices, both domestically and externally, in order to support industrialization. On the domestic side, the prices of foodstuffs were controlled to maintain the real income of the industrial workers and to hold down industrial costs; and on the external side the overvalued exchange rate subsidized the imported inputs of raw materials and capital goods for the industrial sector. Agricultural inputs, however, had to be procured, in general, domestically at inflated prices. Consequently, at the time of the 1964 revolution, the structure of Brazilian agriculture remained basically unchanged from what it had been at the end of World War II. The same primitive methods were still being used in production, and the traditional forms of land ownership remained intact despite recurrent talk about land reform.

The relative decline in average income per worker in the service sector during the 1950s, shown in Table II-4, stemmed primarily from the rapid increase in the working force. The farm workers flooding into the city who were unable to find jobs in the industrial sector moved into the service sector, expanding the working force from 26.4 percent of the total in 1950 to 33.2 percent in 1960. The government accounted for the greatest share in this increase, which grew from 3 percent of the total labor force in 1950 to 7 percent in 1960. The huge expansion of the working force in the service sector reduced the average incomes in this sector to below those of the industrial sector; however, they remained in 1960 more than three times the average incomes in agriculture, more than enough to continue attracting workers into the cities.

Table II-4
SECTORAL DISTRIBUTION OF WORKING FORCE, INCOME
PER WORKER, 1950, 1960, AND 1968

Sector	Labor Force as Percent of Total			Income as Percent of Total			Income per Worker as Percent of Average Income per Worker		
	1950	1960	1970	1950	1960	1968[a]	1950	1960	1968[a]
Agriculture	59.6	53.7	44.2	26.6	22.6	17.7	44.6	42.1	40.0
Industry	13.7	13.1	17.8	23.5	25.2	28.5	171.5	192.4	160.1
Services	26.4	33.2	38.0	49.9	52.2	53.8	189.0	157.2	141.5

[a]Latest year for which sectoral income distribution data are available.
Source: *Conjuntura Econômica*, June 1970, for 1950 and 1960 data; 1968 data from *A Economia Brasileira e suas Perspectivas*, July 1972, Table A.10.

Social Imbalances

Aside from the disparities in regional and sectoral incomes, social imbalances arose from the nature of the industrial growth. The highly concentrated and capital intensive industrialization process aggravated the problem of creating jobs for a rapidly growing population, accelerated the urbanization process, and exacerbated the regressive character of personal income distribution. Employment in the industrial sector increased barely 25 percent during the 1950s, much less than the 40 percent population growth and the 55 percent increase in the working force during this same period. The inability of the industrial sector to create jobs, together with the massive migrations into the cities of the rural population seeking higher paying jobs, not only aggravated the unemployment problem, but also placed additional demands on the already overburdened municipal facilities and intensified an acute housing shortage. The mushrooming of favelos in Rio de Janeiro and the other major cities of the south-central region during these years served to highlight the social and economic inequities in the Brazilian economy.

Brazilian income distribution patterns are among the most regressive of any country in the world, industrial or developing. An analysis of the 1960 census by Albert Fishlow shows that the upper 3.6 percent of the active population received 25.4 percent of total income, while the lower 42.8 percent of the population received only 18.7 percent of total income.[3]

---
[3]Albert Fishlow, "Brazilian Size Distribution of Income," p. 392.

In addition to the inequities involved in urban unemployment and regressive income distribution, the purely economic consequences of the highly concentrated and capital intensive industrialization were ominous. The pyramidal income distribution in regional, sectoral and social terms tended to limit the horizontal extension of markets and eventually to dampen the Brazilian market for industrial produce. Moreover, having grown up under a heavy protective umbrella, industrial production was too high in cost to compete in the export markets. The policy response to this situation by the pre-1964 governments was to enlarge government expenditures of a social and infrastructure investment nature. Since these expenditures never touched the masses at the lower income levels (the rural masses outside the monetary economy gained little from the social programs), they served only to aggravate existing social and sectoral imbalances. The investment expenditures helped to maintain demand for industrial output and industrial employment, but this was at the cost of growing fiscal deficits and inflationary pressures, and these intensified the pyramidal structure of income distribution.

Causes of the Economic Crisis—1962 to 1964

The economic stagnation which began in 1962 and lasted through early 1967 has generated many explanations. Why should an economy that had been growing fairly steadily for a quarter of a century suddenly fall into an economic slump? The previous major economic recession in Brazil had been imported in the early 1930s as part of the worldwide depression. The recession which began in 1962, however, had domestic origins and has no simple explanation. Two diagnoses of the crisis which had significant policy implications were those of the Goulart government and of the Castello Branco government.

The Goulart government's diagnosis of the economic crisis was set forth initially in the Three-Year Plan for Economic and Social Development and later articulated in ECLA documents and in the writing of Celso Furtado, the author of the Three-Year Plan. They explain the Brazilian crisis, as they do the previous industrialization process, in terms of the reversal of two convergent factors, the exhaustion of import substitution as an inducement to invest and the loss of the effectiveness of inflation as a source of forced savings. Both factors involve a decline in the terms of trade for Brazilian exports. Furtado noted that import substitution as an incentive to investment in the industrial sector encountered a barrier in the form of the reduced import capacity. The increased difficulties in substituting domestic production for imported goods led to a rise of the relative cost of equipment and other capital goods and a consequent fall in the rate of investment. This process, Furtado added, was aggravated by the decline in the terms of trade after 1955, while the domestic market had not yet developed adequate incentives for continued investment and growth.

The second factor in this diagnosis of the crisis involved the decline in the effectiveness of inflation as a mechanism for transferring savings to the industrial sector, a circumstance which related to the terms of trade. The favorable terms of trade during the years prior to 1955 had helped to create the income which had been redistributed through inflation to industry without, however, imposing a burden on the other sectors of the economy. But once the terms of trade began to deteriorate after 1955, "the only remaining source that could feed inflation without providing a spiral of prices and costs was lost."[4]

While these two factors comprised the essential elements of Furtado's diagnosis of the Brazilian economic crisis, he also pointed to others: (a) the semi-feudal agricultural structure created an inelastic supply of food for the domestic market, concentrated income in favor of the land-owning classes, and usurped for agriculture part of the industrial sector's increased productivity through a persistent rise in relative prices; (b) the "insufficiency of overhead investment created tensions that increased the economy's vulnerability to inflation";[5] (c) the financial power of foreign firms and their failure to integrate into the national system created rigidities in the economy. In short, the crisis is attributed to everything but unsound economic policies and the industrialization process which they stimulated.

The Action Program of the Castello Branco government attributed the economic crisis to the series of accumulated disequilibria in the economy, especially to the imbalance between the industrial and agricultural sectors, which resulted from misguided economic policies. The Action Program noted that the drought in the southern states had damaged the agricultural harvest and adversely affected industrial production in 1963 due to the rationing of electrical energy. But the Action Program summed up the most important causes of the economic crisis as the "accumulation of distortions in the economy, the hyper-inflation, the sectoral and regional income disparities, the shortage of employment opportunities, and the disequilibrium in the

---

[4]Celso Furtado, *Diagnosis of the Brazilian Crisis*, p. 107.

[5]Ibid., p. 116. Werner Baer, however, argues persuasively that the rise in wholesale prices for agricultural prices did not accrue to the producer but to the middlemen and even in those cases where the producer did not receive the benefit of the higher prices, the proceeds were invested in industry where the returns were higher.

balance of payments."[6] This explanation of the Brazilian economic crisis almost precisely reproduced the diagnosis of the Brazilian economy prepared twelve years earlier by the Joint Brazil-United States Economic Development Commission of which Roberto Campos had been a member. As early as 1952 the joint commission observed several disturbing aspects in the economy: the "concentration of activities in Rio and São Paulo; 60 percent of all private construction, much of which was speculative investments in apartments for high income groups, occurred in these two areas"; the heavy reliance on foreign savings to finance investments; the current account deficit average of about 7 percent of total gross capital formation in 1947-49; the unbalanced growth among regions with regional terms of trade "increasingly unfavorable to the Northeast;" the shortage of power and transportation facilities, with the latter the largest single obstacle; the fact that "inflation is becoming an increasingly ineffectual and wasteful instrument for achieving the transfer of resources into investment;" "the policy of relative overvalued exchange rates and quantitative import restrictions [which] tended to favor internal expansion at the expense of external disequilibrium;" and "the resulting economic distortions and social tensions [that] cannot be shrugged off as unimportant."[7]

The economic program prepared for President Kubitschek in 1956 had included a similar diagnosis of the imbalances and disequilibrium in the economy and recommendations for a set of austerity measures to eliminate these distortions and imbalances before proceeding to the Target Program. Kubitschek apparently put the stabilization and reform portions of the recommended program in his desk drawer, where they remained for the duration of his regime, and proceeded with the more popular "Target Program for Development."

Summary Assessment

It is difficult to assess the long-term consequences of the import substitution industrialization approach to economic development. On the one hand, it did indeed give Brazil one of the highest economic growth rates in its history and an economic growth rate among the highest of any country during post-World War II years. On the other hand, these policies led almost inexorably to economic stagnation,

[6]Ministério do Planejamento e Coordenação Econômica, *Programa de Ação Econômica do Govêrno, 1964-1966*, pp. 19-21.
[7]Joint Brazil-United States Economic Development Commission, *The Development of Brazil.*

international bankruptcy, runaway inflation and an intensified concentration of income. Although the day of reckoning had been postponed through the Quadros regime and well into the Goulart period, when it finally came the intensity of the distortions and imbalances required more serious surgery with a longer convalescent period than if these measures had been taken years earlier. If the growth rates of 8.3 percent of the Kubitschek years, 1957 to 1961, are averaged with the 3.5 percent of the years of austerity from 1962 to 1966, the results of the import substitution policies are less impressive. Another factor which tends to reduce the significance of the high growth rates of the Kubitschek years is the inclusion in the growth data of the rapidly growing coffee production. In 1961, for example, when the growth rate of 10.3 percent is cited, coffee production was 36 million bags, of which about 12 million bags were added to the stockpile. By the time of the 1964 revolution, Brazil's coffee stockpile had reached 60 million bags. The annual buildup in the stockpile alone amounted to almost 1 percent of GNP.

The explanation of the Brazilian crisis necessarily involves a broad range of factors and trends: the traditional secular movement in the terms of trade of primary products; seasonal factors; and, for the first time in Brazil's history, an internally generated cyclical depression in industrial investment and output. The explanation involves the rapidly changing nature of the Brazilian economy, an economy which had been transformed dramatically during the previous decades of industrialization and which now for the first time could produce its own industrial production cycle. It also involves the basic dualism of the economy in that, by 1962, Brazil had developed into a prime example of the dual economy with a highly developed industrial sector existing side by side with a backward traditional agriculture. And within agriculture there was the modern sector producing primarily for export, cohabiting with "pick and hoe" techniques; and a profitable coffee sector with its excessive production, attracting resources from other farm products in short supply. Furthermore, the explanation involves the secular decline in the terms of trade for Brazilian exports, which started downward in 1955 and reached a low point in 1963. The diagnosis also involves the drought and the poor agricultural harvest of 1962, a periodic occurrence in Brazilian agriculture. All of these adverse trends were intensified by the imbalance in policy objectives and instruments, the distortions in the price structure, the structural and financial imbalances, the disparities in income distribution, and the balance of payments disequilibrium. A consequence of the growing economic difficulties was the political instability of 1961 to 1964 which in turn deepened the crisis of

1963 and 1964. To compartmentalize each of these explanations is to ignore the circles of cause and effect sequences which dominate political economy.

An important question for the economic profession is why increases in government spending in the early 1960s did not result in expanded output and employment. The Brazilian experience showed that continued increases in government spending tended only to increase money income, with the usual multiplier effects on prices, but without effect on real income and employment, despite the existing high level of unemployment and excess capacity in the economy. The cause of these developments must be sought in the nature of the Brazilian unemployment, in the relatively inelastic supply of agricultural foodstuffs, and in the other structural and financial distortions in the economy.

The unemployment was of a structural nature; even with a relatively high rate of economic growth, the economy was not providing sufficient jobs for the growing labor force. At the same time there was a shortage of skilled labor due to the inadequacies of the educational system. Agricultural output of foodstuffs did not respond to short-term increases in money demand and had kept pace with population growth rates only as the result of the opening of new lands in the interior rather than any increase in productivity in the coastal areas. Finally, the structural disequilibria created by distortions in the price structure required more than an increase in money incomes to overcome the problems in housing construction and the public utilities.

Under these circumstances the Keynesian economics did not provide an adequate analytical base to explain the seemingly contradictory trends of economic stagnation and excess capacity with rising inflation. More attention had to be given to the composition of the productive structure of the economy. Industrialization of the 1950s was a typical example of unbalanced growth; the leading industrial sector had grown out of proportion to the other sectors, causing structural bottlenecks which only a change in economic objectives, new policy instruments, new institutions, and time could overcome.

While Roberto Campos, Octavio Bulhões, and their fellow economists on the Castello Branco team had a sound diagnosis of the disequilibria in the economy, when the revolution came, these experts were not fully prepared with a comprehensive program. Their initial strategy, objectives, and policy instruments are discussed in the following chapter; their attempts and those of Delfim Netto and his colleagues to implement, innovate, and modify their policy instruments and the results of their efforts are described in succeeding chapters.

CHAPTER III

Strategy for Development, Stabilization, and Reform

> Whatever will be the judgement that History reserves for the Technocratic Period of the Government, it is not likely to be accused of immobilism or of the slavery of routine comfort. For during this period the Brazilian society was more than at any time exposed to what Lippman called, the "acids of modernity."
>
> Roberto Campos
> *Do Outro Lado da Cerca*
> (describing the three-year period
> of the Castello Branco government)

At the time of the April 1964 revolution the Brazilian economy had experienced two years of recession with declining per capita incomes; inflation accelerating above 100 percent per year; growing unemployment and underemployment; increasingly regressive income distribution; and near bankruptcy in the international accounts. Moreover, several financial distortions and structural imbalances served to perpetuate this chaotic state and to hinder any efforts at reform. The agricultural sector, which employed over half the Brazilian labor force but contributed only 20 percent of national output, lacked incentives for investment or for increasing production. The housing construction industry, stagnant for a decade or more, had neither incentives nor financing for investment in housing. The industrial sector began to experience for the first time in its short history an inadequate domestic demand, which, added to a cost level too high to compete in the export markets and a paucity of equity capital, tended to discourage further investments. The foreign trade sector, with disincentives to exports and prohibitive tariffs on imports, had remained stagnant for more than a decade. Excessive growth in the coffee sector had drawn resources from the production of other agricultural products in short supply and the costs of the sixty-million-bag stockpile added to the inflationary pressures. Continuing growth of unproductive public sector expenditures and deficit financing caused rapid inflation and placed a heavy burden on the private sector, both through heavy taxation and the forced savings mechanism. The distorted price structure, stemming from a series of price controls, and the resulting distortions in the financial structure diverted financial savings into inefficient speculative activities and limited the level of savings. Finally, the capital intensive nature of the industrialization created neither sufficient employment opportunities for a growing population nor the effective demand to sustain itself. The only favorable trend in this otherwise dismal picture was provided by the Northeast Development Program which had been building up momentum under the direction of former Planning Minister Celso Furtado. This was the economic situation confronting General Castello Branco as he took over the presidency of the Republic of Brazil in April 1964.

Political Background

The team of economists assembled by President Castello Branco to fill his economic cabinet posts comprised an outstanding group of professional economists. Roberto Campos, former president of the National Economic Development Bank, accepted the newly formed post of minister of planning and general coordination. Octavio Bulhões, a career economist in the Finance Ministry, Superintendent of the SUMOC (Superintendencia do Moeda e do Credito, predecessor of the the Central Bank) and economics professor, accepted the key post of finance minister. To organize the Central Bank Castello Branco called upon Denio Chagas Nogueira, an economics professor and consultant for numerous government commissions. To the presidency of the Bank of Brazil he attracted a prominent São Paulo banker, Luiz de Moraes Barros. Another prominent banker from Rio de Janeiro, Luiz Biolchini, accepted responsibility for straightening out the chaotic foreign exchange and debt affairs, while Casimiro Ribeiro, longtime colleague of Bulhões in the SUMOC and career Bank of Brazil economist, took on the task of managing the Central Bank of Brazil's credit operations. A respected economist from the Getúlio Vargas Foundation, Jose Garrido Torres, became president of the National Economic Development Bank.

These men formed the nucleus of the closely knit team of experts selected by President Castello Branco to assess the Brazilian economic situation and to prepare a strategy for moving Brazil back on the road toward rapid economic development. They brought to their assignments years of experience in the economic profession, in public service, and in banking. Many of them had served on the joint Brazil-United States commissions of a decade earlier; many had helped prepare the unimplemented austerity portions of Kubitschek's Target Program; and many had played a role in implementing the brief stabilization effort of President Quadros in 1961. These men had watched the growth of the distortions and imbalances in the Brazilian economy and had spoken out against the unsound policies with limited success. Their voices had been drowned out by the resounding success of the industrialization effort and the political unpopularity of the austerity measures they were prescribing. Now, with the full political support of President Castello Branco and the military oligarchy which took over the government on 11 April 1964, they had virtually free rein to implement their own development strategy, to build new instruments and institutions, and to restore the economy to the path of balanced economic growth. The problems, however, proved to be less susceptible to quick resolution than had been anticipated.

By the end of Castello Branco's voluntarily limited term of three years, his team of advisers had accomplished a comprehensive job of economic transformation in policies, policy instruments, institutions, and attitudes. They had managed to remove, with a few notable exceptions, most of the major distortions and imbalances in the economy. But most importantly, they had laid the foundation for resumption of a high rate of economic growth in a manner which stressed the social objectives of employment, of housing, and of regional, sectoral, and personal income distribution. By the end of their stay in government in March 1967 they had established the basis for a revolutionary housing program; they had built the Northeast Development Program into a successful industrialization effort for that region; they had changed the behavior of the Brazilian taxpayer; and they had transformed the chronic balance of payments deficit into a surprising surplus.

It was a period of intense and hectic activity on the part of the government planners. It was also a period of austerity and stagnation for the Brazilian economy. As the inflation proved to be more durable than anticipated, the continued austere stabilization measures cut the sources of credit expansion on which Brazilian businessmen had come to depend. Lacking alternative sources of capital, Brazilian business experienced a record number of bankruptcies, creditors' agreements, and liquidity crises. The almost daily volume of new decrees, regulations, laws, and circulars kept the business community in a constant state of confusion. This combination of events, the constant changes in the rules of the game affecting business and the restraints which limited credit availabilities to an undercapitalized business community, precluded development of a favorable investment climate. At the same time there was no alternative investment-generating sector to replace import substitution. The innovation in policies and institutions directed to this end required a long gestation period which precluded any significant impact on investment decisions and demand prior to 1967. The three years 1964 to 1967 constituted a period of rapid change and innovation in Brazilian economic policies and institution building. Roberto Campos described this period of the Castello Branco government as "o periodo do entresafra," the period between the harvests.

Marshall Costa e Silva, who replaced Castello Branco as president in March 1967, committed his government to continuing the general economic strategy and policies of his predecessor. In keeping with Brazilian tradition, he replaced the entire cabinet and all major government posts, including the president and directors of the fledgling Central Bank. However, to ensure continuity in economic policy he appointed to his cabinet and to the leading economic positions a team of economic experts with close ties to the previous government. The outstanding choice proved to be Antônio Delfim Netto as the minister of finance. He had been a professor of economics at the University of São Paulo until 1966 and at the time was serving as secretary of finance of the state of São Paulo. He had also participated in the planning efforts of the Castello Branco team. A private sector management specialist, Helio Beltrão, was appointed minister of planning and general coordination. Beltrão had helped to improve the management of the state oil monopoly, Petrobrás, and had served as management adviser in the organization of the Central Bank. The presidency of the Central Bank was initially filled by Ruy Aguiar da Silva Leme, an economic professor and colleague of Delfim Netto in São Paulo. He was replaced after less than a year by Ernani Galveas who had proven himself an effective director of foreign trade at the Bank of Brazil. Although a career Bank of Brazil economist, Galveas had also served, as have so many other senior Brazilian officials, as an economic adviser in the Finance Ministry. Other promotions within the government included Nestor Jost, from director to president of the Bank of Brazil; and two of the three directors of the Central Bank: Germano de Brito Lyra, promoted from manager to director of domestic credit operations, and Helio Marques Vianna, from manager to director of bank supervision. The third director, Ary Burger, had served as an economics professor at the University of Rio Grande du Sul and as secretary of finance of that state. While his primary interests focused on rural credit operations, he also handled foreign exchange operations until Paulo Pereira Lira was brought back from an assignment as alternate executive director of the International Monetary Fund to become director for Foreign exchange operations.[1] Continuity of policy in two major financial institutions was also assured by the retention of two gifted managers, Mario Trinidade, who had been appointed president of the Housing Bank only two months earlier, and Rubens Costa, president of the Bank of the Northeast since 1964.

The new team brought together by President Costa e Silva, while capable individually, did not initially constitute a cohesive group with accepted leadership as had the Castello Branco economists. But the economic problems confronting them revealed the need for leadership in economic policy making and the man who quickly rose to the task proved to be the young finance minister Delfim Netto. He proved his capacity not only in economic diagnosis and decision making, but also in political manuevering with the military oligarchy and in his ability to attract competent young technocrats into the government. Gradually the more independent economists were replaced by those willing to accept his lead, a process which accelerated in 1969 with the death of President Costa e Silva and his succession by General Emílio Garrastazv Médici, another senior member of the military oligarchy. President Médici broke with Brazilian tradition in retaining Delfim Netto as finance minister and several other effective economic ministers. Médici also strengthened the technical nature of the cabinet by appointing João Paulo dos Reis Velloso as minister of planning and coordination and Marcus Vinicius Pratini de Moraes as minister of industry and commerce. Velloso had served as coordinator of the Office of Applied Economic Research in the Planning Ministry under Roberto Campos from 1964 to 1967 and as deputy planning minister from 1967 to 1969. Marcus Vinicius de Moraes had served as economic adviser to President Costa e Silva. Both were members of the new breed of technical expert who increasingly came to manage the economic affairs of Brazil.

Strategic Options

The immediate problem confronting the Castello Branco government was to stop the inflation which, during the first three months of 1964,

---

[1] The number of Central Bank directors was increased from four to five, including the President, to accomodate Lira.

appeared to be running at an annual rate of 140 percent. At the same time the change in government following the April revolution offered an opportunity to reassess economic and social objectives and policies, and to consider new avenues of approach in order not only to reverse some of the adverse trends, but also to construct the basis for renewed economic development on a sound long-term basis. The occasion presented Roberto Campos, Octavio Bulhões, and their colleagues with four major strategic options: (a) to continue the trend toward greater centralization of economic decision making in the public sector or to reverse this trend and provide greater opportunity for the price mechanism and private sector initiative; (b) to continue the imbalanced growth of import substitution industrialization or to shift to a more balanced economic growth with several leading sectors; (c) to continue the protectionist trade policies or to liberalize foreign trade policies toward an expanding role in world trade; and (d) to continue the emphasis on rapid economic growth at the cost of social objectives or to aim at a greater balance in social and economic objectives at the cost of dampening the growth rate.

The choice between each of these options was not as easy as it might seem in retrospect. Given the tremendous need for infrastructure and the traditional Brazilian paternalism, the Brazilian public sector was destined to continue growing. On the other hand, the rapid growth of public sector expenditures combined with the inability to collect taxes had created an unmanageable inflationary surge and an inefficient bureaucratic apparatus burdening the entire economy. Industrial growth had been the generating force in the economy for many years, and in the longer term would have to resume that role. At the same time, the industrialization process had been at the cost of neglecting agriculture, exports, housing, and other sectors which could provide the domestic demand essential for the continued growth of industry. The protectionist trade policies had also proved to be an effective instrument for promoting industrialization, but again at the cost of neglecting exports and producing a chronic balance of payments disequilibrium. The choice between rapid economic growth and stabilization on the one hand, and more direct social objectives on the other, was no easier to decide than the other options. Concentration of income may facilitate, and postponement of consumption may be essential to, economic growth, but growth also requires for its sustenance the rising demand and consumption which come from a wider distribution of income.

These were the major strategic options which confronted the Castello Branco economists. The strategy which evolved tended to be guided by an economic philosophy which was liberal yet pragmatic, innovative, and eclectic in its implementation. The economists chose to reverse the trend toward a growing public sector in the economy and to give greater, scope to the free price mechanism and private initiative. They opted out of the imbalanced growth posture of import substitution industrializiation in favor of a more balanced growth with agriculture, housing, and exports sharing as growth-generating sectors. They decided to move gradually toward a more liberal foreign trade policy. Finally, while aiming primarily at increasing productivity and efficiency in the economic system, their strategy gave social objectives a key role. Both the housing and agricultural programs, two labor intensive sectors, were designed to increase job opportunities while the housing program carried its own self-validating social objective; the agricultural program also aimed at more equitable income distribution on a sectoral basis while the Northeast Development Program was oriented toward greater equity on a regional basis.

The economic strategy of the Castello Branco government was first outlined in the Action Program for 1964-1966 and later developed in a variety of planning documents.[2] In the foreward to the Action Program, Roberto Campos characterized the general framework of the strategy as "a process through which the economic agents, consumers, [and] enterprises, adequately motivated, learn to mobilize efficiently the human and material resources in order to realize the maximum economic growth potential of the society." Campos emphasized that "a necessary, if not a sufficient, condition to [development] is to want to develop, to adopt the motivation and the line of action which leads to development." He described the publication of the Action Program as a "new step in the sense of seeking the indispensable understanding and participation of all in the task of planning and economic coordination. When the economic chronicle of the Revolution is written, the phase which is hereby initiated will be characterized principally by dialogue."[3]

In more prosaic language, the Action Program has been described as "an analysis of Brazilian economic problems, a statement of policy objectives and an indication of the policy measures to be undertaken to attain those objectives."[4] The diagnosis of Brazilian economic problems, which formed the basis for the Action Program, is summarized in Chapter 2. The economic and social policy objectives included:

---

[2] Ministério do Planejamento e Coordenação Econômica, *Programa de Ação Econômica do Govêrno, 1964-1966.*
[3] Ibid., p. 5.
[4] Benjamin Higgins, "The 1964-1966 Action Program of the Brazilian Government."

(a) accelerating the rhythm of economic development, aiming at a 6 percent growth rate by 1966 and 7 percent in succeeding years;
(b) countering progressively the inflationary process during 1964 and 1965 so as to achieve a reasonable degree of price equilibrium in 1966, which, translated into specific numbers, meant price targets of 25 percent in 1965 and 10 percent in 1966.
(c) alleviating the sectoral and regional disparities and the tensions created by social disequilibria so as to improve the standard of living;
(d) assuring, through investment policy, opportunities for productive employment;
(e) correcting the tendency for uncontrolled balance of payments deficits.[5]

An examination of the policy instruments applied by the Castello Branco government to achieve these objectives forms the major part of this study. Before turning to the specific application of each policy instrument in succeeding chapters, I will discuss the major elements of the strategy of development, stabilization and reform.

Development Strategy—1964 to 1967

The Action Program of the Castello Branco government, as stated, aimed at achieving an annual growth rate of 6 percent in 1965 and 1966 and 7 percent in the succeeding years. Assuming a population growth rate of 3.5 percent, this meant an increase in per capita output of 2.5 and 3 percent respectively.[6] These growth rates appeared to be reasonable inasmuch as Brazil had averaged 6 percent between 1947 and 1961 and 7 percent between 1957 and 1961. The program recognized, however, that resumption of these relatively high growth rates would require a greater investment effort than during the earlier years because of the rising marginal capital-output ratio. The widespread neglect of social infrastructure and the extensive nature of development in the agricultural sector during the 1950s had permitted high growth rates with a relatively low capital-output ratio. The focus of investments in the industrial sector had permitted a high growth in output per unit of capital. With the greater emphasis on increasing

[5] Ministério do Planejamento, *Programa de Ação Econômica*, p. 15.
[6] The population growth rate had been rising steadily from 1.5 percent per year between 1920 and 1940, 2.4 percent between 1940 and 1950 and 3.17 percent between 1950 and 1960. Projecting this upward trend produced a growth rate of 3.5 percent for the 1960s. The 1970 census showed that instead of rising as projected, the population growth rate turned downward to 2.89 percent during the 1960s, permitting proportionally higher increases in per capita output.

agricultural productivity and output, on housing, and on other social infrastructure, the marginal capital-output ratio would have to rise above the level prevailing during the 1950s (estimated at 2) and the level of investments would have to be significantly higher to achieve the same rate of growth in output. For example, on the assumption of a marginal capital-output ratio of 2 and a depreciation rate of 5 percent of GNP, the investment ratio necessary to achieve a 6 percent growth rate would have been 17 percent. Or, assuming a marginal capital-output ratio of 2.5, which is closer to those in the industrial countries, the gross investment ration would have to reach 20 percent to achieve a 6 percent growth rate. A gross investment ratio of at least 18 percent was also essential to increasing employment, another important objective of the Action Program. Estimates of the capital per worker in agriculture and industry indicated that a gross investment level of 18 percent of GNP was essential to absorb the estimated 1.1 million new members entering the labor force each year and to alleviate some of the unemployment and underemployment which had increased during 1962 and 1963.

The key question in the development strategy was how to mobilize domestic and foreign resources so as to achieve the targeted levels of investment and growth. Import substitution policies had been effective in stimulating investment in the industrial sector during the 1950s but these policies no longer served as a major source of investment generation. Also, the forced savings process of inflation no longer served as a mechanism for financing investments. The diagnosis of the crisis had revealed the need to develop alternative investment generating sources and, at the same time, new mechanisms to finance these investments.

How was Brazil to make the transition from an import substitution model to a self-sustaining growth model? The Goulart government gave a response similar to that recommended by ECLA, that is, to expand the public sector investments, "for only the public sector, with its relative significance within the economy, is capable of providing autonomous demand on a sufficient scale to counter-balance the negative effects of the exhaustion of the external stimulus."[7] The Castello Branco economists, however, rejected an increased role of the public sector as detrimental to growth, emphasizing instead measures to stimulate investments in the private sector. At the same time, these private sector investments had to satisfy the social objectives of providing more equitable income distribution on a regional, sectoral, and personal basis.

[7]Economic Commission for Latin America, "Fifteen Years of Economic Policy in Brazil," p. 157.

Treatment of the agricultural sector also revealed the differing development strategies of the Goulart and Castello Branco governments. Whereas the former considered land reform as the major solution to the agricultural problem, the latter diagnosed the agricultural crisis as one of low productivity and inadequate production, and offered as the solution new incentives to investment in agriculture.

In summary, the main lines of the development strategy emphasized the role of the private sector, particularly agriculture. The first order of business was to remove the price controls, quantitative restrictions, and other financial distortions which impaired the incentives to invest in these sectors, even though the change conflicted with an urgent need for price stability. The second order of business was to create new policy instruments and institutions to stimulate savings and to channel these savings into priority sectors. While a degree of price stability and elimination of the distortions in the price structure were essential conditions for investment and growth, they were not sufficient conditions. Also needed were new incentives to investments in the agricultural sector, new mechanisms to expand housing construction, improved machinery for achieving higher growth rates in the northeast region, and new institutions to mobilize savings for the expanded investment effort. In addition, the public sector expenditures had to be restrained so as to release resources for private sector investment. Furthermore, there was a need for development of new incentives for export promotion, new mechanisms for controlling the burdensome foreign debt, and new policies to foster foreign investments.

Stabilization Strategy—1964 to 1967

The achievement of a relative degree of price stability received a high priority in the economic strategy of the Castello Branco government. With prices rising at an annual rate in excess of 100 percent even with the widespread repression of specific prices, there was little hope of achieving other economic and social goals without first restoring some sanity to the price structure. The major questions were how to achieve the necessary degree of price stability and correct the distortions in the price structure with minimum costs to other objectives. The answer to these questions involved two issues: (a) whether the greater part of the burden of stabilization should be imposed on the private or the public sector; and (b) whether stabilization should take the form of shock treatment in the manner of the post-World War II European stabilization programs and as recommended by the International Monetary Fund, or whether it should proceed as a more gradual reduction in prices.

Both the assessment of the cause of inflation and the development strategy supported the conclusion that the stabilization effort should focus on restraining the public sector; yet the Brazilian political and social realities did not permit decisive outright cuts in public spending. The economists realized that they were not able to restrain salary increases for the Brazilian military establishment except in an indirect manner. The military had received a 100 percent salary increase shortly after the revolution and other public sector employees received similar increases shortly thereafter. A wage freeze at that point would have impinged on the salaries of private sector workers, whose wage adjustments normally came towards the end of the calendar year; the result would have been a lower level of real wages for private sector workers than for those in the public sector. The experts considered such a development to be inconsistent with social justice, economic efficiency, and their development strategy, which called for a reduced, not increased, public sector role in the economy. These considerations played a vital part in the solution of the second issue, gradualism versus shock treatment.

The issue of alternative approaches to price stabilization in Brazil had been debated for years without any definitive conclusion. Proponents of the shock treatment, generally of a monetarist inclination, argued that it was not feasible to halt inflation by slow degrees since inflationary expectations did not change gradually but in sudden reversals. The proponents of gradualism, usually of a structuralist bias, generally argued that "the shock required for stability might well result in drastic unemployment, cutback of essential investment programs of the government, or restriction of credit to such a degree that financial panic and business failures would ensue."[8]

In choosing between these alternative approaches to stabilization the Castello Branco economists opted for gradualism and the achievements of the Brazilian economy through 1972 tend to confirm their decision. The financial distortions and structural imbalances in the economy which had developed as a result of years of controls on interest rates, exchange rates, wages, public utility rates, and prices of specific commodities could be eliminated only over an extended period of time. The Brazilian economy had reacted to these controls by building up many institutional and behavioral defenses which could not readily be changed. The proliferation of branch banks and finance companies, a consequence of interest rate controls, had in-

[8]Richard Ruggles, in Economic Commission for Latin America, "Inflation and Growth: A Summary of Experience in Latin America" p. 18.

flated the costs of financial intermediation. The shock treatment approach would have put the 250 finance companies and many of the branch banks out of business overnight with attendant chaos for the financial system. A shock treatment approach would also have damaged the undercapitalized Brazilian industrial corporations. The combination of interest rate controls and the unfavorable tax treatment had induced Brazilian firms to rely excessively on borrowed capital. These firms would not have had time to adjust their capital structures, thus, many otherwise sound business ventures would have collapsed. This approach would also have resulted in abrupt changes in the sectoral composition of demand for goods and services with unfavorable consequences for prices and employment. Imbalances in the structure of demand which had arisen during the years of inflation could only be corrected over a longer period. The overgrown consumer goods industry, a result of the hoarding of consumer durables as an inflation hedge, was an example of such an imbalance. Any abrupt change in demand would result in reduced output and employment without, however, affecting prices which tended to be rigid in a downward direction.

The existence of a high level of residual inflation in the price structure offered an additional argument for a gradual approach to stabilization. Public utility rate controls, rental controls, and controls on food prices and exchange rates had tended to suppress prices in many sectors. Elimination of these controls, while an essential part of the financial surgery, would tend to provoke an inflation of a residual or corrective nature, and in the short-term would offer no off-setting additional supply and employment responses.

The final and perhaps compelling argument for gradualism was that it facilitated achievement of the aim of reducing the public sector's role in the economy. Given the political constraints on reducing consumption expenditures (in current prices), inflation provided a mechanism for reducing these expenditures in real terms.

In addition to the domestic considerations supporting gradualism, the Brazilian economists noted the disappointing results of the shock treatment in other countries. In some instances, they noted, curtailment of the money supply had been partially offset by increases in the velocity of money; the shock approach did not restrain inflation any sooner than the three years envisaged in their gradualist stabilization strategy. In other countries, they found the conditions completely different from those prevailing in Brazil; either the monetary system had been completely destroyed as a consequence of war, hyper-inflation, or major injections of foreign aid; or there had existed no tradition of chronic inflation; or wage bargaining had been abandoned.

In short, adoption of the gradualist approach to stabilization was based primarily on an assessment of what was economically, politically, and administratively feasible in the Brazilian context. The timetable for stabilization indicated that the strategy was a compromise between the liberal framework of the overall economic and social program and the Brazilian economic and political realities; in this sense it was also a compromise between the structuralist and the monetarist positions. The stated objective of the stabilization strategy was to reduce the rate of inflation gradually from the estimated annual rate of 144 percent during the first quarter of 1964 to 80 percent for the year 1964, to 25 percent in 1965, and to 10 percent in 1966. For a country which had experienced an average inflation of 20 percent over a period of twenty years, the 10 percent goal did not appear to be an easy one.

The choice of policy instruments to attack inflation reflected the liberal economic philosophy of the Castello Branco specialists. Of the major instruments for achieving stabilization, fiscal restraint received priority. This meant cutting current expenditures and subsidies to the transport *autarquia*, improving tax enforcement, and restoring confidence in the public debt. The goal of monetary policy, on the other hand, was to give ample scope for private sector credit. Given the irreversibility of inflated costs and the inflationary residuals, an expansion of private sector credit was considered essential to economic recovery. The guiding principle was to permit an expansion in private sector credit in proportion to the increase in the money supply. Because fiscal restraint received the main burden of stabilization, it followed that the smaller the growth in public sector credit needs, the smaller would be the growth in private sector credit. In this sense, monetary and credit policy, which affected only private sector credit, was treated as a residual instrument in the stabilization program.

Initially, the stabilization strategy focused on public sector wage policy and containment of the salaries of government personnel, especially the military, within some acceptable level. The means to achieve the containment was found in the wage policy formula, which essentially limited wage increases to maintaining the average real wage over the previous 24 months. The formula was applied to the public sector wage increases in early 1965 and later in the year was extended to the private sector following recognition that the 35 percent price target in that year would not be achieved without more stringent measures.

The Strategy of the New Economists—1967 to 1972

The strategy outlined in 1967 by Finance Minister Delfim Netto and the new group of economists of the Costa e Silva government was essentially the same as that of the Castello Branco team's Action Program: to pursue balanced economic growth with diversified investment generating sectors; to restrain the role of the public sector while stimulating more rapid growth of the private sector; to stimulate an expansion in foreign trade; and, finally, to give high priority to increasing employment opportunities and other social objectives. The transitional operational plan for implementing the long-term development strategy differed, however, in one significant respect from the Action Program of the Castello Branco team. The new plan aimed at stepping up the pace of economic activity to a full employment level at the cost of the short-term reduction in the rate of inflation. The plan continued the gradualist approach to fighting inflation but, instead of a three-year target as in the Action Program, it called only for a gradual reduction over time. In this sense the implementation of the economic strategy became less doctrinaire and more flexible in response to the changing conditions.

The change in the operational plan from a defined to an extended period of gradualism found its rationale in Delfim Netto's diagnosis that cost-push factors had come to predominate in the inflationary process and that stabilization measures themselves had played a major role in the economic stagnation prevailing since 1962.[9] Periodic attempts by successive governments to restrain excess demand through wage, fiscal, and monetary policies had tended to reduce output and employment with only limited effect on prices. The new operational plan appeared to be a reversion to the pre-1964 years, but there were some very significant differences. Demand stimulation involved primarily wage policy, fiscal policy, and monetary policy. The wage formula was modified to ensure that increases in real wages would be in line with increases in productivity. Political, social, and economic considerations demanded a halt to the decline in real wages which had occurred during the austere wage policy of the previous three years. The tight credit policy of 1966 had already been reversed, following the exchange rate devaluation of February 1966 and the speculative reflows of foreign exchange. On the fiscal side, the government granted business a forty-five-day delay in the payment of the national sales tax, an action which provided the equivalent of a 6 percent increase in credit, interest-free, for nonagricultural purposes.

While wage, fiscal, and credit policies were aimed at stimulating demand in the depressed sectors, pricing and interest rate policies were aimed at limiting the price effects of the demand-stimulating measures. The new look in pricing policies involved a slowdown in

---

[9]Samuel A. Morley, "Inflation and Stagnation in Brazil," pp. 184-203.

the intensity of the corrective price increases and the establishment of a price surveillance mechanism, an Interministerial Price Commission, for reviewing price increases in key industries. Interest rates, which had increased steadily, in real terms, from negative levels in 1964 to very high positive levels in 1967, also received special attention as a cost-push factor in the inflation. The government now attempted through direct intervention (subsidies and interest rate ceilings) to reduce the average interest cost to Brazilian business.

The operational plan also involved a strong element of flexibility in the implementation of policy instruments such as coffee-pricing, interest rate, and exchange rate policies. Once it was accepted that stabilization would not be accomplished in a defined period these prices had to be adjusted more frequently and in a more gradual manner so as to avoid further distortions in the price structure. Thus, a more flexible coffee-pricing policy was initiated in 1967, the trotting peg exchange rate system in 1968, and a more liberal interest rate policy in 1970. The increased flexibility in these prices not only helped to avoid the development of new price distortions, but, perhaps equally important, also helped to moderate the periodic fluctuations in credit availabilities which severely hampered business investment and output. The evolution of each of these policy instruments is developed further in succeeding chapters.

Consequences of the Balanced Growth Strategy

The Brazilian economy responded slowly and unevenly to the transition from an unbalanced to a balanced growth strategy. By the end of its term of office in 1967 the Castello Branco team had achieved neither a relative degree of price stability nor a resumption of economic growth. The stabilization strategy directed at achieving relative price stability in three years proved to be overly optimistic and, in a sense, self-defeating.[10] Also, the balanced growth strategy proved no more effective in stimulating a quick recovery in economic growth than in achieving price stability. Increases in GNP during the years 1964 to 1966 barely kept pace with population growth. As the three-year regime came to an end in March 1967, the industrial sector remained in the same stagnant state which had persisted since 1962. The improved balance of payments and the rapid growth in the Northeast region provided the only relatively bright spots in this

---

[10] Ibid., p. 203. I mean self-defeating in the sense that Morley noted. He suggests that orthodox monetary policy is self-defeating in that tight credit affects supply rather than demand. After a long period of tight credit for the private sector, he says, credit becomes so scarce that firms are unable to finance working capital.

otherwise dismal performance. The more realistic exchange rate and export promotion policies, combined with a recession-induced decline in imports, contributed to a dramatic surplus in the balance of payments and a much-needed buildup in foreign exchange reserves. The Northeast, stimulated by the changes in agricultural and export policies, continued to be the fastest (albeit still at an inadequate rate) growing region of the country.

Not until 1967, three years after the initiation of the Action Program, did the innovation and change in institutions and economic policies begin to take effect. It took these three years to reduce the distortions in the price structure, to develop new instruments and institutions for the mobilization of savings, and to stimulate several significant changes in the productive structure of the economy, all of which eventually rechanneled the economy toward a sustained growth process.

Savings and Investment

The innovative approach of the Castello Branco government proved to be very time consuming. The gradualist approach to stabilization involved a series of unexpected problems which were overcome only through experimentation with old financial institutions and development of new ones. The programs to generate savings and investments required an even greater gestative period to become effective. Whereas the Housing Bank Law was one of the very first measures approved by the Castello Branco government in 1964, the measures to overcome the paucity of capital for housing in an inflationary environment were not undertaken prior to the development and implementation of the three major cornerstones of the program: the Workers' Pension Guaranty Fund, monetary correction, and an effective Housing Bank. The Workers' Pension Guaranty Fund, derived from 8 percent of the salaries of workers who participated in it, provided compulsory savings for the housing program. The application of monetary correction to the savings and loan instruments assured the maintenance of the real value of the workers' pensions and protected the bank resources from future erosion through inflation. The final cornerstone of the housing program, an effective implementing institution, was finally put into place in January 1967 with the appointment of Mário Trinidade to the presidency of the National Housing Bank. Trinidade provided the strong executive leadership needed to administer a program which came to influence about 2 percent of Brazil's national production. With the establishment of these three essential elements, the National Housing Program began in early 1967 to make a major impact on investment demand and within a few months the São Paulo industrial firms were tooling up to meet the anticipated demand from the housing sector.

Two other domestic programs to stimulate investments, the agricultural programs and the Northeast Development Program, progressed at the same slow pace of progress as the housing program. Although the legislation for the agricultural pricing and credit programs was approved already in 1964, the detailed measures and implementation had not been completed at the time of the change in governments in March 1967. Brazilian agriculture began to recover as early as 1965 from the easing of price controls, the elimination of restrictions to exports, and the more realistic exchange rate policy; also, a few commodities benefited from the minimum price guaranty program. But neither the minimum price program nor the rural credit program added any significant incentives to agricultural investment prior to 1967.

The fiscal incentive for investment in the Northeast experienced similar delays. The time required from the initial deposit of the investment credits in the Bank of the Northeast until their release for an approved project was measured in years. Until the end of 1966 the flow of funds into the Bank had served to maintain easier credit conditions in the Northeast than in the other regions of the country, but they had no significant impact on the level of investments in the Northeast until toward the end of 1967.

The Castello Branco government's effort to stimulate foreign investment in Brazil encountered the same time consuming process as its domestic programs. The project evaluation, negotiation, and bureaucratic delays which characterize infrastructure loans from the international financial institutions precluded any significant impact on the level of investments for the first few years after 1964. As a consequence of the cessation of international lending during the years prior to 1964 and the usual time lag between loan authorization and implementation, the international institutions received net repayments on previous loans between 1964 and 1968. Not until 1968 did the flow of new loan disbursements to Brazil exceed the repayments. Meanwhile, there was no alternative to running a large current account surplus, which meant a net foreign disinvestment during each of the years from 1964 to 1966, a development which significantly slowed the pace of stabilization. The current account finally moved into a deficit in 1967, permitting a net transfer of foreign savings into Brazil in that year, while the growing disbursements from the international institutions provided an additional stimulus to investment demand for major infrastructure projects.

The rising investment demand financed by the four major sources—housing, agriculture, the Northeast Development, and the international institutions—generated a resurgence in the Brazilian economy beginning in mid-1967 and continuing through 1972. The combination of the almost infinite investment needs in these four areas and the savings from their respective programs provided the Brazilian economy with four new sources for stimulating economic growth on a sustaining basis. Perhaps the most innovative aspect of these programs was the diverse sources of savings for financing these investments. Compulsory savings in the form of the Workers' Pension Guaranty Fund provided more than ample financing for the housing construction boom which began in 1967. Forced savings through subsidized credit expansion financed new investments in agriculture. Induced savings in the form of the fiscal incentive generated new industrial investments in the Northeast; and foreign savings, derived from the international lending institutions and the mechanism of a current account deficit, financed a growing number of infrastructure projects. The investment demands from each of these sources and their impact on the Brazilian economy are elaborated upon in Chapter IX.

National accounts data show the downward trend of investments from 1964 to 1966 as both private and public sector investments declined sharply. The marginal savings ratio (the ratio of net capital formation to GNP) fell from a relatively high level of 18.7 percent in 1964 to only 8.5 percent in 1966. While several factors adversely affected investments in 1966, the credit crunch in that year, given the heavy reliance of Brazilian business on credit rollovers to finance working capital, clearly played a key role in the sharp decline. Only in 1967, after the several savings-investment programs outlined above became effective, did the marginal savings ratio begin to rise, reaching 19.8 percent in 1968.

Trends of Growth

The Action Program of the Castello Branco government aimed at growth rates of 6 to 7 percent and a relative degree of price stability (below 10 percent) by 1966. In 1966 the actual growth rate reached 5.1 percent which, in per capita terms, meant a 2.2 percent increase (see Table III-1). While this was a significant improvement over the previous two years in which the growth rate had barely kept pace with the population growth, it still fell far short of the growth rates of the late 1950s. Moreover, the recession in the industrial sector at the end of 1966 portended no significant improvement for 1967, indicating

Table III-1

ANNUAL RATES OF GROWTH IN GNP—TOTAL, PER CAPITA, AND BY SECTORS, 1964–1972[a]

Year	Agriculture	Industry	Services	GNP	GNP Per Capita[b]
1964	1.2%	5.5%	2.1%	2.9%	0.0%
1965	14.0	−5.0	2.7	2.7	0.0
1966	−3.2	12.0	5.1	5.1	2.2
1967	5.7	3.0	5.7	4.8	1.8
1968	1.5	13.2	8.5	8.4	6.3
1969	6.0	10.8	9.1	9.0	5.9
1970	5.6	11.1	9.0	9.5	6.4
1971	11.4	11.2	11.3	11.3	7.7
1972	4.1[c]	13.8[c]	10.3[c]	10.4[c]	7.3[c]

[a] Percentage change over prior year in constant prices.
[b] Based upon population growth rate of 2.9 percent per year according to the 1970 census.
[c] Estimated.
Source: *A Economia Brasileira e Suas Persepectivas*, July 1972, Table A.2; For 1972—*Conjuntura Econômica*, February 1973, p. 6.

that the balanced growth strategy had not yet effectively taken hold, that alternative private investment sources had not replaced public sector investment sources. During the years 1964 to 1967, the Brazilian economy remained in the doldrums, with periodic spurts in agricultural or industrial production, but no simultaneous increase in both during the same year. The GNP growth rates remained below 3 percent in both 1964 and 1965, rising to 5.1 percent in 1966 as the result of temporary stimulants to industrial production in late 1965. But at the end of 1966 industrial production again began a decline which continued through the first quarter of 1967.

April 1967 marked in the Brazilian economy the turning point toward a balanced and sustained growth pattern which has persisted through 1973. Despite poor agricultural harvests in 1968, the gross national product in that year rose by 8.4 percent, which in per capita terms, meant an increase of 6.3 percent. This was achieved in spite of a sharp decline in coffee production in that year. The year 1969 proved to be the first year since 1961 in which both the agricultural and industrial sectors combined to produce a growth rate as high as 9 percent. The continuing balanced growth rates of agriculture and industry in 1970 and 1971 showed clearly that this was no accident.

Corrective Inflation

The stabilization effort still had not achieved by 1972 the results targeted in the Action Program for 1966. By the end of the decade, almost seven years after the April 1964 revolution, inflation still had not been reduced to the level projected in the Action Program for 1966, as can be seen in Table III-2.

In examining the reasons for the failure to achieve the target level of price stability, we must distinguish between two periods: April 1964 to March 1967, and March 1967 to December 1972. During the earlier period of the Castello Branco government, stabilization remained a major economic objective. The Castello Branco economists based their three-year stabilization strategy on a compromise between the orthodox approach of the IMF and recognition of the Brazilian realities. Fiscal policy, monetary and credit policy, and wage policy instruments focused on the achievement of a relative degree of price stability. The results, while not a successful as had been anticipated, were significant, as the rate of inflation declined from 91 percent in 1964 to 38 percent in 1966. Nevertheless, frustration over their inability to reduce the inflation to the targeted 10 percent for 1966 provoked the Castello Branco team to impose an extremely tight monetary program during that year, as a result of which the inflation rate dropped to 28 percent in 1967. But the tight credit program also had its adverse repercussions for the industrial sector, particularly the consumer durable industry, which is normally

Table III-2
ANNUAL RATES OF INCREASE IN GENERAL PRICE INDEX, 1964–1972

Year	Targeted[a]	Actual[b]
1964	80%	91.9%
1965	25	56.8
1966	10	37.9
1967	15	28.4
1968	15	24.2
1969	15	20.8
1970	15	19.8
1971	15	20.4
1972	12	15.4

[a]Projection used in annual monetary budgets (described in Chapter IV).
[b]*Conjuntura Econômica*, June 1973.

heavily dependent upon financing. Toward the end of 1966 the industrial sector experienced a sharp cutback in output which was reflected primarily in the production data for 1967.

There were two main causes of the failure to achieve a
relative degree of stabilization during the years 1964 to 1967. The
first was an underestimation of the amount of corrective inflation
needed to eliminate these price distortions. Years of repression in
rents, prices of public services, some basic foodstuffs, interest
rates, and even the exchange rate had created distortions in the
price structure which could be corrected only by more rapid
increases in these prices than in other prices. The alternative of
reducing the prices of other commodities while continuing price
controls was rejected as unrealistic given the downward inflexibility of prices and wages. As the price controls were gradually
removed, rapid increases in prices for housing, public services,
and foodstuffs added to the inflationary pressures. Increased
prices of imported goods, as the result of exchange rate devaluations, also added to the inflation.

The second cause of the incomplete victory over inflation was
the conflict of stabilization objectives with other economic and social
objectives of the government. The industrial recession, aggravated
periodically by on-again, off-again tight monetary programs, induced
the authorities to offer special fiscal stimulants to durable goods purchases in both 1964 and 1965. On the other hand, the stimulants
prevented a greater reduction in the fiscal deficit, which remained a
major source of demand inflation. The agricultural and coffee policies, directed towards increasing output and incomes in these areas,
also resulted in additional inflationary pressures as the 1965 crops,
especially coffee and rice, proved to be unexpectedly large. The
equally unexpected but very welcome surplus in the balance of payments in both 1964 and 1965 further conflicted with the stabilization
objective. A buildup in foreign exchange reserves and reconstruction
of Brazil's foreign creditworthiness were essential to the resumption
of economic growth, but in the shorter term, the surpluses added to
the inflationary pressures.

The transfer of an increasing volume of funds to the Northeast Development program also conflicted with stabilization objectives. While the fiscal cost of the several elements of this program
equalled the fiscal deficit in 1965 and 1966, the economic and
social needs of this impoverished region did not justify any
cutback for stabilization purposes. In short, the stabilization
objective did not stand alone as the major objective of economic
policy. On the contrary, the stabilization program required "an

effort to orchestrate a number of policy instruments to regulate demand—curtailing some sources and stimulating others—in order to slow down the inflation and achieve balance of payments viability, while maintaining employment and an acceptable distribution of income among the principal economic groups, and laying the basis for the resumption of rapid economic growth."[11]

External Equilibrium

While the Castello Branco government moved in the direction of a balanced growth strategy in the domestic economy, it also shifted from a disequilibrium to an equilibrium strategy in the foreign sector. The equilibrium strategy included: (a) a rapid expansion in export earnings, (b) a restructuring of the foreign debt toward longer maturities, (c) restoration of foreign creditworthiness, and (d) attraction of foreign capital. The effectiveness of the measures to achieve these objectives is evident in Table VIII-10. Brazilian exports, which had stagnated at a level of about $1.4 billion for two decades, doubled between 1964 and 1970 and reached $3.7 billion in 1972. Foreign confidence in the Brazilian economy and its ability to service its debts was restored within three years, but this also had required a strong domestic savings effort, for in each of the three years 1964 to 1966, Brazil exported more goods and services than it imported (the current account surplus totalled $558 million), permitting an improvement in its foreign exchange reserves position and a reduction in short-term liabilities.

With the restoration of confidence, foreign capital began in 1968 to flow into Brazil in increasing amounts. Gross capital inflows doubled in 1968 over 1967 and continued sharply upward through 1972. Debt amortization also began to rise rapidly, but net capital inflows, which had averaged only $56 million in the four years 1964 to 1967, rose to $450 million in 1968 and by 1972 had reached an estimated $3.3 billion.

The rapid growth of foreign capital inflows after 1967 permitted Brazil not only to expand imports at a faster rate than exports, but also at the same time, to build up to an adequate level foreign exchange reserves. By 1972 Brazilian merchandise imports, at $4.1 billion, exceeded by three times the $1.3 billion level of 1964, which had also been the average import level for the preceding decade. At the same time, gross foreign exchange reserves rose from $219 million (the equivalent of three months' imports) at the end of 1963 to over

---

[11]Irving Sirkin, "Fighting Inflation in Brazil: Some Tentative Lessons," p. 38.

$4 billion at the end of 1972 (the equivalent of 12 months'imports at the 1972 import level).

The large volume of capital inflows also created an equally large absolute increase in Brazil's foreign indebtedness. Debt service payments increased from $451 million in 1963, about 30 percent of export earnings in that year, to an estimated $1.2 billion in 1971, also about 30 percent of export earnings in that year. This rapid growth in amortization and interest payments required on the part of the authorities constant attention to sound debt management practices, reserve management and a continued increase in exports. These are the major elements of an equilibrium system, for a slackening in the growth of exports is likely to affect the debt service capacity, which in turn affects the level of foreign capital flows.

Trends in Income Distribution

The most controversial aspect of Brazilian economic policies of the eight years following the 1964 revolution has been and continues to be the impact of these policies on income distribution. There are several indications that personal income distribution became more regressive during the initial period of stabilization as a consequence of the decline in real wages of urban workers, the general stagnation in the economy, and the high rate of urban unemployment. Beginning in late 1967 the upward surge of the economy and the stimulation of the labor intensive construction industry tended to reduce the rate of unemployment and, more importantly, the degree of underemployment. Moreover, revision of the wage policy in 1967 had helped to maintain the real wages of urban employees since that time. But, in general, available statistical evidence and observation points to a continuation of the basic dualism of the Brazilian economy with one of the most regressive patterns of income distribution to be found in any country.

Preliminary data from the 1970 census indicates a further deterioration in the personal income distribution shares, even though in absolute terms the incomes of all groups increased during the decade. The incomes of the higher income groups rose faster than those in the lower categories.[12] While personal income shares declined during the 1960s, on sectoral and regional bases there has been some leveling of income shares. The northeast states and most of the other poorer states improved their relative income shares through 1967, the latest

---

[12]Professor Albert Fishlow has provided some preliminary statistical analysis in "Brazilian Size Distribution of Income," pp. 391-402. A more detailed analysis of the 1970 census data has been undertaken by Carlos Langoni, " Distribuição da Renda e Desenvolvimento Econômico do Brasil," pp. 5-88.

date for which detailed national income data are available (see Table II-3). The northeast region did increase its share of total national income, but even with the continued exodus of population from that region—although at lower rates than during the 1950s—the average per capita income of that region rose only moderately. In 1967, the average income per capita of that region remained about half of the national average, only a fifth of the city of Rio de Janeiro, Guanabara, and a quarter of the state of São Paulo. During the years 1960 to 1967, average incomes of the working population in the agricultural sector also improved slightly relative to the higher income industrial and service sectors. The income share of the agricultural sector continued to decline throughout the 1960s, but the rapid rate of movement of the working population into the cities permitted a small relative increase in the average income per worker in agriculture. Still, the average incomes in agriculture in 1967 averaged less than a fourth of the incomes in industry and a third of the incomes in the service sector (see Table II-4).

The mass movement of the Brazilian population from the countryside into the cities continued throughout the 1960s. The urban population increased by 65 percent during the decade while the rural population increased by only 7 percent. By 1970, the urban population comprised 57 percent of the population compared with 45 percent a decade earlier.

Assessment of Balanced Growth Strategy

In assessing the economic and social consequences of the balanced growth strategy pursued by successive Brazilian governments since 1964, we distinguish between two periods, April 1964 to mid-1967 and from mid-1967 through 1972. These two periods are distinguished primarily by varying economic performances, with the first period characterized by stagnation with a rapid decline in the rate of inflation, and the second period by a rising rate of economic growth and moderate declines in the rate of inflation. These two periods also coincide with the regimes of the Castello Branco technocrats, under the leadership of Octavio Bulhões and Roberto Campos, and the new breed of economist under the leadership of Antônio Delfim Netto. The economic strategies pursued by these two regimes remained generally the same throughout the two periods, with the single major exception of price stabilization strategy.

The change from a definite to an indefinite period of gradualism in achieving stabilization had two significant implications for economic policy: first, a more expansive private sector credit policy and, second, greater flexibility in the application of policy instruments. The most important example of the latter is the flexible exchange rate, or trotting peg, system initiated in August 1968.

In retrospect, it would seem that the economic strategy during the period 1964 to 1966 erred in excessive restraint on public sector investments. Public sector investments might have been retained or even increased at the cost of delaying the stabilization period until the new investment-savings programs began to have their impact. At that time the public sector investments could have been phased down concomitantly with expansion from the new investment sources. Instead, the curtailment in public sector investments aggravated the economic recession. And, given the widespread condition of excess plant capacity in the industrial sector, the periodic tax cuts to stimulate demand tended only to increase the purchases of consumer durables with no impact on investment demand. A higher level of public sector investments and a greater degree of flexibility in the application of the policy instruments (for example, interest rates, exchange rates, coffee pricing) might have permitted a higher level of output and employment in these years without jeopardizing the stabilization effort.

The stabilization strategy of achieving a relative degree of price stability within three years proved to be overly optimistic and in a sense self-defeating. By the end of its term of office, the Castello Branco government had achieved neither the relative degree of price stability nor the targeted rate of economic development. Moreover, the excessively tight credit imposed by the Castello Branco team in 1966 contributed to the defeatist attitude toward stabilization which persisted through 1972. The erroneous assessment that credit ease in 1967 brought Brazil out of the 1962-1966 stagnation provided the basis for the liberal credit policy which continued to induce and validate the price increases.

It is interesting to speculate whether the economic recovery in 1967 would have been achieved with a less expansive credit and fiscal policy. Would the growth rates in 1968 and later years have achieved the same high level without private sector credit expansion of 35 percent per year? The answer to this question would depend, in part, upon one's assessment of the amount of corrective inflation remaining in the economic system during these years. While there is some evidence that a number of price distortions, especially in rents, continued as late as 1972, their significance in overall price structure appeared to be relatively insignificant. The liberal credit and fiscal policies of 1967 tended to stimulate additional demand for durable consumer goods, as they had done in 1964 and 1965 when the Castello

Branco government had resorted to similar temporary expedients. They did not serve to stimulate additional investment.

The recovery of investments in 1967 and ensuing years is attributable to the several new investment programs in housing, agriculture, the Northeast, and infrastructure. The simultaneous stimulation of demand for consumer durables in 1967 added largely to the price pressures and served to lock in productive factors from shifting to the new investment sectors. On the other hand, Brazilian business remained in 1967 heavily dependent on loan capital for working capital purposes so that an excessively tight credit policy might have dampened the growth of the new investment sectors. On balance, given the very rapid growth in investments in 1967 and 1968, some dampening of demand would have permitted the same high growth rate with a slight reduction in the rate of inflation.

An important consideration which argued against a tight credit policy was the desire to protect the Brazilian private sector from the public sector and from the foreign private sector. From 1964 to 1966, the investment race was limited to the Brazilian private versus public sector. Foreign investors had little interest in Brazil during these years: the disruption of the economy, the political uncertainties, and the retention of Goulart's Profit Remittance Law served as deterrents. However, as the economic situation brightened and the stability of the military oligarchy seemed more secure, the foreign investors resumed their interest in Brazil, creating a three-way struggle for Brazilian investment resources.

Renewed foreign interest in Brazil in 1967 and 1968 intensified the concern about foreign domination of Brazilian industrial enterprises. The widespread bankruptcies and creditors' agreements resulting from the stabilization measures had forced Brazilian enterprises onto the market at bargain prices for those with access to credit, especially those who had access to foreign credit on more reasonable terms than that available in Brazil. Credit policy came to play an essential role in avoiding foreign takeovers of Brazilian business.

One approach to minimizing foreign takeovers might have been to restrict foreign capital inflows. Instead, the Brazilian authorities pursued a policy mix of attracting foreign investment while ensuring an adequate supply of credit for the Brazilian private sector. In practice, this meant an expansion of private sector credit in proportion to the increase in the money supply. The larger the public sector credit needs and the larger the balance of payments surplus, the larger the increase in private sector credit needed to achieve proportionality with the money supply. Another measure to ensure an adequate supply of credit to the Brazilian private sector was the requirement, implemented in 1967, that at least 50 percent of the assets of each bank be lent to Brazilian firms.

Finally, the impact of the post-1964 economic strategy on income distribution is an essential part of any assessment. In the previous chapter we noted the regressive trends in income distribution on a personal, sectoral, and regional basis during the 1950s. The evidence for the 1960s shows only slight improvement in income distribution shares on a sectoral and regional basis, but a continued deterioration on a personal basis. There is some evidence that much of the deterioration in personal income shares occurred during the 1964 to 1967 austerity period, with some improvement in the following years as the economy moved into high gear. The unanswered question is whether the economy could have returned to a high growth period without the extended period of restructuring and austerity. My assessment, with the benefit of hindsight, is that, given the severity of the imbalances and distortions in the economy in 1964, the stabilization measures and structural changes were essential conditions for a resumption of growth, but that these changes might have been of a shorter duration.

Another important question is whether deterioration in the income distribution is a necessary consequence of rapid economic growth. Is there an essential trade-off between growth and income distribution? My response to this question, based upon my assessment of the Brazilian experience, is that there is no necessary trade-off, that the relationship between income distribution and growth depends upon the nature of the growth, whether labor intensive or capital intensive, and whether balanced or unbalanced. The income distribution-growth trade-off controversy is reminiscent of the earlier savings-investment controversy. Continuation of Brazil's rapid economic growth depends upon more equitable income distribution to ensure the expanding domestic markets to sustain that growth. It also depends upon a mobilization of savings to finance the capital requirements of a high growth rate. In short, continuity of Brazil's rapid growth requires a balance between an expanding domestic market and the resource mobilization to satisfy that market.

CHAPTER IV

Monetary and Credit Policy

Monetary and credit policy in the traditional sense of measures to control the overall cost and availability of credit has played only a minor and passive role in the Brazilian development strategy. Expansionary fiscal policies combined with interest rate ceilings in the inflationary environment imposed severe limitations on the effectiveness of the monetary authorities who, concerned about inflation, restricted credit to the only segment of the economy over which they had any degree of control, that is, the Brazilian private sector. Thus, the history of monetary policy during the period leading up to the 1964 revolution was one of progressive increases in compulsory reserve requirements and a relative decline in private sector credit availabilities. Meanwhile, the public sector and the companies with access to foreign credit expanded rapidly.

In diagnosing excessive public sector expenditures as the cause of inflation, the Castello Branco government emphasized in its stabilization program the containment of expenditures, improvement in revenues, and the development of noninflationary means of financing the deficit. Monetary policy continued to focus on limiting the supply of credit to the private sector with results similar to those in the earlier years.

In 1967 monetary policy received a new look. Frustrated by the combination of continuing inflation and stagnation, Finance Minister Delfim Netto decided to experiment with a new credit-rationing policy, the aim of which was to ensure, despite the stabilization effort, an adequate supply of credit for priority sectors and industries. In particular, the credit-rationing policy aimed at ensuring that the Brazilian private sector received its proportionate share of total credit availabilities and was not squeezed out by either public sector or foreign sector credit demands. In permitting credit to the Brazilian private sector to rise proportionately with the rise in total money supply, the new policy meant that the larger the monetary expansion from public sector or foreign sector operations, the larger the private sector credit necessary to maintain the three-way balance. This new credit policy became the major source for perpetuating the inflation after 1967. Interestingly enough, it is also similar to the approach to credit allocation developed spontaneously during the 1950s, with the important difference that in the earlier period, priority was given to the public and industrial sectors, while in the later period the private sector, agriculture, and exports received priority treatment.

The Monetary Management Apparatus

The traditional distinction between fiscal and monetary policies is not particularly useful in explaining their respective roles in the Brazilian inflation. Fiscal policy is normally limited to the expenditure, revenue, and borrowing policies of the federal government, while the traditional concept of monetary policy involves those measures which affect the cost and availability of credit. In these two policies there is an implicit assumption of separate authorities of the Treasury and the Central Bank managing fiscal and monetary policies respectively. In the Brazilian financial structure both monetary and fiscal policy decisions have been centered in the National Monetary Council (the Council of SUMOC before 1964) with the finance minister as chairman, while the implementation has been largely by the Bank of Brazil which served until 1965 as fiscal agent of the Finance Ministry in addition to its functions as central bank and commercial bank.

While in general fiscal and monetary policies came under the centralized jurisdiction of the finance minister and the monetary council, the latter in fact did not have jurisdiction over a wide range of fiscal policy decisions. Decisions regarding the pricing policies of public autarquia, the contracting of internal and external debts by the autarquia and public enterprises, and pricing policies of the semi-autonomous institutes for coffee, cocoa, sugar, wheat, oil and the social security system—all these were made by separate entities. The National Highway System, for example, under the jurisdiction of the minister of transport, had its own source of earmarked revenues from the petroleum tax, which was not included in the fiscal budget. The minister of transport also had authority to negotiate foreign loans. The minister of mines and energy similarly controlled the pricing and investment policies of the major iron mining company (CVRD) and the electric power company (Elektrobras); the minister of interior managed the oil producing monopoly (Petrobrás); and the minister of commerce and industry set policy for the publicly owned steel companies. Finally, the two major public development banks, the National

Economic Development Bank (BNDE) and the Bank of the Northeast (BNB) came under the jurisdiction of the ministers of planning and interior respectively, and each received earmarked tax revenues outside the federal budget. But whether or not the financial transactions of these agencies, autarquia, and institutes came under the federal budget, the Bank of Brazil was the implementing bank for all of them.

The Functions of the Bank of Brazil. The Bank of Brazil is the key to understanding the Brazilian financial system. It has three major functions: (a) it serves as fiscal agent for the government not only in administering government accounts but also in financing government operations on an open-ended basis; (b) it serves as a commercial bank in competition with the private banks; (c) it has some of the functions of a central bank.

The Bank of Brazil manages on behalf of the Treasury several operations which are outside the normal budget. These operations include the coffee account, the minimum price support program for agricultural products, the sugar and alcohol account, the rubber program, and wheat and oil imports. Revenues for these operations are not included in the budget; thus, whenever there is a deficit in the operation, the bank is required to finance it on an open-ended basis. The coffee account, described in greater detail in Chapter X, is the net result of the purchases and sales of coffee, which involves domestic and foreign prices, production, foreign sales, and reinvestments in the coffee sector. If the crop is large and the Coffee Institute buys large quantities of coffee for the stockpile, the Bank of Brazil may have to finance a large portion of this crop. The financing is accomplished by credit creation, which the bank can do without being limited by reserve requirements.

The Bank of Brazil is also the largest commercial bank in Brazil, with several thousand branches providing about 35 percent of the total credit to the private sector. Again, since it is not subject to reserve requirements, its loans to the private sector are limited only by the overall credit ceilings imposed upon it by the National Monetary Council and by the willingness of the bank's president to adhere to these ceilings. This has not always been the case. From 1959 to 1963, for example, Bank of Brazil loans to the private sector increased over ninefold; in the same period, commercial bank loans increased less than five times.

Prior to establishment of the Central Bank on 1 April 1965, the Bank of Brazil fulfilled many of the functions of a central bank. Regulation of the foreign exchange market was handled by its foreign ex-

change department; control of the rediscounts and reserve requirements of the commercial banks was carried out by the rediscount
department; even the SUMOC was staffed by Bank of Brazil personnel and was generally under the administrative responsibility of
the Bank of Brazil president.

It can be seen from this that the president of the Bank of Brazil
was a powerful official in any administration. With authority over 35
percent of total loans offered at negative interest rates (in real terms),
the president and branch managers of the bank were in a position to
make or break many a businessman. Despite the generally recognized
fact that the personnel of the Bank of Brazil were among the best
trained and most dedicated bureaucrats in Brazil, this authority was
nevertheless subject to abuse.

It can also be seen from this description of the functions of the
Bank of Brazil that its operations may contribute to inflationary pressures independently of the monetary authorities through the extension
of credit either for nonbudgetary government operations or to the
private sector or to both.

The National Monetary Council. The central position of the Bank
of Brazil in the traditional areas of both fiscal policy and
monetary policy required a centralized authority to control both
areas. The first attempt at such an authority was the SUMOC,
established in 1947 at the suggestion of Professor Bulhões. It was
intended to be a temporary and intermediate organization pending
a gradual move toward the establishment of a central bank. For
reasons beyond the scope of this study, SUMOC was not able to
exercise sufficient authority over the Bank of Brazil, and successive finance ministers, who by law were the chairmen of
SUMOC, frequently had to resort to presidential assistance to
control independent-minded Bank of Brazil presidents.

The 1964 revolution and the appointment of Professor Bulhões as
finance minister provided the opportunity to establish a central bank
and to strengthen control over the operations of the Bank of Brazil.
By the end of 1964 the Council of SUMOC had been replaced by the
National Monetary Council with the four central bank directors re-
placing three of the four Bank of Brazil directors. the other members
of the council included the finance minister as chairman, the Bank of
Brazil and BNDE presidents, and two representatives of the private
sector. While the National Monetary Council was expected to control
all fiscal and monetary policy issues, the degree of control in fact
depended largely on the cooperation of the executing agencies, which
differed from time to time.

Even after the establishment of the National Monetary Council, the Bank of Brazil retained most of the functions involving both fiscal and monetary policy implementation. To obtain a comprehensive picture of all the determinants of changes in the money supply it is necessary, therefore, to comprehend operations of both the Bank of Brazil and the Central Bank, the so-called monetary authorities in what is known as the National Monetary Budget.

National Monetary Budget. The first attempt to bring some semblance of unified control over Brazilian monetary policy was initiated in SUMOC in 1962 under the leadership of Professor Bulhões. This took the form of a forecast of the monetary impact of the several determinants of primary reserve money.[1] While in no way changing the control mechanism, the monetary forecast provided the Council of SUMOC with an improved basis for projecting the overall monetary impact of public sector operations both within and without the federal budget. Following the 1964 revolution and the appointment of Professor Bulhões to the position of finance minister, this forecasting process was incorporated into law and was made an essential part of the stabilization effort. The Banking Law of 1964, the same law which transformed the Council of SUMOC into the National Monetary Council and enlarged SUMOC into the Central Bank of Brazil, also stipulated that a National Monetary Budget should be approved annually by the council.

The National Monetary Budget is essentially a forecast of all the major fiscal and monetary accounts which affect changes in the quantity of money. Changes in the assets and liabilities of the Brazilian monetary authorities (which for reasons described above include the Bank of Brazil) are the basic sources of changes in the assets of the private banking system and the public. The distinguishing characteristic of the operations of the Brazilian monetary authorities, compared with other central banking authorities which deal only with the banks, is that, as combined central bank and commercial bank, its operations effect changes in both the commercial bank assets (bank reserves) and assets of the public (currency held by the public and demand deposits in the Bank of Brazil). The major assets of the monetary authorities include: loans to Treasury; loans to the private sector; foreign exchange reserves; and the open-ended credit accounts provided by the Bank of Brazil for the minimum price guarantee program, for the coffee operations, and for purchases of export

---

[1] Eduardo Gomes, an economist in SUMOC at the time and later chief of the economics department of the Central Bank, provided much of the information on the national monetary budget.

and import commodities such as wheat and sugar. The major nonmonetary liabilities are deposits of the government autarquia and the deposits of the Coffee Defense Fund, which in Table IV-2 are reduced by the amount of loans and rediscounts for coffee operations. Increases in deposit accounts of government agencies, which are considered nonmonetary liabilities, tend to reduce monetary liabilities, or more generally to offset increases in assets on the other side of the ledger. The relative significance of each of these major accounts can perhaps best be seen in the balance sheet of the monetary authorities at the end of 1963 (see Table IV-1).

Each of the asset and nonmonetary liability accounts of the monetary authorities affects the money supply through its direct impact on the monetary liabilities of the monetary authorities, known also as primary reserve money. Changes in each major asset and liability account is the consequence of pricing, investment, and other policies in the respective sector. Changes in the Treasury loan account, for example, are determined by policies and developments in the fiscal sector which are described in Chapter VI. Policies affecting foreign asset changes are described in Chapter VIII, while the minimum

Table IV-1

GROSS DOMESTIC PRODUCT AND MONEY SUPPLY INCOME VELOCITY OF MONEY, 1953–1963

(millions of Cr$, current prices)

Year	Gross Domestic Product	Money Supply: Average Monthly Balance	Income Velocity of Money
1953	466	112.6	4.17
1954	623	136.9	4.58
1955	778	162.7	4.81
1956	989	196.6	5.07
1957	1,211	243.3	5.00
1958	1,448	338.7	4.30
1959	1,975	411.7	4.83
1960	2,734	568.7	4.85
1961	4,029	823.1	4.92
1962	6,539	1,266.1	5.21
1963	11,857	2,007.6	5.94

Source: Gross domestic product data from *Conjuntura Econômica*, June 1970; money supply and income velocity data from Simonsen, *Inflação: Gradualismo & Tratamento de Choque*, p. 92.

price guarantee program and purchases and sales of commodities are included as part of agricultural developments in Chapter IX. The monetary impact of coffee pricing policies and other developments in the coffee sector are covered in Chapter X. The remainder of this chapter focuses on private sector credit policies and the overall impact of all these programs and policies on primary reserve money and on the money supply.

Monetary Trends—1953 to 1963

The money supply, we noted earlier, was not a prime target of economic policy in the years immediately prior to 1964. The rate of expansion of the money supply was a residual function of fiscal policy, which aimed at providing adequate credit for the public sector, and private sector credit policy. That the Brazilian inflation was closely related to the increase in the money supply is evident from even a cursory examination of the data. The supply of money, defined in the traditional sense of currency in the hands of the public plus demand deposits in the commercial banks, expanded twenty-two times during the decade prior to December 1963. During the same period the Brazilian price level increased about 15 times. When the growth in GNP is brought into the monetary equation, changes in money supply explain about 97 percent of the increases in prices. The income velocity of money, which increased from 4.17 in 1953 to 5.94 in 1963, explains less than 3 percent of the increase in prices during the period (see Table IV-1).[2]

But to find a high correlation between changes in the money supply and prices is not to say that the monetary expansion was the cause of Brazilian inflation. To find the basic causes of inflation we must look at the sources of monetary expansion which are the result of specific policy actions undertaken by the government. We must in fact examine the impact on effective demand and prices of fiscal sector operations, agricultural pricing and credit programs, coffee operations, private sector credit policies, and foreign exchange operations.

Determinants of Monetary Expansion—1953 to 1963. Examination of the sources of monetary expansion during the decade from 1953 to 1963 reveals the startling difference in the trends of public sector (federal government and federal agencies) and private sector credit. Table IV-2 summarizes the major asset and liability items of the banking

---

[2]Mário Simonsen, *Inflação: Gradualismo & Tratamento de Choque*, pp. 92-93.

Table IV-2
SOURCES OF MONETARY EXPANSION, 1953–1963
(millions of Cr$, current prices)

		1953	1963	Change, 1953–63
A.	Assets of Banking System	149.1	3,254.9	3,105.7
	1. Public sector loans	10.2	1,257.1	1,246.9
	Loans to Treasury to finance the deficit	8.0	915.2	907.1
	Commodity purchase programs	.4	71.3	67.1
	Loans to autarquia	.3	37.8	34.9
	Loans to Treasury for exchange operations	1.5	232.8	237.9
	2. Private sector loans	120.4	1,946.0	1,825.6
	Bank of Brazil loans			
	Commercial bank loans			
	3. Other assets & liabilities (net)	18.6	51.8	33.2
B.	Nonmonetary liabilities	32.5	616.9	584.4
	1. Public sector	9.8	362.2	352.4
	Autarquia deposits	7.4	155.0	147.6
	Counterpart of exchange operations .	2.4	207.2	204.8
	2. Private sector	22.7	254.7	232.0
	Time deposits	17.7	89.4	71.7
	Prior deposits for exchange contracts	5.0	165.3	160.3
C.	Monetary liabilities (money supply)	116.7	2,638.0	2,521.3

Source: *Relatório do SUMOC*, 1953 and 1963.

system for 1953 and 1963 and the changes in these items during the decade. Of the total expansion in the money supply of Cr$ 2521.3 million, public sector loans (less public sector deposit) explain Cr$ 894.5 million and loans to the private sector (again less deposit offsets) explain Cr$ 1493.6 million. The startling aspect of these trends is the fact that the federal government accounted for 35 percent of the credit expansion during this decade while its share of GNP did not exceed 14 percent.

Table IV-3 compares the trends of federal government and private sector credit availabilities in real terms and as percentages of GNP and money supply. In real terms (expressed in 1963 prices and using the implicit GNP deflator), credit to the federal government increased over 9 times between 1953 and 1963 while credit to the private sector increased by only 20 percent. Credit to the federal government rose from 2.2 percent of GNP in 1953 to 10.5 percent in 1963; meanwhile private sector credit declined from 25.7 to 16.6 per-

Table IV-3

FEDERAL GOVERNMENT AND PRIVATE SECTOR CREDIT, 1953 AND 1963

	1953	1963	Change, 1953–63
In millions of Cr$, current prices			
Federal government	10.2	1,257.1	1,246.9
Private[a]...............................	120.4	1,946.0	1,825.6
In millions of Cr$, 1963 prices			
Federal government	136.0	1,257.0	1,121.0
Private	1,612.0	1,946.0	334.0
As percentage of GNP			
Federal government	2.2	10.5	+8.3
Private	25.7	16.6	−9.1
As percentage of money supply			
Federal government	8.8	47.7	+38.9
Private	104.4	74.0	−30.4

[a]Includes state and local government credit
Source: *Relatório do SUMOC*, 1953 and 1963.

cent of GNP. Similar trends are evident when compared with the money supply.

Closer examination of the individual sources of monetary expansion reveals some other significant trends. Loans to the Treasury to finance the deficit were by far the most important source of public sector credit expansion; but loans to the Treasury to cover foreign exchange operations also became a significant and particularly burdensome item. These were loans by the Bank of Brazil for payment of foreign exchange obligations of the Treasury. As they were carried on the books as a foreign currency obligation, these foreign exchange obligations maintained their real value, increasing in cruzeiro terms with each exchange devaluation.

Two other trends of nonmonetary liability items were significant: the declining trend of time deposits (in real terms and as a percentage of the money supply) and the increasing reliance on the part of the authorities to prior deposits for exchange contracts. Time deposits fell off from 15 percent of the money supply in 1953 to 3.4 percent in 1963 as the public found the rate of return on these deposits far less than the rate of inflation and shifted into real assets and into the *letras de cambio* market (see Chapter VII). The prior deposits for exchange contracts increased from 4.3 to 6.2 percent of money supply during the same period. While aimed at limiting import demand and preserving limited foreign exchange availabilities, they also offset in small part the monetary expansion stemming from the growth in loans, thereby reducing further the credit availabilities to the private sector.

Measures for Controlling Private Sector Credit. Private sector credit was the whipping boy of Brazilian monetary policy during the pre-1964 period. Since the public sector had first claim on credit availabilities, occasional attempts at monetary restraint to contain inflationary pressures were usually directed at limiting credit expansion to the private sector. The Brazilian monetary authorities had at their disposal two measures for controlling private sector credit. They could control directly more than 35 percent of private sector credit merely by placing credit ceilings on each of the branches of the Bank of Brazil. Through the use of compulsory reserve requirements, they had an effective measure to control the remaining 65 percent of private sector credit extended by the private commercial banks. Of the three traditional monetary tools, rediscount rates, open market operations, and compulsory reserve requirements, the last was the only effective measure available to the Brazilian authorities. Open market operations, the main instrument for monetary control in the United States and many other developed countries, were not possible in the absence of a money market, particularly a functioning market for government bonds.

The Brazilian authorities did not use rediscount rates, another traditional monetary control measure, for two reasons. In the first place, Brazilian banks viewed their use as an indication of insolvency rather than of illiquidity, so that none of the sounder banks willingly resorted to rediscounts. In the second place, there was no relationship between the level of rediscount rates and bank loan rates. The usury law effectively limited rediscounts to a maximum of 12 percent while commercial bank loan rates exceeded this figure by two or three times. In 1963, for example, the average rate of return on bank loans was 30.5 percent which implied a much higher effective interest rate. Instead of manipulating rediscount rates, the Brazilian tradition has been to establish quantitative ceilings on rediscounts, based upon a fixed percentage of deposits and capital plus reserves. These normal rediscount lines were limited by law to the level of capital plus reserves, but in practice the rediscount department of the Bank of Brazil (now of the Central Bank) fixed the rediscount ceilings at 10 percent of demand deposits; the legal ceiling usually applied only to the larger banks. In addition to the normal rediscounts, the rediscount department also extended special rediscounts for a variety of priority regions, sectors, industries, and commodities such as coffee, cocoa, and cotton.[3]

Since commercial banks tended to maintain a relatively high degree of liquidity in the form of voluntary reserves (cash and deposits at the Bank of Brazil), rediscounts have been relatively unimportant in the Brazilian banking system; they amounted to little more than 4 to 6 percent of deposits during the 1950s. Rediscount facilities were used primarily by the smaller and newer banks which sought a short-term profit from the large disparity between the loan and rediscount rates, and the state banks, which were pushed to the level of illiquidity in their attempts to finance state budgetary deficits. The inflationary impact of the rediscounting operations by the state banks is discussed in Chapter V.

In short, neither rediscount rates nor quantitative ceilings on rediscounts offered effective measures to control bank credit because of the traditional attitudes toward rediscounts, interest rate controls, and the relative insignificance of rediscounts in relation to bank deposits.

The Brazilian monetary authorities overused compulsory reserve requirements to the point of abuse during the decade prior to 1964. Prior to the establishment of the Central Bank in April 1965, compulsory reserves of the commercial banks were deposited in the Bank of Brazil which, being a commercial bank, was free to use these deposits for its own lending operations, including financing the deficit of the Treasury. As reserve requirements were not applicable to the Bank of Brazil, an increase in reserve requirements did not necessarily affect total bank lending capacity; any reduction in commercial bank loans could be, and often was, offset by comparable increases in Bank of Brazil loans to the Treasury or to the private sector.

Compulsory reserves remained at a relatively low level prior to 1956, averaging 3 to 4 percent of deposits; but after 1956 they were gradually raised, as the rate of inflation intensified, reaching a rate of 15.7 percent at the end of 1963 (see Table IV-4). In addition to the compulsory reserves, the banks normally held a fairly high percentage of their free or voluntary reserves in the form of deposits in the Bank of Brazil. Since all bank clearings went through the Bank of Brazil, these deposits formed an essential part of liquid balances. Lacking a money market or other liquid assets as secondary reserves, the banks by necessity maintained extremely high cash reserves. In 1953 they amounted to 18 percent of deposits and by 1963 reached 20.4 percent

---

[3]These special rediscounts provide another measure for channeling credit to priority sectors and to industries for the stimulation of development, but they also contribute to the inflationary propensity of the Brazilian financial structure.

Table IV-4

COMMERCIAL BANK RESERVES AND DEPOSITS, 1953–1972

(end of year data in millions of Cr$, current prices)

Year	Total Reserves[a]	Compulsory Reserves	Voluntary Reserves	Deposits: Demand & Time	Ratio of Reserves to Deposits		
					Compulsory	Voluntary	Total
1953	19.3	3.3	16.0	89.0	3.7	18.0	21.7
1954	23.0	4.1	18.9	105.3	3.9	17.9	21.8
1955	27.2	4.5	22.7	122.2	3.7	18.6	22.3
1956	33.0	6.3	26.7	147.7	4.3	18.1	22.4
1957	53.7	14.5	39.2	200.4	7.2	19.6	26.8
1958	65.8	24.2	41.6	241.9	10.0	17.2	27.2
1959	103.4	37.6	65.8	352.4	10.7	18.7	29.4
1960	144.0	56.5	87.5	485.6	11.6	18.0	29.6
1961	199.4	76.8	122.6	666.0	11.5	18.4	29.9
1962	374.9	166.0	209.2	1,094.3	15.1	19.1	34.2
1963	645.0	280.0	365.0	1,793	15.7	20.4	36.1
1964	1,088	469	618.7	3,218	14.6	19.2	33.8
1965	2,075	1,016	1,058.8	6,042	16.8	17.5	34.3
1966	2,511	1,178	1,333	7,068	16.7	18.9	35.6
1967	3,441	1,911	1,530	11,155	17.1	13.7	30.8
1968	4,834	2,923	1,911	15,922	18.4	12.0	30.4
1969	5,732	3,568	2,164	20,603	17.3	10.5	27.8
1970	6,880	4,492	2,388	26,590	16.9	9.0	25.9
1971	9,870	5,943	3,927	36,288	16.4	10.8	27.2
1972 (Oct.)	11,465	7,331	4,134	44,500	16.5	9.3	25.8

[a]Deposits in BOB plus cash in vaults and compulsory reserves.

Source: 1952 to 1964—*Relatório do Banco Central*, 1965, p. 206; 1963 to 1965—*Relatório Marco*, 1969; 1967 to 1972—*Boletim do Banco Central do Brasil*, December 1972, pp. 28-29, Table 1.9, and pp. 24-25, Table 1.7.

of deposits. Thus, by the end of 1963, 36 percent of bank deposits were tied up in nonearning assets, leaving only 64 percent of assets available for loans to the private sector. This low percentage of earning assets in the commercial banks' portfolios constituted one of the reasons for the high cost of financial intermediation and contributed to the cost-push side of the inflation.

Private Sector Credit Policy and Consequences. Increasing credit constraints on the Bank of Brazil and the commercial banks limited the growth of private sector credit. In real terms, that is, deflated by the implicit GNP deflator, credit to the private sector outstanding at the end of 1963 remained only slightly higher than it had been a decade earlier when the real output of Brazil was only half as large. The relative decline in private sector credit is more pronounced when considered in relation to the money supply and GNP. As a percentage of money supply, private sector credit declined steadily from 107 percent in 1953 to 97 percent in 1963, and as a percentage of GNP, declined fairly steadily through 1962 and dropped sharply in 1963 (see Table IV-5).

The increasing restraints on private sector credit from 1957 to 1963 resulted in a nationalization of credit, development of a high cost

Table IV-5

PRIVATE SECTOR CREDIT AS PERCENT OF MONEY SUPPLY AND GNP, 1953–1963

Year	Private Sector Credit (millions of Cr$)		as % of Money Supply	As % of GNP
	current prices	1963 prices		
1953	120	1,612	107	25.7
1954	152	1,652	111	24.2
1955	171	1,600	105	21.8
1956	205	1,545	104	20.6
1957	255	1,700	105	20.9
1958	312	1,865	92	21.4
1959	401	1,945	97	20.2
1960	565	2,090	99	20.5
1961	781	2,165	95	19.3
1962	1,254	2,240	99	19.2
1963	1,946	1,946	97	16.4

Source: *Relatório do Banco Central do Brasil*, 1965, p. 185; 1963 prices based on implicit GNP deflator; GNP money supply data is based on Table IV-1.

financial intermediation system, denationalization of Brazilian industry, and a dampening of growth in investment and output. With larger increases in credit from the Bank of Brazil and other official banks while credit from the private banks was constrained, private bankers began to express concern about the "nationalization of credit," a tendency which paralleled similar trends toward nationalization of the Brazilian economy during these years. High reserve requirements and interest rate constraints contributed to the development of high cost financial intermediation. Controls on deposit rates, by shifting time deposits from the banks to the letras de cambio market, reduced the private banks' deposit liabilities and earning assets, while repeated increases in reserve requirements further reduced their earning assets. The net impact was to raise per unit bank costs and bank loan rates.

Restrictions on private sector credit tended to affect Brazilian enterprises more than foreign enterprises since the latter had access to foreign sources of credit. Being better credit risks, the foreign companies also received a relatively large share of credit from the Brazilian banks. With domestic credit availabilities declining relative to output and without any form of capital market, Brazilian firms relied increasingly on reinvested earnings for expansion. Some firms found another useful source in delayed payments of taxes, as the penalties for late payment were usually less than the interest rates or profits to be earned on the funds. But on the whole Brazilian firms had less access to credit than foreign firms operating in Brazil. Finally, as private sector credit declined in real terms, both as a percentage of GNP and in relation to the money supply, it is very possible that this credit restraint contributed to the stagnation in private sector investment and output after 1962. To the extent that the capacity constraint on the supply side offset the monetary contractive impact on the demand side, private sector credit restraints may have been self-defeating in the sense that they contributed to the inflationary spiral.

The Role of Monetary Policy—1964 to 1967

In examining the monetary policies and performance during the post-1964 years, we distinguish between two periods: the three years of the Castello Branco government, from April 1964 to March 1967, during which time Octavio Bulhões served as finance minister and chairman of the National Monetary Council, and the period from March 1967 to 1973, during which time Antônio Delfim Netto occupied those posts. While the basic objectives of these two governments remained unchanged, their different approaches to monetary policy and their contrasting results are worth noting.

Monetary policy became one of the three major instruments of the post-1964 stabilization-development program, even though its role was more of a less independent nature than the more autonomous fiscal and incomes policies. Its aims were twofold: to restrict the overall expansion of the money supply and at the same time to rechannel credit from speculative and consumptive to productive purposes. To accomplish these aims, the government pursued two approaches, one general and one selective.

The selective approach discussed in other chapters involved the establishment of a variety of sectoral and regional programs and institutions to channel credit selectively into high priority purpose. Some of the more important of these programs and institutions were the National Economic Development Bank with augmented resources from taxes and the counterpart of international loans; the Rural Credit Law and implementing regulations which channeled 10 percent of commercial bank deposits into agricultural loans; the export credit program; National Housing Program with social security pension funds; the durable goods financing with funds from the *letras de cambio* market; and augmented tax funds for the Northeast Development Program and the Bank of the Northeast.

These selective credit programs conflicted with the second and more general approach of limiting the overall level of monetary expansion, which proved to be the most difficult part of the stabilization effort. Each year the government, either in the Central Bank or the Finance Ministry or both, prepared a monetary budget aimed at gradually descending rates of growth of money supply, based on hoped-for reductions in the rate of inflation and restoring the rate of economic growth. Each year, after approval by the National Monetary Council, these monetary budgets were used in presenting the government's monetary program to the IMF, IBRD, AID, and other international financial institutions as a basis for obtaining international credits, or, as in the case of the IMF, its international blessing. And each year the Brazilian an international authorities were surprised by different sources of excessive monetary expansion or contraction.

The Action Program of the Castello Branco government outlined its monetary policy as one of limiting the monetary expansion "consistent with the objectives of progressive stabilization of prices, avoiding, however, recession in the level of productive activity and any reduction in business savings."[4] The more specific goals of monetary policy included (a) a gradual reduction in the rate of monetary expansion form 70 percent in 1964 to 30 percent in 1965 and 15

[4]Ministério do Planejamento e Coordenação Econômica, *Programa de Acão Econômica do Govêrno, 1964-1966*, p. 15.

percent in 1966; (b) a gradual reduction in public sector financing requirements; and (c) an increase in private sector credit approximately in proportion to the GNP at constant prices, which, as a practical matter, was assumed to be in proportion to the increase in the money supply. The foreign exchange accounts were expected to remain in balance with no impact on monetary flows.[5] Given the alternatives of imposing sharper controls on credit to the private sector, containing public sector credit requirements, or containing both, the Action Program chose to contain public sector financing while permitting increases in credit to the private sector roughly proportionate to the increase in the money supply. This would mean relatively larger increases in private sector than in public sector credit, but to the extent that public deficits were contained and eventually reduced, and/or noninflationary resources found for its financing, the rate of credit expansion to the private sector could also be reduced, permitting a gradual reduction in the money supply.

Beginning of Central Banking. The Action Program included three approaches to more effective monetary control: the development and improvement of the monetary control apparatus; improved control over and a gradual reduction in primary reserve money; and continued use of two of the traditional monetary measures, rediscounts and compulsory reserve requirements.

The monetary control apparatus established by the Banking Law of 31 December 1964 continued the trend initiated in 1945 to establish an independent monetary authority with the necessary tools to control the money supply. A Superintendency of Money and Credit (SUMOC) had been set up in 1945 in part to satisfy the requirements for Brazilian participation in the Bretton Woods institutions, but also as the nucleus for eventual development into a central bank.[6] The Banking Law of 1964 provided the legal foundation for taking SUMOC out of the Bank of Brazil and transforming it into the Central Bank of Brazil, which opened its doors on 31 March 1965, although several years passed before it gathered the necessary staff and operations from other institutions so that it could actually function as a central bank. It has not, in fact, operated independently of the Finance Ministry, since the banking law placed the Central Bank of Brazil under the direct jurisdiction of the National Monetary Council,

---

[5] Ibid, pp. 34 and 64.

[6] Decreto-lei No. 7293 of 7 February 1945 created the SUMOC directly subordinate to the Minister of Finance. Law 4595 of 31 December 1964 established the Central Bank of Brazil to replace SUMOC.

whose chairman is the finance minister. Although it was envisioned that the four directors of the Central Bank with staggered six-year terms would provide a continuity and carry a major voice in the ten-man National Monetary Council, the continuity concept was voided the first time it came up for a test. Following the March 1967 change in governments, Central Bank President Denio Nogueira and the three directors were asked to resign and were replaced by others believed to be more responsive to the wishes of the Costa e Silva government. The concept that the Central Bank Board would carry a major voice in the council also proved to be inconsistent with the actual developments, as the directors frequently failed to present a common front at council meetings.

Under the leadership of Octavio Bulhões, the National Monetary Council gave every impression of being a cohesive and effective team. At least four other members of the council had been close associates of Bulhões at the University of Brazil or in SUMOC, of which he was superintendent prior to the revolution. Denio Nogueira, Central Bank president, and Casimiro Ribeiro, director in charge of monetary operations, were members of Bulhões's and Planning Minister Campos's inner group of economic policy makers. In addition to these four, the Council consisted of Minister of Industry and Commerce Daniel Faraco, Bank of Brazil President Luiz de Moraes Barros, BNDE President José Garrido Torres, Central Bank Directors Luiz Biolchini and Aldo Franco, and two private bankers, Gastão Vidigal and Rui de Castro Magalhães.

As chairman of the National Monetary Council and with control over the purse strings of the Treasury, the Brazilian finance minister is in a position of potentially strong leadership in economic policy making. He is able to influence taxation, expenditures, and borrowing policies at all levels of government. Tariff policies, price controls, rate policies of public utilities, the social security system, and the commodity institutes, such as the Brazilian Coffee Institute, are coordinated under this office. Likewise, in the area of monetary policy, the finance minister, as chairman of the council, has a high degree of influence over banking and monetary regulations. The effectiveness of the finance minister and of the council over monetary policy depends, however, on the cooperation of the implementing agencies, which include the Central Bank and the Bank of Brazil. Despite the harmonious cooperation of these two institutions both with the council and with each other during this period of transition, there was inadequate coordination of various monetary policy measures among the many bureaus and departments within these institutions. Technicians in the foreign exchange department, which remained a part of the Bank of Brazil until 1966, rarely coordinated with those in the banking department, so that the many considerations bearing on a policy issue were not presented to the council in a well-coordinated form. This lack of unified policy was an important causal factor contributing to the large and unexpected fluctuations in the major components of the monetary budget and in primary reserve money. All of this severely limited monetary management.

The monetary stabilization approach of the Castello Branco government focused on improved control over, and a gradual reduction in, the rate of expansion of primary reserve money. As primary reserve money (the monetary liabilities of the monetary authorities) provides the reserves for commercial bank credit expansion, containment of primary reserves was essential to achieving any semblance of monetary control. Containment of the fiscal deficit was only part, albeit the single more important part, of the effort to control primary money. Coffee operations, the minimum price guarantee program, the pricing and investment policies of the federal autarquia, and foreign exchange operations comprised other major sources of expansion in primary reserve money.

Monetary Expansion—1964 to 1966. The budgeted and actual performance of the major monetary and credit accounts for 1964 and 1965 are compared in Table IV-6. The 1964 monetary expansion exceeded the 70 percent expansion target only very slightly, primarily because of an unexpected but welcome surplus in the balance of payments. That all of the other accounts of the monetary budget were close to their respective targets is explained by the fact that the budget was completed in September 1964 with only a few months of the year remaining. Public sector credit was effectively contained within the budget, even though the coffee operations were more expansionary than anticipated, because of an offsetting increase in the deposits of the federal autarquia. Private sector credit expanded by 80 percent, about the same rate as the rate of increase in the money supply, with proportionate increases by both the Bank of Brazil and the commercial banks.

The 1965 monetary experience offers a more typical example of the problems encountered by the Brazilian authorities in forecasting and controlling the sources of monetary expansion. The actual monetary expansion in 1965 was 76 percent, more than double the 30 percent target included in the monetary stabilization program. The Treasury deficit financing requirements were contained well within the budget, but other federal government operations provided disappointingly large sources of monetary expansion. Coffee operations,

Table IV-6
MONETARY BUDGETS AND SOURCES OF MONETARY EXPANSION, 1964–1966
(millions of Cr$, current prices)

	1964		1965		1966
	Budget	Actual	Budget	Actual	Actual
1. Public sector credit (net)	495	434	214	426	−815
Loans to Treasury	753	743	698	270	−190
Coffee operations (net) .	−353	−128	−168	131	−344
Other accounts (net) ...	96	−181	−316	25	−281
Autarquia deposits ..	—	−265	—	−344	−283
Commodity purchases	—	78	—	106	5
Price program ...	—	6	—	243	−3
2. Private sector credit ...	1,682	1,561	986	2,015	1,858
Bank of Brazil	610	543	343	304	902
Commercial banks	1,072	1,018	643	1,711	956
3. Other accounts (net) ...	−222	141	217	1,135	40
Net foreign reserves ...	—	161	—	542	279
Other	—	−20	—	593	−239
4. Money supply	1,955	2,136	1,417	3,576	1,083
(Percentage increase in year)	(70)	(81)	(30)	(76)	(13)
5. Primary reserve money		1,167		1,759	1,009
(Percentage increase) ..		(77)		(67)	(22)

Source: *Relatório do Banco Central do Brasil*, 1965, 1966, 1967.

instead of providing an expected monetary offset of Cr$ 168 million, ended the year with a net expansion of Cr$ 131 million. The main cause was one of the largest coffee crops on record, at 38 million bags more than double the crop registered for the previous crop year. While the coffee support price was held unchanged in 1965 despite the interim 57 percent (year-to-year average) increase in the general price level, the doubling of the nominal support price in the previous year resulted in a sharp increase in coffee sector incomes and in the deficit of the Coffee Defense Fund. At the same time, the decline in coffee exports in 1965 reduced the receipts of the Coffee Institute and added to the stockpile of coffee, which at 70 million bags was one of the highest in Brazil's history. Heavy purchases of rice under the minimum price guarantee program provided another unforeseen circumstance which contributed to the excessive monetary expansion in 1965. The rice support price had been set relatively high with the aim of stimulating rice production but, combined with an exceptionally good crop, it also served to produce a stockpile financing requirement of Cr$ 253 million, almost as large as the deficit financing requirements of the Treasury for 1965.

While domestic agricultural programs created important deviations from the 1965 monetary program, the major source of excessive monetary expansion was the huge and completely unexpected surplus in the balance of payments. The combination of a bold devaluation at the end of 1964 and weak investment demand reduced the 1965 import level to the lowest level since World War II. The resulting balance of payments surplus led to a net inflow of reserves to the banking system of Cr$ 542 million, almost twice the size of the federal deficit. Another exchange transaction which added to commercial bank liquidity was the gradual elimination of "swaps." The swap arrangements with an exchange rate guarantee, that is, a government guarantee to convert the currency swap at the same rate at which it was registered, had been initiated during the Kubitschek regime as part of the effort to attract foreign capital. Recognizing the high cost of these transactions, the Castello Branco government decided to abolish them, and about U. S. $190 million were liquidated in 1965. The average exchange rate guarantee for the swaps outstanding at the end of 1964 was Cr$ 491 per U. S. dollar while the official exchange rate at which the monetary authorities purchased exchange during most of the year was Cr$ 1850 per dollar or higher. The difference between these two rates constituted a loss to the Central Bank, the exact amount of which has not been made public but it was almost the equivalent of the entire federal deficit in 1965.[7]

The expansionary public sector operations and the surplus on the balance of payments (plus other exchange operations) augmented the reserves of the commercial banks which, under heavy loan demand during 1965, expanded their loans by 76 percent. Had the authorities not increased compulsory reserve requirements during the year, commercial bank credit expansion and monetary expansion would have been significantly higher. As it was, the Bank of Brazil held its credit expansion within the 30 percent budgeted for the year so that total private sector credit expansion was limited to 57 percent. Thus we see in 1965 the same uncontrollable growth of primary reserve money as in the pre-1964 period, this time stemming from foreign exchange operations as well as from public sector credit, and the same reliance on Bank of Brazil credit ceilings and compulsory reserve requirements. Once again private sector credit expansion fell significantly below the monetary expansion, as can be seen in Table

---

[7]*Relatório do Banco Central do Brasil, 1965*, Rio de Janeiro, p. 55.

IV-9. As a percentage of money supply, private sector credit continued to decline from 73.7 percent at the end of 1963 to 66.1 percent at the end of 1965; and as a percentage of GNP from 16.6 percent to 15.1 percent.

By the end of 1965 the financial system was exceedingly liquid. Despite the increase in compulsory reserves to the highest average ratio on record, the commercial banks retained a relatively high level of voluntary (free) reserves. Moreover, the decline in the income velocity of money during the year provided an additional degree of liquidity in the hands of the public. A relatively sharp decline in the income velocity of money (from 6.16 to 5.38) had occurred during 1965 as money supply expanded by 76 percent while the price level rose by only 34 percent (December to December). The impact of this overhang of liquidity was felt in 1966.

The 1966 monetary experience afforded a bitter final year for the Castello Branco team of economists. Despite an exceptionally tight and courageous monetary policy, which restricted monetary expansion to only 13 percent for the year, prices continued to rise at the same pace as 1965. (The increase in the general price level from December 1965 to December 1966 was 38 percent.) Both of these trends were unexpected and frustrating. The cut in the rate of monetary expansion from 76 percent in 1965 to 13 percent in 1966 was steeper than had been planned. Yet the rate of inflation failed to decline.

In 1966, with the sale of government bonds exceeding the Treasury deficit, Bank of Brazil loans to the Treasury declined for the first time in a decade or more. A very poor agricultural harvest combined with a cautious pricing policy provided a large offset from coffee operations, and the minimum price program, with the net sale of rice from stocks, remained practically in balance. A continued build-up in autarquia deposits provided another large offset, with the result that the federal accounts in 1966 for the first time in recent history not only moved into surplus, but moved into surplus by a significantly large amount. With these contractive fiscal operations, the authorities felt freer, and, at the end of 1966, even found it necessary, to liberalize Bank of Brazil credit to the private sector. It expanded by 57 percent for the year, although this included some special credits to state governments. A continued surplus in the balance of payments during 1966 contributed another expansive factor, but the surplus in the fiscal accounts held the expansion in primary reserve money to only 22 percent during the year.

Finance Minister Delfim Netto attributed the industrial recession of late 1966 and the early months of 1967 to an excessively restrictive monetary and credit policy during 1966. Total credit to the private sector increased by 34 percent (the Bank of Brazil by 57 percent and the commercial banks by 24 percent), while prices rose by 39 percent, resulting in a decline in credit in real terms and as a percentage of GNP. But as a percentage of money supply, which increased only 13 percent, private sector credit showed a significant improvement. These divergent trends raise serious questions about the use of either money supply or GNP as criteria for assessing, ex ante, the adequacy of private sector credit. The ratio of credit availabilities to GNP provides a reasonable ex post indicator of the shares of savings allocated to the public and private sectors. But ex ante, it can be a case of the dog chasing its tail, because an expansion of private sector credit also affects money supply and nominal GNP.

Available evidence indicates that the slow pace of credit expansion in 1966 was as much the consequence as the cause of the business recession at the end of the year. It is true that the monetary authorities increased compulsory reserves during the year, but voluntary reserves of the commercial banks also remained higher at the end of 1966 than they had been a year earlier. The banks could have expanded their loans at a faster rate had there been an effective demand. The explanation of the slackened loan demand can be found in two developments: first, the poor agricultural harvest of 1966 reduced both agricultural incomes and crop financing requirements; second, the move to positive real interest rates for commercial bank loans, which first occurred in 1966, further slackened the loan demand in an otherwise depressed economy. The causes of the business recession, which were not unique to the 1966 case but cover the entire period since 1962, lie elsewhere, that is, in the lack of investment demand. The resurgence of investment demand in early 1967 raised the Brazilian economy out of the five-year stagnation and into a new period of high growth. An expansion of private sector credit accompanied the revival of growth but its role as a causative factor remains questionable.

The limited growth of money supply during 1966 was the consequence of developments affecting coffee operations, the agricultural price support program, the commodity purchase program, and the sales of Treasury bonds in excess of the deficit. The turnaround in these federal programs from an expansionary impact on primary reserve money of Cr$ 426 million in 1965 to a contraction of Cr$ 815 million in 1966 also had the effect of contracting effective demand, thereby contributing to the recession. In this sense, the slow pace of monetary expansion and the recession stemmed from common causes. The question arises as to why a comparable abatement in the rate of inflation did not occur. Finance Minister Delfim Netto's answer to this question in terms of cost-push inflation resulted in some important shifts in policy in 1967.

Monetary Policy Objectives—1967 to 1972

Although committed to continuation of the stabilization program, the Costa e Silva government's initial objective was to bring the economy out of the industrial recession. This objective dominated all the major economic policies—fiscal, wage and particularly monetary—during 1967. Accepting the diagnosis of cost-push factors as the predominant cause of the recession and continued inflation, the Costa e Silva government embarked on an expansionary monetary policy.[8] Interestingly, the professed target for private sector credit remained essentially unchanged: to maintain private sector credit in approximately constant ratio to nominal product—allowing for physical expansion of product and the overall increase in prices, that is, in proportion to nominal GNP. The emphasis on containment of public sector credit requirements also remained unchanged from the previous government. The essential difference in the approach to monetary policy derived from the different projections of the future rate of inflation. The 1964 Action Program aimed at rather rapid reductions in the rate of inflation, from 70 percent in 1964 to 30 percent in 1965 and 15 percent in 1966. Private sector credit targets based on these overly optimistic rates (the 1966 price increase was 39 percent) inevitably led to declines in real terms. Minister Delfim Netto's approach was to base the credit targets on projections of no more than a small improvement in the previous year's price preformance. This change in price projections raised private sector credit targets and permitted rapid increases in real terms and as percentages of money supply and GNP in the succeeding years. From a role of whipping boy in the pre-1964 period, private sector credit became in 1967 the spoiled child of the economic recovery program.

Determinants of Monetary Expansion—1967 to 1972. The Costa e Silva government's aim of restoring industrial growth through a liberal credit policy dominated the monetary experiences of 1967, but the legacies of the Castello Branco government also played an impor-

---

[8] For a detailed analysis in support of the cost-push thesis the reader may wish to review Samuel A. Morley, "Inflation and Stagnation in Brazil," pp. 184-203. Professor Morley was a member of a University of California team working with the Planning Ministry in 1966 where he met Professor Delfim Netto who also served as a consultant to the Planning Ministry.

tant role in the excessive monetary expansion of that year.The new revenue sharing program and the value-added tax system, both of which were initiated on 1 January 1967, had a strong impact on the 1967 monetary performance. However, Finance Minister Delfim Netto supplemented these expansionary measures with a few of his own. A month's postponement in the federal excise tax collections and payment of overdue government bills (which had accumulated in Minister Bulhões's effort to contain the 1966 deficit) provided additional liquidity to business, while a cut in income taxes, an increase in the price paid to coffee producers, and the limitation of finance companies to consumer goods financing added to effective consumer demand. These several measures provided a turnaround in public sector credit from a contractive Cr$ 815 million in 1966 to an expansionary Cr$ 957 million in 1967 (see Table IV-7).

A balance of payments deficit, primarily the result of the important liberalization program, another Campos-Bulhões measure which took effect in 1967, served as the only major contractive item in the 1967 monetary program. Bank of Brazil credit to the private sector expanded 39 percent, and the commercial banks, relying in part on the 32 percent increase in primary reserve money and in part on drawing down their free reserves, expanded their loans by 64 percent. By the end of 1967 bank free reserves were down to 13.2 percent, compared with 17.7 percent a year earlier. A notable aspect of the trend of free reserves is that excessively restrictive money and credit were diagnosed as the cause of recession and inflation in early 1967; yet by the end of 1967 the economy was surging upward and the inflation had dropped another notch even though bank liquidity had declined from a year earlier. Despite the 43 percent expansion in the money supply during 1967, the general level of prices rose only 25 percent, a reversal of the 1966 experience when money supply rose only 13 percent and the general price level 39 percent.

Professor Mário Simonsen offers several explanations for the lower rate of inflation in 1967 which occured in spite of the more expansionary monetary policy.

> In the first place because income velocity of money naturally tends to fall after the stabilization shock, which occurred during the first semester. In the second place because the level of economic activity increased appreciably between January and December 1967. In the third place because, due to the monetary stringency of the previous year, the year 1967 began with abnormally low indices of real liquidity. In the fourth place because the Costa e Silva government was

especially preoccupied in containing the sources of cost increases, freezing the process of corrective inflation so amply
practiced in the three previous years. In the fifth place because 1967 was a year of exceptional crops, a factor extremely relevant in the containment of the inflationary
rhythm in the short run.[9]

In support of this view, Professor Simonsen points out that the food
component of the cost of living index rose only 14.1 percent in 1967,
and the adjustment of rents, which had been raised 73 percent in
1966, was contained at 44.1 percent.

Monetary developments in 1968 were similar to those in 1967.
Treasury financing requirements, although contained relative to the
earlier year, remained high, due solely to a large offset from
coffee operations—a small coffee crop—and a buildup in deposits
of the federal autarquia. A foreign exchange inflow, following the
initiation of the new flexible exchange rate system in August 1968,
added another expansionary factor. But the main expansionary
factor in 1968 was the 72 percent increase in Bank of Brazil credit
to the private sector. The resulting 43 percent increase in primary
money, together with a relaxed rediscount policy, permitted another huge, 62 percent increase in commercial bank loans to the
private sector and a 42 percent increase in the money supply.
Again the general price increase remained at a relatively moderate
25 percent, as real GNP advanced by 8.4 percent and the income
velocity of money declined from 5.83 to 5.53. A slowdown in the
pace of corrective adjustment of public utility rates contributed to
the slower growth in prices but rental adjustments for the year
were higher than in 1967 and the boom in the construction
industry, underway for its first full year in 1968, pushed construction prices up 32 percent over 1967.

In 1969, Finance Minister Delfim Netto finally achieved the
target of containing public sector credit. With the help of the cut in
the Participation Fund for States and Municipalities from 20 percent
to 12 percent and a sizable sale of government bonds, the Treasury was
able to repay over Cr$ 1026 million of loans from the Bank of Brazil.
Coffee operations and autarquia deposits also continued to provide
large surpluses, offset only in part by expansion of the commodity credit
and purchasing programs, so that overall federal government operations
were in surplus by almost Cr$ 2 billion. Again, large Bank of Brazil
loans to the private sector and a continued buildup in foreign exchange reserves under the effective flexible exchange rate

---

[9]Simonsen, *Inflação: Gradualismo & Tratamento de Choque*, pp. 43-44.

Table IV-7

YEARLY CHANGE IN MAJOR DETERMINANTS OF MONETARY EXPANSION, 1967–1972

(millions of Cr$, current prices)

	1967	1968	1969	1970	1971	Oct. 1972	Accumulated, 1967–Oct. 1972
1. Public sector credit (net)	957	314	−1,942	−2,011	−3,902	−8,832	−15,416
Treasury accounts (net)	699	1,079	−1,026	−832	−3,364	−6,158	−9,602
Coffee operations (net)	48	−597	−641	−919	−493	−422	−3,024
Commodity purchases and sales	145	398	363	343	862	−648	+1,463
Autarquia deposits	65	−566	−638	−603	−907	−1,604	−4,253
2. Private sector credit	4,119	7,448	8,186	9,335	16,595	15,820	61,503
(Percentage change over previous year)	(55.8)	(62.2)	(43.2)	(34.4)	(45.5)	(29.8)	
Bank of Brazil	963	2,468	3,103	3,162	5,748	4,674	20,118
(Percentage change over previous year)	(38.8)	(71.6)	(52.5)	(35.1)	(47.2)	(26.1)	
Commercial banks	3,156	4,980	5,083	6,173	10,847	11,146	41,385
(Percentage change over previous year)	(64.5)	(61.9)	(39.0)	(34.1)	(44.7)	(31.7)	
3. Foreign exchange operations	−112	1,631	4,516	2,523	2,157	7,774	18,489
4. Time deposits	−271	−396	−69	−629	−2,103	−2,510	−5,978
5. All other accounts (net)	−171	−2,617	−3,727	−1,647	−1,506	−1,486	−11,154
6. Money supply	4,522	6,380	6,964	7,571	11,241	10,766	47,444
(Percentage increase over previous year)	(43.1)	(42.5)	(32.6)	(26.7)	(31.3)	(22.8)	
7. General price index							
(Percentage increase Dec. to Dec.)	(25.0)	(25.5)	(20.1)	(19.3)	(19.5)	(13.9)	

Source: *Boletim do Banco Central do Brasil*, December 1972, Tables I.1, I.4, I.8, I.27, and II.49.

system led to a 23 percent increase in primary reserve money and a 33 percent increase in the money supply. The general price level rose by 20 percent and the real GNP grew by 9 percent in 1969.

In the next four years the determinants of monetary expansion remained essentially the same as in 1969. Private sector credit expanded at an annual average rate of about 40 percent. Despite the continuing large monetary contraction from public sector operations —a surplus on Treasury accounts, an offset from coffee operations, and buildup in the deposits of public autarquia—the voluminous inflow of foreign capital kept the private commercial banks sufficiently liquid to permit them to match the credit expansion of the Bank of Brazil. The close correspondence between the trend of money supply and prices is evident in these years, as money supply expanded at an annual rate of 30 percent and prices also rose at a fairly stable rate of about 20 percent (GNP growth rate also average 10 percent). In 1972 private sector credit expansion was restricted to 30 percent, the money supply rose only by 23 percent, and the rate of price increase dropped for the first time since 1967, to about 15.5 percent.

Measures to Control Primary Reserve Money. Perhaps the most significant innovations in Finance Minister Delfim Netto's implementation of monetary policy lie in the several measures to smooth out short-term fluctuations in the sources of primary reserve money. In his studies of the Brazilian coffee problem and foreign exchange movements Delfim Netto had noted the asymmetrical impact of changes in primary reserve money on money supply and prices. The inflationary impact of an expansion in primary money, stemming from, for example, an inflow of foreign exchange or a deficit in the coffee account, was not cancelled by an outflow of foreign exchange or a surplus in the coffee account. Once bank credit had expanded to a new level, the authorities found it impossible to return to a lower level without serious consequences for output and employment, since the prevailing inflationary psychology had already moved the price level up on a one-way street.

Recognizing the ineffectiveness of the traditional monetary instruments in offsetting these large fluctuations in primary reserve money, Delfim Netto introduced measures to moderate the impact of the two major sources of fluctuations in primary money expansion, coffee operations and foreign exchange operations. Coffee operations, for example, experienced variations both annually, as coffee crops varied from year to year, and seasonally, as the Coffee Institute built up its stocks between harvesting and exporting. In his classic study of Brazilian coffee, Delfim Netto pointed out that the price impact of these seasonal fluctuations was asymmetrical because the inflationary impact of the expansion in primary reserve money was not cancelled out when the Coffee Institute sold the coffee and repaid its loans from the Bank of Brazil or rebuilt its deposit account.[10] As a means of moderating the seasonal flows in the coffee account Finance Minister Delfim Netto had already initiated by June 1967 a new policy of more frequent adjustments in the coffee price paid to the producers so as to induce them to hold their coffee until the next price increase.

The impact of short-term movements in foreign exchange provides a classical example of the difficulties of monetary management in Brazil. The policy of one-per-year devaluations pursued between 1964 and 1968 had resulted in alternating periods of heavy inflows and outflows of foreign exchange (see Chapter VIII). As the predictable devaluation time approached there would be a speculative outflow of exchange, followed by an equally heavy inflow of exchange after the devaluation. To illustrate the significance of the amounts involved, the exchange outflow during the months prior to the February 1967 devaluation amounted to about U.S. $200 million, which at the prevailing exchange rate was Cr$ 440 million, or 8 percent of the primary reserve money outstanding. It is therefore no wonder that credit was exceptionally tight prior to the devaluation. Following the devaluation, the reflux of speculative exchange of even greater magnitudes—investors also were waiting for the appropriate time to convert into cruzeiros—augmented primary reserves and provided the basis for a rapid expansion of commercial bank credit, which occurred in 1967. The Brazilian monetary system suffered the same alternating periods of excess liquidity and stringency before and after each devaluation until the implementation of the more flexible exchange rate system, the trotting peg, in August 1968. The more frequent, almost monthly, adjustments of the exchange rate eliminated the speculative exchange movements and the ensuing fluctuations in primary reserve money, thereby permitting for the first time the basis for management of credit and money supply using the traditional monetary instruments.

Monetary Control Instruments. Rediscounts and compulsory reserve requirements proved to be ineffective instruments of monetary control in the face of interest rate controls and violent fluctuations in primary reserve money. The quantitative insignificance of rediscounts further limited their effectiveness as an instrument of policy, while high compulsory reserve requirements, riddled with loopholes, also

---

[10]Antônio Delfim Netto, "O Problema do Café no Brasil," p. 2.

reduced the usefulness of this instrument in offsetting short-term fluctuations in primary money. Moreover, the monetary authorities altered reserve requirements only with great hesitation because of the varying impact of fluctuations in primary reserve money on different banks. An increase in reserve requirements to offset an inflow of foreign exchange, for example, tended to cause severe difficulties for those banks which did not engage in foreign exchange operations and therefore did not benefit from the inflow.

Following the unhappy monetary experiences of 1965 Central Bank President Denio Nogueira became convinced of the need for open market operations as an added instrument of monetary control, and in late 1966 initiated steps to develop an organization within the Central Bank to engage in such operations.[11] Professor Rui Leme, who replaced Denio Nogueira as Central Bank president in March 1967, continued these efforts to develop both qualified personnel within the Central Bank and an appropriate instrument for open market transactions. One such attempt was the ill-fated Operation Tupiquiniquin in 1967, described in Chapter V, an aborted attempt to use government bonds (ORTN) for "open market operations—Brazilian style." Finally, in August 1968, under the third Central Bank president in four years, Ernani Galveas, the Central Bank began to develop the ORTN into a short-term monetary instrument, offering the ORTN to financial institutions at a fixed price with maturities of sixty to ninety days and a guaranteed repurchase price.

These initial operations can in no way be described as open market operations in the traditional sense. The Central Bank played a passive role, reacting to market conditions without any attempt to influence either the cost or availability of credit. The commercial banks purchased the ORTN largely to satisfy compulsory reserve requirements or on behalf of some of their larger customers who wanted to avoid the interest rate ceilings. The biggest drawback for their use by the banks was the difficulty in calculating the interest rate shares for the several holders of the ORTN, since the interest rate earned on them was subject to taxation. Earnings on the ORTN, including the monetary correction portion, were taxed directly if sold prior to maturity, but only the interest portion was taxable if the security was held to maturity, thus providing a built-in incentive to hold them to maturity.

---

[11]His initial step was to invite Mr. Horace Sanford, Vice President of the Federal Reserve Bank of New York, to study Brazil's needs and prospects for engaging in open market operations. He also sent some of his outstanding young officers to the United States to study the U.S. approach from both the official viewpoint of the Federal Reserve Bank and the private viewpoint of the New York dealers. These officers later, in 1969 and 1970, became the nucleus for the Office of the Public Debt which had responsibility for dealing in open market operations.

Despite these shortcomings, the operations in ORTN provided useful initial experiences for many of the Central Bank personnel to deal with private financial institutions on a day-to-day basis; they tended to increase market confidence in government securities; and to a degree they developed a small interbank market. The commercial banks found the ORTN could be used as secondary reserves to increase earning assets while maintaining a high degree of liquidity. In general, the ORTN proved to be unwieldy and ineffective as a monetary control instrument, but did serve as a useful base for the next step in developing a useful monetary instrument.

With the aim of developing a more effective monetary control instrument the Central Bank issued the first Treasury bills in August 1970. Although offered on a discount basis the Treasury bills offered no advantages over the ORTN as monetary control instrument since the Central Bank continued to underwrite the market, buying and selling at fixed prices. On the other hand, the commercial banks found that they facilitated interbank operations, thereby introducing a greater degree of liquidity into the banking system. The Treasury bills carried no monetary correction and the earnings on them were included only in the overall earnings of the holding institutions; they were not taxed directly as were the ORTN.

Development of a market for Treasury bills was a major step forward in providing the Brazilian monetary authorities with a potential instrument for monetary management, but additional policy changes were necessary to make it effective. The first such policy change was a liberation of interest rates from direct controls, which is discussed in the following chapter. Unless the authorities were willing to accept a higher discount rate to push Treasury bills into the market, the authorities would inevitably remain in the passive position of reacting to the market rather than an active force for influencing it. The second prerequisite was the development of a bill market independent of the Central Bank. Only time can tell whether Brazilian financial institutions are sufficiently mature to participate in a market in which a return on a security is not guaranteed. This is essential to evolving a functional bill market within which the monetary authorities can operate to regulate credit.

Assessment of Monetary Policy

Against which objectives should the effectiveness of monetary policy be assessed? If assessed against the traditional objective of promoting relative price stability, Brazilian monetary policy since 1964 has been a failure. The rate of inflation in 1972, eight years after the start of the

Table IV-8
INCREASE IN MONEY SUPPLY
AND GENERAL PRICE INDEX, 1964–1972

| | Annual Percent Rates of Increase | |
Year	Money Supply	General Price Index
1964	84.5	91.9
1965	76.5	56.8
1966	15.8	37.9
1967	43.1	28.4
1968	42.5	24.2
1969	32.6	20.8
1970	26.7	19.8
1971	31.3	20.4
1972	28.6[a]	15.4

[a]Preliminary.

Source: Boletim do Banco Central do Brasil, *various issues.*

stabilization effort, remained above 15 percent. Nor was Brazilian monetary policy particularly effective when matched against the target of controlling money supply, with the single exception of 1966 when money supply increased only 13 percent.

That the expansion in the money supply explains a major part of the continuing inflation appears evident in the data in Table IV-8. While there were large annual or marginal variations in the income velocity of money, or the inverse, the public's willingness to hold money, the average income velocity remained fairly stable, explaining little, if any, of the inflation.

As in the pre-1964 years, the Brazilian inflation continued to be caused by excessive demand, stimulated and validated by the continued increase in the money supply. However, cost-push factors also played an important role, as corrective inflation, the progressive increases in prices and utility rates pursuant to the gradual reductions in controls, contributed significantly to the price increases. High real interest costs, beginning in 1966, also constituted an important cost-push factor to under-capitalized Brazilian businesses. Thus, it may not be very meaningful to categorize the post-1964 inflation as demand-pull, demand-shift, or cost-push. All three factors were important, and it probably is not statistically feasible to distinguish among them at any given point in time. The existence of these several causes of inflation constitutes an important reason for the gradual or corrective inflation approach to stabilization initiated in 1964.

Measured against the objective of improving the capability for controlling inflation, the Brazilian monetary performance has been more effective. In this regard, a number of steps were taken to reduce the demand-pull, to correct the cost-push elements in the inflation, and to improve the instruments of monetary control. Progress in wage policy and interest rates, in the supply of foodstuffs, housing, and imports, and in other areas is discussed in later chapters. Actions directed toward increasing the control over the sources of monetary expansion, treated in this chapter and in Chapter VI, fiscal policy have also met with a degree of success, though this success was slow in coming. Containment of public sector financing requirements, the measures to moderate fluctuations in primary money stemming from foreign exchange and coffee operations, and the initiation of improved instruments for controlling commercial bank loans provide improved bases for eventual control of the money supply and effective demand.

Assessed against the objectives of raising the rates of investment and economic growth, Brazilian monetary policy has produced some mixed results. The question remains as to how much the credit expansion contributed to the increase in real economic growth and how much to the continued inflation. Could Brazil have achieved the same rate of economic growth with a lower rate of monetary and, perhaps, price expansion? Some evidence that it might have is presented in Chapter XI.

Credit to the Private Sector. During the entire post-1964 period monetary policy was guided fairly consistently by the two targets of (a) containing the public sector financing requirements and (b) ensuring an adequate supply of credit for the private sector, which meant proportional increases in private sector credit and money supply (assumed to be proportional to nominal GNP). Both the Castello Branco and Costa e Silva governments were fairly effective in containing public sector credit requirements, but their performances differed significantly in the treatment of private sector credit. As the public sector credit requirements declined, the private sector received a larger percentage share of the total credit, as shown in Table IV-9. The share of private sector credit from the Bank of Brazil and the commercial banks increased steadily from 64.6 percent at the end of 1963 to 73.5 percent in 1966 and further to 95.1 percent by October 1972. Also, the relative increases in private sector credit (in current prices) of the two post-1964 governments were roughly similar. Yet in real terms and as a percentage of GNP and of the money supply, the trends of private sector credit during the two post-1964 regimes differed significantly.

In real terms and as a percentage of GNP and of the money supply, private sector credit expanded rapidly after 1967, compared with declining trends during the previous three years. In constant prices, private sector credit declined by 8 percent from the end of 1963 to the end of 1966; in the following three years, 1966 to 1969, private sector credit almost doubled, and tripled by 1972. As a percent of money supply, private sector credit remained at the end of 1966 below the 1963 level; by 1969 it had reached 95.7 percent. To find relationships between private sector credit and GNP and money supply comparable to that existing in 1969, one must go back to 1956, the year prior to Kubitschek's Target Program. By 1972 private sector credit had risen further to 119 percent of the money supply. Finally, as a percentage of GNP, private sector credit declined from 16.6 percent at the end of 1963 to 13.9 percent at the end of 1966; this trend reversed in 1967 and by 1972 reached 22.7 percent of GNP.

The explanation of the mixed effectiveness of monetary and credit policy during the two post-1964 regimes lies partly in the limitations in the ability of the monetary authorities to control credit and the money supply and partly in the changing targets of monetary policy. The initial attempts of the Castello Branco economists to control the money supply revealed some frustrating limitations. First, the sources of expansion and contraction of primary reserve money proved to be highly unpredictable. Each year a different set of sources seemed to get out of hand; one year it would be foreign exchange accumulation; another year, coffee operations; and yet another, Bank of Brazil loans. Even public sector operations proved erratic and uncertain. Ineffective or inadequate coordination among the policy instruments and sectoral and regional programs constituted a major cause of the unpredictable fluctuations, but external factors, such as the weather and foreign trade, also played a role. Another limitation arose from inadequate control over commercial bank loans, the major source of monetary expansion. Available monetary instruments were not sufficiently flexible to offset the large and unpredictable swings in primary reserve money. Even relatively sophisticated instruments, such as open market operations, had they been available, would not have been adequate for the task. A third limitation confronting the monetary authorities stemmed from the volatile and unpredictable relationships between money supply, prices, and output, with the paradoxical situation of stagnation and inflation with or without an increase in the money supply. These limitations on their capacity to regulate the money supply also tended to weaken seriously the authorities' resolve to impose tight credit conditions.

The mixed effectiveness of monetary policy must also be attributed, in part, to the varying aims of monetary policy during the two post-1964 phases. The Castello Branco government aimed credit policy at stabilization objectives. Together with an extremely effective fiscal restraint, monetary policy helped to bring the rate of inflation down from over 100 percent in early 1964 to close to 25 percent in early 1967. In 1967, Finance Minister Delfim Netto redirected credit policy toward the goal of maximizing the flow of credit to the private sector, with increasing emphasis on allocating the credit to priority sectors (agriculture, exports) and, within the industrial sector, to privately-owned Brazilian firms. The control of inflation as an objective of policy retained only secondary importance, as indicated by the continuing inflation above 15 percent in 1972.

The Brazilian government has been perpetuating inflation (or has shown less concern about halting inflation) since 1967 in the belief that a degree of inflation facilitates the credit rationing system by which the government channels subsidized credit to priority sectors, industries, and firms. In holding interest rates for loans from official institutions, which comprise a relatively large share of total credit, below the rate of inflation, the government provides a subsidy to the recipient of the credit. Given the subsidized rates, the demand for credit will exceed the supply, leaving the credit rationing to official determination. In this way the authorities can insure that priority sectors and industries receive ample credit for growth at rates they can afford to pay. At the same time the excessive expansion of credit through the official institutions provides the base for continued monetary expansion and inflation. This process is described further in the following chapter.

Another motivating factor in pursuing this credit rationing system has a nationalist origin in that it provides the Brazilian authorities with a mechanism for maintaining and perhaps even increasing the ownership and control of industry by private Brazilian firms. During the 1950s foreign investors came to own and control about 25 percent of the Brazilian industrial plant; the government also expanded its share of ownership. Meanwhile, the Brazilian private sector, lacking sources of capital in the inflationary environment, gradually lost out to foreign interests, with foreign sources of capital, and to the government with its access to the printing press. The stabilization effort of 1964-1967, with its stringent credit policy, tended to aggravate the financial problems of Brazilian industry, as indicated by the record number of bankruptcies and the cry of denationalization, the selling out of Brazilian industry to foreign enterprises, became an intensified issue. Through this mechanism of rationing credit the Brazilian government has attempted, since 1967, to ensure that the Brazilian private sector maintains its share of the industrial growth.

The question raised as to why the capital deficiencies of the Brazilian private sector are not resolved by bringing a quick end to

Table IV-9
PRIVATE SECTOR CREDIT, 1964–1972
(millions of Cr$)

Year	Private Sector Credit (current prices)	Total Credit (current prices)	Private Sector Credit (constant prices)[a]	Private Credit as % of Total Credit	Private Credit as % of Money Supply	Private Credit as % of GNP
1963	1,945	3,010	80.4	64.6	73.7	16.6
1964	3,506	5,451	76.1	64.3	73.4	15.3
1965	5,521	8,067	76.4	68.4	66.1	15.1
1966	7,377	10,040	74.0	73.5	70.4	13.9
1967	11,496	14,949	89.8	76.9	76.6	16.3
1968	18,944	23,797	119.1	79.6	88.6	19.1
1969	27,130	31,398	141.3	86.4	95.7	20.6
1970	36,465	40,908	158.5	89.1	101.5	21.1
1971	53,060	56,192	191.6	94.4	112.5	22.7
1972 (Oct.)	68,880	72,430	220.8	95.1	118.9	N.A.

[a] General price index used as a deflator, 1965–1967 = 100.

Source: *Boletim do Banco Central do Brasil*, December 1972, Table 1.8

inflation and by stimulating savings and long-term capital for growth. The answer here lies in the inability of the government to control inflation quickly—as evidenced by the efforts of 1964 to 1967—without adverse repercussions on economic growth. There still remained in 1967 a high degree of corrective inflation in terms of repressed rents and other prices, an inflationary psychology; and adequate instruments and institutions were still lacking to mobilize savings and channel them into long-term investments. The development of these instruments and institutions is the subject of Chapter XI.

Thus, continued inflation is associated with the aim of channeling an adequate amount of credit to priority areas within the private sector and to firms owned by private Brazilians. Without inflation the measures to achieve these aims would be more obvious and would require direct governmental subsidies. This credit rationing mechanism must be viewed as a pragmatic response by the Brazilian authorities to political and economic needs in recognition of the many limitations on their control of money supply and prices. The economic recovery and growth since 1967 provides some evidence of the success of this approach. At the same time, however, the authorities have gradually improved the instruments for controlling the sources of fluctuations in primary reserve money and commercial bank credit and for mobilizing savings for investment purposes, so that by 1972 they were in a position, for the first time, to engage in effective monetary management operations without severely dampening economic growth.

CHAPTER V

The Impact of Interest Rate Policy on Stagnation and Inflation

> During the years in which Brazil lived under a growing inflationary regime, with real rates of interest ever more negative, there crystalized the view that the rate of interest was not an important instrument in the complex of measures needed to restore relative stability and to firm the foundation for sound economic growth. Now that this phase is passed, let us not return to it, since, however recriminating the errors of the past, a reincidence of these same errors would be still less justifiable.
>
> Antônio de Abreu Coutinho
> "A Taxa de Juros e Mercado Financeiro"

Interest rate policies pursued by sucessive Brazilian governments during the 1950s and early 1960s created serious distortions in the financial system, which in turn contributed to the inflation and economic stagnation and impeded the several attempts at stabilization, including the post-1964 stabilization effort. A major theme running through this study of Brazilian financial experience is that the structural imbalances in the Brazilian economy were caused less by the inflationary spiral than by the direct controls on prices which that spiral induced. As prices soared upward, they pressed against existing price ceilings and, fearing the political and social consequences of further price increases, policy-makers tended to strike out at the symptoms rather than the basic causes of inflation. In later chapters we examine the impact of controls on public utility rates, rents, wages, food prices, and foreign exchange rates. The controls imposed on interest rates, discussed in this chapter, provide an object lesson in the adverse consequences of such controls. I will examine first the nature of Brazilian interest rate policies; next, the structure and trend of interest rates; finally, the implications of these policies and trends for the Brazilian economy.

Interest Rate Policies to 1964

It would not be correct to speak of an active interest rate policy during the 1950s since the Brazilian government took no initiative to influence the level and structure of interest rates in the private markets. Interest rates were generally permitted to seek their market levels, as long as they did not exceed the ceiling set by law. Interest rate policy was essentially of a negative nature, along the traditional lines of usury law.[1] But as the rate of price increase exceeded the 12 percent ceiling permitted by the usury law, which it did in each year of the decade prior to 1964, real interest rates tended to be negative whenever the official ceiling was adhered to.[2] There is, however, little evidence that the government actively enforced the usury law for private institutions. Interest rates for most financial transactions tended to exceed the 12 percent limit, with two important exceptions. The official lending institutions, the Bank of Brazil and the National Economic Development Bank, generally adhered to the 12 percent ceiling; and the private banks retained the savings deposit rates below the legal ceiling; this was a mutual agreement of the banks and the monetary authorities. These two deviations became increasingly significant as the rate of inflation accelerated in the early 1960s.

As the general level of interest rates followed prices upward, albeit with a lag, during the 1950s, the monetary authorities became increasingly concerned about the cost-push effects of interest rates and turned more and more to an active policy of providing preferential interest rate treatment to priority sectors and projects. The Bank of Brazil was the primary institution for providing subsidized credit, but the National Economic Development Bank gradually became important in the industrial and infrastructure sectors which received priority attention in the development program.

---

[1] The Usury Law, decreto lei 226.26, of April 1933.

[2] Mário Simonsen, "Inflation and the Money and Capital Markets of Brazil," in Howard S. Ellis, ed., *The Economy of Brazil*, p. 133. Simonsen has pointed out that the gold clause law, also passed in 1933, supported the usury law in impeding the adjustment of the financial markets to inflation. "It was generally understood that the usury law dealt with nominal (and not real) interest rates, and that the gold clause law prohibited any agreement with monetary correction (that is, in which payments are readjusted in proportion to the general rise in prices)."

Interest Rate Trends to 1964

The Brazilian interest rate structure during the postwar years was at once both limited in scope and complicated. Chronic inflation had driven all the long-term instruments, insurance policies, mortgages, and so on, out of the market. In 1952, for example, we find that operations in loan instruments of less than six months duration accounted for practically all recorded loan transactions of both the private commercial banks and the official Bank of Brazil (see Table V-1). But the interest rate structure was also complicated in that no institution was willing to reveal interest rates which exceeded the legal maximum. All the usual forms of evasion prevailed: compensating balances, extra fees and commissions, prior discounting, and a wide variety of under the table methods. In addition, a large proportion of financial transactions were undertaken outside the recognized banking structure. Under these circumstances what can be said about the structure and trend of interest rates? Regression analysis cannot be applied to existing data, but perhaps some broad trends can be sketched.

First, the Brazilian interest rate structure was highly compartmentalized with sharp disparities in the effective interest rates among instruments, institutions and sectors. The average return on commercial bank loans was more than double the Bank of Brazil rates for similar loans. In 1956, the first year for which we have comparable data, the commercial bank loan rates averaged 16.4 percent and the Bank of Brazil 7.0 percent. This divergence in loan rates persisted through 1963 as shown in Table V-2. As the finance companies came into the picture at the end of the 1950s, the rates charged borrowers of letras de cambio were more than double those of commercial bank loan rates, and the rates offered to holders of letras de cambio exceeded by four times the commercial bank deposit rate.

A further disparity in loan rates arose from the official policy of subsidizing loans to priority sectors. The Bank of Brazil, for example, extended loans to agriculture at 6 percent in 1960, while its average return on loans was 9.6 percent. At the same time the average return on commercial bank loans was 19.6 percent and the rate on finance company paper was 42 percent.

Another significant characteristic of the Brazilian interest rate structure during the 1950s was the great disparity between the rates to borrowers and the rates to savers. In 1960 the average interest cost on bank deposits was 4.3 percent compared with the average return on loans of 19.6 percent, and this disparity increased as the rate of inflation accelerated. By 1963 the average return on loans was 30.5 percent, while the average payment for deposits was only 3.5 percent.

Table V-1

OUTSTANDING LOAN BALANCES OF MAJOR FINANCIAL INSTITUTIONS TO THE PRIVATE SECTOR, 1956–1972

(end of year balances, millions of Cr$)

Year	Commercial Banks[a]	Bank of Brazil	BNDE	Finance Companies	National Housing Bank	Total
1956	130	75	7	—	—	212
1957	163	92	12	—	—	267
1958	196	116	21	—	—	333
1959	266	134	37	1	—	438
1960	382	183	54	7	—	626
1961	502	280	70	13	—	865
1962	836	480	116	48	—	1,418
1963	1,210	735	200	81	—	2,226
1964	2,228	1,278	303	245	—	4,076
1965	3,914	1,631	572	695	19	6,831
1966	4,821	2,560	858	872	88	9,199
1967	7,931	3,568	1,421	2,105	451	15,476
1968	12,311	5,737	1,921	4,558	1,873	26,400
1969	16,699	8,489	3,002	6,172	3,582	37,944
1970	23,504	12,178	4,240	7,850	6,231	54,003
1971	31,323	17,927	6,160	10,964	9,927	76,297
1972	41,276	21,359 (Aug.)	7,577 (June)	15,039	12,879 (Sept.)	98,130 (Sept.)

[a]These institutions provided more than 95 percent of total working capital and investment loans in 1968.

Source *Relatório do Banco Central do Brasil*, 1965, pp. 123, 185, 191-192; *Boletim do Banco Central do Brasil*, March 1969, Table 1.27 and December 1972, Table 1.24.

Table V-2
AVERAGE NOMINAL INTEREST RATES ON LOAN
INSTRUMENTS, 1956–1972
(in percent for year)

Year	Commercial Banks	Bank of Brazil	Letras de Cambio (Rate to borrower)	Resolution 63
1956	16.4	7.0	—	—
1957	17.0	8.8	—	—
1958	17.2	8.5	—	—
1959	19.5	9.2	—	—
1960	19.6	9.6	42.0	—
1961	22.3	12.3	52.0	—
1962	25.1	13.5	60.0	—
1963	30.5	14.1	70.6	—
1964	33.3	18.2	81.2	—
1965	34.7	22.8	79.0	—
1966	34.9	25.5	71.5	—
1967	34.1	21.7	49.0	40.2
1968	33.7	34.7	46.2	60.2
1969	30.9	—	44.2	34.2
1970	—	—	44.2	30.7 (July)
1971	—	—	43.7	—
1972	—	—	39.0 (Aug.)	—

Source: Commercial banks and Bank of Brazil data from unpublished reports of SEXPE, Banco Central do Brasil, 4 June 1970 and 26 September 1968, respectively. 1960 to 1961 data was estimated from data on rate to holders of Letras. For 1963 to 1966, unpublished report of SEXPE, Banco Central do Brasil, dated 26 September 1968. For 1967 to April 1970, Departemento Econômico, Divisão Monetaria e Bancaria, Banco Central do Brasil, unpublished report dated 11 May 1970.

This disparity also applied to finance company loans and saving rates, but not to the same degree as in commercial banks and it did not increase with the rate of inflation. In 1960 the rate on finance company paper was 42 percent to the borrower and 21 percent to the saver. By 1963 the rates were 70.6 and 35 percent respectively. The increase in interest rates during this period reflected the increase in the rate of inflation from 29 percent in 1960 to 75 percent in 1963.

Finally, available data indicate that, despite widespread evasion of the usury law, nominal interest rates in Brazil rarely exceeded the rate of inflation, with the consequence that most transactions carried negative real interest rates. And as the rate of inflation accelerated, the gap between the nominal rates and the rate of inflation also increased with the resulting rise in negative interest rates. Table V-3 shows, for example, that in 1963, commercial bank loan rates reached a negative 25.6 percent and the Bank of Brazil loans, a negative 35 percent. Two possible explanations of the increasing lag between nominal interest rates and the rate of inflation are offered: first, that the usury law, while not completely effective, may have had a dampening effect on the entire range of interest rates; second, that the public was unable to anticipate the sharp acceleration in prices. The Brazilian public had long been accustomed to price increases in the range of 25 percent; increases of 75 and 90 percent as in 1963 and 1964 were beyond level of expectation.

Distortions in the Financial Structure

Interest rate controls during the decade prior to 1964 resulted in a series of distortions in the Brazilian financial structure and in the allocation of credit which both reduced the level of financial savings and diverted the savings to consumption goods and lesser productive investments. The financial distortions included (a) a high-cost financial intermediation system; (b) a corporate structure excessively dependent on borrowed capital; (c) a proliferation of finance companies which diverted financial savings to consumer goods financing; (d) low rates of return on financial savings instruments which diverted savings to consumer goods, to lesser productive investments, and into foreign currencies.

Perhaps the most important consequence of the interest rate controls was the development of an extremely high cost financial intermediation system, with the rapid growth of new financial institutions and an expansion of old ones, both of which were unprecedented in Brazilian history. The disparity in the trend of interest rates for bank loans, which were relatively uncontrolled, and deposits, which remained fixed, led to cutthroat competition among the banks for the public's deposits. The result of this cutthroat competition for deposits, according to Mário Simonsen, one of Brazil's outstanding financial economists, was "one of the most curious examples of inefficiency generated by competition. According to the best principles of the adjustment of marginal cost to marginal revenue, the number of bank agencies multiplied, innumerable deposit accounts with small balances and a rapid turnover were opened, excessive employment of

Table V-3

AVERAGE REAL INTEREST RATES ON SELECTED SAVINGS AND LOAN INSTRUMENTS, 1956–1970

(in percent per year)[a]

Year	Loan Instruments				Savings Instruments		
	Commercial banks	Bank of Brazil	Letras de Cambio (Rate to borrower)	Resolution 63	Commercial bank savings deposits	ORTN[b]	Letras de Cambio (rate to holders)
1956	−2.8	−10.8	N.A.	—	−12.5	—	N.A.
1957	+3.6	−4.6	N.A.	—	−8.5	—	N.A.
1958	+4.7	−3.7	N.A.	—	−7.3	—	N.A.
1959	−13.3	−20.8	N.A.	—	−24.0	—	N.A.
1960	−7.4	−15.2	9.9	—	−19.3	—	−6.4
1961	−11.8	−18.0	10.9	—	−23.9	—	−7.9
1962	−17.5	−25.1	5.5	—	−31.6	—	−14.6
1963	−25.6	−35.0	−2.8	—	−41.0	—	−23.1
1964	−30.1	−37.5	−4.9	—	−45.9	—	−24.5
1965	−14.1	−21.7	14.1	—	−34.4	−1.9	−13.3
1966	−2.3	−9.1	24.2	—	−26.2	6.1	−5.5
1967	4.5	−5.1	16.1	9.3	−20.7	1.4	2.3
1968	7.6	8.4	17.7	28.9	−16.6	5.3	4.3
1969	8.4	—	19.3	11.1	−13.7	1.7	6.2
1970	—	—	19.9 (May)	8.6 (July)	—	2.0 (May)	6.8 (May)

[a]The formula for calculating the real rate of interest is

$$d = \frac{100 + n}{100 + d} - 1, \quad \text{where}$$

$\quad$ d = deflated interest rate,
$\quad$ n = nominal interest rate,
$\quad$ d = deflator based on annual change in general price index.

[b]Corrected by monetary correction index of National Monetary Council. Exchange devaluation of 41 percent in 1968 permitted higher return under exchange correction option of 16.2 percent.

Source: See Table V-2.

personnel developed, and so forth. Consequently banks began to have very high operating costs; today few of them are able to lend money for less than 2 percent per month in nominal terms. These cost increases are difficult to reverse in the short run because of labor legislation, excessive fixed investment in buildings and luxurious installations, and so forth. They became one of the most difficult structural problems hindering monetary stabilization.''

The competition for deposits stimulated the establishment of new bank branches throughout the country; the number of branches increased from 5,010 in 1960 to 6,155 at the end of 1963. High bank profits from investment in real estate also contributed to the increase in branch banking. Many of the new branches meant a new building which, financed largely out of deposit expansion, provided leverage for higher real rates of return for the banks. The second factor contributing to the high cost of financial intermediation was the rapid growth and proliferation of finance companies which duplicated the facilities of the commercial banks. Offering interest rates of four to five times the rates offered on savings deposits by the commercial banks, the finance companies attracted an increasing share of the public's savings. In 1959 the letras de cambio held by the public totalled only Cr. $1.3 million or less than 4 percent of bank savings deposits. By 1963 letras outstanding almost equaled savings deposits (see Table V-4).

The economic impact of the financial companies was not limited to their contribution to the high cost of financial intermediation. In channeling a large portion of their assets into durable goods, especially automobiles, they diverted financial savings into consumption goods. Increasing sales of durable goods financing, of course, became essential to the growth of the economy as the industrial capacity grew relative to the capacity of other sectors, but artificial stimulation of durable goods financing during a period of inflation was a case of reacting to the symptoms rather than to the basic causes of economic stagnation.

Another immediate effect of the interest rate policy, particularly the subsidized loan rates, was to distort the internal financial structure of Brazilian firms. The cost of borrowed capital was low in relation to equity capital; thus, firms with access to this cheap credit expanded on the basis of borrowed capital. A good corporate

---

[3]Simonsen, "Inflation and Money and Markets of Brazil," p. 144. Simonsen is typical of the new breed of Brazilian economist, well versed in the traditional economic doctrines, but also aware of the assumptions underlying these doctrines; thus he can apply them in consonance with the institutional and behavioral peculiarities of the Brazilian economy.

Table V-4

VOLUME OF PRINCIPAL FINANCIAL ASSETS HELD BY THE PUBLIC, 1956–1972 [a]

(end of year balances in millions of Cr$)

Year	Commercial Banks, Time and Savings Deposits	Letras de Cambio	ORTN	Letras Imobiliarias	Total
1956	21.1	—	—	—	21.1
1957	24.3	—	—	—	24.3
1958	25.6	—	—	—	25.6
1959	30.7	1.3	—	—	32.0
1960	48.4	7.1	—	—	55.5
1961	56.9	13.0	—	—	69.9
1962	57.7	47.9	—	—	105.6
1963	89.6	81.4	—	—	171.0
1964	148.4	245.0	41	—	434.4
1965	242.0	695.0	417	—	1,354.0
1966	713.0	872.0	1,299	7	2,891.0
1967	1,583.0	2,105.0	2,091	140	5,919.0
1968	2,438.0	4,558.0	2,446	461	9,903.0
1969	2,991.0	6,174.0	4,280	933	14,378.0
1970	4,162.0	—	—	—	—
1971	6,585.0	—	—	—	—
1972	8,200.0 (Oct.)	—	—	—	—

[a] Excluding currency and demand deposits; Bank of Brazil savings and time deposits never amounted to more than 4 percent of the total and are excluded here.

Source: 1956 to 1964 data—*Relatório do Banco Central do Brasil*, 1965, p. 186; 1964 to 1969 data—*Boletim do Banco Central do Brasil*, February and March 1970.

treasurer always tried to meet his working capital requirements, which lost their value with inflation, out of borrowed funds.[4] Equity was invested in real estate and other real assets which did not lose value with inflation. The ensuing high ratio of loan capital to net worth increased interest costs of these firms as interest rates turned from negative to high positive rates in the years after 1966, thus contributing to a record number of bankruptcies and in general providing a serious impediment to stabilization efforts.

The low cost of borrowed capital relative to the cost of other factors of production also contributed excessively to the capital intensive industrialization process and to the other structural imbalances in the economy. The structure and level of interest rates did not reflect the economic cost of capital to the Brazilian economy. As the role of official financial institutions expanded, credit was allocated increasingly on the basis of priorities established by the government. To the extent that the usury law was effective, there was a tendency on the part of the private institutions to allocate credit on the basis of favored customers and family connections rather than on the basis of the customer's ability to pay the price. The rapid expansion of industrial output during the late 1950s indicates that the allocation of credit was relatively effective. But the economic crisis of 1963 would tend to indicate a less efficient allocation of credit as the industrial sector grew too fast relative to other sectors. Moreover, given the inherent subsidies to capital, the industrialization was more capital intensive than might be economically and socially desirable.

The low rates of return on financial savings instruments, due largely to interest rate controls, diverted the flow of savings to consumption goods, to lesser productive investments, and into foreign currencies. Many Brazilians recognized that even letras de cambio failed to offer a positive rate of return and invested in a variety of real estate ventures of speculative and dubious economic values. One such form of investment was in private clubs, country clubs of all forms, summer and winter resorts, and holiday hotels. These clubs were constructed over a period of years at the rate afforded by the monthly contributions of its members. Throughout the Rio area one finds hundreds of partly constructed clubs and hotels which were financed with the savings of thousands of members. The most that a member could hope to receive was a capital gain, assuming that the construction was completed. In many instances the rate of construction was slower than the depreciation. Often the members tired of the never-ending contributions without visible improvement and all con-

---

[4]"It is common practice for companies to work with many different banks, sometimes over forty, scraping a little out of each pot. Other companies have concentrated on very extensive efforts with a smaller number, perhaps four. In either case, contacts have to be maintained at a high executive level. In many companies the financial manager spends one-fourth to one-half of his time calling on bankers—a serious interference with normal management activities. In companies that are too small to have a top-ranking official in charge of finance, this burden falls on the general manager." Lincoln Gordon and Engelbert L. Grommers, *United States Manufacturing Investment in Brazil: The Impact of Brazilian Government Policies*, pp. 96-97.

struction stopped. Another relatively unproductive investment was the construction of residential buildings at the rate the homeowner could afford to pay in cash. Since the construction period dragged on in many cases for several years, the costs of construction increased considerably. On the other hand, there was no alternative to this approach to the housing problem since construction loans and home financing were not available. In the case of apartments, all title-holders initially agreed to contribute a fixed amount per month, and construction proceeded at the rate the poorest titleholder could afford. As inflation continued and construction costs rose, the rate of construction slowed accordingly. Titleholders whose salaries rose with the inflation were able to afford increases in the monthly contribution. However, the pace of construction was slowed to the rate afforded by the titleholder whose salary did not increase or who for some reason was not willing to increase the monthly contribution.

The attraction of the more stable foreign currencies also diverted the flow of financial savings from the domestic financial market. Recognizing that the rate of return on savings instruments was less than the rate of inflation and concerned about political and economic instability, many savers purchased U.S. dollars and other foreign currencies. Some of these monies were sent abroad for investment in bank deposits, stocks and bonds, and mutual funds. But the risks and costs of remitting abroad, especially for the small savers, forced most savers to hold these foreign currencies in Brazil, either under the mattress, in a wall safe, or in a bank deposit box. These currencies paid no return, but at least permitted the saver to maintain the value of his savings while retaining a high degree of liquidity.

The net economic consequence of interest rate policy was to reduce the rate of savings, ex post, to channel savings into a number of unproductive investments, and to divert domestic savings to foreign sources. Thus, interest rate policy contributed to the inflationary pressures, to the economic stagnation of the early 1960s, and to the balance of payments difficulties. It also contributed to the unemployment problem through stimulation of capital intensive industrialization. Finally, the resulting high cost financial structure impeded efforts to stabilize, to resume growth, and to balance the national accounts.

The Monetary Correction Approach to Interest Rates—1964 to 1967

There was no basic change in the official policies affecting the level and structure of interest rates for the first two years after the 1964 revolution. The policymakers focused their attention on the fiscal sector where a great deal of progress was made in reducing the inflationary deficit. Interest rates remained subjected to the usury law, which was in fact reincarnated in the new 1967 constitution. The not surprising result was the continuation of the trend and structure of rates and the same distortions in the financial system which had evolved in the years prior to 1964. Recognition of the need to revise official policies and regulations on interest rates came slowly and even then the measures implemented did not offer satisfactory results.

The first major innovation aimed at correcting the distortions in the interest rate structure was monetary correction. The concept of monetary correction, or the ex post adjustment of financial instruments for price increases, was first applied in July 1964 to tax debts as part of Finance Minister Octavio Bulhões's effort to increase public sector revenues.[5] During the years of high inflation, taxpayers learned to benefit from the premium in postponing tax payments, since the interest rate and other penalties for late payment were less than the interim rate of price increase. Dr. Bulhões pointed out that, "given the bureaucratic slowness of the tax administration and the profitability of indebtedness when the depreciation of money was rapid, many businesses were accustomed until 1964 to remain in debt to the social welfare institutes and the Treasury. Delayed payment of tax debts, despite cumulative penalties, was the best way of increasing working capital."[6] In 1965 the government applied monetary correction to the new issues of government bonds (ORTN) with the aim of restoring confidence in the public debt, a confidence which had been destroyed during the years of inflation.

Success with the application of monetary correction to public debts provided the monetary authorities with the necessary confidence to extend the same correction factor to private debt, which was done in July 1966, two years after the revolution.[7] Finance Minister Bulhões explained the need for monetary correction in this way: "Once the government opted for gradualism in its fight against inflation, which meant a continuation (albeit reduced) of the rise in prices, it was incumbent upon it to offer some guarantee of the preservation of capital values, while the inflation persisted, in order to stimulate

---

[5] The Emergency Tax Reform Law, Law 4357 of 16 July 1964.

[6] Octavio de Gouveia Bulhões, 'Financial Recuperation for Economic Expansion," in Ellis, *Economy of Brazil*, p. 162.

[7] The application of monetary correction to bank deposits and loans was first authorized by the Capital Market Law (4728 of 14 July 1965) but the implementing regulations were not issued until 30 July 1966, with the issuance of Central Bank Resolution 31 which authorized monetary correction for commercial bank operations and Resolution 32 which authorized it for finance company and investment bank operations.

savings. Hence its recourse to monetary correction."[8] Minister Bulhões does not explain why monetary correction was preferable to revocation of the usury law, which would have been a more direct means of accomplishing the same objective. The only answer I can find to this question, is that the usury law in Brazil, as in so many other countries, is based on religious as well as social and economic traditions, that the authorities found it preferable to circumvent rather than confront this law.

The application of monetary correction to private financial transactions met with a mixed reaction on the part of the private sector. The increase in the legal ceilings was welcomed, but neither the commercial banks nor the finance companies accepted the idea of an ex post adjustment of assets and liabilities. The commercial banking associations recommended an alternative of fixed loan and deposit rates with 12 percent interest and an additional amount based upon the anticipation of future inflation or "prefixed monetary correction." They recommended a loan rate ceiling of 30 percent, 12 percent of which was designated as interest and the remaining 18 percent as prefixed monetary correction, and a deposit rate ceiling of 20 to 22 percent per year, depending upon the maturity, including 8 percent interest and 12 to 14 percent prefixed monetary correction. The finance Companies also strongly supported the idea of prefixed monetary correction but with no specific ceiling on the prefixed amount.

What was the effect of monetary correction on the structure of interest rates? The most significant impact was clearly on government bond rates, but monetary correction also provided the official institutions with a legal basis for applying rates above 12 percent. The nominal rate of return on Bank of Brazil loans, we note, rose from 14 percent in 1963 to 25.5 percent in 1966. In real terms this meant a change from negative interest rates averaging 35 percent in 1963 to 9 percent in 1966. Since these average returns include special rates for agriculture and other priority sectors, the rates for normal Bank of Brazil commercial transactions undoubtedly moved to a positive level in 1966. The significance to the National Housing Program of monetary correction is a story in itself. But it is a safe assessment that without monetary correction there would have been no housing boom started in 1967.

The impact on official transactions stands out in sharper focus in the case of readjustable treasury bonds, referred to hereafter as ORTN. The average nominal interest rate on ORTN in 1965 was 53.8 percent and in 1966, 46.4 percent. As the general price index showed

[8]Bulhões, "Financial Recuperation," p. 163.

increases of 57 percent and 38 percent respectively in these two years, the real rate of return on ORTN changed from a small negative rate to a positive rate of 6 percent in 1966. Moreover, these ORTN rates were higher than any alternative financial savings instrument; the nominal return of letras, for example, averaged 36 percent in 1965 and 30 percent in 1966. The result was, as would be expected, a shift in public preferences from savings deposits and letras into ORTN, the volume of which surpassed both savings instruments by the end of 1966 (See Table V-4).

In May 1966 the monetary authorities added an exchange rate correction option to ORTN as a further means of enhancing the acceptability of these public securities and of providing an alternative to dollar purchases.[9] The holder of ORTN was given the option of redeeming the ORTN on the basis either of monetary correction or exchange rate correction, whichever was higher. The amounts of both the monetary correction and exchange devaluations were fixed by the National Monetary Council, but many people felt that the official price index, on which the monetary correction was based, did not reflect the real rate of inflation. This was clearly indicated by the continued widespread purchases of U.S. dollars.[10] The exchange rate option was instrumental in raising the effective interest rates on ORTN from mid-1966 to mid-1968, as the devaluation exceeded the rate of price increases during this period; but since September 1968 the exchange rate correction has been consistently lower than the monetary correction factor.[11]

The monetary correction approach also involved an increase in commercial bank savings deposit rates, even though to an inadequate level. Interest rate ceilings on fixed term deposits of one year had remained at 6 percent until January 1966 when they were raised to 8 percent in connection with the elimination of the 3 percent rate on demand deposits.[12] In July 1966 maximum deposit rates were further increased to 22 percent, which included the eight percent interest rate and 14 percent prefixed monetary correction.[13] The 22 percent rate was sufficiently attractive, despite the higher 30 percent rate of return

[9] Decree Law No. 7, 13 May 1966.

[10] An estimated U.S. $260 million were purchased in 1966. These purchases of dollars intensified as part of the speculative fever prior to the annual devaluations, and some few dollars returned after the devaluation, but the outflow resumed again shortly thereafter.

[11] This was one year after the establishment of the flexible exchange rate system at the end of August 1968.

[12] Central Bank Resolution 15, 28 January 1966.

[13] Central Bank Resolution 31.

on letras, to shift public preferences toward savings deposits, the volume of which tripled in 1966 and doubled in 1967. But the risk factor played an important role in this shift as widespread publicity had been given to the Mannesman case in which holders of letras had lost substantial sums of money. Given the relatively lower rate, the preference for savings deposits proved short-lived as savers reverted to letras in late 1967 and 1968 (See Table 4).

Monetary correction had no effect on effective interest rates on commercial bank loans and finance company operations. Indeed, it was not designed to do so, since these rates were already determined by market forces. The interest rates on finance company paper had been, since its initiation in 1959, relatively free of regulation and were, therefore, most reflective of market conditions. There is no evidence that the application of prefixed monetary correction in any way altered this situation. Commercial bank loan rates had also gradually risen to free market levels which by mid-1966 were approaching a positive level in real terms. The July 1966 accord to set a ceiling of 30 percent on loans appeared to have no more effect on effective rates than did the usury law, since the average rate of return on bank loans was significantly higher than the 30 percent ceiling fixed by the accord.

The July 1966 accord to limit rates on savings deposits to 22 percent and on loans to 30 percent, while the rate of inflation was still running at close to 40 percent, was inconsistent with the general policy of the Castello Branco authorities to permit interest rates to rise to their market levels. Two considerations weighed heavily in their decision. The first was a concern that a deposit rate offering a real rate of return, that is, in excess of 40 percent, would increase bank costs, lead to higher loan rates, and add to the growing bankruptcies and continuing inflationary pressures. Dr. Casimiro Ribeiro, director of the rediscount department of the Central Bank, made this comment to the writer in September 1966. The second consideration was that a higher rate of return on savings deposits would threaten the existence of the finance companies, which were the primary source of the consumer goods financing so vital to maintain the demand for industrial output in an already depressed economy. Planning Minister Roberto Campos expressed this point of view to the writer in August 1966. These two considerations were of an either/or nature, for higher deposit rates would lead to higher loan rates only if they were not effective in attracting additional deposits, which would come largely from the finance companies. On the other hand, if the higher rates were effective in attracting deposits, the banks' earning capacity would also be increased. The monetary authorities eventually moved in the direction of permitting greater competition between the banks and the finance companies, but only after four additional years of experimenting with a subsidy approach to reducing bank rates.

Resolution 63 Transactions

Another financial innovation implemented in 1966 with a potential effect on the interest rate structure was the Resolution 63 transaction, named from its authorizing Central Bank resolution. The monetary authorities had long been concerned about the unequal access of foreign and domestic firms to foreign credit. SUMOC Instruction 289 of 1964 had authorized Central Bank exchange guarantees for foreign credit received by companies in Brazil. This transaction tended to be used largely by foreign firms with parent companies or financial affiliations abroad. The rates on these foreign credits wre significantly lower than those available in Brazil, even when adjusted for exchange devaluations.[14] These cheaper foreign credits, however, were generally not available to Brazilian firms which, although sound credit risks, were not sufficiently known abroad. Resolution 63 was aimed at correcting this situation by improving the access of Brazilian companies to foreign credit sources. The method of accomplishing this objective was to authorize Brazilian investment and commercial banks to act as intermediaries, with investment banks dealing in the transactions in excess of one year and commercial banks in transactions of less than one year.[15] In its first year of operation Resolution 63 transactions carried an effective nominal interest rate of 40 percent, which was less than finance company loan rates of 49 percent but higher than commercial bank loan rates of 34 percent. In 1968, however, nominal effective rates on Resolution 63 transactions reached 60.2 percent, the highest rate for any loan transaction because of the exchange rate devaluations in that year of 41 percent.[16] The more gradual changes in the exchange rates following adoption of the adjustable peg system in August 1968 helped to stimulate both an increase in the volume of, and a decrease in the nominal interest rates

[14] Instruction 289 did not provide an exchange rate guarantee; it merely provided a guarantee that the foreign exchange would be authorized for repayment of the credit, provided foreign exchange was available at the Central Bank.

[15] Resolution 112, 12 March 1969, limited commercial bank participation to transactions between six months and one year.

[16] The nominal effective interest rate to the Brazilian borrower for Resolution 63 transactions is a sum of (a) the rate at which the foreign funds are obtained, usually a couple of percentage points above the prime rates in New York; (b) remittance taxes of about 30 percent of the amount of the foreign interest remission; (c) the Brazilian bank intermediary commission of 4 percent; (d) other charges of about 1 percent; and (e) the exchange devaluation during the period, which in 1968 was 40.9 percent.

on, Resolution 63 transactions. By 1969 nominal effective rates had fallen to the same level as commercial bank loans, thereby offering a source of competition to commercial banks in the loan area.

The Subsidy Approach to Interest Rates—1968 to 1970

In January 1968, the Costa e Silva government initiated a second phase, or subsidy approach, to interest rate policy. Concerned about the cost-push impact of high interest rates and perplexed by the rigidity of nominal rates at the 1965 level despite the reduction in the rate of inflation, Finance Minister Delfim Netto embarked on a course of offering subsidies to banks which agreed to reduce loan rates to specified levels. The subsidy took the form of a reduction in the compulsory reserve requirement which had to be held in the form of non-earning assets, like cash and deposits at the Central Bank. The banks were given the option of satisfying a part of their reserve requirement with ORTN and selected agricultural paper. The objectives were twofold: first, to achieve a reduction in average interest rates through increasing the volume of bank earning assets; and second, to channel the additional credit to priority sectors, specifically agriculture. Bank purchases of ORTN also contributed to financing the government deficit, but this was not the objective in itself. On the contrary, bank holdings of ORTN in lieu of compulsory reserves served to subsidize the banks at the cost of increasing the deficit.

The subsidy approach was initiated with Central Bank Resolution 79 in January 1968. This resolution fixed the official rates for loans which satisfied the criteria for receiving the subsidy at 2 percent per month for loans up to 60 days, 2.2 percent for commercial operations over 60 days, and 2.5 percent for all other loans. On a compound annual basis this meant nominal rates of 26.8 to 33 percent per year. The banks accepted the subsidy but continued to charge what the market would bear. The average rate of return on commercial bank loans in 1968 was 33.7, and this included a significant amount of agricultural credits at 14 to 18 percent per year. In June 1969, the monetary authorities increased the subsidies to the commercial banks, again in the form of a higher percentage of ORTN which could be included in compulsory reserve requirements. Under Resolution 114, 1 June 1969, banks which reduced loan rates to the official ceilings were permitted to satisfy up to 50 percent of their compulsory reserve requirements with ORTN. At the same time interest rate ceilings were reduced to a maximum of 2.2 percent, or an annual rate of 28 percent. Again most banks accepted the subsidy but managed to earn an average of 30.0 percent on their loans in 1969, which again included some agricultural paper at the lower rates.

The attempt to reduce interest rates through the subsidy approach continued through February 1970. There are some indications that the issuance of Resolution 134 in February 1970 marked the turning point in interest rate policy. On the one hand, Resolution 134 reduced the official ceilings to a maximum of 1.8 percent per month or 24 percent per year, again with no greater effect on actual rates than the earlier resolutions. On the other hand, it eliminated the ceilings on commercial bank loans for consumer purposes. This resolution, together with an earlier authority to issue certificates of deposit without rate limitation, gave the banks the authority needed to compete with the finance companies in the profitable consumer loan business.

Finally, the market for finance company (and investment bank) paper, the letras de cambio, and aceites cambiais remained relatively unaffected by the official ceilings on interest rates. Rates in this market sought their market level with the expected result that financial savings continued to be channeled to the finance companies. (see Table 4). And although nominal rates declined in this market after 1969, the rate of decline was much slower than the decline in the rate of inflation so that, in real terms, the interest rate level continued to rise (see Table V-3). Concerned about the growing real rates for letras de cambio, the monetary authorities in June 1969 also decreed a 10 percent reduction in these rates.[17] However, the finance companies were no less ingenious than the commercial banks (the same officials serve in both institutions) in evading the official ceiling. Reported interest rates declined following the decreed reductions, but the official ceiling had no effect on nominal interest rates. The method used by finance companies in evading the ceiling was to offer letras with the required 10 percent reduction in rates but with shorter maturities (described as "giving away days"). This policy of reducing interest rates by decree was further extended to the investment banks in March 1970, again without noticeable effect on the effective interest rate level.[18] Increasing competition from the commercial banks following the issuance of Resolution 134, and from abroad under Resolution 63, is more likely to have had an impact on interest rates than administrative control of rates.

Direct Intervention in Interest Rate Market

The Brazilian authorities have, at various times, advanced five arguments in support of direct intervention to affect the level and struc-

---

[17] Resolution 115, effective 15 June 1969.

[18] Resolution 136, effective 2 March 1970, reduced by 10 percent the cost of financing from investment banks.

ture of interest rates: (1) the high cost financial intermediation system; (2) the vested interest in the finance companies; (3) high interest rates as an inflationary cost push factor; (4) interest controls as a political offset to wage controls and price surveillance; (5) the use of the interest rate as a selective instrument for subsidizing priority sectors. A sixth argument in favor of an experimental course to affect interest rates is that so little is really known about the impact of interest rates on the major economic objectives. Since the economic profession has not been able to agree on the effects of interest rates, it is not difficult to understand why the Brazilian authorities decided upon an experimental course.

The high cost structure of the commercial banking system developed during the years of inflation, it was argued, precluded any significant reduction in commercial bank rates without some offsetting financial inducement. In its 1969 annual report the Central Bank of Brazil described the high interest rate level as "an impediment to the deceleration of the rate of inflation".[19] Mário Simonsen suggests that "the commercial banking system today is reasonably well adapted to 30 to 40 percent annual inflation but not to stable prices, since real interest rates charged on loans would become unbearably high" and that the high cost system "is one of the most difficult structural problems hindering monetary stabilization."[20] The aim of the subsidy approach was to permit the banks to lower their loan rates by increasing their earning assets, but there is no evidence of any resulting reductions in effective bank loan rates. On the contrary, the subsidies perpetuated the high cost financial structure by protecting the less efficient institutions. This seems to have been recognized by the new measures taken in 1970 which permitted greater competition between the banks and other financial institutions. Active use of this authority by the commercial banks should tend to attract savings deposits from the letras de cambio market, and over time lead to incorporation of the finance companies within the structure of the commercial banks. This rationalization of the financial structure should enhance the possibilities for lowering interest rates.

The Central's Bank's acceptance of prefixed monetary correction on commercial banks deposits in lieu of full *ex post* monetary correction was based largely on a concern that if interest rate constraints were removed from the commercial banks, there would be a real threat to the continued existence of the finance companies. In July 1966 the Central Bank accepted the 22 percent ceiling on deposit rates because of the belief that a competitive rate at that time, espe-

[19]*Relatório do Banco Central do Brasil*, 1969, p. 46.
[20]Simonsen, "Inflation and Money and Markets of Brazil," pp. 144-145.

cially following the Mannesman Case, would put the finance companies out of business overnight. Planning Minister Roberto Campos and Central Bank President Denio Nogueira were concerned about the adverse economic repercussions of a sharp curtailment of letras de cambio, which was the major source of durable consumer goods financing, on the sales and output of durables. As a result of the continued flow of financial savings to the finance companies, which tended to invest a relatively high proportion of their assets in consumer financing, there arose in 1966 the anomalous situation of relatively tight bank credit while durable goods sales, financed by finance companies, were booming. Finance Minister Delfim Netto, who took office in 1967, evidenced an even greater concern about the economic impact of a decline in sales of durables and limited the finance companies solely to financing of durables. Meanwhile, the continued existence of duplicate facilities perpetuated the high cost financial structure. The establishment of a private investment banking system in 1967 contributed further to these high costs.

A third argument frequently expressed in Brazil in favor of direct intervention to reduce interest rates is that high interest rates were a cost push factor which impeded the stabilization effort. Brazilian business, heavily burdened with a high debt structure, tended to pass the interest cost on to the consumer. Several questionable assumptions underlie this line of reasoning. The first is that direct intervention, either by direct controls or subsidies, actually reduces effective interest rates. The evidence points to the contrary. Commercial banks have been charging what the traffic will bear on loans while enjoying subsidies or otherwise claiming to meet the rate ceilings. A second questionable assumption is the existence of a simple relationship between bank loan rates and interest costs to the business. To the extent that bank lending capacity is increased as a result of higher savings deposits, business credit needs may be satisfied by banks instead of by other sources or by the parallel market, at significantly higher rates. The net effect may well be a lowering of the interest rates for firms previously borrowing from non-bank sources. Finally, there is the assumption, more valid in the case of Brazil than elsewhere, that interest cost is a significant element in total business costs. Nevertheless, even though Brazilian firms developed a high debt ratio during the period of negative real interest rates, for most industrial and commercial firms interest costs as a percentage of sales is relatively small compared with other costs. As important as the cost of credit is a dependable supply.

A fourth consideration in support of some form of interest rate ceiling is the political motivation. With continuing controls on wages and a price surveillance system, it did not seem politically expedient to eliminate interest rate controls, even though there was no significant popular or military pressure against high interest rates.

Finally, subsidized interest rates have long been used in Brazil as a selective instument for subsidizing priority sectors. During the 1950s this instrument was used extensively to subsidize industry and infrastructure. In more recent years it has been used more for the agricultural sector and export industries. Official interest rates for these two sectors remain well below the annual increase on the rate of inflation (a negative real interest rate). Infrastructure loans from the National Economic Development Bank during 1970 averaged a zero real rate of interest. At the nominal interest rates for rural credit prevailing in 1970, farmers received a subsidy of about 7 percent of the amount of their credit. The advantage in providing low interest rate loans as a means of subsidizing priority sectors is that the extent of the subsidies is concealed to all but the sophisticated observer. If the rate of inflation were eliminated, the interest rate subsidies would be sharply curtailed and some provision for farm subsidies would have to be included in the budget, where they would become more obvious. It is interesting to speculate whether perpetuation of inflation might be a policy insofar as it is useful in maintaining interest rate policy as a selective instrument for subsidizing priority investment sectors.

Other Developments Affecting the Interest Rate Structure

The structure of interest rates in Brazil has been increasingly influenced by three developments in the financial markets: more intensive competition from foreign sources of credit, increased competition between commercial banks and finance companies, and establishment of a treasury bill market.

The rapid increase in the inflow of foreign credits during 1968 and 1969 provided a degree of competition with commercial bank loans. Given the foreign confidence in the Brazilian economy, foreign sources of credit have opened up to Brazilian borrowers. Resolution 63 provided an instrument for Brazilian firms to obtain foreign credit through domestic banks at rates which have gradually fallen, as the exchange devaluations have decreased, to a level competitive with commercial bank rates. While the monetary authorities have limited Resolution 63 operations, high interest rates in Brazil continue to attract a large inflow of foreign credit, registered with the Central Bank under Law 4131. Another aspect of the large inflow of foreign credit is the expansionary impact on domestic credit. Within a given

monetary budget the authorities have to sterilize larger than anticipated net foreign reserves with contractive domestic operations, such
as through government bond sales which tend to push interest rates
up. Thus we have both the competitive impact of lower foreign rates
pushing rates down, and the offsetting sterilization operations which
tend to push them up.

In 1970 increased competition between commercial banks and
finance companies was stimulated by elimination of interest rate ceilings on commercial bank loans to individuals. Central Bank Resolution 134, together with an earlier authority to issue certificates of
deposits without limitations on rates, gave the commercial banks
scope to compete with finance companies in the consumer financing
market. Active use of this authority by the commercial banks tended
to attract savings deposits form the letras de cambio market, and led
to incorporation of the finance companies within the structure of the
commercial banks, thus rationalizing the financial structure and enhancing the possibilities for lowering interest rates.

A third development which will have a significant impact on the
interest rate structure in Brazil is the development of a treasury bill
market. In authorizing the sale of treasury bills[21] the monetary authorities have provided the basis for attacking another source of the
high costs in the financial structure, that is, the high voluntary cash
reserve requirements commercial banks are forced to maintain in
absence of a secondary interbank market. Lacking a liquid instrument
or market for investing excess reserves on a short-term basis, the
commercial banks have traditionally maintained high voluntary reserves (12 percent of total deposits at the end of 1968 but as high as 20
percent in earlier years). Development of a market in treasury bills
will, over time, give the banks the interbank market they need to
reduce their cash reserves and increase their earning assets.

Summary of Post-1964 Interest Rate Policies

Official policies affecting the structure of interest rates evolved
through three overlapping stages between 1964 and 1970. For the first
two years after the revolution the dominating factor continued to be
the usury law which limited interest rates to 12 percent per year. In
practice, this ceiling was evaded by all financial institutions, with two
major exceptions, loan rates from official institutions and deposit
rates in private commercial banks. The second stage began with the
application of monetary correction, first, in 1964 to tax liabilities; then

---

[21]Central Bank Resolution 150, issued 24 July 1970.

in 1965 to government bonds; and finally in 1966 to all major long-term financial instruments. While monetary correction had little impact on the effective level and structure of rates in private markets, its significance in providing the legal basis for bringing interest rates in official institutions closer to market levels and in permitting an increase in bank deposit rates cannot be underrated. Finance Minister Delfim Netto initiated a third phase of interest rate policy in January 1968 with extension of financial inducements to the commercial banks in return for reducing their nominal loan rates. Nominal bank loan rates had tended to stabilize at the 1964 level and, since the rate of inflation had declined rapidly, real rates had risen to relatively high levels. But the financial inducements proved to be no more effective than usury law in effecting a reduction in real interest rates. In January 1970 the monetary authorities may have embarked on yet another phase of interest rate policy in permitting the commercial banks greater scope for competition with the finance companies and other financial institutions. This phase of policy, with greater reliance on competition, should permit some reduction in the costs of financial operations and eventually in nominal and real rates of interest.

CHAPTER VI

Fiscal Policy for Growth with Inflation

Fiscal policy evolved in Brazil during the 1950s into a powerful instrument for promoting industrial growth. High protective tariffs interwoven with an overvalued exchange rate system gave the initial impetus to industrial growth, while an increasing array of fiscal incentives and subsidies provided additional stimulation to this sector. The high rate of growth in the industrial sector during the 1950s provides ample evidence of the effectiveness of these policies as an instrument for growth. But Brazilian fiscal policies and the fiscal system which evolved from them during the 1950s proved to be as ineffective in achieving other major economic objectives, that is, price stability, equitable income distribution, full employment, and balance of payment equilibrium, as they were effective in achieving growth.

The revenue system, instead of providing the sort of automatic stabilizers known in the industrial countries, became more and more inflation prone. The narrow concentration of investment incentives in the industrial sector, a normally capital intensive industry, was at the cost of neglecting the labor intensive industries, housing construction, and agriculture, which were severly restricted by a shortage of investment capital in the inflationary environment. This also meant an inequitable concentration of income in the urban industrial region of south-central Brazil. And finally, the entire set of policies intensified the chronic deficit in the balance of payments which required debt reschedulings in 1961 and again in 1964.

The post-1964 governments retained fiscal policy as an active instrument for affecting the level and direction of investment and economic growth, but shifted the emphasis from the single-minded devotion to industrial development to multiple objectives of price stability, economic efficiency, more equitable income distribution,

118

and balanced sectoral and regional economic growth. The shift in emphasis required greater use of the income tax as an active instrument for affecting sectoral and regional investments as well as the overall level of saving and investment.

The importance of fiscal policy as an instrument for growth is largely attributable to three facts in the Brazilian economy: the absence of money and capital markets as a source of investment financing, the large role of the public sector in the economy, and the nature of the Brazilian tax system.[1] In this chapter we examine the nature of the tax system and the role of the public sector and how they contributed to growth—and to inflation. The scope of fiscal policy included in this chapter is the

> body of measures relating to the tax system, public expenditures, contracting of internal and external debt by the states and the operations and financial situation of the autonomous and semi-public agencies and bodies, through the medium of which the amount and distribution of investment and public consumption as components of national expenditure are determined and the amount and composition of private investment and consumption are influenced directly or indirectly.[2]

Fiscal Policy in the Decade Prior to 1964

Federal deficit spending was the primary cause of Brazilian inflation during the decade prior to 1964. Increases in federal government spending in excess of revenues contributed directly to the excessive demand for goods and services; and the rising budgetary deficit, financed by currency issued by the Bank of Brazil, provided the basis for a multiple expansion of the money supply and private sector spending. The inflationary impact of federal government operations is traced in Table VI-1. Expenditures rose from 8.4 percent of GNP in 1953 to 12.1 percent in 1963, while tax revenues remained fairly stable at 7.9 percent of GNP during the decade. The resulting deficit grew from 0.4 percent of GNP in 1953 to 4.2 percent in 1963.

---

[1] The Brazilian experiences with fiscal policy contrast with those of Mexico where the effectiveness of fiscal policy as an instrument for promotion of growth (and stabilization) is limited because the general level of taxation and government savings is relatively low. Tax revenues of the federal government have ranged between 8 and 12 percent of GNP. See Dwight S. Brothers & Leopoldo M. Solis, *Mexican Financial Development* p. 52. The authors also noted that the Mexican fiscal system is less effective as an instrument of policy because the responsiveness of tax revenues to increases in gross national product is markedly lower than in the wealthier countries whose systems of taxation are more progressive.

[2] Victor L. Urquidi, *Fiscal Policy for Economic Growth in Latin America*, p. 2.

Table VI-1

FEDERAL EXPENDITURES, REVENUES, AND DEFICITS, 1953,
1958 and 1963

(millions of Cr$, current prices)

	Expenditures		Revenues		Deficits	
Year	Cr$	Percent of GNP	Cr$	Percent of GNP	Cr$	Percent of GNP
1953	39.0	8.4	37.0	7.9	2.0	0.4
1958	130.4	8.9	102.0	6.9	28.4	1.9
1963	1,435.0	12.1	930.0	7.8	505.0	4.2

Source: *Conjuntura Econômica*, December 1969.

The main causes of the burgeoning federal expenditures were (a) the mushrooming personnel payroll, and (b) the accelerating subsidies to public autarquia, particularly the transportation autarquia.

The inflationary growth in federal government expenditures for personnel and subsidies to autarquia is seen more sharply when viewed in constant prices. Table VI-2 shows the acceleration in personnel expenditures from a 40 percent growth between 1953 and 1958, to 105 percent between 1958 and 1963. Autarquia subsidies, which had been an insignificant portion of current expenditures in 1953, multiplied by 15 times during the five years prior to 1958 and doubled again by 1963. In the latter year subsidies to autarquia accounted for 70 percent of the federal deficit. These were distributed as follows:

	(in million Cr$)
State Railroads	177.6
Merchant Marine	37.0
Social Security	30.7
National Highways Dept.	31.2
State Steel Works	19.9
Northeast Development Agency	12.7
Others	54.6
Total	363.7

If we explore further why these two items in the budget rose so rapidly compared with other government expenditures, we find the answer in the policy responses to two of the major problems of the time: the high and rising levels of both unemployment and inflation. In each instance the policy response of successive governments was to attack the symptoms instead of the causes. Rising unemployment, the consequence of the concentration of growth in the capital inten-

Table VI-2

CURRENT EXPENDITURES OF THE FEDERAL GOVERNMENT, 1953, 1958 and 1963

(millions of Cr$, 1963 prices)

Year	Personnel	Purchases of Goods & Services	Transfers to Consumers	Subsidies to Autarquia	Total
1953	159.8	174.6	82.6	6.7	423.7
1958	224.0	136.5	137.2	104.8	602.5
1963	460.0	121.5	158.0	204.5	944.0
Percentage increase					
1953/58	40	−22	66	1,460	42
1958/63	105	−11	15	96	57

Source: *Conjunctura Econômica*, December 1969.

sive industrial sector and the stagnant productivity and low growth rates in the agricultural sector, induced a migratory flood to the cities. The Brazilian government tried to alleviate the problem of growing unemployment by adding more and more people to the public payroll, a response which was consistent with the "traditional propensity of the Brazilian government to distribute jobs without providing work."[3]

The policy response to inflation, like the response to unemployment, attacked the symptoms rather than the causes. To moderate the growth of prices, the government contained the freight and passenger rates for shipping by railway, air and sea. As the inflation continued, the rates charged by these transportation agencies became grossly inadequate to cover their current operating expenses, let alone their investment requirements. The government also limited rate increases for privately owned, usually foreign, telephone, electricity and gas utilities, with the consequences a neglect of investments and a deterioration in services to near chaotic levels.

Much has been written about government investments as a major cause of the Brazilian inflation.[4] But this examination of federal investments does not reveal any significant inflationary impact from public sector investments source after 1958. During the five-year period 1953 to 1958 investment expenditures doubled in real terms. But

[3] Mário Simonsen, "O Crecimento do Sector Publico na Economia Brasileiro," p. 15.

[4] Eugenio Gudin, "The Chief Characteristics of the Postwar Economic Development of Brazil," in Ellis, *Economy of Brazil*, pp. 3-25. The new federal city of Brasilia, for example, is reported to have cost more than Cr$ 620 million during the first ten years of its construction, or an average of Cr$ 62 million per year. The significance of this expenditure, if such was the cost, can be seen when compared with total federal government investments in 1963 of Cr$ 212.7 million.

Table VI-3

**INVESTMENT BY FEDERAL GOVERNMENT, FEDERAL
AUTARQUIA AND SOCIAL SECURITY,
1953, 1958 AND 1963**

(millions of Cr$, 1963 prices)

Year	Federal Government	Federal Autarquia	Social Security	Total Investment
1953	66.7	26.6	12.0	105.4
Percent of total	(63.4)	(25.3)	(11.4)	(100)
Percent of GNP	(1.1)	(0.4)	(0.2)	(1.7)
1958	109.5	76.7	22.8	209.0
Percent of total	(52.4)	(36.7)	(10.9)	(100)
Percent of GNP	(1.3)	(0.9)	(0.2)	(2.4)
1963	78.9	119.8	14.0	212.7
Percent of total	(37.1)	(56.2)	(6.7)	(100)
Percent of GNP	(0.7)	(1.0)	(0.1)	(1.8)
Percentage increase				
1953/1958	64	188	90	98
1958/1963	−19	56	−38.5	2

Source: *Conjuntura Econômica*, December 1969.

during the five years from 1958 to 1963, federal investments remained almost constant in real terms, as shown in Table VI-3. This table also shows the shift in investments from the federal government to the autarquia during these years. Investments undertaken directly by the federal government declined from 63.4 percent of total federal investments in 1953 to 37.1 percent in 1963, while autarquia investments constituted a growing share, rising from 25.3 percent of the total in 1953 to 56.2 percent in 1963.

Comparison of the federal government subsidies to the autarquia with investments by these enterprises shows clearly that unrealistic pricing policies of these autarquia lie at the heart of the Brazilian budgetary problem. In 1953 the subsidies to the autarquia totalled Cr$ 6.7 million (Table VI-2) while investments were four times as much at Cr$ 26.6 million. By 1958 subsidies exceeded autarquia investments which meant that the government was subsidizing current operating expenses of the autarquia out of budgetary revenues. By 1963 subsidies to the autarquia were almost double the level of investments.

Salient Characteristics of the Brazilian Tax Structure

The main characteristics of the Brazilian tax structure include its federal nature; regressivity with heavy stress on consumption taxes; federal government sharing of revenues with state and municipal governments; inflexibility due to heavy reliance on earmarking of tax revenues; inflationary propensity owing to an absence of the automatic income stabilizers; and finally, its potential effectiveness in affecting the level and direction of investments and growth.

The Brazilian tax structure is a federal system with separate tax authorities for federal, state, and local governments. The federal government, including social security and autarquia, collects about 63 percent of total taxes, but disburses only 48 percent of total expenditures. The state governments collect about 33 percent of total revenues and disburse 39 percent of total spending, while the municipalities collect only 4 percent and disburse 13 percent. Both federal and state governments rely heavily on excise (consumption) taxes while the local municipalities rely on land taxes and transfers from the higher echelons of government.

Another way of looking at the role that the several layers of government play in the Brazilian economy is in terms of their purchases of goods and services and tax revenues as a percentage of GNP, as in Table VI-4. The centralized accounts of the federal union, comprising the federal government, the social security system, and the federal autarquia, accounted for 8.3 percent of the final goods

Table VI-4
TAX REVENUES AND EXPENDITURES IN FINAL GOODS AND SERVICES, BY LEVEL OF GOVERNMENT, 1967
(as percentage of GNP)

Level of Government	Tax Revenues	Expenditures Goods and Services
Federal union	11.1	8.3
Federal government	7.2	5.6
Social security	2.3	1.2
Autarquia	1.6	1.5
States (including state		
autarquia)	6.0	7.6
Municipalities	1.0	1.6
Total public sector	18.1	17.5

Source: *Conjuntura Econômica*, December 1969.

and services consumed and invested in Brazil in 1967, but collected revenues amounting to 11.1 percent of GNP. Expenditures of the states, on the other hand, accounted for 7.6 percent of GNP while collecting revenues equivalent to 1.6 percent. Finally, the municipalities accounted for 1.6 percent of expenditures and 1 percent of revenues.

Secondly, the Brazilian tax system is highly regressive, with great stress on the consumption, or indirect, taxes. Indirect taxes comprised 64 percent of total taxes in 1967 (compared with 43 percent in the United States in 1967) Even these figures understate the use of indirect taxes because all social security collections in Brazil are considered direct taxes, as noted in Table VI-5, while in the United States statistics, the 50 percent of social security collected from the employers is considered an indirect tax.

One explanation for the low level of direct taxation in Brazil is notorious evasion of taxes, particularly of the income tax, but even consumption taxes are evaded regularly.[5] The changeover to the value-added tax in 1967 was justified in part as a potent weapon against tax evasion, since it is to the advantage of each business to ensure compliance by previous businesses in the productive process. The fiscal incentives so widely used by the post-revolutionary governments have also added to the basic regressivity of the Brazilian tax system to the extent that they permit the large taxpayers to retain control over funds which otherwise would be used to pay taxes. On

Table VI-5
DIRECT AND INDIRECT TAXES,
BY LEVEL OF GOVERNMENT, 1967
(as percentage of total taxes)

Level of Government	Direct Taxes	Indirect Taxes	Total
Federal Union	53	47	100
Federal government	31	69	100
Social security	100	—	100
Autarquia	45	55	100
State governments	2	98	100
Municipalities	53	47	100
Total public sector	36	64	100

Source: *Conjuntura Econômica*, December 1969.

[5]Shoppers are frequently asked if they wish a receipt for their purchase; if the shopper requests one, the price is raised by the amount of the tax.

the other hand, the fiscal incentive funds are available only on the condition that they be used for investments with high social and economic priorities.

Revenue sharing, a third basic feature of the Brazilian tax system, is provided for in the 1945 Constitution. Both the federal and state governments have collected taxes for transfer to the local municipalities. The entire proceeds of the tax on minerals, 60 percent of the taxes on electricity, and 38.7 percent of the taxes on petroleum are transferred to the local governments. Nevertheless, revenue sharing remained relatively small and most of the funds remained earmarked until the initiation, in January 1967, of the new revenue sharing programs described later in this chapter.

A fourth feature of the Brazilian tax system is its inflexibility due to heavy reliance on earmarking of tax revenues for specific public agencies, states and municipalities, and fiscal incentives for specific use in the private sector. Almost 42 percent of total taxes collected by the the federal government in 1967 were earmarked for specific purposes, including 11 percent for states and municipalities and much of the remainder for the National Economic Development Bank, Petrobrás, the Federal Electricity Fund, and the Highway Construction Fund.

Earmarked taxes totalled Cr$ 355 million of total federal government revenues of Cr$ 854.5 million in 1963. Of total direct taxes, primarily the income tax, of Cr$ 251.1 million, the federal government transferred, as earmarked funds, Cr$ 151 million to the states and municipalities and other sources. Fourteen percent of the income tax was transferred to the states and municipalities, and 100 percent of an income tax surcharge was transferred to the National Economic Development Bank. Of the indirect taxes of Cr$ 603.4 million, the Brazilian government transferred Cr$ 204.5 million, including 15 percent of the stamp tax to education, health, and social pioneers; 14 percent of the excise tax to the states and municipalities and to the Federal Electricity Fund; all of the excise taxes on autos to Petrobrás; 8 percent of import duties to the National Port Fund; and 100 percent of duties on vehicles to Petrobrás. Other earmarked taxes included:

penitentiary tax—100 percent to the penitentiaries;
single tax on electrical power—40 percent to the Federal Electricity Fund, 50 percent to the states, 10 percent to municipalities;
clearance tax—100 percent to various funds;
union tax—100 percent to the Social Fund;
lighthouse duties—100 percent to the Naval Fund;
racetrack taxes—70 percent to the commission on breeding horses, 24 percent to the army cavalry.

Rationale for the widespread use of earmarking include the linkage between the uses of the services and the taxes collected for them and avoidance of the annual legislative appropriations process. On the other hand, earmarking limits the government's flexibility in controlling inflation through cutting expenditures. The fiscal incentives, directed toward increasing investment incentives in priority sectors, add another degree of inflexibility to the tax system. The fiscal incentive for investment in the Northeast, for example, permitted until 1970 a deduction of 50 percent of the income tax liability to persons or firms willing to invest in the Northeast region. In 1966, the Castello Branco government also authorized a fiscal incentive of 10 percent for individuals and 5 percent for firms for investment in the capital market.[6] The fiscal incentive approach, offering deductions from the income tax liability, was later extended to investments in the export, fishing, forestry, beef raising, and agricultural sectors. In addition to their use for development purposes, fiscal incentives were directed toward stabilization objectives. In February 1965 fiscal incentives were offered (under Portaria 71, 23 February 1965) to firms which agreed not to raise prices during the remainder of the year, except where costs had risen more than 7 percent. With some modification the Portaria 71 incentives were continued until 1967.

Fifth, the Brazilian tax system is inflation prone. The automatic stabilizers, the progressive income tax and social security payments, which have been effective in the United States and other countries in moderating the movement in demand, both upward and downward, have not been effective income stabilizers in Brazil. The marginal tax revenues, as a percentage of GNP, have been less than average revenues. As GNP rises, tax revenues tend to rise at slower rates. Federal government revenues remained fairly stable, at about 8 percent of nominal GNP, from 1959 to 1963, while prices rose continually from an annual rate of 38 percent in 1959 to 75 percent in 1963 (see Table VI-6). Aggressive tax enforcement and tax reform measures in 1965 and 1966 raised federal revenues above 11 percent in 1966 although they declined in 1967 due to one-time tax deductions directed at stimulating the economy.

There are several reasons for the failure of the automatic stabilizers in Brazil. The simultaneous existence of stagnation and inflation offers the first explanation. These stabilizers cannot serve to increase overall effective demand and employment and, at the same time, reduce the inflationary impact of excessive effective demand. A second explanation is that the Brazilian tax structure has not been an

---

[6]In 1970 the 10 percent for individuals increased to 12 percent and the 5 percent for firms was eliminated.

Table VI-6

PRICE INCREASES, REAL GNP GROWTH AND FEDERAL REVENUE AS PERCENTAGE OF GNP, 1956–1967

Year	Annual Rates of Increase		Federal Revenue as Percent of GNP
	Consumer price index	Real GNP	
1956	19	3.2	6.8
1957	14	8.1	6.3
1958	13	7.7	6.9
1959	38	5.6	8.0
1960	29	9.7	8.0
1961	37	10.0	7.9
1962	52	5.3	7.6
1963	75	1.5	7.8
1964	91	2.9	8.3
1965	57	2.7	8.9
1966	38	5.1	11.1
1967	28	4.8	9.6

Source: *Conjuntura Econômica*, December 1969.

effective counterinflationary instrument because of the relatively small size of the progressive income tax, less than 10 percent of total tax revenues (compared with about 50 percent in the United States) and because of the failure to keep tax payments on a current basis. The personal income tax was not placed on a pay-as-you-go basis until 1966 and corporate income taxes still are not on this basis (as of 1972). Given the high rates of inflation, taxpayers tended to delay tax payments and accept the fines which could be paid with profit with a deflated cruzeiro. A third explanation is the nature of the public sector transfers which are only slightly connected with unemployment benefits, but are largely subsidies and retirement benefits. The upward trend of these transfers during the years of real GNP growth indicates that they are not of a stabilizing nature. The fourth and final reason for the failure of the automatic stabilizers is that the Brazilian tax system relies heavily on indirect taxes of an ad valorem nature. The revenues from these taxes remain fixed as prices rise, thus declining in real terms.

The major positive feature of the Brazilian tax structure was its effectiveness in affecting the level and direction of investments and output. The performance of the Brazilian economy during the postwar period, 1947 to 1961, and again from 1967 to 1972, would tend to bear out this conclusion. The effectiveness of the Brazilian tax structure in stimulating investments and channeling them to priority sectors lies, on the one hand, in the opportunity it affords for capital accumulation through compulsory (forced) and induced savings programs and, on the other, the large incentives it offers for investments in priority sectors. Its inflationary bias contributed to a higher rate of economic growth through inflationary forced savings during the 1950s, even though this contribution was at best short-lived. More significant are the earmarked taxes and social security programs. The major arguments against the Brazilian tax system as an instrument for growth are (a) that the most efficient firms tend to pay the highest taxes, thereby limiting their ability to accumulate capital; and (b) that the earmarking and fiscal incentives tend to channel investments to less efficient sectors and regions than if market forces were permitted free play.

Fiscal Policy since 1964

The 1964 Action Program of the Castello Branco government shifted the main lines of fiscal policy from the single-minded emphasis on industrial development to multiple objectives of price stability, economic efficiency, more equitable income distribution, and a more balanced economic growth. The Action Program outlined the fiscal objectives for each of the three major instruments of fiscal policy, expenditures, taxation, and public sector investments: (a) to contain government expenditures through disciplining consumption and public sector transfers, and to improve the composition of expenditures so as to reduce the government deficit and alleviate progressively inflationary pressure; (b) to strengthen tax collections and correct the distortions of tax incidence so as to combat inflation, stimulate savings, improve the orientation of private investments, and diminish the regional and sectoral economic inequalities; (c) to orient public sector investments in such a way as to strengthen the economic and social infrastructure of the country, creating the external economies necessary for development of private investment and to reduce the regional and sectoral disequilibria.[7] How effective was the government in achieving these aims of fiscal policy?

Expenditures. Containment of federal government expenditures received first priority on the stabilization agenda. Containment of ex-

---

[7]Ministério do Planejamento Coordenação Econômica, *Programa de Ação Econômica do Govêrno, 1964-1966*, p. 15.

penditures in nominal terms, while prices continued to rise at a higher rate, meant a decline in expenditures in real terms. The 1963 expenditure level of Cr$ 1.4 million had reached a record 12.1 percent of GNP with revenues covering only two-thirds of the total, and the remainder financed by inflationary borrowing from the Bank of Brazil. Projections of expenditures made by the Finance Ministry indicated that the 1964 expenditures would be Cr$ 3.65 million, or about 150 percent higher than the previous year, and the deficit would amount to Cr$ 2.0 million, or 55 percent of expenditures.[8] These projections provided ample evidence of the need for a deep cut in government expenditures. The ensuing 1964 containment program aimed at suppressing the two major causes of rising expenditures: personnel expenditures and subsidies to the public transportation autarquia.

Reducing the wage bill for public servants, both military and civilian, meant cutting the excessive number of employees on the public payroll and holding their wage increases to some noninflationary formula. The first part of this program was not acceptable in the short run because it would have created serious unemployment problems, and the latter part was undercut, for 1964 at least, by the 100 percent increase in salaries given to the military shortly after the revolution. Civilian public servants also needed a catch-up salary increase which was also settled at 100 percent. The political problems involved in containing public sector salaries pointed to the need for a wage policy that would relate public sector wage increases to some reasonable price formula, which is discussed at greater length in Chapter VII.

Subsidies to the public transportation autarquia had grown as a result of the effort to contain inflation through maintaining the rates on public utilities. By 1963 subsidies to the autarquia had become 22 percent of current expenditures of the federal government, equivalent to 40 percent of the budget deficit in that year. But cutting the subsidies also meant that transport rates had to be raised, thus adding to corrective price increases. Elimination of uneconomic railway and other transportation lines and nationalization of these services were other elements of the program not amenable to short-term action and results.

The effectiveness of the expenditure containment effort is traced in Table VI-7. The Castello Branco government cut federal expenditures from 12.1 percent of GNP in 1963 to 10.0 percent in 1967. The

---

[8]Ibid., p. 54. This is not to say that, had there been no change in the government, the budget would have been as projected. The Goulart government would have used many of the same measures used by Finance Minister Bulhões to contain expenditures, especially measures such as postponing the payment of bills, that is, the carryovers of unpaid bills to the following fiscal year, which accounted for CR$ 434 million of the budget cut.

Table VI-7

FEDERAL GOVERNMENT EXPENDITURES, REVENUES AND DEFICITS, 1963–1972

(millions of Cr$)

Year	Current Prices			Constant Prices[a]			As Percentage of GNP		
	Expenditures	Revenues	Deficits	Expenditures	Revenues	Deficits	Expenditures	Revenues	Deficits
1963	1,435	930	505	—	3,843	2,086	12.1	7.8	4.2
1964	2,617	1,890	727	5,677	4,100	1,577	11.4	8.3	3.2
1965	3,825	3,232	593	5,290	4,470	820	10.5	8.9	1.6
1966	6,496	5,910	586	6,516	5,928	588	12.2	11.1	1.1
1967	8,039	6,814	1,225	6,280	5,323	957	11.3	9.6	1.7
1968	11,502	10,275	1,227	7,234	6,462	772	11.6	10.4	1.2
1969	14,709	13,953	756	7,661	7,267	394	11.2	10.6	0.6
1970	19,932	19,194	738	8,666	8,345	321	11.5	11.1	0.4
1971	27,652	26,980	672	9,983	9,733	250	11.8	11.5	0.2
1972	38,254	37,738	516	11,806	11,647	159	N.A.	N.A.	N.A.

[a] Deflated by general price index, 1965-1967 = 100.

[b] The large increases in revenues and expenditures in 1966 are attributed to the inclusion in the budget for the first time the revenues from the petroleum tax and the earmarked expenditures for road building and railways. The petroleum tax amounted to Cr$ 896 million, or 1.7 percent of GNP, in 1966 and comparable amounts in later years.

Source: Boletim do Banco Central do Brasil, December 1972; Conjuntura Econômica, February 1973, p. 66.

explanation of this decline in expenditures lies in the reduction in the wage bill for public personnel and in the subsidies for the transport autarquia, the two major elements of the expenditure containment program. Following the 100 percent increase in salaries of government personnel in 1964, there was no salary increase in 1965, despite the 57 percent rise in the general price index in that year. As a consequence, federal personnel expenditures, in constant prices, fell sharply. In 1966 government personnel were given salary hikes of 39 percent, and total personnel payments, in constant prices, moved upward but, as noted in Table VI-8, remained well below the 1963 level. Successive wage increases in accord with the wage guidelines gradually increased the total government wage bill but it had not returned to the 1963 level by 1971. Federal government transfers to the transportation autarquia did not decline as precipitously as personnel payments. Nevertheless, continuing efforts at rationalizing the operations of these agencies permitted a significant reduction in the level of subsidies, in constant prices, by the end of the 1960s.

Tax Policy. During the Kubitschek years tariff policy had been the basic stimulant for industrial development. While retaining the tariff structure, the post-1964 governments changed the emphasis to the income tax as an active instrument for affecting sectoral and regional investments as well as the overall level of savings. The Castello Branco economists initiated the expanded income tax incentives for investment in the Northeast, in the capital market, in the agricultural sector, and in specific industries previously bypassed in the industrialization process, such as fishing, forestry, and tourism. At the same time they were confronted with the problem of reforming a tax structure which had grown up in a compartmentalized, uncoordinated manner with each tax serving different purposes, not infrequently at cross purposes with each other. There was little coordination within the federal government and even less among the states and between the states and federal government.

The 1964-66 Action Program diagnosed two major shortcomings of the Brazilian tax system: first, it was inflation prone. Revenues failed to rise at the same rate as expenditures and GNP. The marginal rate of growth of revenues was lower than the average rate—as a percentage of GNP. And second, the incidence of the tax system was both inequitable and uneconomic. In terms of priorities, the first aim of tax policy was to increase revenues so as to diminish the inflationary impact of the huge deficit. The measures to increase revenues included: (a) intensified tax enforcement; (b) an increase in excise taxes of 30 percent and imposition of a 10 percent tax on compulsory

Table VI-8

**FEDERAL GOVERNMENT EXPENDITURES ON PERSONNEL
AND TRANSFERS TO TRANSPORTATION AUTARQUIA,
1963–1971**

(millions of Cr$)

	Expenditures on Personnel			Transfers to Transportation Autarquia		
Year	Current prices	Constant prices[a]	% of total expenditures[b]	Current prices	Constant prices[a]	% of total expenditures[b]
1963	460	1,900	32	205	847	14
1964	847	1,837	32	385	835	15
1965	909	1,257	24	637	881	17
1966	1,474	1,478	23	798	800	12
1967	1,917	1,497	24	1,224	956	15
1968	2,280	1,434	20	1,389	874	12
1969	3,158	1,645	21	1,026	534	7
1970	3,949	1,717	20	1,416	616	7
1971	4,888	1,765	18	2,097	672	8

[a]Deflated by general price index, 1965-1967 = 100.
[b]Based on total expenditures in Table VI-10.
Source: 1963-1968—*Conjuntura Econômica*, October 1970, p. 85; 1969-1971—
—unpublished Finance Ministry data.

re-valuation of corporate assets; (c) a 3 percent levy on worker payrolls for a workers' indemnification fund (to be invested in government bonds); and (d) a shift in the income tax system to
pay-as-you-go.

Of equal importance with increasing revenues was the need for
revisions in the tax system aimed at reducing the inequitable burden
of taxes and providing incentives to investment in underdeveloped
sectors and regions of the country. Thus, tax policy also included a
number of measures which tended to reduce revenues, such as the
extension of the fiscal incentive system, the virtual elimination of
taxes on exports, and the initiation of a revenue sharing system which
transferred up to 20 percent of federal income and excise tax revenues to the state and municipal governments. While these measures
were essential to stimulating growth in priority sectors, increasing
employment opportunities, reducing regional and sectoral income
disparities, and reducing the balance of payments deficit, they also
contributed to the budgetary deficit and thus to inflationary pressures.
Despite these tax reductions, revenues continued to rise in constant
prices and as a percentage of GNP as shown in Table VI-7.

Revenues increased in constant prices in each of the years 1964 to 1966, with fairly high increases of 14 percent in 1965 and 12 percent in 1966. The setback noted in 1967 was due to two major actions of a one-time nature: first, the transfer of 14 percent of the income and excise tax revenues to the states and municipalities in connection with the changeover to the value-added tax system initiated in January 1967; and second, the one-month postponement in the collection of the excise tax in July 1967 aimed at stimulating a more rapid growth in the economy. In 1968 tax revenues in constant prices rose by 21 percent and in the following years increased more rapidly than GNP. By 1971 federal tax revenues had reached 10 percent of GNP, compared with 7.8 percent in 1963.

Financing the Deficit. During 1964 and 1965, the expenditure containment and tax policy efforts reduced sharply the fiscal deficit, in constant prices. After a brief setback in 1967 for reasons described earlier, the reductions in the deficit continued consistently through 1972 as shown in Table VI-7. As a percentage of GNP the fiscal deficit fell from 4.2 percent in 1963 to 0.2 percent in 1971. While the thrust of the post-1964 stabilization effort aimed at reducing the budgetary deficit through the containment of expenditures and the strengthening of tax receipts, the authorities also developed a complementary set of actions to finance the deficit in noninflationary means in recognition of the fact that the deficit was not likely to be eliminated for some years. These actions to restore confidence in the public debt and to develop a market in government bonds became essential to the stabilization effort.

Rebuilding the market for public securities in an inflationary environment presented the Brazilian government with two major hurdles: the usury law and the lack of confidence in government securities. The usury law prohibition of interest rates in excess of 12 percent per year would obviously not produce savings when prices continued to rise by three to four times that level. There were two alternatives to overcoming this hurdle—abolish the usury law or offer a means of avoiding it. The authorities decided to retain the usury law, largely in anticipation of a rapid elimination of inflation and a return to a degree of price stability by 1966. As an interim measure they decided to issue a new form of security with monetary correction, known in other countries as an index bond. These securities, officially designated National Readjustable Treasure Bonds and popularly called ORTN, were first issued in July 1964 (Law 4357, 16 July 1964) with maturities of one to five years and interest of 6 percent plus monetary correction. The monetary correction factor was a quarterly correction of the principal of the security by the amount of inflation during the quarter once removed, with the wholesale price index as the bases for the correction.

Despite the seemingly high rate of return on ORTN, they did not sell well in 1964 and 1965 largely because of the public's loss of faith in government securities during the years of hyper-inflation and negative real interest rates. Another factor, however, was that the Brazilian public did not trust the domestic price index and had grown accustomed to valuing their assets in terms of dollars. To overcome this latter attitude the monetary council added in 1966 a corrective factor option based on the change in the exchange rate during the maturity of the ORTN. Thus a bond purchased in November 1965 could be redeemed in November 1966 with a correction based on the exchange rate or the wholesale price index, whichever was higher. Although the exchange rate was devalued only once during this period (by 20 percent) while the wholesale price index increased 41 percent, the exchange rate option proved to be helpful in building confidence in government bonds.

A second step directed at restoring confidence in the public debt was to permit commercial banks to satisfy their compulsory reserve requirements by holdings of ORTN. This measure contributed significantly to increasing the sale of ORTN during 1965 but was of no help in providing a noninflationary means of financing the deficit. In fact, this option was slightly more inflationary than direct borrowing from the Bank of Brazil since the monetary correction paid on the ORTN added to the deficit in the following year. The Bank of Brazil, on the other hand, received no monetary correction on its loans to the Treasury.

The third step in restoring confidence in the public credit was to refund the existing debt which, with interest rates limited under the usury law and without monetary correction, had lost most of its real value through inflation. Decree Law 263, dated 28 February 1967, established the conditions for refunding the domestic federal debt. It was accomplished by an exchange of ORTN with five-year maturities. The value of the securities was established by the current market price for securities issued after 31 December 1964 and Cr$ 10 for those issued prior to that date. Excluded from the refunding was the public debt held by the monetary authorities.[9] Evidence of the effectiveness of the several measures to develop noninflationary means of financing the deficit is offered in Table VI-9. From 1964 to 1968 the deficit was financed almost entirely by the monetary authorities, that is, through Bank of Brazil credit to the Finance Ministry. Beginning in 1969 and

---

[9] *Relatório do Banco Central do Brasil, 1969*, p. 102.

Table VI-9
FINANCING THE DEFICIT, 1963–1972
(millions of Cr$, current prices)

Year	Deficit[a]	Financed By Monetary Authorities	Financed by the Public ORTN and bills	Other
1963	505	426	N.A.	78
1964	727	736	N.A.	−9
1965	593	270	N.A.	323
1966	586	−191	324	453
1967	1,225	699	648	−122
1968	1,227	1,079	705	−557
1969	756	−1,026	−91	1,873
1970	738	−832	1,471	99
1971	672	−3,364	1,383	2,653
1972	516	−7,766	8,283	N.A.

[a]Includes ORTN, bills and other.

Source: *Boletim do Banco Central do Brasil*, December 1972; *Conjuntura Econômica*, February 1973, p. 66.

continuing through 1972 the deficit has been more than covered by sales of securities to the public permitting the federal government to repay a large part of its debt to the monetary authorities.

State Borrowing Policy. The previous chapter discussed the impact on the banking structure of interest rate controls during a period of hyperinflation. These conditions induced state governments, as well as private companies, to establish banks in order to ensure an adequate supply of credit or to avoid losses on their financial transactions. These state banks gradually came to serve not only as financial agents for the state governments but as important sources for financing deficits in the state budgets. As the deficits grew, the bank assests became increasingly frozen in state bonds and with increasing frequency they were forced into the Bank of Brazil for rediscounts to cover claims against them. This chain of events turned into a form of financial blackmail, for, if the Bank of Brazil refused to clear a check drawn on a state bank, the bank would be forced into bankruptcy with an adverse impact on the state governments and the economy. Finance Minister Bulhões finally put a stop to this practice in 1966 when he advised the state banks, particularly the state banks of Guanabara, São Paulo and Minas Gerais, to reduce their rediscounts at a fixed rate, in a sort of domestic IMF standby arrangement, or be forced into bankruptcy. To our knowledge, no banker called Minister Bulhões's hand. Instead, the states turned in 1967 and 1968 to an alternative method of financing their deficit. In issuing state bonds with monetary correction and interest rates more attractive than those offered on ORTN, the states created another problem for the federal government. The high interest rates offered on state bonds tended to conflict with the federal government objective of reducing interest rates to business, and again the finance minister was forced to take action. In October 1969, Finance Minister Delfim Netto issued a prohibition against the issuance of state bonds of any type until 29 October 1971.[10] Excepted from this prohibition were securities issued in anticipation of revenues, not to exceed a fourth of the revenues anticipated during the financial period. The debt was to be liquidated within thirty days after the end of the financial period.[11] Responsibility for exercising control over the issuance of state and municipal securities was delegated to the Central Bank.[12]

Revenue Sharing. The immediate motivation for initiating a broad revenue sharing program on the part of the federal government was the changeover on 1 January 1967 from a turnover tax to a value-added tax as the primary source of state and local revenues. To compensate for an anticipated reduction in revenues from the value-added tax, the 1967 constitution provided for a transfer of 20 percent of current federal excise and income tax revenues to states and municipalities. As noted above, the concept of revenue sharing for specific purposes stems from the 1945 constitution, but the transfer of significant amounts of funds to the states and municipalities without strings attached was an innovation creating problems of its own.

The Participation Fund for States and Municipalities, which the revenue sharing plan is called, derives its resources from a fixed percentage of the federal excise and income taxes. While the constitution fixed the percentage at 20 percent, this was reduced to 14 percent in 1967 to help keep the federal deficit to a manageable level. The percentage was increased in 1968 to 20 percent, but experiences with this level quickly prompted the federal government to reduce the amount to 10 percent, where it remains. The funds are allocated

---

[10] Federal Senate Resolution 58, 23 October 1969.

[11] *Relatório do Banco Central do Brasil, 1969*, p. 103.

[12] Resolution 101, 8 November 1969. The 1967 Constitution empowered the federal government to intervene in the financial affairs of the state governments if they adopt measures or implement programs that are not in accord with the overall program of the federal government.

equally to the states and municipalities.[13] Initially there were no restrictions on the use of these funds except that they be used equally
for current expenses and investments.

The criteria for distributing the funds among the state governments are area, population, and per capita income. Of the states'
share, 2½ percent is distributed on the basis of area; the remaining
47.5 percent is distributed in direct proportion to the ratio of the
state's population to the total population and inverse of the ratio of
the state's per capita income to the average for the entire country.
The 50 percent share of the fund going to the municipalities is distributed primarily on the basis of population: 5 percent of the share is
distributed to state capital cities in relation to population and in inverse proportion to per capita income; the remaining 45 percent is
distributed among the other municipalities on the basis of population
alone. The Participation Fund is also distributed on the basis of current revenue. Earlier revenue sharing measures had been calculated
on the basis of the previous year's revenues, a practice which, during
a period of inflation, inevitably resulted in a loss in real values. This
was, for example, the experience of the Amazon and the Northeast in
the revenue sharing programs in the 1945 constitution.

The Participation Fund resulted in rapid increases in the revenues of state and municipal governments in 1967 and in 1968, and
many of these governments, unaccustomed to such a large windfall,
used the funds on elaborate town halls, football stadiums, and other
luxury projects instead of on improvment of the educational, health,
sewage, and water facilities. Recognizing the uneconomic use of the
Participation Funds and feeling the pressures of the continuing high
federal deficit, Finance Minister Delfim Netto took advantage of the
extraordinary authority offered by Institutional Act No. 5 of December 1968 to reduce the fund from 20 percent to 10 percent with an
additional 2 percent allocated to a Special Fund. The criteria were left
unchanged, but the federal government gave itself the authority to
withhold the transfer pending approval of the investment projects, the
commitment of local funds to the projects and a gradual assumption
of additional functions by the local governments.

The cut in the Participation Fund from 20 percent to 10 percent
at the end of 1968 created particular hardships for the northeast states
where it accounted for more than 25 percent of revenues. For some
states, like Maranhão and Piauí, it accounted for over 50 percent of
total revenues. On the other hand, it accounted for a very small share
of the revenues of the wealthier states in the south-central region—

---

[13] In 1967 there was 3973 municipalities, 22 states, 3 federal territories, and a federal
district.

less than 1 percent for Guanabara (formerly the federal district of Rio de Janeiro) and São Paulo. Recognizing of the difficulties imposed on the northeast states, the government decided to distribute the Special Fund, comprising 2 percent of income and excise tax revenues, to these states and in addition persuaded some of the wealthier states to forego their share of the Participation Fund in favor of the northeast states.

The Brazilian experience with the Participation Fund, or revenue sharing without strings, is too brief to reveal all the implications but, compared with the alternatives, revenue sharing has proved to be an effective economic instrument. The Participation Fund was initiated as a substitute for the loss in revenues to state and local governments resulting from the shift to the value-added tax and loss of other tax sources. The basic concept of the revenue sharing program was to give the states and local governments a source of revenue as a substitute for other tax sources which tended to discourage investments and exports or had other undesirable economic effects. The loss of state authority to impose export taxes, for example, and the eventual elimination of these taxes by the federal government contributed to the increased competitiveness of Brazilian exports and to the improved balance of payments after 1964. The main disadvantage of the Participation Fund has been the loss of funds to the federal treasury, averaging 7.7 percent in recent years as shown in Table VI-10. To the extent that the revenues shared with the states and municipalities added to the federal deficit, the program contributed to the inflationary pressures. On the other hand, the additional revenues received by the states and local governments tended to reduce their budgetary deficits, which in some instances at least were financed through inflationary borrowing from official state banks or through issuance of state bonds. In either case, a reduction in state deficits may be as anti-inflationary as the reduction in the federal deficit would have been had there been no revenue sharing program. The net inflationary impact of this program therefore cannot easily be weighed. Another important aspect of the Participation Fund is that it is an instrument for improving the regional distribution of income. The distribution formula provides a greater share to the poorer states, since it is distributed on the basis of per capita income and population.

While the Participation Fund was designed as an instrument for decentralizing the economic and political decision-making process in Brazil, this aspect of the revenue sharing program has been neglected. Brazilian officials have tended to look at the federal government as the most efficient governing unit and have been impatient at the time-consuming and wasteful economic and political decision-making pro-

Table VI-10

**PARTICIPATION FUND FOR STATES AND MUNICIPALITIES,
1967–1972**

(millions of Cr$, current prices)

Year	Participation Funds[a]	Percent of Total Expenditures
1967	586	7.3
1968	1,433	12.4
1,969	1151	7.8
1970	1,532	7.7
1971	2,085	7.5
1972	2,999	7.8

[a] Includes Special Fund of 2 percent.

Source: *Boletim do Banco Central do Brasil*, December1972, Table III. 60;
Conjuntura Econômica, February 1973, p. 66.

cesses at the lower levels of government. They have, therefore, tended to increase federal government control over the Participation Fund. If the aim of the Brazilian government is to extend economic and political liberties and decentralize decision-making, one of the first changes should be to reverse the tendency toward centralized control over the Participation Fund. Political and economic development at the local level would be encouraged by an expanding interest in planning and management of local projects, where the potential taxpayers are able to see for themselves the results of their own efforts.[14]

Role of the Public Sector in the Brazilian Economy

Small republics have sometimes derived a considerable revenue from the profit of mercantile projects. The republic of Hamburg is said to do so from the profits of a public wine cellar and apothecary's shop. The state cannot be very great of which the sovereign has leisure to carry on the trade of a wine merchant or apothecary.[15]

[14] The Subcommittee on Interamerican Economic Relations of the Joint Economic Commission noted that "the traditional minor role assigned to local governments is a dampening force on economic and social development." U.S. Congress, Joint Economic Committee, *Hearings before the Subcommittee on Interamerican Economic Relations*, 87th Congress, May 1962.

[15] Adam Smith, *The Wealth of Nations*, Book 5 (New York: Everyman's Library, 1934), p. 299.

During the postwar years the Brazilian public sector increased rapidly in terms of direct participation in the economy and in terms of control over economic decision making. In its diagnosis of this trend, the Castello Branco government concluded that the high degree of nationalization halted the process of economic development. Federal government investments alone were estimated at 60 percent of total investments and government expenditures (both current and investments) totalled 33 percent of GNP. On the basis of these estimates, the Action Program called for limiting the role of the public sector expenditures and investments so as to provide greater scope for private sector growth. In this section there is a brief deviation from the main theme in order to outline the role of the public sector in the Brazilian economy. Thus, the actual and potential contribution of the public sector to the social and economic welfare can be assessed. Earlier the inflationary impact of the acceleration in federal government expenditures and the role of tax policy in inducing economic growth in the industrial sector was noted. In Chapter XI I will examine the public sector's potential for maintaining a high and stable level of investments and growth in the Brazilian economy.

The degree of government involvement in the economy can be partly illustrated by three indicators: first, by its direct share in the economy; second, by its participation in key sectors; and third, by its control over decision-making in other sectors. Public sector expenditures of final goods and services rose from 13.4 percent of GNP in 1947 to 17.4 percent in 1963.[16] During the same sixteen-year period, gross tax collections increased from 15 percent of GNP to 18 percent. Total public sector expenditures plus subsidies and transfers to the private sector rose from 17.1 percent of GNP in 1947 to 23.6 percent of GNP in 1963. The upward trend of public sector expenditures on final goods and services reversed and declined to 15.7 percent in 1968, while gross tax collections continued upward to 26.8 percent in 1968, and total expenditures, transfers and subsidies rose to 24.9 percent in 1968.[17] Compared with other countries in a similar state of development the revenue figures show a relatively high involvement of the government in the economy. The industrial countries collect between 25 and 30 percent of GNP in revenues; the less developed countries collect from 8 to 15 percent. On the other hand, the Bra-

---

[16]The public sector in this sense includes states and municipalities as well as the federal government, social security system, and federal autarquia.

[17]Total public sector spending of 25 percent of GNP is significantly lower than previously published data have indicated. Previous data showed that public sector spending was 31 percent of GNP, which was among the highest in the world and was comparable with the most developed countries. Sources of this data are Fundação Getúlio Vargas, *Conjuntura Econômica* 24, nos. 6 and 10.

zilian government transfers a high portion of its revenues to the private sector so that its expenditures on final goods and services is relatively low compared with other countries in a similar stage of development.

Gross capital formation of the public sector rose from 2.7 percent in 1947 to 4.1 percent of GNP in 1963 and further to 5.6 percent in 1969 (see Table VI-11). Public sector investments as a percentage of total investments show an increase from 14.5 percent in 1947—although this was an exceptionally low year—to 25 percent in 1963, rising to 31 percent in 1967 and falling again to 25 percent in 1968 as private sector investment picked up. This is not an exceptionally large percentage of total investments when compared with other countries. Mexico had 41 percent in 1965; Turkey, Greece, Spain and Portugal show even higher figures.

In addition to its large direct roles in the economy as a whole, the Brazilian government participated directly or indirectly in a number of key sectors and industries. It owns or controls practically all the public utilities, the telephone system, railway system, airlines, shipping companies, electrical production and distribution networks, the major iron mining company, the oil refining monopoly, and the three major steel companies which comprise 75 percent of the industry's output. In the credit area, the five major federal financial institutions (the Bank of Brazil, the National Economic Development Bank, the National Housing Bank, the Bank of the Northeast, and the Federal

Table VI-11

PUBLIC SECTOR SAVINGS AND INVESTMENTS, 1963–1969

Year	Current Account Savings[a]			Investments		
	Current prices	Constant prices[b]	% of GNP	Current prices	Constant prices[b]	% of GNP
1963	37	153	0.3	488	2,016	4.1
1964	−43	−93	—	964	2,091	4.2
1965	317	438	0.9	1,617	2,237	4.4
1966	1,581	1,586	3.0	2,140	2,146	4.0
1967	380	297	0.5	3,190	2,492	4.5
1968	3,173	1,973	3.2	4,099	2,578	4.1
1969	1,182	616	0.8	7,432	3,871	5.6

[a] Current account savings are defined as current receipts less current operating expenses.
[b] Deflated by general price index, 1965-67 = 100.
Source: *Conjuntura Econômica*, June 1970.

Savings Institutions) accounted for 39 percent of total outstanding credit to the private sector in 1970. State banks accounted for another 2.6 percent of total credit in that year. In the labor area, the government exercises a profound influence over union policies and leadership through its authority to collect union dues on behalf of the unions. Over 40 percent of total foreign trade is controlled directly by the government. On the export side, the Brazilian Coffee Institute controls the pricing policies for Brazil's most important export, accounting for 36 percent of total exports in 1970; it had been as much as 70 percent in the 1950s. Sugar and cocoa are also controlled by public institutes while iron ore exports come almost entirely from the government-owned company, Vale do Rio Doce. On the import side, the government directly imports for resale all wheat, through Cibrazem, and oil, through Petrobrás, which together comprised over 32 percent of total imports in 1967. The government even has its own large share of the foreign debt, about 45 percent of the total outstanding debt at the end of 1970. The government has also been directly involved in the manufacturing industries; it started the first automobile factory, which it sold in 1968 when the competition got too intense. It also created a meat packing plant which it sold in 1970 for similar reasons.[18]

Finally, the Brazilian government has a strong influence over private sector decision making. Given its diagnosis of the excessive degree of nationalization of the Brazilian economy, justified by the second and third aspects just set forth, the Castello Branco government's economic development program aimed at reducing the role of the public sector and stimulating growth in the private sector. The measures which it undertook in this regard included tax policy, monetary policy, development of a capital market, guarantees for foreign investors, and the establishment of credit institutions and programs for the private sector. Tax exemptions were granted to stimulate investment in the northeast; in specific industries like forestry, fishing, tourism, agriculture; and in the capital market. The protective tariff system, which had stimulated the growth of Brazilian industry in the 1950s still provided ample protection for private industry. The new Capital Markets Law and the fiscal incentives helped to stimulate growth of a capital market in which the private sector could obtain the necessary capital for expansion. Foreign investors received Central Bank guarantees for conversion of capital under Instruction 289, while United States investors also benefited from the Investment Guarantee Agreement. The National Economic Development Bank

[18]*Boletim do Banco Central do Brasil*, December 1972, Table 1.24.

and the Bank of Brazil provided special funds for private sector investments. Finally, the Housing Bank and the Agricultural Credit Program provided direct credit to private entrepreneurs in these sectors.

Assessment of Fiscal Policy

During the postwar years fiscal policy evolved in Brazil into an effective policy instrument for influencing the level and direction of investments and economic growth. By the mid-1960s the federal government influenced, directly or indirectly, over 80 percent of total investments in Brazil. During the 1950s, tariff and exchange policies and direct government investment stimulated investments in the industrial sector and infrastructure. The post-1964 governments shifted the emphasis to other sectors and other instruments of fiscal policy. Tax policy became an effective vehicle for inducing private sector investments into priority areas such as industrial investments in the northeast, the capital market, tourism, forestry, and fishing. Through revenue sharing with the states and municipalities, the federal government became increasingly involved in the level and nature of investments made by these lower echelons of government. Federal expenditure policy aimed at minimizing the level of current expenditure so as to maximize the level of government investments, not only through direct federal government investments but through influencing the investments made by public enterprises, including iron mining, steel, electric power production and distribution, communications, and oil refining, many of which are financed by earmarked taxes. Finally, public debt policy has been implemented, at least since 1967, with an eye to its impact on the availability of credit to finance private sector investments.

Supplementing the traditional fiscal policy instruments in affecting the level and trend of investments are several other major public sector programs. The National Housing Program, an extra-budgetary program under the control of the Minister of the Interior, was developed into an instrument for generating savings from the workers' pension funds which are directed to investments in housing and the construction industry in general. Investments in agriculture have been to a degree influenced by the Agricultural Credit Law and its implementing regulations. The minimum price program for agricultural products has also been used to influence the decisions to invest in the production of specific crops, and fiscal incentives were extended to agricultural investment in 1970. Finally, credit from official financial institutions plays an important role in financing private sector investments. The Bank of Brazil provides 62 percent of total credit for rural production and investment purposes; the National Economic Development Bank provides a major portion of the credit for industrial and commercial investments; and the Development Bank of the Northeast is the major source of investment capital for that region. Both of the latter institutions also receive taxes for investment purposes. The impact of these federally controlled programs on investments, both the total level and the composition, portend well for the stability and growth of investments and national output (see Chapter XI).

While the Brazilian fiscal structure has evolved into an effective instrument to promote economic growth, it has not been as effective an instrument for achieving price stability. The fiscal deficit, it has been noted, was the primary cause of the hyper-inflation of the early 1960s, and, despite some achievements in controlling expenditures and increasing revenues, the federal government deficit still remained a source of inflation in 1970. Preliminary data for 1972 indicate that, for the first time in recent history, the Brazilian federal government is likely to run a surplus.

What should be the role of fiscal policy in a developing country? Keynesian economics places heavy emphasis on the role of fiscal policy in influencing the aggregate levels of demand, output, and employment. In the industrial countries this focus on the aggregates has been relatively effective in providing desired changes in the levels of employment and prices, with an expansionist policy tending to increase employment and a contractive policy tending to stabilize prices. But this Keynesian focus on the aggregates provides no solution to the simultaneous problems of rising unemployment and inflation which are typical problems of many developing countries. This was also the situation facing Roberto Campos and Octavio Bulhões when they were appointed ministers of planning and finance respectively in the Castello Branco government in April 1964. Growth in gross national product in the previous two years had not kept pace with the population growth rate; unemployment, which had been increasing even in the 1950s when the growth rate had averaged 7 percent per year, worsened with the stagnation in output after 1961; prices continued to grow at an accelerated pace, reaching 75 percent in 1963 and running at an annual rate of over 100 percent in the early months of 1964. In this situation, a policy of stimulating aggregate demand would tend only to reinforce inflationary pressures with little or no impact on employment or output; a policy of contracting aggregate demand, on the other hand, would tend to contract inflationary pressures but at the cost of reducing output and employment.

The prescription offered by Bulhões and Campos was in part the classical one of emphasizing the allocative function of fiscal policy, to stimulate savings so as to ensure more resources for investment and less for consumption. But neither they nor their successors left the allocation of investments entirely to free market forces, as prescribed in the classical economic texts. They helped market forces on their way with a series of fiscal incentives and compulsory programs directed both at increasing the level of private sector savings and investments and at channeling these investments into socially desirable sectors and regions. As the major instrument of economic policy, fiscal policy played a key role in this effort, with the expenditure containment and debt management programs directed primarily at price stabilization and tax policy directed toward influencing the level and direction of investments.

CHAPTER VII

Wage Policy

These persons clamor for a system in which each person may have at least, "a standard of living compatible with human dignity." But the question is NOT, UNHAPPILY, HUMAN DIGNITY but PRODUCTIVITY; even reducing the level of inequality to the minimum compatible with the functioning of any system, the size of the "pie" is not sufficient to give to each and everyone a slice corresponding to that standard.

Eugenio Gudin
Análise de Problemas
Brasileiros, 1958-1964

What is an appropriate wage policy for a developing nation? Should wage policy be aimed at increasing labor's share in the national income or should it be aimed at limiting labor's share so as to increase savings? Can either of these objectives be achieved by wage policy instruments such as official minimum wage legislation, wage fixing by official formula, or other public sector legislation? Or should wage determination be left for market forces? How much of labor's share should be distributed in the form of job-related wages to increase work incentives, and how much in the form of indirect benefits, like social security, to increase savings?

The Brazilian wage policy experiences of the years leading up to the 1964 revolution and the years since the revolution have offered for urban industrial workers contrasting periods of feast and famine and for agricultural workers a fairly continuous, but improving, period of famine. President Getúlio Vargas first attempted in 1954 to use wage policy as an instrument for increasing labor's share in the national income. João Goulart intensified this effort after he came into the presidency in 1962. As a reaction to the hyper-inflation of 1963 and

1964, the post-revolution government of Castello Branco implemented an austere wage policy aimed at maintaining labor's share in
the national income while at the same time ensuring that excessive
wage adjustments did not add to inflationary pressures. Contrasting
wage objectives, policy instruments, and results, in terms of the
trends of real wages, form the substance of this chapter. The Brazilian wage policy experiences during these two periods lead to the
conclusion that wage determination in developing nations, as in developed nations, should preferably be left to market forces. At the same
time, the Brazilian experience shows that government policies can
increase the level of savings through influencing the distribution of
wages between direct and indirect payments.

Wage Policy Prior to 1964

Wage policy gradually evolved during the 25 years prior to the 1964
revolution into an active instrument of economic and political policy.
The specific measures to influence wages included minimum wage
regulations and wage standards for civil servants and employees of
public and semi-autonomous agencies. But the government also developed a strong potential influence over wages through its control
over labor unions and the labor courts.

President Getúlio Vargas issued the first minimum wage decree
during the "Estado Novo" period in 1941 and adjusted the rate upward in
1943; from that time until 1951 the minimum wage level remained unchanged, despite a more than 100 percent increase in prices. Following
his election in 1951 Getúlio Vargas raised the minimum wage level by
about 200 percent, and less than two years later, in an attempt to woo the
labor vote, he announced another 100 percent increase.[1] In the ensuing
years minimum wage adjustments became larger and more frequent to
keep up with the rising rate of inflation. The Café Filho and Kubitschek
governments each waited two years before making new adjustments in

---

[1] Thomas E. Skidmore, *Politics in Brazil, 1930-1964: An Experiment in Democracy*, p.
134. Skidmore describes the role João Goulart, then minister of labor, played in the 100
percent increase. Goulart submitted his recommendation for a 100 percent increase
(from 1,200 to 2,400 cruzeiros per month) on 22 February. Vargas accepted his resignation on the same date. However on 1 May Vargas "pointedly praised the work of his
former Minister of Labor as" an "indefatigable friend and defender of the workers." In
deciding on the 100 percent increase, Vargas acted against virtually every economic
advisor he consulted. The National Economic Council, for example, recommended
scaling down Goulart's suggested 100 percent to 40 percent. The fact was that Getúlio
Vargas had decided to court working class political support by means of a handsome
increase in real wages, regardless of the consequences on other sectors of opinion.
Skidmore outlines this decision as the beginning of the end for Vargas, who committed
suicide on 24 August of the same year.

the minimum wage level; but since 1959, as the rate of inflation accelerated, successive governments have revised the minimum wage on an annual basis.

It is a simple matter to decree increases in the official minimum wage level, but it is quite another matter to legislate changes in effective wages paid to the workers. Even to the extent that nominal effective wages are influenced by the official minimum, there is the question of real wages, that is, whether the effective wage adjustments are sufficient to compensate for the inflation since the last wage adjustment.

Trends of Private Sector Wages Prior to 1964. Can the government legislate changes in effective real wages? The limited information available on the Brazilian wage structure and level during the years prior to 1964 leads to the conclusion that government legislation was no more effective in influencing real wages than in controlling interest rates or other prices in the Brazilian economy. Private sector wage rates were determined by the market demand and supply for the several categories of labor. In some regions, few workers received as high a wage as that set by the official minimum. The government recognized these regional differences in setting lower minimums for the poorer regions, such as the Northeast, than for the higher income regions. Moreover, few of the higher salaried employees appeared to be affected by adjustments in the minimum wage. Nevertheless, some studies show that a significant number of workers in the urban industrial sector appeared to be employed at the minimum rate and their nominal wage rates were adjusted with changes in the official minimum rates. A Labor Ministry study indicated that close to 25 percent of the total working force had their salaries adjusted on the basis of changes in the minimum wage.

This apparent relationship between adjustments in the minimum wage rate and adjustments in effective nominal wage rates for a relatively large proportion of the urban workers appeared to lend strong economic and political significance to these adjustments. Of particular significance was the trend of the minimum wage level in real terms, taking into account changes in the cost of living during the interval between wage adjustments. This became increasingly important as the rate of inflation accelerated toward the end of the 1950s. Its significance was further enhanced by the absence of any other statistical series on which to trace the trend of wage rates in the Brazilian economy. The minimum wage rate became the accepted indicator of the trend of real wages. Yet there is some evidence that it did not in fact reflect the trend of effective wages, either in nominal terms or in real terms.

The real minimum wage rates in the city of Rio de Janeiro, that is, the nominal rate deflated by the cost of living index for that city, increased at an annual rate of 3.6 percent, a total rise of 42 percent, between 1947 and 1961, according to a Ministry of Planning study.[2] In tracing this trend, the Brazilian Planning Ministry noted that it displayed an "irregular behavior" with large gains during the 1952 to 1956 period and a decline thereafter until 1960. This trend and the irregular behavior of the real minimum wage rate are also clearly outlined in Table VII-1, which illustrates the oscillations in the real minimum wage rate, not only between the 1956 and 1959 adjustments but even in 1960 and 1962 after the adjustments had been made an annual affair. By 1963 the real minimum wage level had declined close to the 1952 level. Even the 100 percent increase in the nominal rate in February 1964 failed to provide any improvement in the real minimum rate as the rate of inflation between wage adjustments exceeded the nominal wage adjustments (see Table VII-2). At the time of the April 1964 revolution the minimum wage rate in real terms had fallen, despite sharp increases in nominal terms, for three straight years, to a level only slightly above the 1952-1954 average.

Did the minimum wage rate reflect the trend of effective wage rates in the Brazilian economy? There are no data on the trend of

Table VII-1
INDEX OF AVERAGE ANNUAL REAL MINIMUM WAGE—RIO DE JANEIRO

Year	1952–1964 (1964 = 100)
1952	91
1953	85
1954	103
1955	113
1956	114
1957	127
1958	111
1959	128
1960	111
1961	128
1962	109
1963	102
1964	100

Source: Based on data collected by Peter Gregory, "Evolution of Industrial Wages and Wage Policy in Brazil, 1959-1967," Table 5.

[2] Estados Unidos do Brasil, *Three-Year Plan for Economic and Social Development, 1963-65*, p. 20.

Table VII-2
MINIMUM WAGE AND COST OF LIVING CHANGES—RIO DE JANEIRO MAY 1943–FEBRUARY 1964

Month and Year	Rio de Janeiro Minimum Wage (Cr$ per month)	Percentage Wage Increase	Rio de Janeiro Cost of Living Index	Percentage Increase from Previous Wage Increase
January 1952	1.20	215	1.17	105
July 1954	2.40	100	1.80	54
August 1956	3.80	57	2.73	52
January 1959	6.00	57	4.04	48
October 1960	9.60	60	6.89	71
October 1961	13.44	40	9.53	38
January 1963	21.00	56	16.30	71
February 1964	42.00	100	34.10	111

Source: Based on data collected by Gregory, "Evolution of Industrial Wages and Wage Policy in Brazil, 1959-1967," Table 5.

wages in the agricultural sector which employed more than half of the Brazilian labor force, but all evidence points to a decline in real wages in that sector during the years prior to 1964. That the official minimum wage rate did not reflect the trend of effective wage rates in the industrial and service sectors is indicated in two studies. Sampling data cited in the Gordon-Grommers study indicate that the actual wage rates for skilled and unskilled workers failed to keep pace with the increase in minimum wage rates between 1952 and 1957-59. These data show that the spread between effective rates of unskilled workers and the official minimum declined from 1.25 in 1952 to 1.15 in 1959, and for skilled workers from 2.19 in 1952 to 1.59 in 1959.[3] This would tend to indicate that as the government adjusted the minimum rate above market levels, the effective wage adjustments failed to keep pace.

A more extensive study of the average earnings of persons employed in industrial establishments provides additional evidence that the official minimum wage rate did not accurately reflect the trend of real wages. A study by Peter Gregory concluded that the average earnings of persons employed in industrial establishments increased from 1959 to 1964, despite reductions in the real minimum wages

[3]Lincoln Gordon and Engelbert Grommers, United States Manufacturing Investment in Brasil: The Impact of Brazilian Government Policies, 1946-1960 (Boston: Harvard University Press, 1962), p. 118. The rates for skilled and unskilled workers were based on inquiries conducted by the American Chamber of Commerce for Brazil and published in Brazilian Business, September 1959 and June 1957.

during these years. In explaining the divergence between the minimum salary and actual wage payments, he distinguished between two
periods, from 1959 to 1962 and from 1963 to 1964. The first period
was one of high level prosperity and rapid economic growth with
money wages rising faster than the price level. "In the presence of
rightward-shifting demand schedules for labor and a less than perfectly elastic supply of quality labor, market forces alone should have
been capable of producing a rise in real wages."[4] He noted:

> The following two years present something of a paradox, a
> sharply rising real wage level in the face of a general deterio-
> ration of economic conditions. Not only did the pace of
> inflation accelerate but the rate of growth of the economy
> contracted sharply. In the face of conditions usually consid-
> ered most favorable to increases in real incomes of wage and
> salary recipients, real earnings actually rose by about 14
> percent over the two-year period.[5]

This rise in real earnings, he continued,

> cannot be explained as a product of labor market conditions.
> With real output increasing less than one percent during 1963
> over 1962, it is probable that the minimum labor require-
> ments of the industrial sector actually declined. Year-end
> total employment in manufacturing appears to have regis-
> tered a decline of approximately five percent.

Loose labor supply conditions in 1964 also braked the rate of increase
of real earnings in that year.
    In addition to the increase in real wages, Professor Gregory
noted that two new measures contributed to the flow of cash receipts
to workers: effective December 1962 was a new year-end bonus or
"thirteenth month salary" equal to one-twelfth of a worker's December wages times his number of months in the enterprise's employment during the year; and, in December 1963, the Goulart government initiated a family allowance program to provide workers with
children below the age of fifteen allowances equal to 5 percent of the
monthly minimum wage per child, payable monthly. These two measures added roughly 11.7 percent to the average receipts per worker,
supplementing a fairly comprehensive system implemented in earlier
years, including the following: "In addition to payment for actual
hours worked, workers receive the equivalent of a day's pay for
Sunday, twenty days annual vacation, an average of ten holidays and

[4]Peter Gregory, "Evolution of Industrial Wages and Wage Policy in Brazil, 1959-
1967," p. 2.
[5]Ibid., p. 1.

fifteen days annual sick leave, all of these remunerated at the normal rate of earnings.[6]

In summarizing the trend of real wages plus legally required fringe benefits, Professor Gregory notes that all evidence points to a sharp increase in real income of industrial wage and salary earners during 1963 and 1964:

> Since the institutional forces that were operative in increasing wages, salaries and other benefits in industry were not operative to the same extent in most other sectors, prices, as well as rates of remuneration of productive factors, lagged, producing a shift in real income and command over resources to the industrial wage and salary class.[7]

An increase in real wages during a period of economic stagnation and hyper-inflation would indicate a wage-push inflation during 1963 and 1964. At the same time, the upward push of wages was only possible because of the simultaneous pull of demand. To put the problem of causation of inflation in its proper perspective we may point to Sir Dennis Robertson's analogy with the stalactite of inflated demand and the stalagmite of cost-push. "When the two meet in an icy kiss, it would tax the ingenuity of man to say which was the dominant factor."[8] Even if the increase in real wages played an active role in the "icy kiss," that does not say that the minimum wage policy played a role. The evidence is not clear, as we have noted, that the minimum wage had a direct impact on effective real wages. Its impact, if any, was more likely of a permissive nature, along with very liberal treatment of wage increases by the government controlled labor courts. The same cannot be said of public sector wage policy.

There is substantial evidence that public sector wage increases played a major causal role in the Brazilian inflation. The inflationary impact was of two kinds: first, in setting the pace for private sector wage demands and, second, in creating the public sector deficits which constituted the basic source of Brazilian inflation. It was not so much the salaries of public servants, which were established by the National Congress, as the salaries of workers for the autonomous public enterprises, particularly the transportation autarquia, that stimulated inflationary pressures. Eugenio Gudin estimated that the salaries of railway workers increased 127 percent in real terms between 1940-43 and 1960, compared to a 48 percent increase in the minimum salary

[6] Ibid., p. 23.
[7] Ibid., p. 29.
[8] International Economic Association Conference Report of 1959, p. 456.

during the same period.[9] Pédro Cipollari concluded in his study of the Brazilian railway industry that, from 1960 to 1963, the average real wages of railway workers rose by 98 percent, while productivity rose only 7 percent.[10] The merchant marines and the dockworkers also benefited from the independence of these state enterprises from the interventions of the National Congress. On 17 November 1961, Professor Gudin noted the inflationary wage increase of the Port of Santos dockworkers:

> A week ago the Minister of Transportation Sr. Tancredo Neves signed an agreement with the dockworkers, conceding a general increase in salaries of 40 percent, plus another 40 percent when it drizzled, plus a month extra salary for Christmas, plus another month vacation, plus 25 percent during holidays, plus 20 percent for handling cargo considered unhealthy, etc. The previous month the minimum salary had been increased 40 percent, which corresponded to a 50 percent increase in real terms over the salary fixed, after careful study, by President Vargas in 1952.[11]

In addition to their direct inflationary impact, the uncontrolled wage increases in the public autarquia created inequities and distortions in the wage structure and in the economic system. The salary increases for railway, maritime and dockworkers led to disparities among workers within the public sector, and between the public sector and the private sector, for workers exercising similar functions. "Employees exercising equal functions, in similar positions in ministries and in the autarquia, received unequal salaries: there are cases in which those who serve in the autarquia earn double what the traditional civil servants in the union earn."[12] Following the portworkers' accord in late 1963, Professor Gudin noted that unskilled floor sweepers in these unions earned nine times the salary received by similar workers in other places.[13]

The maritime, port, and railway workers during 1962 and 1963 became what Professor Gudin described as the "millionaire proletariats," earning higher salaries than university professors.[14] Uncon-

---

[9] Gudin, *Análise de Problemas Brasileiros*, p. 484.

[10] Pedro Cipollari, "O Problema Ferroviario no Brasil," p. 46-47.

[11] Gudin, *Análise de Problemas Brasileiros*, p. 501.

[12] Ibid., p. 502.

[13] Ibid., p. 505.

[14] Ibid., p. 507. A railway worker in the Northwest, he noted, earned Cr$ 70,000 to 80,000 per month compared with Cr$ 14,000 for a university professor in the same region. He failed to note, however, that few, if any, university professors relied solely on their university salary for a living, but normally held two to four jobs simultaneously.

trolled wage payments to the transport workers contributed to a variety of economic distortions; one example is the stagnation in export earnings. High stevedore salaries at the Port of Santos contributed to the decline in the use of this port from more than 1.1 million tons in 1958 to less than 200,000 tons in 1963. It cost, in 1963, $30 to load a ton of cocoa at the Brazilian port of Ilheus, compared with only $2 in African ports. Freight charges for manganese from the Brazilian port of Macapa to Santo totalled $30, compared with less than $4 from Macapa to New York. These are just a few examples offered by Professor Gudin of the impact of autarquia salaries on transportation costs both within Brazil and to other countries.[15]

In sum, the government's wage policy, as reflected in the minimum wage developments, salaries of public servants, and a liberal attitude to wage accords in the labor courts, contributed to perpetuating and expanding the Brazilian inflation. Wage policy contributed on both the cost-push and demand-pull side of the price equation. Minimum wage increases and a permissive attitude in the labor courts provided a stimulant to wage increases in the private sector while public sector deficits, stemming in large part from autarquia and public employee wage increases, provided the commercial banks with the necessary reserves to expand private sector credit, with the result that prices rose to validate the private sector wage increases.

As to the impact of wage policy on labor's share in the national income, available evidence points to a reduction between 1947 and 1962 as real wages failed to rise as fast as labor productivity.[16] In absolute terms the real income of the workers increased form 1947 to 1962 but not to the full extent of the increase in productivity, with the consequence, according to Professor Werner Baer, that there occurred a "redistribution of the *increment* in the real product to the producing sector."

During 1963 and 1964, on the other hand, real wages rose faster than the average level of productivity with the effect of improving labor's share of national income. This improvement was partly at the expense of property owners, as rental controls contained rental increases to about half the increase in money wages; and agriculture, as price controls and export limitations on foodstuffs helped to move the

---

[15] Ibid., p. 507.

[16] Werner Baer (*Industrialization and Economic Development in Brazil*, p. 123) comes to this conclusion in his study of wage trends to 1960, as does Peter Gregory, ("Evolution of Wages in Brazil," pp. 1-2) who continues in 1959.

terms of trade against this sector. But the improvement in labor's share of national income proved short-lived. Economic stagnation, structural imbalances and hyper-inflation eventually caught up with real wages and they started to decline in 1964 "before the stabilization program and wage policy had become effective."[17]

Post-1964 Wage Policy

The Castello Branco economists reacted strongly to the inflationary wage policy of the Goulart government, but only after a year of eating bitter fruit. Public sector wage adjustments in 1964 of 170 percent for the military and 110 percent for the civilian employees provided a strong additional stimulant to the inflation. Private sector wage adjustments in 1964 followed suit with increases of 80 to 90 percent. The inflationary impact of these wage adjustments, together with other inflationary sources like coffee stockpiling, the minimum price program, foreign exchange inflows, and the continued high rate of inflation (about double the target rate) provoked the authorities to impose a restrictive across-the-board wage policy in 1965. A new wage formula, developed in 1964 but not implemented in that year, was applied to both the public and private sectors. Strict application of this wage formula in 1965 through 1967 led to continuing real wage reductions for all wage adjustments under the formula.

The 1964 Action Program outlined the basic principles of wage policy in this way: (a) to maintain the share of wage earners in the national income; (b) to prevent excessive salary adjustments from reinforcing the inflationary process; and (c) to correct wage distortions, particularly in the Federal Public Service, in the autarquia, and the semi-autonomous economic institutions controlled by the Union. To ensure comparability among wage levels and adjustments the government established a National Wage Policy Council with authority to approve or reject all wage changes. Initially the principles were applied only to salaries previously affected by the government, that is, the minimum wage rate, public sector salaries, and salaries of private firms subsidized by the government in one form or another. To ensure compliance with these principles in the adjustment of wages, the government approved a precise formula which included three criteria or coefficients: (a) a coefficient for restoring the average real wage of the previous two years; (b) a coefficient for increases in

---

[17] Gregory, "Evolution of Wages in Brazil," p. 33.

productivity, and (c) a coefficient for the inflationary residual.[18] The inflationary residual was determined by the National Monetary Council on the basis of planned expansion of the primary money and the money supply.

Prior to implementation of the wage formula in late 1964, adjustments in the official minimum wage had been calculated on the basis of the rate of inflation during the period since the previous wage adjustment. This meant peak-to-peak wage adjustments with high real wages at the time of the wage increase, gradually declining inversely to the rate of inflation until the next wage increase. Planning Minister Roberto Campos claimed that this peak-to-peak approach perpetuated the inflation: "To try to maintain the peaks of real wages, achieved fleetingly in the face of inflation, would be precisely to sanction the continuation of the previous rate of inflation, not to contain it."[19] To substitute for the peak-to-peak approach the new wage formula included a coefficient aimed at restoring the average real wages during the preceding twenty-four months. This coefficient in the wage formula was fairly cut and dried, based as it was on the cost of living index and the money wage rate in force during the twenty-four months. If the wage formula had been limited to this coefficient alone, or even if a small increment had been added for productivity increases, the result would have been a continuing decline in average real wages as long as prices continued to rise. To compensate for the projected rate of inflation under the gradualistic Action Program, an additional coefficient was essential if average real wages were to be maintained. This inflationary residual coefficient constituted one-half of the rate of inflation projected by the National Monetary Council for the next twelve-month interval until the next wage adjustment. However, the inclusion of this coefficient in the wage formula created a balancing act problem for the monetary authorities. Overly high projections of future inflation would have a self-fulfilling tendency in the sense that they would be used by the private

---

[18]The wage policy formula was:

$$W_0 = \sum_{i}^{24} \frac{W_i}{-IC_i} \left(1 + \frac{R}{2} + P\right)$$

Where, W_0 is the newly adjusted wage level

W_i is the money wage rate in force during the preceding 24 months

c_i is a price index with a base of 1.00 in month 1, the last month prior to the effective month of the new adjustment

r is the expected rate of inflation over the coming 12 months, or the "inflationary residual"

P is the national average rate of increase in productivity.

Ministério do Planejamento e Coordenação Econômica, *Programa de Ação Econômica do Govêrno, p. 84.*

[19]Robert Campos, Do Outro Lado da Cerca, *p. 128.*

sector in price setting. Low projections of future inflation, on the
other hand, would inevitably result in declining real wages. In the
latter event, the Monetary Council assessment of the impact of the
stabilization measures would be overly optimistic.

The new wage formula was supposed to serve as a guideline for
private sector wage adjustments at the end of 1964, but, following the
100 percent increase in the minimum wage in February and the 110
percent increase in public sector wages in July, private sector negotiations concluded with average increases ranging from 80 to 90 percent
(see Table VII-3). This unhappy experience led the monetary authorities to implement an austere wage policy for 1965. Public sector
salaries remained fixed during the entire year, and an austere version
of the wage formula was applied to all private sector wage adjustments (Law 4725). The latter was accomplished by projecting the
"inflationary residual" at 10 percent despite the prevailing inflation
rate of about 50 percent, and by omitting entirely the productivity
coefficient. The difference between the projected and actual rates of
inflation resulted inevitably in a decline in average real wages under
the formula. This decline in real wages was noted by the Castello
Branco economists but, believing that industrial wages were above
the value of their marginal product and determined to force a deep cut
in inflation, they held the wage formula virtually unchanged for 1966
wage adjustments. The only change in the formula was the addition of
a productivity coefficient of 2 percent. Again, real wages under the

Table VII-3

**AVERAGE SIZE OF ANNUAL WAGE ADJUSTMENTS UNDER
OFFICIAL WAGE FORMULA, 1964–1972**

(percentage increases)

Year	Private Sector	Public Sector	Average Cost of Living Increase
1964	80–90	110	91.4
1965	40–45	—	65.8
1966	30–35	35	41.3
1967	21.0	22.1	30.9
1968	23.5	24.9	22.0
1969	24.4	23.4	22.6
1970	24.0	24.1	22.3
1971	22.3	22.4	20.2
1972 (June)	22.8	22.9	17.7

Source: Labor Ministry, National Wage Department, quarterly reports.

formula declined as the inflation continued at three times the projected inflationary residual.

In 1967 Finance Minister Delfim Netto and the new group of economists decided to halt the decline in real wages as part of the humanization policy of the Costa e Silva government, which took office in March of that year. When the next round of wage adjustments came up for negotiation in mid-1967 the new monetary council increased the allowance for residual inflation from the 5 percent of the previous two years to 7.5 percent, to bring it more in line with the actual cost of living increases (see Table VII-4). While even this was inadequate to halt decline in real wages—inflation continued at a rate of 20 percent—the council was hesitant to project an inflation rate higher than 15 percent. Instead, the council added another coefficient to the wage formula, an allowance to compensate for differences between the projected inflationary residual and the actual rate of inflation during the previous contract period.

With this new coefficient the wage policy formula in 1968 consisted of four coefficients or allowances for wage adjustments: (a) the basic coefficient for restoring average real wages during the preceding twenty-four months; (b) the inflationary residual coefficient; (c) the productivity coefficient; and (d) the allowance to compensate for losses due to differences between projected and actual inflation rates. These four allowances have provided since 1968 for slight increases in real wages under the wage formula.

What has been the trend of real wages in Brazil since 1964? Has Brazilian labor borne the major brunt of the stabilization effort? To answer these questions we must define clearly what we mean by *real*

Table VII-4

WAGE FORMULA ALLOWANCES, AUGUST 1964–AUGUST 1970

(percentage increases)

Period during Which Effective	Allowance for Inflationary Residual	Allowance for Productivity
August 1965–July 1966	15.0	—
August 1965–July 1966	5.0	—
August 1966–July 1967	5.0	2.0
August 1967–July 1968	7.5	2.0
August 1968–July 19 1969	7.5	2.0
August 1969–July 1970	6.5	3.0
August 1970–July 1971	6.0	3.5

Source: Labor Ministry, National Wage Department, quarterly reports.

wages and *labor*. By Brazilian labor we refer only to the urban industrial and service employee; the more than 50 percent of the
working force in agriculture have not been subject to wage policy and
have not received in general the minimum wage. No specific data are
available to indicate the level and trend of wages of agricultural
workers. Real wages are defined here as the average monthly earnings, which include payment for actual hours worked and fringe benefits paid directly to the worker. The focus of attention on the monthly
wage rate, as reflected in the minimum wage and wage policy formula, neglects the number of hours worked and the host of fringe
benefits legally payable to the worker. There are no data on hours
worked which permit us to consider this factor; but data are available
on the fringe benefits paid directly to the worker; these benefits
amount to 48 percent of a worker's wages. In addition to the fringe
benefits received directly, the Brazilian worker is legally entitled to a
series of indirect benefits averaging 34.4 percent of his wages (see
Table VII-5), which brings the total wage bill to the Brazilian firm to
about 82 percent of wages (wage per time unit worked). All of these
benefits, both the direct and indirect, came into force prior to 1964 so
that, while they significantly affect the level of real wages, they do
not affect the trend since 1964. The trend of average monthly earnings
or real wages, then, has been affected by wage policy, as reflected in
the wage formula, and the labor market conditions, which is best
measured by the actual earnings of labor.

Average monthly earnings in real terms, as measured by the
wage formula, declined about 20 percent between 1964 and 1968. The
actual monthly earnings of employees in manufacturing industries
shows a similar trend. Professor Gregory's index of real earnings
shows a decline from 114.6 in 1964 to 96.4 in 1967, which was very
slightly below the index level for 1962.[20] But the timing of the decline
in real wages differs between the wage formula approach and empirical study of monthly earnings. The monthly real wages yielded by
the wage formula declined steadily from 1964 to 1967 and then leveled
off, with perhaps 2 percent decline per year thereafter. Empirical
studies of monthly earnings, on the other hand, show that most of the
decline in real wages occurred between 1964 and 1965, explained by
the sharp increase in prices at the end of 1964. From late 1965 to 1968
the data indicate "virtual constancy in average monthly earnings"
(see Table VII-6). The explanation for the divergence in the trends
indicated by the wage formula and the actual monthly earnings seems
to be a "conscious policy on the part of the employers to prevent a

---

[20] Gregory, "Evolution of Wages in Brazil," p. 12.

Table VII-5
FRINGE BENEFITS AND PAYROLL TAXES REQUIRED BY LAW
AS A PERCENT OF WAGES/PER NORMAL WORK PERIOD[a]

Purpose	Percent
Indirect Benefits	
Retirement pensions	8.0
Training programs support	3.0
Agriculture development	0.5
Education support	1.4
Accident insurance	8.0
Worker contingency account	8.0
Other charges	10.5
Subtotal	39.4
Direct Benefits	
Sunday pay	18.4
Vacation	7.1
Holidays	3.5
Sick Leave	1.9
Time for employment search	2.2
13-month salary	10.6
Family allowance	4.3
Subtotal	48.0
TOTAL	87.4

[a]Normal work period is defined as 365 days less 52 Sundays, 20 days vacation, and 10 holidays—or 283 working days a year.

Source: Gregory, "Evolution of Industrial Wages and Wage Policy in Brazil, 1959-1967," Table 7.

further erosion in the real income position of their employees by conceding periodic wage increases in addition to the annual adjustment."[21]

Summary of Post-1964 Wage Policy

To sum up, it seems clear that urban industrial workers did not fare very well from the wage policy formula pursued by the Castello

[21]Ibid, p. 12.

Table VII-6
EARNINGS OF EMPLOYEES IN MANUFACTURING
INDUSTRIES, 1962–1970

Year	Average Monthly Earnings (Cr$)		Index of Real Earnings (1964 = 100)
	Current Prices	Constant Prices[a]	
1962	20.40	147.83	89
1963	39.22	162.07	98
1964	76.45	165.84	100
1965	115.78	160.14	97
1966	153.08	153.54	93
1967	196.53	153.54	93
1967	187.12	146.19	88
1968	252.00	158.49	96
1969	307.00	159.90	96
1970	385.00	167.39	101

[a] Deflated by general price index, 1965-1967 = 100).

Source: For 1962–1967, based on Gregory, "Evolution of Industrial Wages and Wage Policy in Brazil, 1959-1967," Table 1. (Professor Gregory's concept of monthly earnings is "average earnings of all persons employed in industrial establishments." While recognizing that this is a less than ideal concept, he concludes that it offers "a reasonably accurate picture of the course of wages in recent years at least in their broad outline if not in precise detail.")

For 1967-1970, based on reports to the minister of labor required under the "Law of Two-thirds." (That law requires that two-thirds of the employees of firms in urban centers be Brazilian nationals. The number of employees included here comprises only a sample of total employed.)

Branco government from 1964 to 1967, but if the 1964 level of wages was, as it appeared to be, above sustainable market levels, given the supply of labor, labor productivity, and the demand for various labor skills, the decline in real wages of industrial workers during these years was essential to restoring equilibrium in the economy. Certainly, wage policy did not contribute to inflationary pressures after 1965 when wages for both the private and public sectors declined. One development which contributed to both equity and economic considerations was the application of the public sector wage policy to the autarquia. Containment of autarquia expenditures for personnel constituted a major element in the stabilization efforts. Finally, from a savings viewpoint, the reorganization of the retirement pension funds (8 percent of wages) into the National Housing Bank created an important means for protecting the personal savings of the working man and also a compulsory savings program for transforming financial savings into real savings in the form of housing (see Chapter XI for further treatment).

Wage Policy for a Developing Nation

The Brazilian wage policy experience of the past two decades leads to the conclusion that wage determination in developing countries, as in developed countries, should preferably be left to market forces. Measures designed to influence real wages or labor's share in the national income are largely ineffective, are in part counterproductive and, at the most, affect wages of only a small part of the working force. Moreover, to the limited extent that wage policy has been effective in improving the wages of the Brazilian industrial worker, it has been at the expense of the remainder of the working force, in terms of both lost employment opportunities and income redistribution through forced savings. Thus the authorities had little to lose and much to gain in refraining from wage controls. On the other hand, Brazilian social legislation has proved to be uniquely effective in increasing the level of savings out of wages. Each of these points deserves further elaboration.

The Brazilian experience both in the years prior to 1964 and the years since 1964 indicate that wage setting by administrative action or wage formula has had only limited and temporary impact on effective real wages. Real wages tended toward a level dictated by market conditions, not the level established by the Wage Policy Council or other administrative unit. During the pre-1964 years much of the benefit of the high nominal wage increases was quickly lost through inflation. Real wages tended to increase with, but not quite as fast as, the improvement in labor productivity. Real wages reached their peak just after the 100 percent increase in nominal wages in February 1964, at the very time when the rate of inflation was running at an annual rate of about 140 percent. Yet by the time of the next wage adjustment in February 1965 the inflation had dissipated all the gains from the previous wage increase. The decline in real wages between 1964 and 1967 was consistent with labor market conditions during these years as the economy lay fallow and there was little incentive for private firms to raise wages. The recovery in the Brazilian economy since 1967 also helps to explain the recovery in real wages since that time.

Brazilian experiences also indicate that measures designed to influence real wages have been counter-productive. They contributed to sharp fluctuations in real wages as the wage increases were concentrated around the adjustments in official wage changes while prices rose steadily month after month, resulting in alternating periods of feast and famine for the workers. They also contributed to inequitable and uneconomic wage differentials for workers in different industries, depending upon whether they were affected by wage policy measures or not. Uncontrolled wage increases without regard to productivity in some industries, like the transportation autarquia, had a direct causal impact on the inflation; and to the extent that personnel salary increases substituted for investments in these industries, they also dampened the rate of growth. Suppression of wages in other industries may also have limited the growth rate, as noted by Arthur Smithies: "In a changing and growing economy, legal prices and wages are necessarily unadapted to the current economic situation. And the industries that are most likely to be prejudiced are those that are growing most rapidly and are embarking on new lines of economic endeavor. In short, control systems, in practice, are prejudicial to the process of growth and change."[22]

The Brazilian experience reveals that wage policy measures affect only a small portion of the working force. At the most, 50 percent of the workers in the urban industrial and service sectors appeared to be influenced by public sector wage policy. This left unaffected the remaining 50 percent of the urban workers and all of the rural workers, which, in the case of Brazil, constituted more than half of the total working force. Assessment of the Brazilian income trends indicates that some of the gain in real income by the urban industrial worker during the 1950s and early 1960s was at the expense of other workers. This took two forms. First, the real income of agricultural workers was suppressed through forced savings resulting from inflation and various governmental measures designed to minimize the impact of inflation on the urban industrial worker. Second, the large wage differentials between industrial and non-industrial workers contributed, along with other governmental measures, to a relatively high degree of capital intensive industrialization, thus creating fewer jobs than would have been desirable. In commenting upon wage policy prior to 1964, Leff and Cohen pointed out that the minimum wage policy of the Brazilian government established a level of wages approximately twice as high as the level paid to rural workers even in areas near the city of São Paulo. "To the extent that this differential is not justified by transfer costs and differences in the cost of living, urban employers must pay a wage which is unnecessarily high. Because of this distortion, they may be led to substitute capital for labor ... The possibilities for such substitution are greater than is some-

---

[22] Arthur Smithies, "Inflation and Development in Latin America," p. 18.

times assumed." Leff and Cohen conclude with an important lesson
for developing countries:

> Government policy artificially raising the minimum in-
> dustrial wage may aggravate difficulties of "labor absorp-
> tion," both in inducing substitution of capital for un-
> skilled labor and in accentuating any effects in this
> direction caused by insufficient supply of skilled labor.
> Hence, governments in underdeveloped countries should
> realize that perhaps one of their few options in efforts to
> increase "labor absorption" to the full extent to which
> technology and economic considerations permit might be
> a policy of permitting real wages to fall toward the lower
> levels dictated by market conditions.[23]

Gains in real income by the urban industrial workers during the
1950s were in part disadvantageous to rural workers; however, some
of the losses in real income by the urban industrial workers since 1964
have benefited the rural workers. Unfortunately, the evidence to support this assessment is not as susceptible to simple arithmetic as is the
wage formula and the cost of living index which so loudly proclaims
the decline in real wages of the Brazilian urban industrial worker. The
claim of improvement in real income of agricultural workers since
1964 is based upon a broad assessment of the trends in the agricultural sector, included in Chapter X.

While the measures to influence the overall level of wages have
tended to be ineffective, counter-productive, and limited in scope,
social legislation has been effective in increasing savings out of
wages. The heavy reliance in the Brazilian wage structure on indirect
fringe benefits relative to direct job-related wages has been an important factor in the increase in domestic savings and economic growth
since 1967. Inadequate attention to job-related wages also has the
uneconomic result, as pointed out by Peter Gregory, of reducing the
effectiveness of wages in providing incentives to work and attracting
labor to rapidly growing industries. He noted that "transferring a
larger proportion of the cost of labor to the basic job rate per time
unit worked would place a higher direct reward on effort, would make
incentive systems of pay much more attractive and effective, and in
general increase the efficiency of the allocative function of the wage
in the economy."[24] In weighing the needs of the worker for work
incentives versus the need for job and income security, the Brazilian
government has traditionally opted for the latter. Brazil has one of the

---

[23]Benjamin I. Cohen & Nathaniel Leff, "Employment and Industrialization Comment," p. 162.
[24]Gregory, "Evolution of Wages in Brazil," p. 42.

more advanced social security systems among the low income countries. In part this undoubtedly grew out of the paternalistic systems prevailing in the Brazilian fazendas, described so well by Gilberto Freyre; in part it is also attributable to the political ambitions of such Brazilian leaders as Getúlio Vargas; and in part to the desire to avoid the instability and insecurity of other industrial societies. To a large degree the Brazilians have succeeded in achieving a greater degree of economic stability over the years than most countries. Prior to the stagnation of 1962-67, for example, Brazil had experienced almost three decades of relative stability in addition to rapid growth during the 1950s.

The post-1964 governments have not altered the traditional emphasis on income security, but have in fact expanded upon it in the form of improved social security and housing programs and the Fund for Social Integration, to be elaborated upon in Chapter XI.

To what extent have wage policy and the wage formula perpetuated the Brazilian inflation? Since 1967 the rate of inflation has hovered between 20 and 25 percent, and the wage formula has permitted wage increases of about this same percentage. This relative stability in the rate of inflation contrasts with the marked decline from above 90 percent in 1964 to 25 percent by the end of 1967, a period in which the real wage rates under the wage formula also declined markedly. Does this mean that the rate of inflation can only be further reduced by limiting wage increases under the formula? Since the available evidence has not demonstrated that the wage formula has had any major impact in restricting private sector wages, it is difficult to conclude that it is perpetuating the Brazilian inflation. The cause of Brazilian inflation since 1967 has been excessive expansion of private sector credit, which in each year from 1967 to 1969 far exceeded the rate of wage increase. Under the booming economic conditions that have prevailed since 1968 the private sector has granted liberal wage increases in the knowledge that monetary and credit expansion would validate these increases in the form of higher prices. A more restrictive credit policy would have the effect of dampening the private sector's liberality toward wage increases. A reasonable guideline to achieve this would be to hold the rate of credit expansion below the increase in wage adjustments. Such a policy was recommended by Edward Bernstein when serving as Director of Research at the International Monetary Fund:

> The most efficient method of dominating inflation is to taper off the rhythm of the wage price spiral and end the massive increases in salaries [with] a system of small readjustment in salaries at smaller intervals . . . thus in three or four stages,

the impulse of credit should not accompany even the modest
readjustments in salaries, but should be in smaller increases
than salary adjustments until stabilization is achieved.[25]

This assessment of wage policy concludes with a quotation from
Peter Gregory's study.

> Income redistribution goals are not likely to be achieved
> simply by legislating wage rates or fringe benefits alone. The
> fiscal mechanism is more suited to this goal, in the short run,
> and ... Over the long run, ... a frontal assault should be
> made on the underlying conditions which determine the pre-
> sent distribution, the persistence of various kinds of monop-
> oly, inefficiencies in the distribution system of goods, the
> low productivity of large segments of the labor force, the
> scarcity of high quality human resources, etc.
>
> Wages are low in Brazil largely because the productivity
> of labor is also low ... The most enduring approach to ...
> an improvement in labor productivity is through the exten-
> sion and improvement of education and training programs
> which are consistent with the requirements of a modern in-
> dustrial society. Not only is continuing improvement in the
> quality of the labor force probably a necessary concomitant
> of sustained growth, but it should have the agreeable by-
> product of contributing to a redistribution of income in a
> more egalitarian direction.[26]

---

[25] Gudin, "Análise de Problemas Brasileiros," p. 491.
[26] Gregory, "Evolution of Wages in Brazil," p. 40-41

CHAPTER VIII

Foreign Exchange and Trade Policy

The contrasting use of policy instruments between the pre- and post-1964 Brazilian governments is nowhere more pronounced than in the application of foreign exchange and trade policies. For almost a decade prior to 1964 the Brazilian authorities pursued a policy at first spontaneously, later deliberately, of maintaining a balance of payments disequilibrium. Whether spontaneous as in 1951-52, or deliberate, as in the years after 1957, the disequilibrium in the balance of payments became an effective instrument for assuring a continuing net flow of foreign real resources and real savings into Brazil, as well as for inducing foreign and domestic investments in the industrial sector. Net foreign savings (current account deficit) averaged $290 million per year from 1957 to 1963, the equivalent of about 8 percent of total Brazilian investments during these years. This high level of net foreign saving was achieved by the heavy import pressure and a stagnation in exports, both stimulated by an overvalued exchange rate. But it was also obtained at the cost of neglecting Brazil's own savings potential, its export potential and an unsustainable debt service burden. As autonomous financing and investments were not sufficient to finance the current account deficit, an increasing part was financed by commercial arrears, swap transactions, short-term bank credits, and, finally, debt consolidation and rescheduling. The short-term nature of the financing served only to postpone from year to year the eventual day of reckoning. By December 1963 Brazil had received about $1 billion in compensatory financing, that is, loans acquired as a result of debt reschedulings and refinancing. At the time of the 1964 revolution, the Goulart government was actively seeking another rescheduling.

Celso Furtado, one of the most prolific spokesmen for the development and trade policies during this period, explained the rationale for the balance of payments disequilibrium in terms of the lack of an alternative: it was either balance of payments disequilibrium or domestic stagnation. In his view any attempt at correcting the disequilibrium through devaluation and other policies would lead to a reduction in the rate of economic growth. He saw a "basic incompatibility . . . between the equilibrium in the balance of payments, as obtained by a fluctuating exchange rate or by successive devaluations, and a development policy aimed at an increase in capital formation."[1]

The Castello Branco government totally rejected the disequilibrium system in favor of balance of payments equilibrium at an ever-increasing level of trade. A unified and realistic exchange rate, export promotion, import liberalization, and a restructuring of the foreign debt toward longer maturities were all part of the overall program to achieve this equilibrium. But the turn-about in these policies took time and their impact on the Brazilian economy became evident only after four years of trial and error innovation. During the first three years, 1964 to 1966, the surplus in the current account of the balance of payments averaged $186 million, which meant net foreign dissaving during these three years of $558 million.

With the unification and simplification of the exchange rate in 1965 and 1966 and the import liberalization of March 1967, the current account moved into deficit in 1967, averaging $320 million over the ensuing three years and thereafter rising sharply to an estimated $1.5 billion in 1972. The export promotion efforts, highlighted by the trotting peg exchange rate system implemented in August 1968, gave an impetus to exports which resulted by 1972 in an almost threefold increase in exports above the 1960-63 average. At the same time the large inflow of long-term capital, stimulated by renewed confidence in the soundness of trade and exchange policies, permitted a restructuring of the foreign debt and an increase in international reserves to the highest level in Brazilian history. By 1968, Brazilian trade policy was clearly contributing, in all its aspects, to the economic recovery of Brazil. And, in 1973, the prospects remained good for the continued contribution of foreign trade to Brazilian investment and growth.

Pre-1964 Policies—"The Disequilibrium System"

Import Policy as the Key to Industrialization. Import policy lay at the heart of Brazilian industrialization, initially as a spontaneous reaction to exchange shortages, but increasingly as a deliberate policy of pro-

---

[1] Celso Furtado, *Development and Underdevelopment*, p. 167.

tecting the domestic market for industrial products and channeling the scarce foreign exchange into priority imports. As these protectionist and selective aims became a more conscious part of economic policies, the methods for achieving them evolved through essentially three stages: from quantitative controls implemented by an import licensing system (1947-53), to quantitative controls implemented by a multiple category exchange auction system (1953-57) to a modified exchange auction-ad valorem tariff system (1957-64).

By 1953 the existing import licensing system superimposed on a specific tariff schedule had lost all effectiveness as an import regulating measure. The steady inflation since the war combined with maintenance of the exchange rate at the highly overvalued prewar rate highlighted the serious limitations of this approach. Large subsidies to the importers who received licenses, the attendant inducements to bribery and corruption, and the loss of government revenues from this source eventually brought about a change, albeit a limited one. In 1953 the import licensing system was abolished in favor of a five-category exchange auction system, but no changes were made in the specific tariff rates and the quantitative limitations. The exchange authorities (SUMOC) continued to allocate the scarce foreign exchange among each of the five import categories, which were then sold at weekly auctions. The effective exchange rate for each category, set at the auctions, reflected the amount of exchange allocated and the demand for commodity imports included in each category. In addition, preferential exchange rates were fixed by the government for special purposes, such as wheat, oil and oil products, newsprint, and imports for government agencies. During the years from 1953 to 1957 about half of Brazilian imports entered under these preferential rates.[2]

In March 1957 a new tariff law replaced the specific duties, prevailing since 1934, with a system of ad valorem duties ranging from 10 to 100 percent for producers' goods and 100 to 150 percent for consumers' goods. The exchange rate system also continued to be used as an import control device, but the five-category auction system was reduced to two categories, a general category and a specific category, with exchange quotas for each allocated by SUMOC.[3] Although the Quadros government abolished in 1961 the exchange rate auction system, the exchange system continued to be used as an import control

---

[2]Lincoln Gordon and Engelbert L. Grommers, *United States Manufacturing Investment in Brazil: The Impact of Brazilian Government Policies, 1946-1960*, p. 20.

[3]The general category includes raw materials, equipment, and other production goods, as well as current consumer goods of which the supply in the internal market is not satisfactory. The special category includes goods of restricted consumption and other items of any nature of which the supply in the internal market is considered satisfactory.

device. As the foreign exchange crisis intensified in 1962 and 1963, the government resorted more and more to the technique of delaying delivery of foreign exchange for several months after the exchange was sold to importers. The costs, in terms of interest rates, of the delay in delivery added to the effective cost of exchange and of imports. Through varying the interval of the delay in releasing the exchange, the authorities could continue to preserve scarce exchange for priority imports and add to the costs of lower priority imports. While the accumulation of these prior deposits for imports served as a monetary contractive measure during the years just prior to 1964, they also served to expand money supply as the trade and payments system was freed of encumbering restrictions during the years after 1964.

Another important protectionist instrument used increasingly during the late 1950s and 1960s was the Law of Similars. The basic aim of this law was to prohibit the importing of a product which the government recognized as being available domestically. Any commodity registered as a similar received broad protection through both high, almost preclusive, tariffs, and its classification in high foreign exchange rate category. Moreover, similar commodities "cannot be imported by most public corporations, mixed (partly owned by the government) companies, public authorities, or by an importer who receives any special treatment such as exemption from required advance deposits, government financing for investment, etc."[4]

How well did import policy serve the objectives of stimulating economic growth and maintaining balance of payments equilibrium? Their effectiveness in inducing investments in the industrial sector has been chronicled by many writers, a summary of which is included in Chapter II. Their contribution to the chronic balance of payments problem of Brazil has not received equal attention. Contrary to expectations that the import substitution policies for industrialization would tend to reduce the relative demand for imports, the import coefficient (ratio of imports to GNP) remained relatively stable during the decade prior to 1963 (see Table V.III-1). The explanation of this phenomenon given by professors Antônio Delfim Netto and Nathaniel Leff is that the income creation effect on imports heavily outweighed the import substitution effect; that is, that the increased demand for imports stimulated by higher national income more than offset the foreign exchange saved by domestic production of goods formerly imported.[5] They con-

---

[4]Joel Bergsman, *Brazil's Industrialization and Trade Policies*, p. 34. Bergsman provides a more detailed explanation of the Law of Similars, which dates back to 1911 but has been enforced with varying degrees of strictness.

[5]Nathaniel Leff and Antônio Delfim Netto, "Import Substitution, Foreign Investment, and International Disequilibrium in Brazil," p. 219.

Table VIII-1

**BRAZILIAN IMPORTS, GROSS DOMESTIC PRODUCT,
AND IMPORT COEFFICIENT, 1947–1964**

(millions of Cr$, current prices)

Year	Imports C.I.F.	Gross Domestic Product	Import Coefficient (imports as % of GDP)
1947	22.8	165	13.8%
1948	21.0	195	10.8
1949	20.6	230	9.0
1950	20.3	272	7.5
1951	37.2	323	11.5
1952	37.2	397	9.4
1953	25.2	470	5.3
1954	55.2	627	8.8
1955	60.2	783	7.7
1956	71.6	996	7.2
1957	86.5	1,218	7.1
1958	103.0	1,458	7.1
1959	161.0	1,989	8.1
1960	201.0	2,756	7.3
1961	299.0	4,052	7.4
1962	512.0	6,601	7.8
1963	782.0	11,929	6.6
1964	1,243.0	23,055	5.4

Source: *Conjuntura Econômica*, June 1970, pp. 89-106; APEC, *A Economia Brasileira e Suas Perspectivas* July 1972, Table I.10.

cluded that import substitution and increasing foreign investment may be highly successful from the viewpoint of income creation and growth, but are unlikely to solve the balance of payments problem.

These authors attribute the high multiplier effect of import substitution investment on national income to the high marginal propensities to consume and invest in an inflationary environment. Under the circumstances prevailing in Brazil, the investment multiplier did not have the usual leakages in the form of private savings, public savings, or limitations on other investments. Also, the low marginal propensity to import, compared with other countries, meant that an increase in imports did relatively little to restrict the expansive effect of an increase in spending. They pointed out that the government could have tightened import restrictions, but "to cut back imports drastically, it was feared, would have a bottleneck effect on output and growth." They concluded that Brazilian imports were limited on the upward side by the inelastic supply of foreign exchange and on the downward side by the bottleneck effect that too restricted a supply of imports would have on the growth of the rest of the economy.[6]

Overvalued Exchange Rates. An overvalued exchange rate played an essential supporting role to import policy in regulating both the level and composition of imports during most of the postwar period through at least 1964. The overvalued exchange rate created the steady high demand for imports which was an essential condition for the policy of allocating to priority uses. Through this mechanism, the overvalued rate became, initially unconsciously and later more deliberately, an important means for subsidizing priority sectors of the economy, essentially the industrial sector.

In its supporting role, exchange rate policy followed import policy through three major phases: a unified fixed rate system (prior to 1953), a multiple exchange auction system (1953 to 1961), a relatively unified adjustable rate system (1961 to 1964). From 1937 to 1953 the Brazilian exchange rate was fixed at 18.72 cruzeiros per U.S. dollar despite the intervening 80 percent inflation. The major reason for maintaining an overvalued rate during these years was the objective of maximizing exchange earnings from coffee exports, although concern about the inflationary impact of higher import prices and a desire to facilitate imports were also considerations.[7] In addition to the rates for preferential imports such as wheat, petroleum, and newsprint, the Brazilian authorities initiated in October 1953 a new system of multiple exchange rates for each of the five categories of imports previously regulated by import licenses, such as wheat, petroleum, and newsprint.[8] As noted above, the exchange anthorities (SUMOC) held weekly auctions for

---

[6]Ibid., pp. 226-227. This analysis led Leff to conclude that the failure of imports to keep pace with the economy's growth eventually played a key role in the economic stagnation of 1962 and following years. The problem, he claims, stems from a lack of foreign exchange, not excessive import controls. The decline in imports in 1961 and 1962, he writes, "imposed a ceiling on marginal output which interrupted the economy's previous upward movement of self-reinforcing growth and investment" and "the lack of raw materials and other inputs from abroad may inhibit the ability of domestic producers to respond elastically to the additional demand for their products." N.H. Leff, "Import Constraints and Development: Causes of the Recent Decline of Brazilian Economic Growth," p.494.

[7]Bergsman, *Brazil's Industrialization and Trade Policies*, pp. 27-37.

[8]The preferential exchange rate for newsprint was also used effectively by Brazilian governments as a means of obtaining favorable press coverage, a means of press censorship which is not very subtle, but is more acceptable in a capitalist society.

each of the five import categories. The exchange rate for each category reflected the amount of exchange allocated to, and the demand for commodity imports included in, each category. About half of the exchange available to SUMOC was allocated to these categories and the remaining half was allocated to special products and purposes at preferential rates, for example, wheat. In connection with the Tariff Law of 1957, the five categories were reduced to two categories, but otherwise the essential features of the exchange auctions system remained unchanged. In 1961 the Quadros government finally abolished the exchange auction system in an attempted move toward a unified exchange rate system. The move was of short duration, however, as a consequence of the critical shortage of foreign exchange, which led to a debt rescheduling in 1961, and the resignation of the Quadros government. In reacting to the continuing exchange crises in 1962 the new Goulart government restored most of the essential features of the multiple exchange rate system which had existed since 1953: the overvalued rate, exchange allocations to priority sectors fixed by the government, and highly subsidized rates for preferred sectors. The extent of the overvaluation is shown in a study by Joel Bergsman, which points out that, in 1963, for example, the average export rate was only 553 cruzeiros per U.S. dollar, while the effective input rate, including protection, was 1,670 cruzeiros per U.S. dollar.[9]

Professor Benjamin Higgins aptly described the Brazilian exchange system at the time of the 1964 revolution.

> On the eve of the March Revolution, the exchange system, as a consequence of the many measures adopted during the preceding two and a half years, was characterized by its complexity and by its limiting and restricting conditions as regards current transactions. Unrealistic exchange rates; plurality of markets; stagnation in the level of compulsory deposits at 100 percent of the value of contracts and, in some cases, rising to 200 percent; prohibition of certain imports; quantitative restrictions on the purchase of foreign currency; paralysis of remittance of profits and dividends; maintenance of bilateral payment agreements unfavorable foreign exchange margins; subsidies on certain imports and premiums on certain exports, were among the measures in force.[10]

Stagnant Exports. Export policy vied with agricultural policy as the most neglected of Brazilian policies during the postwar period. The

[9]Joel Bergsman, *Brazil, Industrialization and Trade Politics* (New York: Oxford University Press, 1970), Table 3.2, p.38.
[10]Benjamin Higgins, "The 1964-1966 Action Program of the Brazilian Government," part 4, p. 1.

exception in both cases was coffee. With a defeatist attitude to export expansion the Brazilian authorities concentrated on maximizing the foreign exchange earnings from their major export, coffee. Maximizing coffee export receipts, in the logic of the time, required that the cruzeiro exchange rate should remain overvalued. Devaluation, it was thought, would mean a decline in the foreign currency price of coffee and, since the demand was inelastic, a decline in total receipts. More sophisticated economic thinkers also may have accepted the overvalued cruzeiro on the grounds that it was the only way, in the face of the politically powerful coffee growers to contain the price of coffee and thus to minimize the excess coffee production.[11]

Maintenance of a fixed exchange rate during the immediate postwar years, despite the growing domestic inflation, had a disastrous impact on non-coffee exports, which declined in both relative and absolute terms from the end of the war to 1952. By 1952 non-coffee exports were only 26.2 percent of total exports, compared with 64.5 percent in 1946. In dollar value terms, non-coffee exports declined from $635 million in 1946 to $371 million in 1952 (see Table VIII-2). The increase in export earning during these years was attributable entirely to the increase in the world market price for coffee.

The stagnant condition of Brazilian exports was a major factor in the devaluation and change in the exchange rate system in 1953. The new system included separate exchange rates for different export products and bonuses to stimulate exports of particular products. Between 1953 and 1963 the average exchange rate for exports rose faster than the domestic price level, and more and more export products were transferred to the official export rate.[12] After 1959 only coffee, cocoa, mineral oil, and castor oil beans carried special export rates.

The increase in the real export exchange rate had a favorable impact on non-coffee exports, which, although rising steadily from 1953 to 1963, had by the 1960s barely returned to the 1946 level. Taking a three-year average to offset the effects of temporary conditions, we find that non-coffee export earnings during the three years prior to the 1964 revolution remained below the level of fifteen years earlier. Moreover the increase in non-coffee earnings after 1953 was barely sufficient to offset the decline in coffee earnings, stemming from the decline in the world market price for coffee. Total Brazilian export earnings in 1963 were at almost exactly the same level as in 1952. Again taking a three-year average, total exports declined from $1503 million in 1952-54 to $1342 million in 1961-63. During the same period Brazilian GNP in real terms had almost doubled.

[11]/See Chapter VI for a more detailed discussion of coffee policy during the 1950's.
[12]/See Bergsman, *Brazil's Industrialization and Trade Policies*, Table 3.2, p. 38.

Table VIII-2
BRAZILIAN EXPORTS AND NON COFFEE EXPORTS,
1946–1964
(millions of US$)

Year	Total Exports	Non-coffee Exports	Non-coffee Exports as % of Total Exports
1946	985	635	64.5
1947	1,131	717	63.4
1948	1,173	682	58.1
1949	1,089	458	42.1
1950	1,359	494	36.4
1951	1,771	712	40.2
1952	1,416	371	26.2
1953	1,540	450	29.2
1954	1,558	610	39.2
1955	1,419	575	40.5
1956	1,483	453	30.5
1957	1,392	546	39.2
1958	1,244	556	44.7
1959	1,282	538	42.0
1960	1,269	557	43.9
1961	1,403	695	49.5
1962	1,214	572	47.1
1963	1,406	659	46.9
1964	1,430	670	46.9

Source: APEC, *A Economia Brasileira e Suas Perspectivas*, July 1972, Ano XI, Tables G. 3 and I. 14.

What was the explanation for the stagnation of Brazilian export earnings? In the case of coffee, both the volume and average price had increased over the postwar period, but the variable trend of coffee prices in world markets created more than its share of problems. Record high coffee prices in the post-Korean War boom stimulated domestic investment in coffee, adding to inflationary pressures, and—of significance in the context of export policy—provided the eventual rationale for attributing Brazil's economic problems to the declining terms of trade. Coffee prices gradually declined from the $87.00 per sack (132 pounds) in 1954 to $38.00 in 1963; yet the 1963 price was still

35 percent higher than the coffee prices prior to the Korean War boom. To attribute the decline in export earnings to the decline in the commodity terms of trade, the usual explanation of Brazil's foreign exchange crisis, the trend must be calculated from the peak years of coffee prices in the early 1950s. The Brazilian authorities might well have benefited from a closer reading of the parable of Joseph and stored up some foreign exchange during those eight years, 1950 to 1957, of relatively high coffee prices.

The trade explanation of Brazil's foreign exchange crisis is more acceptable when centered on fluctuations in the terms of trade rather than in the long-run deterioration in the prices of primary products. The prices of Brazil's exports, primarily coffee and a few other traditional primary products, have been subject to greater fluctuations than the prices of exports of other Latin American countries and other developing countries, and have been much greater than the prices of its imports. The high export prices in the early 1950s came at a convenient time to finance the growing import requirements of the rapid industrialization. As the industrialization boom continued through the later 1950s, while export prices sagged, the financing gap was taken up increasingly with foreign credits and private investment, until President Goulart limited this source with the Profit Remittance Law of 1962, thereby intensifying the foreign exchange crisis.

The main explanation of the stagnation of Brazil's exports during the years prior to 1963 was an overvalued exchange rate. From the end of World War II to 1953 the real rate for exports declined sharply as the nominal rate remained fixed in the face of steady price increases. Despite the upward trend of real rates for exports after 1953, the cruzeiro remained overvalued during the entire period. The degree of overvaluation changed during these years, with real rates falling about 40 percent from 1946 to the minimum value in 1952, and then rising gradually thereafter to 1962, but "the problem has been the maintenance of existing over-valuation, not a continuous increase in over-valuation."[13] In a joint study with Arthur Candal, Bergsman also noted that "exports were discouraged not only by the bias in exchange rates, but also by fluctuations in the real export exchange rate, since the nominal rate was adjusted infrequently in the face of a continuous inflation." The average month-to-month fluctuation in the real rate, according to his calculations, was over 3.8 percent, and in forty-nine

---

[13]Ibid., p. 47. Bergsman noted that the cruzeiro was substantially overvalued in 1945/46. "The evidence for this was that Brazil's balance of trade was in serious deficit, and that the nominal export rate had remained constant while Brazilian prices had risen about 80 percent more than U.S. prices during the period 1937 to 1945." The same assessment is also made by Gordon and Grommers, *United States Manufacturing Investment in Brazil*, p. 15.

months during the period 1948 to 1966 inclusive the fluctuation was over 5 percent.[14]

Another factor explaining the stagnant export sector, shown by Bergsman, was the strong bias to produce for domestic consumption rather than for export. Non-coffee exports, he notes, carried an implicit tax which averaged 31 percent during the years 1954 to 1963. Commercial policy, he concludes, discriminated against agricultural exports (excluding coffee) roughly to the extent of the implicit export tax, and, in terms of value added, by an even higher amount, roughly 37 percent between 1954 and 1964.[15]

The strong bias against exports during this period is explained by Professor Nathaniel H. Leff as resulting from (a) the considerable pessimism concerning the possibilities of expanding exports because of the low income elasticity of world demand for most primary products; (b) the fact that the government approached export possibilities with an implicit "exportable surplus" theory of trade—according to this doctrine, a country exports only the surplus which is left over after the domestic market for the commodity has been adequately supplied, domestic demand taking priority, however, and being supplied even if internal prices are lower than the world market prices; and (c) the concern of government officials with the instability and risks of depending on exportation as a source of income and supply. As Professor Leff notes, "These considerations were reinforced by ideological currents stressing the importance of import substitution and industrial development as a means to modernization and emancipation from colonial dependence on the world economy."[16]

Evidence that the stagnation in Brazilian exports was not attributable to world market conditions is provided in Table VIII-3. Brazil's share of world exports declined from 2.1 percent in 1953 to 1 percent in 1963; similar declines occurred relative to exports of the Latin American countries and other developing countries. If Brazilian exports in 1963 had maintained the same relative percentage of developing country exports that they had had from 1948 to 1953 (recognizing that the exports of industrial countries have been rising at a faster rate) exports would have amounted to $2.3 billion instead of $1.4 billion. Or if Brazil had retained its relative share of Latin American exports, it would have had export receipts of $1.9 billion in 1963. If Brazil had retained its share of total world exports it would have received $5.4 billion in 1963.

---

[14]Joel Bergsman and Arthur Candal, "Industrialization: Past Success and Future Problems," in Howard S. Ellis, ed., *The Economy of Brazil* p. 33.

[15]Ibid., p. 45.

[16]Nathaniel Leff, *Economic Policy-Making and Development in Brazil 1947-1964*, p.80.

Table VIII-3

BRAZILIAN EXPORTS AS PERCENT OF EXPORTS OF LATIN AMERICA, DEVELOPING COUNTRIES, AND TOTAL WORLD— 1948, 1953, AND 1963

Year	Latin America	Other Developing Countries	Total World
1948	20.1	7.3	2.2
1953	22.2	7.8	2.1
1958	16.7	5.3	1.3
1963	15.6	4.5	1.0

Source: International Monetary Fund, *International Financial Statistics*.

Foreign Investment Policy and Performance. Brazilian policies toward foreign private investment made two about-faces during the postwar years. Through 1953 foreign investments remained at a very low level as the result of limits imposed in 1943 on the repatriation of capital and remittances of profits.[17] From 1947 to 1953 the annual inflow of risk capital averaged $15 million, while profit remittances averaged $47 million for a net outflow of $32 million per year. A more positive attitude to foreign investment began in 1953 with the abolition of the earlier restrictions on capital transfers and remittances and the establishment of a free exchange rate market for these transactions. Two years later, in 1955, SUMOC Instruction 113 extended a further attraction to foreign private investment. By enabling foreign investors to import capital without exchange cover, Instruction 113, in effect, offered them an advantage over domestic investors. "In importing capital goods directly, the foreign investor avoided sending dollars to Brazil at the free market rate and using the cruzeiros thus obtained to repurchase dollars at a higher price in the auction market." The measure of the advantage, or subsidy, was the difference between the cost of foreign exchange in the relevant auction category and the free market rate.[18] According to Professor Gudin, nearly half of the cruzeiro cost of imported machinery was subsidized during the years 1955 to 1960. Professor Gudin, who was Finance Minister at the time Instruction 113 was implemented, computed the cost of these subsidies at $850.6 million (the subsidy multiplied by the value of suppliers' credits) during these years. This, he claims, was the cost of industrialization to the consumers in general and to agriculturalists in

---

[17] Ministério do Planejamento e Coordenação Econômica, *Programa de Ação Econômica do Govêrno, 1964-1966*, p. 143.

[18] Gordon and Grommers, *United States Manufacturing Investment in Brazil*, p. 20.

particular.[19] The Instruction 113 scheme was incorporated in the Tariff Reform of 1957 and further augmented by the Kubitschek Government in offering importers of industrial machinery and equipment assurance of foreign exchange at the coffee export rate, an exceptionally favorable exchange rate for importers.

These subsidies and the domestic market potential offered sufficient inducements to foreign investors to expand their annual rate of investment in Brazil several-fold, to an annual average of $91 million during the years 1954 to 1961; meanwhile, the annual profit remittances dropped to $33 million. By 1961, however, foreign investment had begun, once again, to fall off as a result of the restrictions imposed on profit and capital remittances[20] by the Goulart government. The consequences of the Profit Remittance Law of 1962 do not seem particularly unfavorable to Brazil if one can accept the balance of payments data on the net flow of private foreign investments and remittances of profits and dividends during 1962 and 1963. While the rate of foreign investment declined, so did the outflow of profits and dividends. The resulting small reduction in the net flow can hardly explain the intensified balance of payments difficulties of those years. To find the full impact of the Profit Remittance Law one has to include the declining trend of net capital flows, which occurred despite the rescheduling of part of the 1962 and 1963 debt repayments, the net outflow in 1963 of swap transactions (which in part were a substitute for direct investments) and the many other accounts in which remittances abroad were concealed. Underinvoicing of exports and overinvoicing of imports were commonplace activities during the years through 1967. Purchases of dollars in the "parallel market," the Brazilian euphemism for the black market, was another of the host of approaches used by innovative Brazilians and foreigners resident in Brazil to send their capital abroad. The 30 percent remittance tax and compulsory deposit requirements on remittances provided strong inducements to remit outside the official channels. Estimates of the outflow of foreign exchange through the parallel market during these years range from $100 to $150 million per year, and a significant part of this outflow constituted capital flight and remittances of various forms.[21]

Balance of payments disequilibrium. The Brazilian balance of payments remained in relative equilibrium from the end of World War II through 1956, with the exception of the two Korean War years of 1951

---

[19]Eugenio Gudin, "The Chief Characteristics of the Postwar Economic Development of Brazil," Ellis, *Economy of Brazil,"* p.11.
[20]Law 4131 of 3 September 1962.
[21]In the balance of payments statistics this net outflow has been allocated on an arbitrary formula of 40 percent foreign travel, 30 percent factor payments and 30 percent short-term capital outflow.

and 1952 (see Table VIII-4). Widespread concern that the availability of imports would be severely curtailed as a consequence of the Korean War, as they had been during World War II, led the Brazilian authorities to an excessively liberal import policy during these two years. The liberal import policy, combined with the overvalued exchange rate which had persisted for several years, resulted in an 80 percent increase in imports and an accumulated deficit during the two years of over $900 million. When the expectation of a Korean War scarcity proved to be unfounded as imports poured into the country, the authorities restored the tight quantitative import restrictions, at the same time revising the control mechanism from an import licensing system to a multiple category exchange auction system. During the following four years, 1953 to 1956, the Brazilian balance of payments remained in approximate equilibrium, but an equilibrium which was both artificial, dependent as it was on severe import restrictions, and tenuous, based upon a rather shaky trade surplus. The average annual trade surplus of $340 million during these four years was adequate to cover comparable payments for services and remittances of dividends, profits and interest. But it depended upon two temporary factors: record high coffee prices and the large import inventory built up during 1951 and 1952. The first maintained export earnings at a relatively high level and the second permitted a reduced level of imports without limiting the industrial growth rate. These trends proved to be very short-lived.

The overvalued exchange rate and the neglect of noncoffee exports finally caught up with the Brazilian authorities in 1957, as Brazil's balance of payments moved into a chronic deficit which persisted through 1963 (see Table VIII-4). The trade surplus, which had averaged $340 million from 1953 to 1956, fell to $107 million in 1957 and turned into a small deficit in 1960. The decline in export earnings from both coffee and noncoffee exports and the rise in imports contributed to the drop-off in the trade surplus. With the drawing down of the 1951-52 inventory stockpile, an increase in imports proved to be essential to the continued growth in the economy despite the rapid growth in domestic production of import substitutes. Starting in 1960, services and remittances of dividends, profits, and interest, which had remained relatively stable, also began to add to the deficit as a result of the accumulation of foreign investment and short-term borrowings of earlier years. These trends added up to an accumulated deficit during the seven years 1957 to 1963 of $1.5 billion, this despite a net accumulated inflow of autonomous foreign capital of about $1.1 billion.

Financing the Deficit. The Brazilian government financed the accumulated deficit of about $2.5 billion during the period 1950 to 1963 pri-

Table VIII-4

BRAZIL'S BALANCE OF PAYMENTS, 1955–1963

(millions US$)

	1955	1956	1957	1958	1959	1960	1961	1962	1963
Exports FOB	1,419	1,483	1,392	1,244	1,282	1,269	1,405	1,214	1,406
Imports FOB	1,099	1,046	1,285	1,179	1,210	1,293	1,292	1,304	1,294
Trade balance	320	437	107	65	72	-24	113	-90	112
Net interest & dividends	-78	-91	-93	-89	-116	-145	-145	-136	-87
Other services and donations	-240	-289	-278	-224	-267	-309	-188	-163	-139
Current account balance	2	57	-264	-248	-311	-478	-222	-389	-114
Gross Capital Inflow	143	338	497	508	559	475	615	491	310
Amortizations	-140	-187	-242	-324	-377	-417	-327	-310	-364
Capital account balance	3	151	255	184	182	58	288	181	-54
Errors and omissions	12	-14	-171	-189	-25	10	49	-138	-76
Net change in reserves	17	194	-180	-253	-154	-410	115[a]	-346	-244
Level of foreign exchange reserves, end of year	491	611	476	465	438	428	563	417	219

[a]Net increase was due to debt rescheduling in 1961.

Source: *Boletim do Banco Central do Brasil*, various issues.

marily by short-term borrowings in which the government participated either as the direct borrower or as the provider of an exchange guarantee. Foreign exchange reserves accumulated during World War II financed about $500 million of the deficit. Through 1961, however, the government succeeded in maintaining an adequate level of gross foreign exchange reserves for window dressing purposes. Publications of the IMF show, for example, Brazilian reserves as of December 1961 at $563 million, which, at five months' import requirements, was a reasonably adequate level.[22] But by 1961 all of Brazil's gold stock of $285 million was held by foreign banks as a guarantee for foreign loans. Much of the remainder of Brazil's reserves at the end of 1961 could be attributed to the debt rescheduling of that year. In the next two years, having exhausted its sources of short-term credits, suppliers credits, swap transactions, and every other type of financial arrangement, the Brazilian government was no longer able to maintain its window dressing reserves. By the end of 1963, Brazil's foreign exchange reserves, less the $150 million in gold earmarked for gold guarantee loans, added up to $69 million, barely enough to finance ten days' import requirements.

Not only had the reserves been depleted by the end of 1963, but also Brazil's capacity to borrow had been exhausted. In financing the continuing deficits, the government had accumulated almost $2 billion of compensatory and short-term liabilities. The service on this debt, added to the service on the autonomous investments and loan capital, created an unbearable drain on Brazil's limited export earnings. The debt rescheduling of 1961 alleviated the debt service pressures in that year, but the renewed high deficits of 1962 and 1963 brought Brazil to the point of international bankruptcy. The debt rescheduling of 1961 had served only to postpone the need for fundamental changes in the economy. Brazil's creditors did not wish to engage in an additional rescheduling operation without more assurance that these fundamental changes in policy would be made. The only alternative, from the Brazilian viewpoint, was a unilateral debt moratorium.

Foreign Indebtedness. At the end of World War II Brazilian foreign indebtedness was probably at the lowest level in recent history. Brazilian debt had been refinanced in 1943 and, with net repayments during the war, Brazil's annual debt service (repayments on principal and interest) fell to less than 3 percent of export earnings in 1951. The debt service began to rise rapidly in 1954 as payments on the 1951-52 imports became due and by 1957 took 19.7 percent of export earnings.

---

[22]Three months' import requirements has normally been considered an adequate level for most developing countries.

By 1960, with the heavy reliance on foreign borrowing to finance the balance of payments deficit, the debt service took a record 36.6 percent of Brazil's export earnings. Brazil's growing debt problem was not, however, the overall level of the debt, which had grown only slightly faster than Brazil's GNP, but the short-term nature of the debt. A long history of defaults and rescheduling had reduced Brazil's credit standing in international financial markets so that even after World War II, when Brazil's financial situation was fairly good, neither private nor public institutions were able to obtain long-term financing except through a few official institutions, such as the Export Import Bank (Eximbank) and the World Bank. Since these sources of capital were limited, most of the Brazilian debt took the form of short-term suppliers credits, commercial bank loans with gold collateral, and commercial arrears. The huge deficits of 1951 and 1952, for example, were financed almost entirely by commercial arrears estimated at $900 million to $1 billion at the end of 1952.[23] These arrears were liquidated

Table VIII-5
BRAZIL'S DEBT SERVICE RATIO, 1950-1964
(millions of US$)

Year	Amortization of Debt	Interest Payments	Total Debt Service	Exports of Goods and Services	Debt Service Ratio (total debt service as % of exports)
1950	85	29	114	1,402	8.1%
1951	27	22	49	1,833	2.7
1952	33	26	59	1,485	4.0
1953	46	35	81	1,654	4.9
1954	134	51	185	1,663	11.1
1955	140	39	179	1,542	11.6
1956	187	69	256	1,636	15.6
1957	242	73	313	1,592	19.7
1958	324	61	385	1,410	27.3
1959	377	93	470	1,441	32.6
1960	417	118	535	1,463	36.6
1961	327	117	444	1,540	28.8
1962	310	121	431	1,299	33.2
1963	364	90	454	1,502	30.2
1964	277	133	410	1,548	26.4

Source: *Boletim do Banco Central do Brasil*, December 1972,Publicação Especial, pp. 6-13. For later years, see Table 17, Chapter 8.

[23] Henry J. Bitterman *Refunding of International Debt*, p. 121.

in 1953 with credits from the Eximbank, a number of private commercial banks, and a drawing from the International Monetary Fund. From the end of 1956 to 1961 Brazil drew $142 million of medium-term credits from the IMF. In the following years the Brazilian government relied increasingly on supplier credits, commercial bank lines of credit, and other short-term transactions to finance the balance of payments deficits. As these sources began to dry up, the government was forced to turn more and more to swap transactions, which tripled in volume between 1958 and 1961. Even these very unfavorable transactions failed to provide adequate financing and commercial arrears began to pile up in 1960 and 1961.[24]

The short-term structure of Brazil's foreign debt made its balance of payments particularly vulnerable during the political crisis of 1961 and 1962. An estimated 23 percent of the debt outstanding at the end of 1961 carried maturities of less than one year, compared with an estimated 13 percent six years earlier. At the time of the Quadros government's debt negotiations in early 1961 the scheduled repayments of principal and interest were slightly more than half the total foreign exchange earnings.[25] Similar amounts were projected for the next five years. (About 40 percent of the principal was due in 1961 and 1962, and 78 percent within a five-year period.

If rescheduling action had not been undertaken in 1961, the Brazilian balance of payments deficit in that year would have been only slightly less than the $800 million of scheduled debt service; lacking reserves and borrowing capacity to cover this deficit, the alternative was a unilateral default on the Brazilian debt. The consolidation and

[24]The swap transaction was a foreign exchange transaction in which the Bank of Brazil purchased foreign currencies from a foreign creditor at the current rate of exchange but with a guarantee to resell the foreign currencies at the the same rate, regardless of the exchange rate at the time of the resale. With the continuing inflation and successive devaluations these transactions proved to be very costly to the monetary authorities. As an example, a $100 swap transaction in December 1959 at the going exchange rate of Cr$ 76 per U.S. dollar would give the foreign investor Cr$ 7,600. At the end of one year, the investor was able to repurchase the $100 with the same Cr$ 7600. In the interim, the exchange rate had been devalued to Cr$ 90 per dollar. To get the $100 of exchange to cover this transaction, the Bank of Brazil had to give up Cr$ 9,000, the exchange rate prevailing in December 1960. The difference of Cr$ 1,400 constituted a net gain to the investor, a net loss to the Bank of Brazil, and of even greater significance, it meant a net monetary expansion of approximately this amount for each of the $228 million of swaps outstanding at the end of 1959, or Cr$ 3.2 billion. This amounted to 4.2 percent of the federal deficit in 1960 which, while significant, was still not a major cause of the failure of the stabilization efforts of May and June 1961 as claimed by ECLA. "Fifteen Years of Economic Policy in Brazil," *ECLA Economic Bulletin for Latin America*, vol. 9, no. 2 (November 1964), p. 203.

[25]About 40 percent of Brazil's debt outstanding at the end of 1960 was estimated to be due in two years. The outstanding principal was variously estimated at 3.4 to 3.8 billion and interest payments ran about $118 million for the year. Bitterman, *Refunding of International Debt*, p. 9.

rescheduling of Brazil's debt undertaken by the Quadros government in cooperation with the European banks (the Hague Club), private and official U.S. institutions, the Japanese banks, and the International Monetary Fund was announced as a $2 billion financing package aimed at alleviating the debt burden over the next few years. The debt burden for 1961 was indeed cut back from the record 1960 level of 36 percent to less than 29 percent of export earnings. Unfortunately, the Brazilian government was unable to persist with the stabilization measures which had been an essential part of the consolidation agreement, and the political crisis following the resignation of Quadros and the confusion during the early years of the Goulart government served only to exacerbate the foreign exchange and debt servicing problem. By the end of 1963 Brazil's foreign debt had grown another $700 million to about $3.6 billion (see Table VIII-6). Government projections of debt service totalled $600 million, or about 40 percent of export earnings, for 1964 and only slightly less for 1965.[26]

In short, the 1961 debt rescheduling served only to buy a few years' grace. The Brazilian government had failed to implement the necessary domestic and foreign policies necessary to restore some semblance of order to the balance of payments and the debt structure. In 1963 Finance Minister San Tiago Dantas had already initiated negotiations for another round of rescheduling, but the international and national institutions were hesitant to participate anew without more evidence of Brazil's willingness and capacity to make the necessary difficult decisions. This hesitation was removed after the revolution of 1964 and the installation of the Octavio Bulhões-Roberto Campos team in positions of financial leadership.

Assessment of the Balance of Payments Crisis. An objective assessment of the causes of the Brazilian balance of payments crisis of 1961 and 1963 must include three factors: (a) the declining terms of trade after 1954; (b) the inadequate level of long-term capital, and (c) inadequate attention to the Brazilian export potential. It was certainly true that the terms of trade moved against Brazilian exports after 1954, although it was also unreasonable to assume that coffee prices—and coffee constituted about 70 percent of export earnings—would remain at the record

---

[26]Estados Unidos do Brasil, *Three-Year Plan for Economic and Social Development, 1963-65*, p. 51. Principal repayments were projected at $465 million and interest at $132 million. Foreign Minister Carvalho Pinto reported on 4 July 1963 that foreign debt totalled $3 billion and that amortization and interest scheduled for 1963-65 would amount to $1.8 billion or about 43 percent of export revenue for that period.

Table VIII-6

BRAZILIAN FOREIGN DEBT OUTSTANDING AT YEAR-END, 1951–1963

(millions of US$)

Year	Foreign Debt	
	Including IMF	Excluding IMF
1951	1,177	1,111
1952	1,791	1,753
1953	1,772	1,706
1954	1,957	1,891
1955	1,921	1,855
1956	1,972	1,934
1957	2,104	2,029
1958	2,401	2,289
1959	2,583	2,491
1960	2,979	2,839
1961	3,209	3,029
1962	3,517	3,355
1963	3,347	3,188

Source: Author's estimates, based upon an analysis of balance-of-payments data, using 1969 data as a reference point and cross-checking with several earlier sources, such as Gudin, "The Chief Characteristics of the Postwar Economic Development of Brazil," in Ellis, ed., *Economy of Brazil*, pp. 12-13.

high levels of 1954. It is also true that long-term capital was not forthcoming on an adequate level and that Brazil was forced into excessive reliance on short-term credits to finance the necessary imports. Too much of the longer-term capital was provided on an emergency—or compensatory—basis after Brazil had already overindulged in suppliers credits, short-term bank credit, swaps, and commercial arrears. Of the total outstanding debt in 1963 of $3.2 billion, $1 billion had been provided in the form of balance of payments support provided by official institutions (compensatory financing) and another $900 million was of a short-term nature. Only $1.5 billion or about 40 percent of Brazil's foreign debt had been received in the form of project loans and supplier credits. Finally, it was also true that the Brazilian government had neglected its export sector. The export stagnation during the fifteen years prior to 1964 and the upward trend of Brazilian exports after 1964 provide ample evidence that this was so.

Post-1964 Policies—"The Equilibrium System'

Objectives. At the time of the 1964 revolution, the Goulart government had been attempting for several months to negotiate the rescheduling of Brazil's debts for the second time in three years. The Castello Branco government continued these negotiations and within three months was able to conclude a new Hague Club agreement with participation of all Brazil's major creditor nations.[27] According to data published by the Brazilian government, the debt rescheduling provided relief from scheduled repayments in 1964 and 1965 of $243.8 million, including $149.9 million from the Bilateral Consolidation Agreement (Act of Paris of 1 July 1964) with the United States, Germany, France, Netherlands, United Kingdom, Italy, Switzerland, and Japan. The U.S. Treasury postponed a 1964 repayment on an Exchange Stabilization Fund credit of $25.3 million; the Eximbank deferred repayments of $25.6 million from 1964 to 1965 through 1967; and the IMF spread out repurchases of $106 million due in 1964 over a period of twenty-five months.[28] This rescheduling of debts and additional new credits provided largely by USAID prevented the import constraint from taking on more serious proportions while the new government had time to make the necessary revisions in exchange and trade policies.

Based on their revised assessment of the causes of the balance of payments crisis, the Castello Branco advisers laid out new reforms for each of the main instruments of foreign trade and exchange policy: export policy, exchange rate system, foreign investments, and foreign debt. Export expansion was assigned a major role in the trade program, with realistic exchange rates, a simplification of the bureaucratic processes, fiscal incentives, and improved export financing as the means for achieving this target. A unified, realistic, and flexible exchange rate system, with the exception of a special rate for coffee exports, constituted another important set of targets. Encouragement of foreign investments was to be achieved through modification of the Profit Remittance Law and simplification of registration procedures.[29] Finally, the Action Program aimed at lengthening the maturity of the existing debt by limiting supplier credits and seeking longer terms on all new debt. The Action Program did not include liberalization of the high protective tariff systems as an integral part of its reform movement

---

[27]So named after the group of creditors which first met at the Hague to reschedule Brazilian debts in 1961.

[28]Ministério do Planejamento, *Programa de Ação Econômica*, pp. 129-130.

[29]Ibid., p. 49. Specifically articles 31, 32 and 33 of Law 4131, 3 September 1962, were to be abolished. This was the law, implemented by the Goulart government, which destroyed the favorable investment climate of the 1953 to 1961 period.

The need for this measure only became obvious after the experiences of 1964 and 1965.

Reform of the Foreign Exchange System. According to the Action Program for 1964-66.

> The reform programmed for the foreign exchange system would seek to correct the defects of the inadequate policy followed principally since the end of 1961, which had resulted in a progressive deterioration in the balance of payments and an expansion of the external debt. The principal objective is to simplify the exchange system with the unification of exchange operations in a free and flexible exchange market, which reflects the domestic and external price tendencies as well as the conditions in the market.[30]

The above statement of objectives for reform of the exchange system included three essential principles for a sound exchange system: unification, realism, and flexibility. The first phase of the reform program, already initiated in May 1964, was the simplification and unification of the rate system. This included a series of measures to revoke the exchange subsidies for wheat, petroleum products, and newsprint; to tranfer sugar and cocoa to the free export rate; to abolish the 200 percent prior deposits on imports; and to reduce compulsory deposits for imports and financial transactions.[31] This unification and simplification process continued throughout 1965 and 1966 so that by the end of 1966 the Castello Branco government had eliminated virtually all exchange subsidies for import commodities, special rates for exports (except for coffee), and compulsory deposits and guarantee for imports and financial transactions.[32] The exchange system presented to the Costa e Silva government in March 1967 was the most simplified and unified rate Brazil had experienced since

---

[30]Ibid., p. 48.

[31]SUMOC Instructions 270 of 9 May 1964, 275 of August 1964, and 277 of August 1964.

[32]Measures taken to liberalize and unify the exchange system include (a) November 1965—elimination of the 15 percent surcharge on imports; reduction of the 30 percent surcharge on remittances to 15 percent; elimination of compulsory prior deposits on imports of 50 percent; (b) January 1966—reduction of guaranty deposit from 100 to 25 percent; (c) April 1966—elimination of guaranty deposit of 25 percent; (d) June 1966—elimination of weekly limit of $50,000; (3) August 1966—elimination of 1.1 percent stamp tax, to be effective January 1967; (f) 17 September 1966—elimination of requirements that exchange contract be closed prior to issuance of an import license; (g) 24 September 1966—elimination of the 15 percent surcharge on remittances, and the 100 percent limit on licenses to purchase special category imports; (h) 1966—2000 items shifted from the Special to the more liberal General category as part of a five-stage program.

1952, and, more important, the maintenance of this rate did not require quantitative import restrictions, as they did in the earlier year, because of the more realistic rate.

The second element of the exchange rate reform was to maintain a realistic rate, defined as a free rate "which reflects the domestic and external price tendencies as well as the conditions in the market."[33] This definition calls to mind the Purchasing Power Parity Concept that the exchange rate should somehow relate domestic costs and prices with similar costs and prices abroad. The shortcomings of this concept have been adequately described by Enke and Salera.[34] Its application in the context of the Brazilian exchange reform is even less appropriate inasmuch as the many measures taken to simplify and unify the exchange system also had an important impact on the effective rate itself. The elimination of the prior and guarantee deposits and other measures affecting imports tended to reduce the effective import rate, while the transfer of some export commodities to the free export rate tended to increase the effective rate for these commodities and therefore the average export rate. On the other hand, the huge inflow of foreign capital, especially from the U. S. government, tended to hold the rate lower than it would have been in its absence. The net result of all these measures, added to the exchange devaluation, can only be assessed in terms of their impact on the major items in the balance of payments, particularly imports and exports. They cannot be assessed in isolation.

If only the free market rate is considered, in isolation from the measures cited above, one finds that the effective exchange rate did not maintain its realism in terms of the purchasing power parity concept. From 13 March 1964 to 13 February 1967, the date of the last devaluation of the Castello Branco Government, the exchange rate depreciated, in terms of dollars, by 55 percent. During the same three-year period, the value of the cruzeiro, in terms of the domestic general price index, fell by 76 percent. Yet the evidence points to a significant decline in the following three years. Since February 1967, the devaluations have kept up fairly well with the general price increases when foreign price increases are taken into account, as shown in Table VIII-7.

Despite the movement toward unification and realism of the exchange rate, the Brazilian economy experienced serious difficulties as a consequence of the inflexibility of the prevailing exchange rate system. The continued price increases inherent in the gradual approach to stabilization necessitated periodic devaluations to keep the

[33] Ministério do Planejamento, *Programa de Ação Econômica*, p. 48.
[34] Stephen Enke and Virgil Salera, *International Economics*, p. 134.

Table VIII-7
OUTSTANDING VALUE OF SHORT-TERM FOREIGN
OBLIGATIONS, 1964–1972
(millions of US$)

End of Year	Instruction 289 (14 January 1963)	Resolution 63 (21 August 1967)	Law 4131 (9 March 1962)	Total
1964	—	—	N.A.	—
1965	137	—	N.A.	137
1966	261	—	N.A.	261
1967	179	41	N.A.	220
1968	361	285	470	1,116
1969	374	433	799	1,605
1970	381	653	1,250	2,285
1971	295	983	1,915	3,193
1972	207	2,018	3,303	5,528

Source: *Boletim do Banco Central do Brasil* October 1970, p. 108, and June 1973, pp. 108-109.

rate realistic. The speculative exchange cycles before and after each of these quasi-predictable devaluations carried several adverse repercussions for the Brazilian economy. In addition, the peculiar annual timing of the devaluations, coming as they did between late November and early February of each year, created particular hardships for agriculture. In deciding upon the timing of the annual devaluations, the authorities had a special eye on the impact on the annual round of wage increases, which took place largely during September and October. For this reason all the major devaluations between 1964 and 1968 occurred between 13 November and 15 February. This timing was particularly unfavorable for Brazilian farmers since the harvest season, May and June, followed the devaluations by several months. Because they could not afford to hold their crops off the market until the next devaluation, they found their export profits eaten away by inflation during the ensuing period.

As the almost annual pattern of exchange devaluations emerged following the 1964 revolution, private businessmen began to engage more and more in short-term speculative exchange operations. As the time for the next devaluation approached, private speculators engaged increasingly in a variety of techniques to maximize their foreign exchange holdings. Postponement in closing exchange contracts for exports, advance payments for imports and foreign debts and shenanigans with coffee exports were commonly used techniques. But perhaps the most used and least justifiable technique was the use of Instruction 289 transactions. A brief look at these operations will give an idea of the extent and repercussions of the exchange speculation.

Instruction 289 is a short-term credit operation established by the SUMOC, named after the implementing regulation, and used as a substitute for the swap transaction. Whereas the swap carried an exchange rate guarantee, the Instruction 289 transaction carried only a guarantee of convertibility, provided foreign exchange is available, at the prevailing exchange rate. This transaction provided to foreign companies operating in Brazil a useful instrument for obtaining foreign credit with maturities of 180 days or more at the lower interest rates prevailing abroad. Even with the exchange risk these transactions were profitable as the interest rates in Brazil grew in 1966 and 1967 to exceptionally high positive levels. (By 1969 they had reached a level of 20 percent in real terms.) To the extent that the exchange risk could be avoided, the transaction became doubly profitable. Here the predictability of the annual devaluations served to enhance their profitability. As the annual exchange devaluation approached, the companies holding Instruction 289 funds would seek temporary sources of cruzeiros to cover their working capital requirements. In so doing they intensified the competition for the ever-tight credit and drove interest rates higher. Since they tended to be the large foreign companies with good credit ratings, they usually received the requested credit at the expense of reduced credit availabilities for the smaller companies with lesser credit ratings, which, of course, tended to be Brazilian firms. To make matters worse, the outflow of foreign exchange reserves associated with the liquidity of the Instruction 289 transactions reduced over-all credit availabilities at the same time that the demand from the foreign companies was increasing.

Immediately following the devaluation, the timing of which was expedited by the speculation, the entire process reversed itself. The foreign firms registered new 289 contracts with the Central Bank at the higher exchange rate (that is, receiving more cruzeiros per dollar than had been given up a few days or weeks earlier for the same dollar), repaid the domestic loan, and added the difference between the exchange profit and interest costs to the company profits. With the inflow of foreign exchange and the repayment of credit, domestic credit availabilities eased and interest rates tended to decline but were held up by the renewed upward price pressures.

These annual speculative cycles had three unfortunate repercussions on the Brazilian economy. On the external side, they complicated the management of the exchange markets and foreign exchange reserves. They forced the authorities into premature devaluations which increased import prices and kept imports at a lower level than desirable—as in 1965—in terms of stabilization objectives.

On the domestic side, the annual speculative cycles made monetary management virtually impossible. As credit tightened during the weeks or months prior to the inevitable devaluation, the authorities, lacking the capability of easing credit selectively, were regularly pressured to reduce reserve requirements to alleviate the excessive tightness in the credit markets. Following the reflow of foreign exchange after the devaluation, on the other hand, the monetary authorities were reluctant to increase reserve requirements because of the impact of this blunt instrument on the many banks which did not benefit from the exchange flow. On both sides of these operations the need for a more flexible monetary instrument, such as open market operations, was sorely felt.

A third unfortunate aspect of these 289 operations lay on the political plane. Their benefits were received primarily by the large foreign companies while those suffering most from the periodical speculative cycles and alternating periods of credit stringency and ease were Brazilian firms. This inequitable situation added fuel to the nationalist temper long existing in the Brazilian business community. For years they had experienced inequitable treatment as a result of other policies to stimulate foreign investment; the validity of their new complaint was finally recognized and acted upon by the Costa e Silva Government in 1967.

Shortly after the Costa e Silva government took office in March 1967 it implemented the first of three measures directed at equalizing the access to credit of Brazilian and foreign firms. The first measure, which prohibited Brazilian banks from extending more than 50 percent of its loans to foreign companies, turned out to be a purely psychological measure. Because of the vague character of the definition of foreign company and the generosity of the 50 percent limit, this measure did not adversely affect the access of foreign companies to cruzeiro credit. More effective in expanding the access of Brazilian firms to foreign credit was the Resolution 63 transaction, the objective of which was to do for Brazilian firms what Instruction 289 did for foreign firms. To overcome the lack of foreign credit sources available to small- and medium-sized Brazilian firms, the Central Bank, through its Resolution 63, authorized the commercial banks and investment banks to serve as intermediaries, with the former in credits of less than one year and the latter in longer-term credits. These transactions received the same Central Bank guarantee as the Instruction 289 but again with the exchange risk borne by the borrower. Initially the Resolution 63 transactions carried higher interest rates than for comparable domestic credits, but by 1970, as they became more acceptable, their rates came down to competitive levels. Their high degree of acceptance and use in the market is shown by the Table VIII-7.

While the implementation of the flexible exchange rate system in August 1968 was not motivated by a desire to equalize Brazilian and foreign credit availabilities, it tended to have that effect. In eliminating the inducement to foreign firms to borrow periodically, the flexible rate system provided a greater degree of stability in credit availabilities for Brazilian firms, and in so doing reduced their need to hold credit for strictly precautionary purposes—that is, to cover them during the recurrent periods of credit stringency.

A third form of financial transaction which must be cited at this point are the 4131 funds, initiated by Law 4131 of 9 March 1962, aimed at regulating the credit flows between foreign companies and their Brazilian affiliates. Foreign funds are registered at the Central Bank under this law for the same purposes as Instruction 289 funds; they can be of long-, medium-, or short-term duration, and they can be for investment or working capital purposes. They differ from Instruction 289 only to the extent that they do not carry a foreign exchange guarantee. The guarantee was important when Brazil's foreign exchange position was tight from 1964 to 1968, but as Brazil's reserve position became stronger, its significance disappeared. Central Bank data on the 4131 funds do not indicate the actual levels outstanding during the years prior to 1968 because of the backlog in the registering of funds following the institution of the law in 1962. Central Bank data show large increases in 1965 and especially in 1966, which reflect registrations of funds which had entered Brazil in earlier years, probably prior to 1962. In fact, there was a net outflow of 4131 funds between 1964 and 1968. With the restoration of confidence of foreign investors in Brazil in 1969 and the tighter management of the Instruction 289 funds, more and more of the foreign money was registered under Law 4131.

The Trotting Peg Exchange Rate System. By 1968 the need to eliminate the exchange speculation through some improvement in the exchange system was only too apparent. The implications of the exchange system for reserve and credit management, for farm incomes, and for the politically explosive denationalization issue forced the authorities to reassess the prevailing system and look about for an alternative. One such alternative widely discussed in Brazil was a freely fluctuating rate system with the rate determined by the supply and demand for exchange in the market. Finance Minister Delfim Netto had himself

Table VIII-8
BRAZILIAN EXCHANGE RATES,
PERCENTAGE DEVALUATIONS AND GENERAL PRICE
CHANGES, 1964–August 1972

Date	Exchange Rate[a] (Cr$ per US$)	Percentage Devaluation in Terms of US$	Change in General Price Index during Year	Change in U.S. Consumer Price Index
1964	—	*204.2*	*90.5*	
Jan.	600	N.A.		
Feb.	1,160	93.3		
Aug.	1,215	4.7		
Sep	.1,550	27.5		
Dec.	1,825	17.7		
1965	—	*20.54*	*56.8*	
Nov. 16	2,200	20.54		
1966	2,200	0	*37.9*	*3.1*
1967	—	*22.72*	*28.4*	*2.8*
Feb. 13	2,700	22.72		
1968		*40.93*	*24.2*	*4.1*
Jan. 4	3,200[b]	18.6		
Aug. 27	3,630[c]	13.35		
Sep. 24	3,675	1.37		
Nov.19	3,745	1.89		
Dec. 9	3,805	1.59		
1969		*13.66*	*20.8*	*5.4*
Feb. 4	3,905	2.61		
Mar. 19	3,975	1.78		
May 13	4,025	1.25		
July 7	4,075	1.23		
Aug. 27	4,125	1.22		
Oct. 3	4,185	1.45		
Nov. 14	4,265	1.90		
Dec. 18	4,325	1.40		
1970		*13.76*	*21.9*	*5.9*
Feb. 4	4,380	1.38		
Mar. 30	4,460	1.81		
May 18	4,530	1.56		
July 10	4,590	1.32		
July 24	4,620	0.65		
Sep. 18	4,690	1.51		
Nov. 4	4,780	1.91		
Nov. 18	4,830	1.04		
Dec. 22	4,920	1.85		

Table VIII-8—Continued
BRAZILIAN EXCHANGE RATES,
PERCENTAGE DEVALUATIONS AND GENERAL PRICE
CHANGES, 1964–AUGUST 1972

Date	Exchange Rate[a] (Cr$ per US$)	Percentage Devaluation in Terms of US$	Change in General Price Index During Year	Change in U.S. Consumer Price Index
1971		*13.82*	*19.7*	*4.3*
Feb. 9	5,000	1.62		
Mar. 27	5,080	1.59		
May 3	5,160	1.66		
June 11	5,250	1.73		
Aug. 5	5,370	2.27		
Sep. 13	5,470	1.85		
Nov. 10	5,600	2.36		
1972		*10.36*	*15.5*	*4.9*
Jan. 28	5,750	2.66		
Mar. 16	5,810	1.04		
May 8	5,880	1.01		
July 14	5,930	0.85		
Sep. 5	5,990	1.01		
Oct. 17	6,060	1.16		
Nov. 22	6,130	1.16		
Dec. 15	6,180	0.82		

[a]Central Bank purchase price

[b]Converted to new cruzeiros where 1,000 previous cruzeiros equals one new cruzeiro.

[c]Initiated gliding peg exchange rate system.

Source: 1964 to 1971—*Conjuntura Econômica*, November 1972, Table 1, p. 78; for 1972—*Conjuntura Econômica*, February 1973, p. 52.

espoused such a system when he was studying at the University of São Paulo, the problems of Brazilian agriculture. Concern about speculative excesses of a free rate, however, caused the authorities to turn to a compromise solution.

The trotting peg exchange rate system announced by Finance Minister Delfim Netto on 27 August 1968 has proved to be among the most effective of the many innovations implemented by post-1964 Brazilian government.[35] In this new system (also described as an adjust-

---

[35]I prefer to describe the Brazilian flexible rate system as a trotting peg to differentiate it from the smaller rate changes of the industrial nations, commonly called the crawling peg system. See also Juergen B. Donges, *Brazil's Trotting Peg: A New Approach to Greater Exchange Rate Flexibility in Less Developed Countries.*

able peg system, a crawling peg, and even, in its Brazilian application, a galloping peg), the exchange rate is fixed and supported by the government. The only variation from the system which preceded it is that the exchange rate is changed by smaller amounts and at shorter intervals. Through the end of 1972 the government modified the rate thirty-five times by an average change of 1.5 percent, with a range from a low of 0.65 to a high of 2.66 percent. The time interval has averaged forty-four days with the shortest interval fourteen days and the longest seventy-eight days. The size and timing of the rate changes are determined on the basis of several criteria, including the relative changes in domestic and foreign prices, interest rates during the interval, the trend of non-traditional exports, and the trend of foreign exchange reserves.[36]

From August 1968 when the flexible rate system was implemented through the end of 1972, the exchange rate in terms of U. S. dollars has been devalued by 60 percent. During the same interval the general price index in Brazil has doubled. Assuming 6 percent price increases per year on the part of Brazil's major trading partners, the Brazilian devaluations have just about kept up with the inflation, but not quite. On the other hand, the trend of exports and foregin exchange reserves indicates that the devaluations may have been excessive.

Non-coffee exports had expanded fairly rapidly—by 46 percent —in the first four years (1964-67) following the revolution, but they rose by 126 percent in the next four years. By 1972 they exceeded the 1960-64 average by more than four times. Private capital inflows likewise reacted favorably to the new exchange system. And as a result of these trends in exports and capital flows, gross foreign exchange reserves mounted from $251 million at the end of September 1968 to over $3 billion at the end of 1972 (and to over $6 billion at the end of 1973). It is not possible to divorce the effects of the exchange rate system from the many measures in the domestic and foreign areas, the export expansion program, and the investment boom which started in 1967. Nevertheless the trotting peg exchange rate system played a key role in promoting exports and attracting foreign investments, both in terms of direct economic costs and benefits and in terms of stimulating foreign confidence in the Brazilian financial policies and prospects. The combination of these measures has resulted in a large and continuing balance of payments surplus which in turn has been the major source of the monetary expansion, as shown in Chapter IV.

---

[36]The government has not officially announced the specific criteria for determining the rate changes but various public officials have mentioned these as the most significant criteria.

Export Expansion and Diversification Program. No sector of the Brazilian economy was more profoundly affected by the economic policies of the post-revolutionary governments than the export sector. In distinct contrast with the previous focus on import substitution industrialization as the leading growth sector, the experts of the military governments emphasized the need for an agressive policy of expansion and diversification of exports, not as the leading sector, but as one of several leading sectors in the revival of economic growth.

Despite the stagnation of Brazilian exports during the decade prior to 1964 and the pessimistic outlook for exports embodied in the prevailing Prebisch doctrine, the Castello Branco economists placed their confidence in export expansion as a major growth sector. To achieve the export expansion targets, they drew upon the entire gamut of measures, including (a) realistic exchange rate; (b) rationalization of export procedures;[37] (c) exemption from the value-added, stamp, and federal excise taxes; (d) drawback from taxes previously paid (income and customs)—this was initiated in April 1961 but rarely used because of bureaucratic obstacles; (e) export financing through the foreign exchange department of the Bank of Brazil (SUMOC 278 and 279, dated 9 October 1964); (f) export guarantees; and (g) new credit lines with other Latin American countries.[38]

These were the plans. How well did they do in implementing them? We described earlier the exchange rate policy and the trend of real exchange rates. Regarding the remaining measures, it is safe to conclude that they were implemented with a fair degree of thoroughness if not dispatch. By July 1970 the incentives to export included (a) federal income tax exemption (Exporters of manufactured products were permitted to deduct export profits from taxable income.); (b) exemption from the federal excise tax (IPI) on manufactured goods; (c) state excise tax (ICM) exemption (This exemption was incorporated in the Federal Constitution of 24 January 1967.); (d) drawbacks or refunds, usually in the form of a tax credit of import duties on the imported components of exported products; (e) preferential financing of export sales and production for export.[39]

---

[37]At one count in 1965, there were thirty separate documents and an equal number of offices for approval of exports. By 1968 Central Bank President Ernani Galveas could boast that the exports could be delivered to the docks with one set of papers.

[38]Ministério do Planejamento, *Programa de Ação Econômica, pp. 131-133.*

[39]Joel Bergsman, "Foreign Trade Policy in Brazil," pp. 21-23. In his analysis of these export incentives, Dr. Bergsman concludes that "They have completely erased the earlier strong bias against exports; on the average, export sales are now roughly just as profitable as domestic sales. However, the average covers a wide range of variation among different products."

It is impossible to separate the effects on exports of these several incentives from the effects of the many other measures to stimulate domestic production of agricultural products, mining, and manufactures. The combined impact of these measure, however, has been dramatic, as can be seen by the rapid growth of non-coffee exports since 1964 (see Table VIII-9). Excluding coffee (which was not subject to the same exchange rates and other measures discussed here), exports of primary agricultural products in 1971 exceeded by three times the 1960-64 average, rising from 20 to 30 percent of total exports. Exports of manufactured products, which are even more directly influenced by the export measures, tripled between the 1960-64 average and 1967, and by 1971 were nine times the 1960-64 level. During the 1960-64 period exports of manufactured goods comprised less than 5 percent of total exports; by 1971 they comprised 20 percent of a much larger export level.

Export earnings from coffee rose only 15 percent between the 1960-64 average and 1971 (mostly due to improved prices), so that coffee earnings as a percent of total exports declined from 53 percent in 1960-64 to 26 percent in 1972.

Table VIII-9
BRAZILIAN NON-COFFEE EXPORTS, 1964–1972
(millions of US$)

Year	Total Exports	Non-Coffee Exports	Annual Percentage Increase	Non-Coffee Exports as % of Total Exports
1960–64 Average	1,344	630	—	47
1964	1,430	670	6.3%	47
1965	1,596	889	32.7	56
1966	1,741	968	8.9	56
1967	1,654	922	4.8	56
1968	1,881	1,084	17.6	58
1969	2,311	1,465	35.1	63
1970	2,739	1,758	20.0	64
1971	2,904	2.082	18.4	72
1972	3,991	2,934	40.8	74

[a]Estimated.

Source: *Boletim do Banco Central do Brasil*, June 1973, pp. 120-121.

Import Liberalization

The heavy pressure on imports in the face of an overvalued exchange rate and a shortage of foreign exchange did not permit the Brazilian authorities to consider import liberalization measures in their 1964-66 Action Program. Imports had remained at $1.2 billion for the previous four years and, given the import pressures, no reduction from that level seemed imminent. Their projections for 1965 and 1966 assumed imports to grow in proportion to GNP at 6 percent per year, reaching $1.4 billion in 1965 and $1.5 billion in 1966.[40] The $200 million decline in imports in 1964 from the $1.2 billion level served only to provide welcome relief from the persistent foreign exchange pressures. Not until the 1965 import figures became available, with the lowest import bill since 1950, did the authorities begin to consider seriously the need for tariff reductions. At $941 million the 1965 import level fell short of the projected level by more than $450 million. Despite a recovery in 1966 the import level in that year still remained $200 million below the targeted level of $1.5 billion.

Examination of the causes of the decline in imports in 1964 and 1965 and the slow rate of recovery thereafter revealed that all the major components of imports had shared in the decline, including capital goods, intermediate goods, and consumer goods, and that these declines stemmed primarily from the general stagnation in the domestic economy. Recovery of the economy, therefore, was essential to restoration of the level of imports, but merely to restore the previous level was not enough.

Two additional considerations bore on import policy: the stress on exports as a leading sector in the economic recovery program, and the renewed large inflow of foreign capital. Export expansion as a major target of economic policy meant that imports would also have to increase in some comparable proportion or Brazil would wind up as a net exporter of resources (goods and service) and as a net foreign investor. Such a development made no sense for a country whose objective was to maximize its rate of economic growth. The renewed interest of the developed countries and international institutions in extending loans and concessional aid to Brazil added another important factor. With these additional resources import policy could seek to achieve not merely a balance in the current account, but a deficit large enough to permit the transfer of real resources into Brazil.

The current account surpluses in 1964 to 1966 and the long-term capital inflows served a useful function in permitting Brazil to pay off

---

[40]Ministério do Planejamento, *Programa de Ação Econômica*, p. 134.

its short-term obligations and restore its foreign exchange reserve position to an adequate level, but they also served to aggravate domestic inflationary pressures. A larger volume of imports would have been useful during these years as an anti-inflationary measure. In the longer term a relatively larger volume of imports and a current account deficit are essential if foreign savings are to contribute to Brazilian economic growth.

Recognizing the need for higher level of imports, the Brazilian authorities took a series of steps in 1965 and 1966 to reduce the costs of imports, but did reduce tariffs. Import surcharges and the interest cost of compulsory deposits and guarantee deposits were reduced in five successive steps from January 1965 to April 1966. The special-category commodities were transferred to the general category between January and November 1966 and the special-category was eliminated in March 1967 by Central Bank Resolution 41. Despite these measures imports failed to respond adequately. In mid-1966 Ministers Campos and Bulhões instructed a special committee under the chairmanship of José Vilar de Queiroz, economic advisor to the Planning Ministry, to formulate a program for tariff reductions. Within a few weeks the Queiroz Committee had recommendations for a complete revision of tariff rates. These recommendations were approved by the Brazilian Congress, Law 37 of November 1966, effective March 1967.

The general reduction in the tariff structure in March 1967, the elimination of import surcharges and advance deposits for imports, and the elimination of the special category constituted "a dramatic and sweeping liberalization" of imports over the three years 1964 to 1967.[41] These measures cut the average tariff rates plus exchange premiums by one-third of the 1964 level, and "when allowance is made for devaluation relative to domestic prices, the ratio of the price index of potential imports to the price index for domestic substitutes is now less than two-thirds of 1964." [42] Moreover, the tariff reductions of 1967 constituted a marked narrowing in the spread of protection among different commodities. . . . In 1964 the differential between the most protected fifth and the least protected fifth was a minimum of 200 percent and on up to 400 percent, whereas today it is as little as 30 percent and on up to 100 percent. This means that the price advantage given to the most favored producers over other producers has been sharply narrowed, though the remaining differentials ought still to be sufficient for an instrument of industrialization

---

[41] Paul G. Clark, "Brazilian Import Liberalization," p. 1.
[42] Ibid.

policy.[43] Put into effect in March 1967, just at the time of the change in governments, the new tariff structure contributed to the 10 percent increase in imports in that year and, together with the investment boom set off in 1968, to the 29 percent increase in 1968, the highest level in Brazil's history (10 percent higher than the exceptional levels of 1951 and 1952. Most important, these increases in imports turned the current account surpluses of the three previous years to fairly large deficits, permitting a net transfer of resources and foreign savings into Brazil.

In December 1968 the trend toward import liberalization suffered a reversal because of concern about the 29 percent increase in imports in 1968, the more nationalistic tendencies of the Costa e Silva government, and the recognition that the across-the-board cuts had created some inequities in the tariff structure.[44] Table 13 gives a fairly reasonable view of the impact of the increase in tariffs, relative to the pre-1966 and the 1967-68 levels in terms of net product protection. In terms of "effective protection" Dr. Bergsman concluded that the December 1968 tariff increases "restored the net effectiveness protection too close to the levels in effect before the March 1967 reforms."[45]

Despite this reversal toward greater protection, imports continued upward in 1969 and 1970. Whether Brazilian import policy was excessively restrictive during these years depends upon an over-all assessment of the balance of payments. In view of the significance of the import constraint on the Brazilian economic development, the import policy and trend of imports cannot be divorced from the trend of export earnings described earlier, and net foreign capital flows, a discussion of which now follows.

Foreign Investment Policy. Brazilian businessmen had become increasingly concerned during the 1950s about the extensive foreign investments in industry. Although they had been generally opposed to the economic ideologies of the Goulart government, Brazilian industrialists did not necessarily object to the restrictions on foreign investment imposed by such measures as the Profit Remittance Law. This negative attitude to foreign investment placed economists of the Castello Branco government in a somewhat ambivalent position. On the one hand they recognized that foreign capital and technology were essen-

---

[43]Ibid.

[44]Bergsman traces the trend of net product protection from 1966 to 1967 in his "Foreign Trade Policy," p. 42.

[45]Ibid., p. 38. The "effective protection" concept measures "the tariff on the product relative to the price at which the product can be purchased from abroad, the effect or value-added tariff regulates the domestic value added in the production process relative to the value added in the process in the absence of protection."

Table VIII-10

BRAZIL'S BALANCE OF PAYMENTS, 1964–1972
(millions of US$)

	1964	1965	1966	1967	1968	1969	1970	1971	1972
Merchandise exports, fob	1,430	1,596	1,741	1,654	1,881	2,311	2,739	2,882	3,990
Merchandise imports, fob	−1,086	−941	−1,303	−1,441	−1,855	−1,993	−2,507	−3,245	−4,200
Trade balance	344	655	438	213	26	318	232	−363	−210
Net interest and dividends	−132	−175	−199	−258	−231	−261	−353	−420	−480
Other services and donations	−73	−113	−187	−193	−250	−338	−441	−524	−720
Current account balance	*139*	*367*	*52*	*−238*	*−508*	*−281*	*−562*	*−1,307*	*−1,410*
Gross capital inflow	359	299	470	471	934	1,374	1,839	2,696	4,910
Amortization	−277	−304	−350	−444	−484	−524	−824	−850	−1,100
Capital account balance	*82*	*−5*	*120*	*27*	*450*	*850*	*1,015*	*1,846*	*3,810*
Errors and omissions	−217	−31	−19	−34	37	−20	92	−9	
Net changes in reserves	*4*	*331*	*153*	*−245*	*32*	*549*	*545*	*530*	*2,400*
Level of gross foreign exchange reserves, end of year	245	484	425	199	257	656	1,187	1,746	4,183

Source: *Boletim do Banco Central Do Brasil*, various issues.

tial to economic development; on the other, they knew that the development of a national entrepreneurial class competitive with foreign firms, not only in the domestic area but also in the export sector, was also essential to growth, and that Brazilian business was a major source of political support. As a result, modification of the Profit Remittance Law proved to be more difficult than anticipated. Even simplification of investment and loan registration procedures and elimination of bureaucratic bottlenecks to foreign investments faced their ups and downs, depending upon who was assigned to implement them. The one positive measure to stimulate foreign private investment was the Investment Guarantee Agreement with the United States.

The combination of the stagnant investment opportunities related to a stagnant economy and the uncertainty about the official position on foreign investments resulted in a net outflow of private capital during 1964 and 1965. The private capital inflow did not pick up significantly until 1968 when the economy had resumed the high growth rates typical of the 1950s.

Table VIII-11 shows the net flow of private capital for investment and working capital purposes from 1956 to 1972. The explanation for the seemingly unjustified inclusion of swaps and Instruction 289 transactions with direct private investments and 4131 funds in this table is the serious problem of distinguishing private investments from short-term capital movements. A significant part of both the swap and the Instruction 289 transactions must be considered as part of direct private investments, Both were used primarily by Brazilian subsidiaries or branches of foreign companies as a source of working capital. Both offered significant financial incentives, and, registered as short-term, opportunities to pull out in the event of political disturbances. The financial incentives of these operations relative to direct investments were several: (a) they were not subject to the 15 percent tax on new capitalization; (b) interest payments on these instruments were deductible for income tax purposes; and (c) they avoided the ceiling on profit remittances.[46] Finally, both the swap and the Instruction 289 transactions offered the inducement of short-term gains from speculation in the exchange rate movements.[47] A final piece of evidence that swaps

---

[46]There was no absolute ceiling on the remittance of profits, but the graduated remittance tax made it an effective ceiling.

[47]The Instruction 289 flows during 1967 and 1968 reveal the extent of the speculation. During the final months of 1967 Instruction 289 contracts were liquidated heavily as an exchange devaluation became imminent. Following the devaluation on 4 January 1968, these funds came back to Brazil, with a net inflow of $182 million for the year, following a net outflow of $82 million in 1967. Because of these speculative movements around the exchange rate changes it would be more appropriate to average the 1967-68 flows to arrive at a figure for private capital flows in these two years. The flexible exchange rate implemented in August 1968 has elimininated this particular problem.

Table VIII-11
NET FLOW OF PRIVATE CAPITAL
FOR INVESTMENT AND WORKING CAPITAL, 1956–1972
(millions of US$)

End of Year	Swaps (net)	Instruction 289 (net)	Resolution 63	Law 4131	Direct Foreign Investment (net)	Total
1956	−20	—	—	—	89	69
1957	20	—	—	—	143	163
1958	−30	—	—	—	110	80
1959	115	—	—	—	124	239
1960	47	—	—	—	99	146
1961	73	—	—	—	108	181
1962	47	—	—	—	69	116
1963	−30	—	—	—	30	—
1964	−51	—	—	—	28	−23
1965	−190	137	—	—	70	17
1966	−12	124	—	—	74	186
1967	−99	−82[a]	41	—	76	−64[a]
1968	−12	182	244	—	61	475
1969	—	13	148	273[b]	124	553
1970	—	7	220	451	108	756
1971	—	−86	330	665	124	1,133
1972	—	−88	1,035	1,388	337	2,672

[a] Reflects exchange rate speculation.
[b] Estimated.
Source: Banco Central do Brasil, annual reports.

and Instuction 289 might preferably be considered as private investment is the relative stability of the total amount of these transactions
over the years. Swaps outstanding at the end of 1963, for example,
totalled $364 million; by 1969 they were completely replaced by In-
struction 289, which were valued at $374 million. The Instruction 289
transactions would have been higher at the end of 1969 had not the
monetary authorities limited the amount.[48] With limitations on the
volume of Instruction 289 transactions, there was a sharp increase in
the demand for Resolution 63 transactions, which as noted, increased

[48]Concerned about the growing level of the short-term debt, the authorities decided to
place a ceiling on the amount of debt falling due on any given month. Once this limit
had been reached, new registrations of Instruction 289 were approved only with longer
maturities. By 1972 the new registrations carried maturities of seven years, compared
with the one-year maturities that had prevailed earlier.

in volume from $41 million at the end of 1969, when these operations too came under similar limitations as to maturities.

Development Assistance. Prior to 1964 Brazil had received relatively little development assistance from the major international and national financial lending agencies. Brazil had financed its import requirements in part through direct private investment, but primarily with short-term credits and compensatory financing—a euphemism for debt rescheduling. International lending agencies had contributed more through the series of debt consolidations and reschedulings of 1953, 1961, and 1964 than they had through loans. The 1964-66 Action Program created a new air of confidence that the necessary economic reforms would be undertaken. But an examination of the actual capital inflows reveals that only the United States Agency for International Development and the Inter-American Development Bank had sufficient confidence and inventiveness to invest any capital in Brazil during the critical years immediately after 1964.

The World Bank Group (the IBRD and the IFC) gave an expression of confidence with large loan authorizations in 1965 and 1966 but their preparations were too slow and their operations too cautious. During the first five years after the 1964 Action Program these institutions reduced by $15 million their outstanding loans to Brazil. Due to the lag between the initial authorization and actual disbursements, disbursements on World Bank loans did not exceed loan repayments until 1967, and did not reach a significant amount until 1969. The net flow of capital to Brazil (loan disbursements less repayments) averaged less than $100 million during 1964 to 1967, but picked up rapidly in 1968 and the following years.

Over the years Eximbank has been Brazil's major source of long-term financing. At the end of 1963 Eximbank held in its portfolio loans of about $700 million which constituted about 20 percent of the total Brazilian debt estimated at $3.3 billion. Incidentally, this was also about 25 percent of Eximbank's total loan portfolio. About two thirds of the Eximbank's loans, or $466 million, had been granted to Brazil as a consequence of the 1953 and 1961 debt reschedulings and were used to pay off previously incurred commercial arrears and other forms of short-term borrowing. With 20 percent of the outstanding Brazilian debt, Eximbank president Harold Linder understandably was concerned about the bank's excessive exposure in a country with Brazil's record of economic and political instability. Following the 1964 rescheduling, Eximbank embarked on a course of reducing its Brazil portfolio. The net outflow during the next six years totalled $200 million, of which $68 million were repayments on project loans and $132 million were repayments on compensatory financing. In 1967 in recognition of Brazil's economic recuperation, Eximbank began to increase its loan authorizations, but disbursements did not exceed loan repayments until 1971.

Only two institutions, the Inter-American Development Bank (IDB) and USAID, both instruments of Alliance for Progress, accepted the huge risks in providing the large amounts of capital needed to support the economic reforms of the Castello Branco government. The IDB had been expanding its loans to Brazil at a fairly rapid pace since its founding in 1961; its annual rate of disbursements continued steadily upward from $35 million in 1964 to $64 million in 1967 while repayments on the relatively new loans remained low. To keep its capital moving into Brazil during these crucial years of the early 1960s the IDB extended, according to severe critics, some loans for rather risky and perhaps unjustifiable ventures. On the other hand, the continued capital flow from the IDB served to stimulate investments in a stagnant economy and to provide needed foreign exchange—to the extent that the loans included local cost financing—at a time when other major sources of capital, with the exception of USAID, were pulling out of Brazil.

USAID, the bilateral economic assistance arm of the U.S. government, reacted quickly to support the economic reform program of the Castello Branco government. Brazilian balance of payments data already showed a net inflow from USAID in 1965 of $147 million and an accumulated total of $488 million for the four years from 1964 to 1967. The program loan, a loan concept included in the 1961 AID legislation to provide overall balance of payments support to sound economic programs, was the main instrument of development assistance. These figures do not include about $150 million in Public Law 480 agricultural credit sales, which are repayable in cruzeiros, grants of Public Law 480 foodstuffs, and technical assistance grants. During these critical four years, AID provided over 80 percent of the net inflow of long-term capital. By the end of 1967 AID had come close to replacing Eximbank's position as Brazil's largest creditor, with about 17 percent of the total registered Brazilian debt.

Table VIII-12 summarizes the capital flows to Brazil during the years from 1964 to 1967 and from 1968 to 1971. In sharp contrast with the pre-1964 years long-term credits comprised the largest form of financing. The net inflow of $1.6 billion in long-term credits and $1.8 billion of medium-term loans and supply credits permitted Brazil to repay more than $450 million in compensatory financing and to restore its position in the IMF. This expanded flow of long-term capital also helped Brazil to restructure its foreign debt from excessive reli-

Table VIII-12

NET CAPITAL FLOWS TO BRAZIL,

1964–1971

(millions of US$)

	1964–1967	1968–1971	1964–1971
Net long-term loans	594	1,052	1,646
U.S. AID	488[a]	435	923
Export-Import Bank of U.S.	−46	50	4
Inter-American Development Bank	172	266	438
World Bank	−30	188	158
International Finance Corp.	10	15	25
Other official sources	—	98	98
Net medium-term credits[b].............	66	1,745	1,811
Net short-term credits[c]	−201	917	716
Net compensatory financing[d]			
International Monetary Fund			
Drawings outstanding	−29	−138	−167
Other net capital flows	—	−26	−26
Net capital flows	354	3,169	3,523

[a]Excludes about $150 million of local currency repayable PD-480 credits.

[b]Suppliers' credits and Law 4131 credits.

[c]Bank credits, commercial arrears, swap transactions, Instruction 289 and Resolution 63 transactions.

[d]Credits rescheduled in 1961 and 1964.

Source: Prepared on basis of Central Bank debt reports for December 31, 1969, 1970 and 1971 and extrapolated back to 1963 on basis of balance of payments data.

ance on short-term sources to a more balanced debt position, to improve its capacity to service outstanding debt, and to restore its international credit worthiness and all that that means for the stimulation of private sources of investment and capital.

Foreign Debt Burden. The increased flow of long-term capital from USAID and the IDB between 1964 and 1971 permitted the Brazilian authorities to undertake a fundamental transformation in the maturity structure of the foreign debt. By the end of 1971 the Brazilian foreign debt stood at $6,870 million, about twice the level at the time of the 1964 revolution (see Table VIII-13).[49] At the same time, the composi-

[49]The first exhaustive compilation of the Brazilian foreign debt was made on 31 December 1969. Previous data on the Brazilian debt were estimates based upon only partial registrations. To obtain an idea of the trend of the foreign debt one must rely on the balance sheets of the foreign lending institutions and backward extrapolation of balance of payments data, which has been done in compiling the tables in this study.

Table VIII-13

MATURITY STRUCTURE OF BRAZIL'S FOREIGN DEBT,
December 1963 and December 1971

(millions of US$)

Maturity of Debt	December 1963		December 1971		Change
Long term[a]...........	919	28.9%	2,531[e]	36.8%	1,612
Medium term[b]........	949	29.8	2,760	40.2	1,811
Short term[c]...........	562[c,d]	17.7	1,278[f]	18.6	716
Compensatory financing[d].........	758	23.8	301	4.4	−457
Total	3,188	100.0	6,870[g]	100.0	3,690
IMF drawings outstanding	167	—	—	—	−167
Total debt, plus IMF .	3,347	—	6,870	—	3,523

[a]Includes debt held by the IDB, IBRD, IFC, USAID, Eximbank, the German Kreditanstalt, the National Bank of Denmark, the external consolidated debt and diverse loans as the Brazilian Light Traction Group and those resulting from the expropriation of power and telephone service companies.

[b]Includes Law 4131 loans, excluding those due within a year (see f) and suppliers' credits.

[c]Includes identifiable items as commercial arrears, swaps and external bilateral agreement balances totalling $562 million. Much of the unidentified difference is explained by the delay in registration of foreign debt in 1963. Debt registrations were not brought up to date until 1968.

[d]Includes consolidated and rescheduled debts from 1961 and 1964, but excludes drawings outstanding from the IMF.

[e]Includes $196 million of cruzeiro repayable loans from the IDB. While not strictly a foreign loan, these loans do carry a maintenance-of-value clause so they retain their value in foreign exchange and can be used by the IDB as a substitute for foreign exchange in future loans.

[f]Includes Instruction 289, Resolution 63, $10 million of diverse credits and $173 million of Law 4131 loans due in 1970.

[g]Estimated on basis of balance-of-payments data and working backwards from the 1969 debt data.

Source: 1963 data:—*Relatório do Banco Central do Brasil*, 1965, p. 140; 1969 data—*Boletim do Banco Central do Brasil*, 1965, p. 140; 1969 data—*Boletim do Banco Central do Brasil*, July 1970, pp. 108-109.

tion of the debt had taken on a longer term aspect than in the earlier year. By the end of 1971 medium- and long-term loans comprised 77 percent of the total debt, compared with less than 59 percent six years earlier. About 23 percent of the 1969 debt involved short-term transactions (Instructions 289 and Resolution 63 transactions) and compensatory financing which had comprised 42 percent of the 1963 debt. The basic changes, then, in the Brazilian debt during the eight years from the 1964 revolution to the end of 1971 were, on the one hand, a doubling of the total debt, and on the other, a move toward longer maturities.

What are the consequences of these changes for Brazil's capacity to service its existing debts and take on the additional debts needed to finance the continuing current account deficits? Can Brazil afford its 1971 debt and, if so, can it afford to take on additional debt? What are the prospects for another of the financial crises which periodically plagued Brazil in the 1950s and the early 1960s? The answer to these questions resides, not in the total level and structure of the debt, but in five trends: the trend of annual debt service (both principal and interest,) on existing and new debt; the adequacy of foreign exchange reserves; the trend of export earnings; the availabilities and terms of foreign capital; and finally, the trend of the Brazilian economy. My assessment of all these trends concerning the Brazilian capacity to service existing debt and take on additional debt is favorable.

The most immediate considerations in assessing the debt service capacity of a country are the level of foreign exchange reserves (which is discussed in the next section), the trend of exports, and the ratio of debt service to export earnings or the debt service ratio.

Table VIII-14

BRAZIL'S DEBT SERVICE RATIO, 1963–1972

(millions of US$)

Year	Amortization of Debt	Interest Payments	Total Debt Service	Exports of Goods and Services	Debt Service Ratio (total debt service as % of exports)
1963	364	90	454	1,502	30.2
1964	277	133		1,548	
1965	304	166	470	1,757	26.7
1966	350	162		1,882	
1967	444	202	646	1,839	35.1
1968	484	154		2,086	
1969	493	204	697	2,601	26.8
1970	672	284	956	3,117	30.7
1971[a]	850	302	1,152	3,325	34.6
1972[b]	1,100	360	1,460	4,100	35.6

[a]Preliminary.
[b]Estimate.

Source: *Boletim do Banco Central do Brasil*, December 1972, Publicação Especial, pp. 6-13. For earlier years, see Table 7, p. 360. 1971 and 1972 data — *Conjuntura Econômica*, February 1973, p. 58.

Table VIII-14 traces the trend of the debt service ratio from 1963 to 1971. As of 1971 approximately one out of every three dollars earned by Brazilian exporters is being used to finance previously incurred debt. This heavy debt burden contributed to the recurring financial crises in the years from 1960 to 1964. By 1969, with the help of current account surpluses from 1964 to 1966 and the lengthening maturity of the debt, the debt service ratio had declined to 26.8 percent, still a high level when compared with most other developing countries. In 1970 the debt service ratio began to move upwards again as a consequence of the voluminous inflow of private foreign capital. The significance of this high debt service depends upon a deeper analysis of the nature of the debt, quality of debt management on the part of the Brazilian authorities, and the effectiveness of policies to expand export earnings. After fifteen years of stagnation, Brazilian export earnings reacted favorably to the export promotion program of the post-1964 governments, increasing about 170 percent in the ensuing eight years. Given the continuing emphasis on export expansion in Brazilian government policies, the prospects for continuing the export growth are good. The trend toward higher growth rates in the Brazilian economy since 1967 also augurs well for the Brazilian debt service capacity. The faster Brazil grows, the easier it will be to generate the domestic savings eventually necessary to substitute for foreign savings (that is, a current account surplus).

The renewed interest of the World Bank (with a $1 billion loan program extending over a five-year period) and Eximbank in extending loans to Brazil should permit a continued high level of long-term capital inflow for the coming years.[50] These loans, together with the loans of IDB and other official sources, offer the Brazilian authorities an opportunity to extend further the average maturities of the Brazilian foreign debt. Another significant development affecting the Brazilian debt structure and debt service capacity is the active control by the Brazilian Central Bank over the composition and maturities of the debt. Central Bank Director Paulo Pereira Lira strengthened control over the debt through limiting the amount scheduled for repayment at any given date. This is a key element in Brazilian debt policy, for the foreign debt has not been excessive, even in 1961 and 1964, in terms of the Brazilian GNP and capacity to repay over a longer period; the periodic financial crises have always arisen as a result of the short-term nature of the debt, as in December 1960 when commercial arrears and short term obligations comprised 43 percent of the total debt. By limiting the amount of foreign debt repayments scheduled for any given month,

---

[50] In 1968 the World Bank announced a $1 billion program over five years; in 1971 the Bank gave evidence of having doubled the annual commitment level.

Director Lira is inducing the foreign creditors and Brazilian borrowers to extend their maturities and, more importantly, in so doing is reducing the possibilities of a renewed foreign exchange crisis arising from a mass flight of short-term money.

Adequacy of Reserves. The surplus on the Brazilian balance of payments permitted the Brazilian authorities not only to reduce their short-term and compensatory liabilities, but also to increase the level of foreign exchange reserves. Gross foreign exchange reserves, which stood at $72 million at the end of 1963, increased to an estimated $4183 million at the end of 1972, a net increase of over $3 billion.[51] The trend of reserves relative to Brazil's import requirements is traced in Table VIII-15.

The adequacy of foreign exchange reserves to maintain debt service and essential import requirements during a period of decline in export earnings or capital inflow is normally stated in terms of import requirements measured in months. In these terms, Brazilian gross foreign exchange reserves at the end of 1972, about nine months' imports, exceeded the reserve levels of most developing countries and many industrial nations. And in terms of the trend, the 1972 figures were a tremendous improvement over the two weeks' import level of December 1963. Balanced against this favorable level and trend of reserves is the high degree of fluctuation in Brazilian export earnings and capital flows. In 1962, for example, export earnings dropped $241 million, or by 16 percent, as a consequence of a poor harvest. Despite a more active export policy after 1964, exports also declined in 1967 but by a smaller amount, for the same reason. Dependent as it is on primary exports for a large percentage of its export earnings, Brazil needs a higher than average level of reserves. The possibilities of capital flight also indicate a need for a higher than average level of reserves for Brazil. The $5.5 billion of capital registered in the form of Instruction 289 and Resolution 63 and Law 4131 funds, even though a large portion is needed for working capital purposes, presents an ever-present threat of a drain of reserves in the event of domestic crisis. This can be moderated in part by domestic credit policy, but a higher level of reserves is needed to forestall a crisis initiated through any run on reserves. Given the degree of fluctuation in Brazil's export earnings and the higher than average

---

[51]The IMF reports show Brazilian reserves in 1963 of $219 million, which includes gold holdings of $150 million. Central Bank reports reveal that $147 million of the gold holdings were held by foreign banks as guarantees for loans. A more accurate picture of the reserves available for use by the monetary authorities in 1963 is obtained by excluding this tied gold.

Table VIII-15
**FOREIGN EXCHANGE RESERVES AND IMPORT
REQUIREMENTS**
(millions of US$)

End of Year	Gross Reserves[a]	Imports[b]	Month's Import Requirements
1963	72	1,569	0.55
1964	157	1,330	1.4
1965	454	1,280	4.3
1966	425	1,703	3.0
1967	199	1,878	1.3
1968	257	2,378	1.3
1969	657	2,628	3.0
1970	1,187	3,297	4.3
1971	1,746	4,181	5.0
1972	4,183	5,703	9.0

[a]Gross reserves (the IMF concept as included in the IFS, less gold holdings included in IMF gross reserve concept but held by foreign banks as guarantee for loans) amounted to $147 million in 1963, $88 million in 1964, $30 million in 1965.
[b]Imports of goods and services; factor payments not included.
Source: *Relatório do Banco Central do Brasil*, 1965, 1968, p. 124, and 1969, p. 127; International Monetary Fund, *International Financial Statistics*.

risks of short-term capital flight, Brazil should preferably maintain reserves above six months' import requirements, which at the 1972 level of imports would be $2.9 billion. Two arguments against this relatively high level of reserves are that Brazil can ill afford to maintain idle deposits abroad in the face of its own immense need for resources, and that development aid of a concessional nature cannot be justified to a country which maintains such a high level of reserves.[52] A realistic argument in support of a high level of reserves is the confidence they inspire in Brazil' debt service capacity. International bankers and investors, like small town bankers, prefer to lend to those who have money. A few billion dollars in deposits in New York and European banks and a clear account at the IMF provide an immeasurable degree of confidence in Brazil's financial situation.[53]

[52]The deposits need not be idle. In 1969 an increasing portion of Brazilian reserves were invested in Euro-dollar deposits earning 8 percent or more interest.
[53]In addition, since 1963 Brazil has repaid outstanding drawings from the IMF so that $262 million of drawing rights were available in the event of an unforeseen decline in export earnings.

With this confidence, the Brazilian authorities can afford to choose among the alternative sources of finance ready to bestow their capital on Brazil. Without this confidence, they would be running to Washington, London, and Paris with their hands out, as in 1953, 1960, and 1963.

Assessment of Foreign Exchange and Trade Policy

Brazilian experience of the 1960's provides an object lesson in the consequences, both favorable and unfavorable, of trade and exchange policy. During the periods both before and after 1964, Brazil used trade policy as an active instrument for stimulating investment and economic growth. In both periods efforts were made to maximize foreign savings, albeit by divergent approaches: in the early years by inducing disequilibrium and, in the later years, through equilibrium in the balance of payments. In terms of objectives, the major divergence between the two periods lies in the treatment of exports. The policies of the earlier years neglected exports while in the later years export expansion became an essential part of the economic reform program. The Brazilian experience has shown that a developing country can expand its export earnings, given sound policies and persistence. Persistence is perhaps a key element here because the results are not immediate, as shown by the case of Brazil, which required four years of innovative effort.

The Brazilian experience also reveals that developing countries have a larger number and variety of policy options in pursuing trade policy than do the industrial countries. The industrial countries are confronted with limitations in their use of tariff policy, exchange rate policy, and even export incentives through their participation in international agreements and institutions such as the General Agreement on Tariffs and Trade (GATT) and the International Monetary Fund (IMF). Developing countries have a greater degree of flexibility in the use of these instruments. which they should not overlook. The Brazilian experiences reveal the potential effectiveness of these instruments in maximizing economic growth without encountering the traditional constraints.

Four sets of trade and investment policy instruments including tariff policy, exchange rate policy, export policy, and investment policy are available to developing countries in pursuit of a variety of policy objectives. These four instruments can be adopted flexibly in pursuit of their development objectives. The Brazilian experience has also revealed some significant constraints on the use of these policy instruments: the transfer constraint, the elasticities constraint, the constraint imposed by the availability of foreign capital, and the foreign retaliation constraint. The transfer constraint is determined by the level of foreign savings, or the net inflow of goods and services which can be sustained over time.[54] Excessive use of exchange devaluations, export incentives, and tariff policies quickly push up against the transfer constraint, as experienced by the Castello Branco government from 1964 to 1967 when Brazil ran large current account surpluses, or net foreign dissaving. Less aggressive use of exchange devaluations and more rapid action to liberalize the restrictive import structure would have been of immeasurable benefit in reducing the inflationary pressures during those difficult years. On the other hand, inadequate exchange devaluation and export incentives may just as readily lead to a level of foreign savings which cannot be sustained, because of the unavailability of foreign capital to fill the gap.

The elasticities constraint is determined by the elasticities of supply and demand for Brazilian exports and imports. Excessive concern about the inelastic demand for coffee led Brazilian authorities in the 1950s to pursue an overvalued exchange rate policy, to the detriment of other potential Brazilian exports. In more recent years Brazil has shown that a combination of export taxes for coffee and export incentives for price elastic commodities can be an effective means of stimulating exports while limiting the domestic impact of excessive incomes in the coffee sector. Brazilian experience also provides clear evidence that the demand for primary products is not as price inelastic as the doctrines of the 1950s held them to be.

The foreign capital constraint is determined in part, but not entirely, by the debt service capacity of a country which is, in turn, a function essentially of the level and trend of export earnings. The stagnation of exports during the 1950s reduced Brazil's debt service capacity, and in so doing, gradually closed the doors of the international and national lending agencies and forced Brazil to rely more and more on short term financing which served only to intensify the need for more capital. In contrast, the growth of export earnings since 1964 has been accompanied by increasing inflows of long-term capital, initially by AID and the IDB, and later by the IBRD, the Eximbank and private foreign institutions. Thus, the more Brazil pushes exports and narrows the foreign savings gap, the more foreign capital becomes available. In turn, the more foreign capital, the less Brazil has to pursue an aggressive export promotion policy to finance

---

[54]The concepts of resource transfer, which excludes transfer payments, and of net foreign disinvestment, which is equated with current account deficit or net foreign savings, are also frequently used to express the same idea.

its imports. These trends, which built up in 1969 and 1970, have created another policy constraint, that is, the inflationary impact of large capital inflows not accompanied by an increase in imports.

Brazil did not experience the foreign retaliation constraint in its aggressive pursuit of export promotion policies during the 1960s, but continued aggressive pursuance of exchange devaluations and export incentives is very likely to raise the issue of competitive devaluation. To offset this line of attack Brazil can fall back on the purchasing power parity theory and show that the devaluations in recent years have not kept up with domestic inflation. Excluded from the exchange rate and price data, however, are the substantial benefits to exports received from the many tax exemptions, drawbacks, subsidized credit, and other incentives. Critics of the trotting peg exchange rate system also state that if all countries pursued the same approach, Brazil would derive no benefit from it. Such criticisms, whether valid or not, are likely to stimulate various forms of retaliation against Brazilian exports, should they continue to grow at the 20 percent pace of the late 1960s and early 1970s.

Within the limits of these constraints, an optimum policy mix would seem to be aggressive use of exchange rate policy and export incentives to stimulate exports and to achieve a sustainable level of foreign savings, that is, current account deficit. Foreign investment policy, to include debt management and reserve policies, would be coordinated with exchange rate and tariff policies to maximize the sustainable level of the current account deficit. Tariff policy would be directed primarily at influencing the import product mix, to achieve the degree of protection necessary to stimulate investments in priority sectors. The Brazilian experience provides evidence that this policy mix can be effective in promoting a rapid rate of economic growth on a sustainable basis while maintaining equilibrium in the balance of payments.

CHAPTER IX

The Crisis in Agriculture

> Once there are investment opportunities and efficient incentives, farmers everywhere will turn sand into gold.
>
> T. W. Schultz
> *Transforming Traditional Agriculture*

> All studies and surveys connected to the causes of the relative backwardness of Brazilian agriculture, of its low productivity and of the depressed condition of the rural populations, lead inevitably to the identification of its origin within the country's deficient agrarian structure . . . the absurd and anti-economic distribution of land . . . which stands as the most serious obstacle to a rational improvement that might afford production the flexibility exacted by the process of development of our domestic economy, made necessary by the rapid population growth.
>
> Estados Unidos do Brasil
> *Three-Year Plan for Economic*
> *and Social Development, 1963-65*

Stagnant productivity and a low growth rate of Brazilian agricultural output contrasted sharply with the high productivity and rapid growth of industrial production during the decade prior to 1961. These diverging trends created a supply crisis in the Brazilian economy which contributed significantly to the hyper-inflation, overall economic stagnation, and near international bankruptcy persisting through the mid-1960s. The quotations above reflect two extreme reactions to the problem of deficient agricultural output and productivity. Are price incentives alone sufficient to induce needed investments in agriculture? Or can the problem be solved by a more equitable distribution of land, by rural education, by agricultural research, or by other structural reform? The answer in any given case depends upon the diagnosis of the problem and its causes.

Perhaps the most controversial of Brazilian economic policies in recent years has been the diagnosis and policy response to agriculture. Success in achieving high rates of industrial and overall economic growth rates during the 1950s tended to divert the attention of Brazilian economic authorities from the growing imbalance in the agricultural sector. Aside from coffee, agriculture received no special attention in the development strategy pursued during the 1950s. On the contrary, the entire range of policy instruments, fiscal, monetary, foreign exchange and trade, and pricing policies, tended to subsidize industrial investments at the cost of agriculture. The existence of a growing crisis in agricultural production and productivity was not recognized until the supply shortage of 1962. The response of the Goulart government to this crisis was a land reform program.

Agricultural policies in the post-1964 years were characterized by the same emphasis on the market mechanism and innovative trial and error process which characterized other economic policy areas. The economists of the Castello Branco government diagnosed the slow growth rate in agriculture as the consequence of erroneous government policies and responded with a mix of policies aimed at restoring market incentives for agricultural production and export. First priority was given to the gradual reduction and eventual elimination of controls on food prices, elimination of quantitative export restrictions, and provision of a more favorable exchange rate for exports, overwhelmingly agricultural in origin. In the short term these policies tended to put an upward pressure on food prices, thus reinforcing existing inflationary pressures and complicating the stabilization efforts. The second phase consisted of a new set of measures, including a minimum price support program, a rural credit program and an input subsidy program, essentially for fertilizer and tractors. These special programs had only a marginal impact on agricultural output compared with the macro-economic policies which restored the price incentive to investment, production, and export of agricultural commodities.

Agricultural Policies to 1964

Success in achieving high rates of industrial and overall economic growth rates during the postwar years diverted the attention of Brazilian authorities from the growing imbalance in the agricultural sector. During the 1950s agricultural output increased at an annual average rate of about 4 percent, which was slightly above the rate of increase in population. But the aggregate growth rates of agricultural output tended to conceal the growing structural imbalance both within agriculture itself and between agriculture and other sectors of the economy. Agricultural output in the older coastal regions stagnated, with a decline in productivity per person and per hectare. Declining agricultural incomes in these regions encouraged the workers to migrate to the cities, where income levels were three to four times higher, and to newer and more productive areas in the interior. The rapid urbanization, industrialization, and rising incomes created new and shifting demands for agricultural products which traditional techniques were not equipped to satisfy.

The prevailing economic ideologies of the 1950s tended to reinforce the Brazilian authorities in their neglect of agriculture as the industrial road to economic development was preached from the academic podium and international credits were readily available for industry but not for agriculture. The major exception to the general neglect of agriculture was coffee. The problem of coffee was excessive, rather than insufficient, production, although coffee shared with agriculture the problem of stagnant productivity. The existence of a problem in agriculture was first recognized only after the supply crisis of 1962. The Goulart government attributed the deficiencies in the agricultural growth rate to structural factors, primarily the anti-economic distribution of land. Given this diagnosis, which is outlined in the Furtado Plan of 1962, the recommended cure was a land reform program, which became the key element in the Goulart government's development program.

During the 1950s the entire range of economic policy instruments, fiscal, monetary and credit, foreign exchange and trade, and pricing, tended to stimulate new investments in industry at the cost of agriculture. The highly overvalued exchange rate reduced the costs of imported capital goods and raw materials to the benefit of industry. At the same time it held down the cruzeiro return to exports, largely agricultural products, and the returns to the farmers did not rise proportionately to the increase in domestic costs. It is of note that the terms of trade between agricultural and industrial products turned against agriculture in 1953, the year in which the multiple exchange rate and overvalued rate policy was solidified. Finally, the overvalued exchange rate damaged the competitiveness of Brazilian agricultural exports in foreign markets and contributed to the stagnation of Brazilian exports. The net impact of the exchange rate policy was to tax the agricultural sector and subsidize the industrial sector, thus reducing incentives to investment in agriculture relative to industry. Because of the relatively high comparative advantage of Brazilian coffee, incentives to invest in coffee remained excessive even with the exchange confiscation.

Fiscal policy, as the major source of inflation, also served to tax agriculture. Inflation, combined with controls on agricultural prices, played a key role in the entire set of developments which served to extract forced savings from agriculture to finance industrialization. Monetary and credit policy instruments also contributed to the transfer of savings from agriculture to industry. The structure of the Brazilian banking system tended to channel credit to the industrial and service sectors rather than to the high risk agricultural sector. The National Economic Development Bank and the Bank of the Northeast provided addtional credit for industry. The only general program which tended to have a favorable impact on agriculture was the road building program. In opening access to the frontier the new roads provided an outlet for the growing population and an increase in agricultural production which was not forthcoming from the older regions. But as the production of foodstuffs and raw materials extended deeper into the interior, transportation costs inevitably raised prices to the increasingly urbanized east coast consumer.

The few programs designed specifically to improve agricultural incentives and output were not sufficiently effective to offset the adverse impact of the more general economic policies.[1] The minimum price guaranty program was never effective because, with prices rising at rates in excess of 25 percent per year, the floor price set for agricultural commodities was unrealistically low by the time the farmer sold his crops. The rural credit program was limited almost entirely to the financing of crop marketing, not for fixed investment or production loans. Much of the credit, it appears, went to middlemen to finance the movement of goods to market, or at times to withhold goods from the market pending further rises in prices.[2] Fi-

---

[1] George Edward Schuh, *The Agricultural Development of Brazil*. In his evaluation of Brazilian agricultural policies during the post-war period Schuh says that "although it has probably had some positive effect on the agricultural sector, it has most likely had less effect than the set of general economic development policies followed, which had other primary objectives. Most notable among these were the overvaluation of the currency and the prohibition or limitation of exports. The principal policy objective of the government prior to this was rapid industrialization. The set of policies used to attain this, involving principally import-substitution industrialization, discriminated rather heavily against the agricultural sector." (p. 293)

[2] Judith Tendler, "Agricultural Credit in Brazil," p. 5.

ly, the fertilizer subsidies benefited only about 5 percent of producers on farms and this was the larger and more advanced segment.[3]

Trends in Agricultural Output and Productivity—1947 to 1964

Agricultural performance can be measured in terms of total output, total output per capita, total output per capita real income, food production per capita, agricultural exports, productivity per hectare, and productivity per farm worker. Each of these measures of performance will be examined.

Brazilian agricultural output increased at an annual average rate of about 4 percent from 1947 to 1964.[4] This rate of growth would seem adequate to satisfy the needs of a population growing at a rate of about 3 percent per year. But the growth of agricultural output fell short of expectations when compared with the more rapid growth of industrial output, about 8 percent per year during this same period. U.S. Department of Agriculture studies (see Table IX-1) indicated that Brazil's agricultural output per capita compared unfavorably with the more rapidly growing countries, such as Mexico and Japan, as well as with the developed countries.

Brazil's agricultural performance also fell short of expectations when the growth of domestic income is taken into account. Per capita real income was growing in Brazil during the period 1950 to 1968 at an estimated compound rate of 2.3 percent per year. Assuming an income elasticity of demand of 0.5, domestic demand for agricultural output was rising at a compound rate of 4.2 percent, leaving a deficit in agricultural production of 0.4 percent per year. Yet these aggregative figures do not tell the whole story. If we examine the high protein foods, such as meat products, we find that the deficit in production is significantly greater.[5] Rising prices of these products relative to other prices were the first to attract the attention of the authorities, who reacted by imposing price controls and export restrictions in order to maintain the real income levels of the urban citizens. Price controls tended to aggravate the supply problem as the farmers refused to bring beef and other meat products to market at prices which failed to cover their costs.[6]

---

[3] Gordon Smith, "Agricultural Policy, 1950-1967," in Howard S. Ellis, ed., *The Economy of Brazil*, p. 238.

[4] We have divergent statistics on this point. The Getúlio Vargas Foundation data indicate 4.3 percent per year, while studies by USDA indicate a growth rate of 3.8 percent.

[5] Brazilian production of meat products was rising at an estimated 2 percent per annum.

[6] The problems with wheat, another commodity with a high income elasticity of demand, are described in Peter Knight's *Brazilian Agricultural Technology and Trade*.

Table IX-1

GROWTH IN AGRICULTURAL OUTPUT,
SELECTED COUNTRIES, 1950–1968

	Compound Annual Percentage Increases In—		
	Total agricultural output	Total population	Per capita agricultural output
Brazil	3.8%	3.0%	0.8%
Mexico	5.1	3.3	1.8
Latin America	3.3	2.8	0.5
Developing countries	2.8	2.5	0.3
Japan	3.3	1.0	2.3
Developed countries	2.7	1.2	1.5

Source: U.S. Department of Agriculture, *Economic Progress of Agriculture in Developing Nations, 1950-1968*, Foreign Agricultural Economic Report No. 59, Washington, D.C., 1970.

Brazilian agricultural productivity per unit of land remained stagnant during the entire postwar period. One study of twenty-four crops shows practically no change between 1947 and 1965.[7] The only items which experienced an increase in productivity were livestock and livestock products (0.7 percent on a gross basis and 1.4 percent on a pure yield basis).[8] Brazilian crop yields compared unfavorably with most other developing countries. In a study of crop yields per hectare in forty developing countries during the period 1950 to 1968, only six countries showed a poorer record than Brazil.[9]

International comparisons of yields of some basic crops indicate that Brazil lagged far behind, and that the lag became greater during the period from 1952-56 to 1962-66. Data collected by the USDA (see Table IX-3) indicate that grain yields increased only 0.2 percent per year compared with 2.5 percent per year for Mexico. Peter Knight's

---

[7]Louis F. Herrman, "Brazil: Room to Grow," Table 52, p. 135. This study concluded that "gross crop yields showed almost no increase. After eliminating the effects of shifts among locations and crops, pure yields declined about 0.1 percent a year" (p. 134).

[8]Ibid., Table 51, p. 134. The improved productivity seems to have been limited to meat other than beef, poultry, and eggs. Knight's study of Rio Grande du Sul indicated a decline in beef productivity between 1952-56 and 1962-66.

[9]John R. Schaub, "Agriculture's Performance in the Developing Countries," Table 5, p. 16. Output per hectare of major field crops increased at a compound annual growth rate of 0.2 percent from 1950 to 1968. Argentina was 1.4 percent, Colombia, 1.6 percent; India, 1.5 percent.

Table IX-2

CHANGE IN GRAIN OUTPUT, AREA AND YIELDS, SELECTED COUNTRIES, 1950–1968

	Compound Annual Percentage Increases In—		
	Grain production	Grain area	Grain yields
Brazil	4.3%	4.1%	0.2%
Argentina	2.5	1.1	1.4
Mexico	5.7	3.2	2.5
Developing countries	3.0	1.5	1.5
Japan	2.4	−0.8	3.2
Developed countries	2.9	−0.1	3.0

Source: U.S. Department of Agriculture, *Economic Progress of Agriculture*, Tables 1 and 5.

study of rice, wheat, soybeans, corn, and beef in Rio Grande do Sul points out that, in the earlier period, Brazil's yield of rice, for example, was about half the U.S. yield per hectare.[10] In the later period the yield in Brazil was only one-third the U.S. rice yield per hectare. During this period, U.S. yields had increased 52 percent, while brazilian yields increased only 7 percent. The same trend is true of corn. Brazilian yields of wheat and soybeans actually declined during the two periods.

Output of grain per worker on Brazilian farms seems to have fared somewhat better than output per hectare. Brazil's 3 percent annual increase in grain production per farm person was significantly higher than the increases for other developing countries, but also significantly lower than the developed countries and Mexico (see Table IX-3). Moreover, the increased yields per farm person were attributable almost entirely to more hectares per farm person. Two factors contributing to the increase in output per worker were the heavy migration to the cities and into the interior and the increased availability of more fertile land in the interior. As a result of this migration, the farm population increased by an estimated 1.3 percent per year while crop area per person on the farms increased by 2.8 percent per year.

[10]Peter Knight, *Brazilian Agricultural Technology and Trade* (New York: Praeger Company, 1971), Table 25, pp. 150-151, from FAO, *Production Yearbook*, 1967. In commenting on this table, Knight concluded that the overall picture was one of yield stagnation for these crops (p. 152). Productivity in beef, he noted, has been stagnant or declining in the postwar period.

Table IX-3

CHANGE IN GRAIN OUTPUT AND GRAIN AREA PER FARM PERSON, 1950–1968

| | Compound Annual Percentage Increases In— | | | |
	Grain output	Total farm population	Grain output per farm person	Grain Area per farm person
Brazil	4.3%	1.3%	3.0%	2.8%
Mexico	5.7	1.7	4.0	1.4
Argentina	2.5	1.9	0.6	−0.8
Developing countries	3.0	2.4	0.6	−0.9
Japan	2.4	−4.5	6.9	3.7
Developed countries	2.9	−1.6	4.5	1.5

Source: U.S. Department of Agriculture, *Economic Progress of Agriculture*, Tables 2, 5, and 6.

Agricultural Exports—1947 to 1964

The crisis of Brazilian agriculture is most clearly evidenced by the stagnation in exports of agricultural products. Because of the special circumstances surrounding coffee this product is excluded from our analysis. Excluding coffee, agricultural exports in 1964 totalled $488 million, significantly less than the $519 million of earnings from this source a decade earlier. Noncoffee agricultural exports averaged 36 percent of total exports in 1955 and exactly the same percentage in 1963, reflecting the stagnation in total exports, which remained almost constant at $1.4 billion between 1950 and 1963. A decline in the prices of primary products during the 1950s accounts for a part of this stagnation in Brazilian exports but more important were the stagnation in agricultural productivity, the overvalued exchange rate system, and the export quota system. This is clearly evidenced by the trend of exports of other Latin American countries, where exports rose 32 percent, and of other developing nations, where exports rose 39 percent, between 1955 and 1963, while Brazil's exports remained static (see Table IX-4).

Diagnosis of the Agricultural Crisis

The statistics presented above paint a fairly clear picture of the supply crisis in Brazilian agriculture during the 1950s and the early 1960s. It was a picture of moderate increases in total output, as the

Table IX-4

EXPORTS BY VALUE: BRAZIL AND OTHER COUNTRY GROUPS, 1955 AND 1963

(millions of US$)

	1955	1963	Percent Increase
Brazil	1,423	1,406	—
Other Latin American countries	5,917	7,784	+32
Other developing countries	20,877	29,000	+39
Total world	83,220	135,300	+62

Source: International Monetary Fund, *International Financial Statistics.*

farm population migrated into the interior states to cultivate more productive lands. Productivity, or yields per hectare, remained relatively stable with increases in the new lands barely offsetting declines in the old, as the farmers applied the same primitive techniques to the new lands as they had applied to the old. These trends were accompanied by increasing economic and social costs: by the early 1960s there were indications that opportunities for further expansion into the frontier were becoming exhausted (at least in the southern states of Rio Grande do Sul and Parana). As increases in output were derived more and more from the frontier areas, transportation, storage, and other marketing costs increased; and infrastructure needs in the interior added to the demand for scarce resources. In addition to increasing costs, the picture of Brazilian agricultural production through the 1960s is one of failure to meet the demands of a rapidly growing urbanized and industrial economy. This was particularly true of the changing mix of commodities while income rose as the demand for beef, milk, and wheat grew relative to the low income staples, such as rice and beans. Finally, stagnant productivity and increasing costs of agricultural output perpetuated the low real incomes of Brazilian farmers, who accounted for over 50 percent of the total Brazilian labor force in 1960.

The growing imbalance in Brazilian agriculture was not recognized by the governments preceding the 1964 revolution. The Furtado-Dantas diagnosis as presented in their 1963-65 development program noted that "the disparity between agriculture and industry should not be interpreted as a crisis in agriculture, for this is a basic condition consistent with development in this sector."[11] The 1963-65

[11]Estados Unidos do Brasil, *Three-Year Plan for Economic and Social Development*, p. 94.

program also accepted as natural the sharp rise in the prices of farm products: "the intensive growth of the primary product demand, as a result of a rapid industrialization and the relative rigidity of the primary sector—causes a sharper rise in farm-product prices than that of industrial prices, as occurred in Brazil during the period 1947-1960."[12]

The Dantas-Furtado diagnosis led to the conclusion that agriculture had benefited during the 1950s relative to industry: "the terms of trade are increasingly favorable to agriculture as a whole over the entire period," and, "this real benefit is flagrant between 1950 and 1960, having compelled industry to relinquish increasing shares of its income to agriculture."[13]

While they did not recognize a crisis in Brazilian agriculture, the Furtado-Dantas report identified the "archaic, primitive agrarian structure," particularly the "absurd and anti-economic distribution of land" as the cause of the relative backwardness of Brazilian agriculture, of its low productivity and of the depressed condition of the rural population.[14] Thus, land reform was recommended as one of the basic elements of their economic stabilization and development program. "The existing agrarian structure constitutes a serious obstacle to the accelerated development of the nation's economy, and adjusting it to the requirements and needs of progress of the Brazilian community is imperative."[15]

The Dantas-Furtado report noted that 34.5 percent of the farming establishments operated only 1.3 percent of the land (less than ten hectares). On the other hand 3.4 percent of the farming establishments had 62.1 percent of the land. The report noted the negative effects of such unequal land distribution; the excessive concentration of labor on the small farms; large tracts of land left idle or applied to cattle-raising with scarce opportunities for employment; the acute seasonality of employment on the larger tracts with resulting underemployment; and the regressive distribution of rural income.

Assessment of Pre-1964 Agricultural Policies and Performance

The functions expected of agriculture in a developing country are to provide (a) an economic surplus for financing industrial growth, (b) a labor surplus for an expanding industrial sector, (c) an adequate

---

[12] Ibid., p. 94.
[13] Ibid., p. 95-98.
[14] Ibid., p. 106.
[15] Ibid., Table 57, p. 107.

supply of foodstuffs for urban workers and raw materials for the
industrial and service sectors, (d) sufficient foreign exchange earnings
to finance growing import requirements, and (e) a growing domestic
market for industrial output. How well did Brazilian government satisfy these functions? (a) While Brazilian agriculture provided an economic surplus during the 1950s, it was far from sufficient to finance
the rapid pace of industrialization. During the 1950s, industrial output
grew at an annual average rate of about 8 percent, one of the highest
rates both in Latin America and in all the underdeveloped world
during this period. The high rate of investment in the industrial sector
was financed largely from three sources: reinvested earnings, agricultural savings, and foreign investments. A high level of reinvested
earnings was achieved through the set of economic policies which in
effect taxed agriculture and subsidized industrial investments. This
was probably the most important method by which forced savings of
agriculture were transferred to the industrial sector. In addition,
coffee growers made some direct investments in the São Paulo industrial sector. But to an exceptional degree Brazilian industrialization was financed by foreign investments. These investments, induced by the overvalued exchange rate and other industrial subsidies,
created a very heavy debt service burden and placed an unduly large
segment of the industrial sector in the hands of foreign owners. Brazilian economic performance of the 1950s would have been much
more laudatory if the industrial growth had been financed to a larger
extent from domestic savings; even with the large volume of forced
savings, Brazilian agriculture did not provide the economic surplus
which it could have.

(b) Agriculture served only too well the function of providing a
labor surplus. Census data indicate that seven million people migrated
from the country into the cities during the 1950s. This flood of unedu-
cated and untrained workers, attracted by salaries three to four times
those in agriculture, created intense competition for a limited number
of industrial jobs and served to keep the industrial wages for unskilled
workers at a relatively low level.[16] With industrial employment increasing at a rate of only 2 percent per year, less than the 3 percent

---

[16] Per capita income in the agricultural sector was only 25.2 percent of income in the
industrial and services sectors in 1947, and, while it grew by an estimated 60 percent to
1963 compared with an 18 percent increase in the other sectors, it remained only 34
percent of per capita incomes in the other sectors in the later year. This income
differential between the rural and urban workers attracted a flood of migration to the
cities; the rising per capita income in the primary sector was due more to this outmigration of labor from the rural to the urban centers than to any increase in productivity. By 1960, about 54 percent of the working force was still employed in agriculture,
down from 60 percent in 1950.

population growth rate, industry did not provide sufficient jobs even for the urban population.[17] Without education and training few of the rural migrants found employment in industry; most went into the lower-compensated service sector or into the expanding lists of unemployed. The migrants also aggravated the immense housing problem and the desperate shortage of all forms of urban infrastructure, schools, transportation, communications, water, and sewage.[18] Thus, while agriculture provided a labor surplus, it failed to provide adequate incomes in its own sector to moderate the migration to the cities and to the interior, both of which intensified the need for new infrastructure. In these migrations we find part of the explanation for the expanding governmental expenditures. Successive Brazilian governments tended to react to the problem of unemployment by creating government jobs without providing work, in keeping with the traditional Brazilian paternalism. On the other hand, urban infrastructure, being largely in private hands, was neglected. The big infrastructure expenditures, consistent with Kubitschek's thrust to the interior, were on highways to open the interior of Brazil.

(c) Brazilian agriculture is highly diversified and peculiarly suited to supplying a great variety of foodstuffs and raw materials. Yet even in this area Brazilian agriculture did not perform well during the 1950s. The output of foodstuffs increased about 4 percent annually, which on the surface would seem adequate to feed a population growing at an annual rate of 3 percent. Yet sharp changes in population tastes and income created new and rising demands which agriculture was not able to satisfy. An urban population growing at an

---

[17]Notable is the indication that the share of the working force occupied in industry declined from 14.2 percent in 1950 to 13.9 percent in 1960. The big growth in the labor force was in the service sector, especially government, which employed 21.9 percent of the working force in 1960, up from 16.3 percent in 1950. The employment trends of the 1950s were in distinct contrast with the 1940s when the industrial working force had increased at 4.6 percent per year, the service sector only 2.4 percent, and agriculture 0.6 percent.

[18]The flood of migration to the cities created tremendous demands for housing, the usual social services, and for employment. Those who visited Rio de Janeiro or any other major city in recent years have been struck by the mass of favelas, hastily constructed mud and thatched shanties thrown up overnight on the steep hillsides or along the swampy shores of smelly storm sewers and lakes. These favelados invaded the cities to seek the higher rewards of urban living, only to find that neither jobs, nor housing, nor any of the other conveniences of life were available to them. Few jobs were available in industry. The capital intensive industrial sector created new jobs at the rate of only 2.3 percent per year, while the urban population, adding the migration, was growing by 5.6 percent per year. The growing numbers of urban unemployed created great pressures for employment in the lower productivity service industries, especially the public payrolls, which expanded at an annual rate of 5.2 percent. As a consequence of the outmigration, the rural working force grew by only 1.7 percent per year during the 1950s.

annual rate of 5.7 percent was not able to supplement its table with food from the traditional vegetable garden. Also, per capita income was rising at a rate of 2.3 percent per year which meant, assuming a 0.5 income elasticity of demand for food, a food deficit of 0.4 percent per year. Finally, the rising incomes and urbanization meant a shift in the pattern of food consumption with increased demand for wheat, livestock, and meat products, the production of which increased at a very slow rate. Meat production, for example, expanded at a rate of only 2 percent, resulting in a deficit of 2.2 percent per year. As the deficit in wheat and meat products grew, their prices rose rapidly; the reaction of the authorities was to impose price controls, but the controls tended only to aggravate the supply problem. As costs rose more rapidly than prices, farmers refused to bring their beef to market; wheat farmers turned to other products and domestic production stagnated. Increased imports of wheat intensified the foreign exchange shortage even though much of the wheat was financed under the PL-480 program of the United States.

(d) Brazilian agriculture failed to perform the function of financing the growing import requirements of an expanding economy. Agricultural exports stagnated during the 1950s and since over 90 percent of total Brazilian export earnings were secured from agricultural products and their derivatives (80 percent from seven major products—coffee, cocoa, cotton, sugar, tobacco, sisal and pine—during 1949 to 1951 and 76 percent during 1961-1964). The stagnation in agricultural exports meant a stagnation in total exports. The dollar value of Brazilian exports in 1963 was less than it had been a decade earlier. Part of the decline in the value of exports after 1954 was caused by the decline in the prices of primary products in world markets after the Korean War boom had subsided. But by 1963 the prices of many of these primary products had returned to mid-1950 levels. Moreover, Brazil had the capacity to produce and export a wide range of products, the demand for which was rising in world markets. Beef is an important example, but soybeans, corn, and other farm products offered good markets which Brazilian agriculture failed to take advantage of.

(e) Stagnation in agricultural productivity and exports, and the relatively slow growth of agricultural output meant an equally slow growth of agricultural incomes and of demand from the agricultural sector for industrial output.

Lacking an expanding domestic market and unable to compete in international markets, Brazilian industry headed toward a standstill.

Agricultural Policies since 1964

Brazilian agricultural policies during the post-1964 period were characterized by the same emphasis on the market mechanism and the innovative trial and error process which characterized other economic policy areas since 1964. The Action Program diagnosis of Brazilian agriculture clearly indicated the adverse impact of national economic policies on agricultural output and productivity; the first remedial phase was to revise those policies which tended to discourage production. This meant gradual reduction and eventual elimination of price controls on beans, milk, beef, and other consumer products; elimination of quantitative export restrictions; and provision of a more favorable exchange rate for exports. While stimulating to agricultural production, these measures tended, in the short run, to aggravate domestic price pressures and to conflict with the stabilization effort. In the longer term, however, offering the farmer a fair price for his production was essential to stimulating production in this bottleneck sector.

The second phase was to improve upon existing agricultural programs as a means of increasing production and productivity. Existing programs in varying stages of effectiveness included the minimum price support program, the rural credit program, and the input subsidy programs, essentially for fertilizer and tractors. Each of these programs are discussed briefly.[19]

The Action Program analysis of the agricultural problem rejected the idea of land reform as a solution to the agricultural supply crisis. "In keeping with the traditional significance of the expression, Agrarian Reform is fundamentally a profound change in the ownership relations of the land with the objective of improving the distribution of agricultural income and of increasing the efficiency of the use of land. Moreover, in its traditional sense, Agrarian Reform should only be an adequate remedy for malformation of the structure in which there exists an excess of labor, relative to the systems and techniques prevalent in the use of the land. This does not appear to be the case in Brazil. On the contrary, the most frequent causes of the need for structural change identified in Brazilian agriculture are situations in which there is a reduction in the per capita output, as a consequence of the decline in the productivity of labor, and a fall in output per hectare, as a result of the incapacity to maintain the fer-

---

[19]For a more thorough discussion, see Gordon W. Smith, "Agricultural Policy, 1950-1967," in Ellis, *Economy of Brazil;* Schuh, *The Agricultural Development of Brazil;* and Knight, *Brazilian Agricultural Technology.*

tility of the land."[20] Despite this diagnosis the Campos report recommended an Agrarian Reform Law as a "democratic option to stimulate private property, in the right of the worker to the fruits of his labor, in the increase of productivity" and for the general social welfare. However, the report gave equal emphasis to colonization of the interior.

The Minimum Price Guaranty Program. A form of minimum price support program for basic commoditites like rice, corn, and beans (also cotton, peanuts, soybeans, manioc, and sisal in the Northeast) had been in force in Brazil since 1951 but it was virtually neglected and ineffective until 1963. With the constant increase in prices, averaging 25 percent per year, the minimum prices set at the beginning of the planting season were rarely effective at harvest time. Moreover, the program was little known to a majority of the farmers and even for many of those who were aware of it, the implementing institutions were not readily accessible (geographically and sometimes bureaucratically) to them.

The minimum price program first received attention after the food supply crisis of 1962, so described because of the poor harvest in that year and the rise in agricultural prices relative to the general price level. (The wholesale prices of agricultural products deflated by the general price index rose to 111.3 in 1962, with 1949-1953 equal to 100.) While the main solution of the Goulart government to the agricultural problem had been land reform, as an interim measure the government also activated the minimum price program and took steps to set up an effective operational network in the interior.[21]

The first improvement in the minimum price program by the Castello Branco experts was the application of monetary correction to the support prices for the 1965 crop. But even with this major improvement, the effectiveness of the program was largely limited to a few commodities, such as cotton, peanuts, and particularly rice, as the government purchased almost a third of the 1965 rice crop. The cost of financing and purchasing the 1965 commodity stockpile amounted to Cr$ 253 million, more than twice the previous high point in 1963 even after adjusting for the increase in prices, and more than 10 percent of the federal government deficit in that year. The inflationary experience of 1965 led to an overcautious and perverse approach to price setting for the 1966 crop, and this, added to poor

[20]Ministério do Planejamento e Coordenação Econômica, *Programa de Ação Econômica do Govêrno, 1964-1966*, pp. 105-106.
[21]Smith, "Agricultural Policy," in Ellis, *Economy of Brazil*, p. 245.

weather, contributed to the decline in overall agricultural output in that year.

The experiences of 1965 and 1966 revealed the need for another modification of the minimum price program so as to achieve some sort of balance between (a) the inflationary impact of the program which occurred in 1965 and (b) provision of an adequate incentive to the farmers to improve production and productivity, which was partly lacking in 1966. At the same time the government had to take into account its limited capability to manage the stockpiling and sales of agricultural commodities. Thus the 1967 program, in addition to setting more realistic minimum prices, concentrated on non-recourse financing instead of purchasing the crops out-right. The decision was left to the farmer to withhold his crops from the market and to arrange for storage and for sales when the market seemed most profitable. With this change in emphasis, loans comprised about 80 percent of the 1967 program compared with 30 percent in previous years, and by 1969 the direct purchases had been virtually eliminated in favor of non-recourse financing.

Most students of Brazilian agriculture have concluded that the minimum price program was not effective prior to 1967, except for peanuts, cotton, and rice in 1965. The gradual improvement and extension of the program, especially the application of monetary correction and the shift to loan financing, developed it by 1967 into an effective instrument for stabilizing agricultural prices during the crop cycle and for providing an incentive to expanded production. Nevertheless, there is little evidence as yet of its contribution to improved agricultural productivity.

Rural Credit Program. Subsidized credit for agricultural purposes through the Bank of Brazil has long been a principal policy instrument of Brazilian governments, stemming largely from the failure of the commercial banking system to provide credit to farmers.[22] In the prevailing inflationary environment Brazilian private banks preferred short-term commercial and industrial credits to the longer-term credit requirements of agriculture. The Brazilian banking system with its extensive branches throughout the country, served largely to channel savings from the countryside into the main branches in the major urban centers. The undue reliance on the commercial bill doctrine, that is, the rediscounting of commercial bills, also served to concentrate credit on the financing of the exchange of goods rather than on

---

[22]Ibid., p. 239. Interest rates on Bank of Brazil credit to agriculture have not exceeded 19 percent while prices have been rising annually by 25 percent or more, resulting in a negative real interest rate.

their production.[23] Finally, inflationary conditions created a continuing high demand for credit, so that banks were in position to be very selective, limiting credit to only the very best credit risks, a criterion which most farmers outside the coffee sector rarely met.

With the active participation of the Bank of Brazil, agriculture received about 17 percent of total private sector credit by the end of the 1950's. This was a step forward but was still inadequate in terms of agriculture's contribution to GNP, about 27 percent. The food supply crisis of 1962 further stimulated the government to improve the rural credit program, which expanded rapidly in 1963 and 1964, the Bank of Brazil accounting for the entire increase. By 1964 total credit to the agricultural sector had reached a reasonable level in terms of agriculture's share of total bank credit, the regional distribution of credit and agriculture's share of GNP.[24]

On the other hand, analysis of the composition and distribution of this credit revealed serious shortcomings. First, most of the credit was of a short-term nature for crop marketing; very little was for medium and long-term loans for investment or working capital purposes of the type needed to increase productivity and output. Practically all of the commercial bank credit was extended to middlemen for financing the movement of crops to market. Second, most of the credit was distributed to relatively few farmers with geographic and other access to branches of the Bank of Brazil, and was concentrated on a relatively few major crops. A Planning Ministry study showed that in 1961 only 17 percent of the total cultivated area of eight major food crops benefited from Bank of Brazil credit.[25] One crop, coffee, received about 30 percent of total agricultural credit in 1956. The focus of agricultural credit in the Bank of Brazil was also a major limiting factor to its wider distribution. While the Bank of Brazil with its 500 branches throughout the country extended two-thirds of total agricultural credit, the more than 6,000 branches of the private commercial banks participated in rural credit only to the extent of financing the retailing and wholesaling of crops. There was little or no direct credit from the private financial institutions to finance farm production.

Improvement in the rural credit program ranked high on the list of priority measures taken by the Castello Branco government. The Rural Credit Law, approved on 14 July 1964, outlined a series of

---

[23] Under the commercial bill doctrine the financing of the movement of goods to market was considered non-inflationary.

[24] Tendler, "Agricultural Credit in Brazil," p. 16.

[25] *Estados Unidos do Brasil, Three-Year Plan for Economic and Social Development 1963-1965*, p. 124.

measures for improving the existing system and for establishing new institutions with the objective of extending credit to farmers to whom credit had not previously been available.[26] The major innovation in the new program was a series of measures directed at bringing the private commercial banks into rural credit operations. The steps taken to involve the private banks were of two forms, one voluntary with financial inducements and the second compulsory with financial penalties. The voluntary approach, already implemented in 1964, permitted the banks to count specified rural loans as part of the compulsory reserve requirements. This meant that the banks could obtain a rate of return on an additional portion of their assets which otherwise would have been sterilized as reserves with the monetary authorities. This new measure appeared to have an impact in its first year as the commercial banks increased their rural credit applications in 1964 by 40 percent (in constant prices).

The compulsory reserve requirement proved, however, to be an ineffective instrument for selective allocation of credit to agriculture. One the one hand, the use of compulsory reserves to channel funds to agriculture complicated the problem of monetary control. In permitting the banks to satisfy their compulsory reserve requirements with rural paper, this selective measure reduced the effectiveness of the reserve requirements for limiting the overall credit expansion. On the other hand, there was no means of ensuring that the credit was in fact in addition to what the banks might have lent to agriculture without this selective measure. In October 1968, the government decided to terminate the selective approach by giving the banks the option of satisfying their reserve requirements with government bonds or rural credit. Interest rates on the bonds, at 6 percent plus monetary correction, were far more attractive than the rates on rural loans, 12 percent plus 6 percent commission. With inflation continuing at 20-25 percent, monetary correction plus 6 percent amounted to an annual rate of 26-31 percent compared with the 18 percent available from rural paper, which also carried a higher risk factor. With this rate differential, the commercial banks quickly shifted into government bonds.

The compulsory approach took the form of a legal requirement that the commercial banks commit 10 percent of their deposits to rural loans of specified terms and conditions.[27] Although this legal

[26]The Rural Credit Law, Decreto 54, 019, 14 July 1964, was modified by Decreto 54, 129 of 13 August 1964. Central Bank Resolution 5 of August 1965 formalized the measure permitting the banks to satisfy 10 percent of their compulsory reserve requirements by rural loans.

[27]Central Bank Resolution 69, September 1967.

requirement had been included in the Rural Credit Law of 1964, the implementing regulations were not issued until September 1967 under the initiative of Central Bank Director Ary Burger.[28] The banks were given a month to comply with the new 10 percent requirement. To the extent that a bank could not lend directly for agricultural purposes, which was the case with many banks lacking country branches, it was required to deposit an equivalent amount of funds in a special fund for agriculture (FUNAGRI) in the Central Bank. These funds would be used for rediscounting agricultural paper from other banks which had greater portfolio of rural paper. The initial regulations had two major shortcomings. First, they provided incentives to banks to invest in commercial paper rather than investment or production credits. The commercial banks were induced to meet their 10 percent requirement largely by loans to intermediaries to finance the movement of crops to market on a sixty- to ninety-day basis. For commercial credits, banks were permitted to discount the interest from the principal at the time the loan was made, a practice specifically prohibited for other agricultural loans. The second shortcoming of the mandatory credit program was that, in permitting higher rates for larger loans, it encouraged the commercial banks to concentrate on loans to large farmers and intermediaries rather than to small- and medium-size farmers.[29]

In recognition of these shortcomings, the National Monetary Council revised its rural credit regulations effective May 1969 (Resolution 97, August 1968). The revisions required that (a) at least one-third of the rural credit must be for working capital or investment purposes (excluding coffee and sugar which had separate credit programs); (b) specific portions of the credit had to go to medium and small scale farmers; (c) banks which did not have an approved agricultural credit department could invest up to 50 percent of its rural credit directly, the rest to be deposited with FUNAGRI at 6 percent; and (d) the working capital and investment credits had to be associated with extension services offered by the bank itself or by one of the approved agricultural extension services.

---

[28] In recognition of the great diversity of institutions and policies affecting rural credit, the government created in 1964 a National Coordination Commission for Rural Credit with responsibility for systematizing the criteria and priorities for rural loans. On 3 September 1965 this function was incorporated into the Central Bank as the Office of Coordination of Rural and Industrial Credit (GECRI). Dr. Burger, an economics professor and former president of the Development Bank of the Southeast and secretary of finance of the state of Rio Grando do Sul, was appointed director for GECRI in February 1967.

[29] Tendler, "Agricultural Credit in Brazil," p. 30.

The rural credit program has been effective both in increasing the total supply of credit to the agricultural sector and in channeling an increased proportion of this credit through commercial banks as opposed to the official institutions. On the other hand, the program as it was operated through May 1969 was still not fully effective in fulfilling the objectives of greater decentralization of the credit to smaller farmers and for investment purposes. The financial incentives in the program still encouraged the private banks to lend for marketing purposes and to large farmers.

A major complication with the rural credit program arises from the interest rate policy during this period. Private banks were required to lend to farmers at interest rates of about 19 to 20 percent, which were negative rates in real terms during this entire period; these rates were also at least 25 percent below the rates which banks received from other customers. Yet from a farmer's viewpoint private bank rates were higher than for similar loans from official institutions (about 15 percent). This raises the question as to whether a more effective and economical rural credit program would not have been to channel all credit through the Bank of Brazil.[30]

The interest rate ceiling on rural credit was, however, generally conssitent with interest rate policy and as such was subject to the same criticisms as described in Chapter V. Interest rate controls on agricultural credit, as on bank deposit rates and on loan rates in general, are a departure from the basic policy of relying on the markit for determination of prices. In this sense interest rate policy was more a continuation of, rather than a break with, the pre-1964 policy responses to inflation, which included price, wage, and utility rate controls. In the Brazilian setting, interest rate ceilings have not been effective. There was usually a jeito (a way around the controls) either in the form of evasion or avoidance. In either case, the authorities did not have the supervisory personnel to ensure compliance.

Subsidies to Farm Inputs. Various forms of subsidy to farm inputs, especially fertilizer and to a lesser degree farm machinery, have been an instrument of farm policy since World War II. Through 1961 the subsidy took the form of preferential tariff and exchange rate treatment for imports of farm inputs. With the devaluation and change in the exchange rate system in 1961 the subsidy method was also changed to an interest rate subsidy through Bank of Brazil loans.[31] Farm credit was being offered by the Bank of Brazil at interest rates

---

[30] Ibid., pp. 44-45.
[31] Schuh, *The Agricultural Development of Brazil*, pp. 294-5.

of 14 to 19 percent per annum at a time when prices were rising at an annual rate of 50 to 90 percent and interest rates on non-farm credit were 60 to 100 percent.

The Castello Branco government continued the interest subsidy approach to subsidizing farm inputs. The only significant change in the program was to extend the subsidies to private commercial bank loans through the creation in 1966 of a Fund for the Financial Promotion of the Use of Fertilizers and Mineral Supplements, better known by its acronym, FUNFERTIL. This fund offered interest rate rebates on bank loans for the purchase of fertilizers.

The Brazilian fertilizer subsidy effort met with a small measure of success as Brazilian farmers responded with increased use of fertilizer.[32] But the methods used to implement the program had serious shortcomings. Since it was not supervised or tied to any meaningful standards which would limit diversion of the funds to other uses, it benefited only about 5 percent of Brazilian farmers, probably the more technologically advanced producers. The great majority of farmers were not touched by the program.[33] As with the minimum price and rural credit programs, the effectiveness of an input subsidy program as an instrument for improving farm productivity and output was limited to the modern segments of agriculture which respond to market incentives. For the majority of Brazilian farmers market incentives are not sufficient; they must be supplemented with rural extension services, education, research, and, in some areas, changes in the land tenure system. But one student of Brazilian agriculture argues that a strong case can be made for a fertilizer program as the leading edge in the process of agricultural modernization. In his study of fertilizer usage in the state of Rio Grande do Sul, Peter Knight concluded that even without subsidized prices, fertilization would be highly profitable for a wide range of commodities. He adds that fertilizer is a democratic innovation because it aids small as well as large farmers; it is more labor intensive than mechanization; it does not depend on topography of the land; and it is relatively neutral with regard to the type of crop. In view of these factors, he writes, fertilizer can play a central role in the process of technological change in agriculture. It is the critical element in moving from an extra-active activity to a modern agriculture dependent upon manufactured inputs for an increased output.[34]

---

[32]Smith, "Agricultural Policy," pp. 226-7.

[33]Ibid., p. 238

[34]Knight, *Brazilian Agricultural Technology*, p. 180.

Fiscal Incentives to Investment in Agriculture. A new approach taken to improve agricultural productivity is the application of fiscal incentives to investment in agriculture similar to the fiscal incentives which have prevailed for investment in industry and in the Northeast. The income-tax liability has been cut in half for corporations investing in agriculture or other approved enterprises in northeast and north Brazil. A two-year tax holiday and reductions for an additional two years has been granted to corporations formed to engaged in agriculture; special incentives have been offered for investment in fertilizer production and distribution facilities; duties on imports of agricultural inputs have been removed; and many agricultural inputs and exports are exempt from the 15 to 18 percent value-added tax.

Agricultural Trends since 1964

The overall trend of agricultural output the 1964 revolution has not changed significantly from the pre-1964 trend of about 4 percent growth per year, with the usual annual variations due to weather conditions. The decline in the population growth rate from 3.2 during the 1950s to 2.7 during the 1960s permitted only a small increase in per capita agricultural output—1 percent per year. But there has also been a significant shift in the composition of Brazilian agricultural output during the years since 1964 stemming primarily from the relative decline in coffee production. By the end of the 1960s Brazil's average coffee production had fallen to only two-thirds of what it had been at the beginning, the nature and cause of which are examined in the following chapter. Meanwhile, the output of other agricultural commodities, particularly food crops, increased in proportion to the decline in coffee production. The production of non-coffee agricultural commodities, particularly food crops, increased at an annual rate of about 5 percent, with the biggest jumps in 1965 and 1967. It may be significant that agricultural output (excluding coffee) continued to increase slightly in 1968 and 1969 despite the poor weather conditions. The declining importance of coffee production in the total agricultural picture also has implications for greater stability of output and incomes in the agricultural sector.

The most dramatic impact of the post-1964 policies on agriculture, other than coffee, was in the export field. Exports of agricultural commodities, other than coffee, tripled between 1964 and 1972 after remaining stagnant for the previous decade. The upward trend of world prices for primary products in the world market contributed to this trend, but the major factors were the improved price incentives offered through the more realistic exchange rate, removal of the export quota system, and the other incentives to domestic production.

In summing up the trends in agricultural performance during the eight years since the 1964 revolution, I find that significant and even dramatic results were achieved in reducing excessive coffee production and in stimulating exports of non-coffee agriculutral products. The decline in coffee production was offset by increases in output of other agricultural products, especially foodstuffs, but the overall increase was only slightly greater than during the earlier years. The increase in the output of foodstuffs, for example, was not adequate to reduce the food deficiency, especially the deficiency in high protein foods.

Assessment of Post-1964 Agricultural Policies and Performance

The most critical policy issue confronting the post-1964 government was how to increase agricultural productivity and output. Agricultural output had not increased fast enough during the 1950s and early 1960s to satisfy the rapidly growing demand. The increase in output which had taken place was the result of more extensive farming in the interior, while productivity in the older agricultural areas remained stagnant.

The Castello Branco government attacked the agricultural supply crisis by a series of measures designed to restore and improve upon market incentives: the elimination of agricultural price controls and quantitative export restrictions, more favorable exchange rates for exports, an improved minimum price guaranty program, enlarged credit availabilities, and continued subsidies to agricultural inputs like fertilizer and farm machinery. Consistent with its emphasis on market incentives the government placed a high priority on investments in transportation, particularly feeder roads and highways, and in communications and other marketing facilities. But inadequate attention was given to relating the market incentives to agricultural extension services, to research, and, in some areas, to improving the land tenure system. Progress in these structural areas was slow, hesitant, and clearly inadequate in terms of the tremendous need. Education and training and extension services were carried on largely by the states, with some improvement evident only in São Paulo, Rio Grande do Sul and Minas Gerais.

The most effective of the post-1964 policies for agriculture, in my assessment, were the macro-economic policies. Just as the pre-1964 macro-policies had a greater impact on agriculture than the policies relating specifically to agriculture, the post-1964 macro-policies also had a more beneficial impact than the programs relating directly to agriculture, The minimum price guarantee, rural credit, and input subsidy programs applied only to a small group of farmers, usually the large farmers in the south-central region of Brazil who had access to the financial institutions administering these programs. Thus, Brazilian agriculture responded to the market incentives as might be expected. The modern segment of agriculture responded with dramatic increases in production, especially for export; but there was little apparent improvement in the productivity and output of the more traditional segment of agriculture which produced primarily for the domestic market. This emphasis on market incentives tended to enhance investment and growth opportunities in agriculture but at the same time to intensify the basic dualism between the modern and traditional segments of Brazilian agriculture.

CHAPTER X

The Contribution of Coffee
to Inflation

> With a more thoughtful policy we could have
> achieved the same development effort with
> lower costs; or more development with the
> same costs.
>
> Antônio Delfim Netto
> "Sugestoes para uma
> Politica Cafeeira"

Brazil's experience with coffee exemplifies the problems of a country which is heavily dependent upon a single commodity. The problems arise not only from the fluctuations in export prices and in domestic production—both of which are uncontrollable in the short run—but also from the domestic monetary impact and the relative incentives to produce alternative crops, especially food crops for domestic consumption. The importance of coffee in the Brazilian economy is suggested by the following data: coffee exports exceeded 55 percent of total exports in each year through 1964; coffee output was more than 10 percent of total agricultural output; land cultivated for coffee comprised more than 10 percent of the total cultivated area and some of the best land in Brazil; an estimated 7 percent of the total working force was occupied in the coffee sector; and the coffee stockpile, at the end of 1963, was estimated at 60 million bags which, at the world market price, would be valued at $260 million, a significant capital investment for a $25 billion economy.

Coffee policy during the 1950s stands out in sharp contrast to the general agricultural policies outlined in the previous chapter. The Brazilian coffee sector did not suffer the same neglect as the agricultural sector in general. Investments in new coffee trees rose sharply during the mid-1950s and coffee production doubled; since the volume of exports remained relatively stable, a large share of the increased output was placed in storage. By the end of 1963, the Brazilian stockpiles of coffee, 60 million bags (132 pounds per bag), was almost equal to total world consumption for one year. With this stockpile, Brazil was underwriting the cost of guaranteeing a stable supply of coffee to satisfy world consumption. The costs of this policy to the Brazilian economy, in terms of adding to the inflationary fuel and of opportunities foregone to produce alternative crops for domestic consumption and for export, were enormous.[1] In this chapter we examine the Brazilian policies for influencing the price and quantity of coffee production, exports, and domestic consumption and in turn the impact of these policies on national economic objectives.

During the 1950s and early 1960s coffee policy had an adverse impact on all the major objectives of economic policy. The evidence tends to support the thesis that coffee policy (a) tended to intensify the regional disparities in income; (b) was a major factor in the stagnation in export earnings; (c) stimulated inflation from both the demand and supply sides; and (d) contributed to the economic stagnation of the mid-1960s. In addition, the policies pursued with regard to coffee in the international sphere stimulated production in other countries and reduced steadily Brazil's share in the world coffee market.

The magnitude of the coffee problem first became vividly clear to the Castello Branco government in 1965 with the adverse economic repercussions of a 38-million-bag coffee crop, almost half of which was added to the already burgeoning stockpile. A series of policy changes, initiated in that year, helped to modify public attitudes and to reduce the incentives to invest in the coffee sector which, together with some bad weather, reduced the average coffee output for the following five years well below domestic and export demand. By the end of 1970 the coffee stockpile was reduced to an estimated 30 million bags, less than half the 70 million bag stockpile at the end of 1965. (Statistics on coffee production, exports, domestic consumption, and estimates of the stockpile are provided in table X-1.) The reduction in the stockpile had an important contractive impact on the monetary budget. The policy changes were even more important in terms of stimulating production and export of alternative crops, not only in the coffee zones but in other regions of the country. In sum,

---

[1] By the end of the 1950s the coffee stockpile amounted to one to two percent of GNP, or about 5 to 10 percent of aggregate Brazilian savings and gross investment during these years. Nathaniel H. Leff, *Economic Policy-Making and Development in Brazil, 1947-1964*, p. 30.

Table X-1
COFFEE PRODUCTION, EXPORTS, CONSUMPTION AND STOCKS, 1946–1970
(millions of bags)

Coffee Crop Year[a]	Production Registered at IBC	Exports for Calendar Year	Domestic Consumption[a]	End-of-Year Coffee Stocks[b]
1946/47	14.0	15.6	3.0	38.0
1947/48	13.6	14.7	3.0	34.0
1948/49	17.0	17.5	3.0	30.0
1949/50	16.3	19.3	3.0	24.0
1950/51	16.7	14.8	3.0	23.0
1951/52	15.0	16.4	3.0	19.0
1952/53	16.1	15.8	4.0	15.0
1953/54	15.1	15.6	4.0	10.0
1954/55	14.5	10.9	4.0	10.0
1955/56	22.0	13.7	2.2	16.0
1956/57	12.5	16.8	6.3	6.0
1957/58	21.6	14.3	4.2	10.0
1958/59	26.8	12.9	5.0	19.0
1959/60	44.1	17.7	7.0	38.0
1960/61	29.8	16.8	7.0	44.1
1961/62	35.9	17.0	7.0	56.0
1962/63	28.7	16.4	6.2	47.6
1963/64	23.1	19.5	6.7	59.6
1964/65	18.0	14.9	7.5	48.0
1965/66	37.8	13.5	8.1	65.3
1966/67	17.5	17.0	8.1	62.7
1967/68	23.4	17.3	8.6	60.0
1968/69	16.8	19.0	8.7	49.7
1969/70	18.9	19.6	8.7	36.3
1970/71	11.0	17.1	8.9	24.4
1971/72	24.6	18.4	8.1	23.5

[a]1 October to 30 September.
[b]Estimated.
Source: *Relatório do Banco Central do Brasil*, 1968-72.

the combination of policies affecting coffee (a) reduced inflationary pressures (on the demand side) from the coffee sector; (b) stimulated an increase in output in alternative crops; (c) contributed to the sharp expansion in total exports; and in so doing (d) ameliorated the regional disparities in income. Moreover, containment of coffee production also improved the imbalance in the world demand and supply picture for coffee. On the negative side, the reduction in coffee output tended to aggravate unemployment and personal income distribution problems in the south-central coffee producing regions. To the extent that producers shifted from coffee, a very labor intensive crop, to beef raising, for example, a large number of workers suffered a loss of jobs and income.[2]

Coffee Policies Prior to 1961

What were the policies which stimulated the over-production of coffee during the 1950s and early 1960s? The basic objective of coffee policy during the entire post-war period through 1965, as I have frequently emphasized, was to maximize foreign exchange receipts from coffee. Coffee produced as much as 74 percent of total export earnings in 1952 and averaged well over half of total exports in each year through 1965 (see table X-4). Use of an over-valued exchange rate as a deliberate policy choice was the consequence of three basic considerations. First, the ideological: the impact of the Prebisch doctrine on Brazilian policy makers during the 1950s has been noted. In holding that the limiting factor to the growth of the developing countries was the import constraint, stemming from the general decline in the terms of trade of the developing countries, this doctrine implanted a defeatism into the assessment of policy makers regarding the possibilities of expanding total exports. A second consideration was the concern about the domestic price impact of devaluation. The third consideration, partly derived from the previous two, was the aim of maximizing foreign exchange earnings for coffee in the face of an inelastic demand.[3] On the assumption of an inelastic demand, any reduction in the price through a devaluation of the exchange rate would not result in any significant increase in export volume, but would instead tend to reduce total export receipts. On

---

[2] Carlos Viacava, director of the Coffee Institute, pointed out in 1971 that the increase in the labor costs in São Paulo was one of the principal factors for the reduction of coffee planting in that state. Also salaries in the coffee areas are the highest in the agricultural sector.

[3] The price elasticity of demand for coffee was estimated at 0.25. Any reduction in the Brazilian price through devaluation, it was believed, would be followed by retaliatory devaluation by the other coffee producers.

the domestic side, the low cruzeiro return to the the producer, it was believed, would tend to dampen the tendency to overproduction. At the same time the government stood ready to purchase any coffee offered at the fixed price.

Withholding of coffee stocks from the world market to maximize foreign exchange earnings had long been a part of Brazilian policies. In the 1920s the Brazilian coffee stocks were financed by external borrowing. In 1931 the Vargas government shifted to a policy of domestic financing, which resulted in the building up and eventual destruction of 78 million bags of coffee.[4] And domestic financing of coffee stocks served a useful function during the 1930s, as pointed out by Celso Furtado: "It is therefore quite clear that the recovery of the Brazilian economy which took place from 1933 onward was not caused by an external factor but by the pump-priming policy unconsciously adopted in Brazil as a by-product of the protection of the coffee interests."[5]

But use of an overvalued exchange rate as the basic instrument of coffee policy proved to be not only deficient, but also just short of disastrous in terms of results, in regard to both the balance of payments and the domestic economy.

In terms of the objective of maximizing foreign exchange earnings, the coffee defense policies had two basic defects. First, Brazil voluntarily assumed the position of residual supplier in order to sustain the price level. Second, receipts were not necessarily maximized since, even if they were larger during the earlier years, eventually increased competition from new coffee suppliers reduced the level of receipts. As a consequence, Brazil's share of the world coffee market fell from 60 percent in 1950 to only 39 percent in 1963.

The unfavorable results of the overvalued exchange rate on the domestic side were also significant. Perhaps most significant was the adverse impact on the production and exportation of alternative agricultural commodities. Despite the exchange confiscation from the overvalued exchange rate, investments in new coffee plantings were still profitable, especially relative to alternatives in the agricultural sector, because to many the coffee culture was a prestigious way of life and returns on alternative investments would have to be significantly higher to induce a shift out of coffee. Other crops did not carry the benefits of a guaranteed minimum price, ample financing, warehousing facilities, and a sympathetic ear in the presidential palace; with domestic prices and costs rising almost twice as rapidly as the

---

[4]Fundação Getúlio Vargas, *Conjuntura Econômica* 27 (May 1973), p. 89.

[5]Celso Furtado, *The Economic Growth of Brazil*, p. 212.

exchange rate devaluations, agricultural crops other than coffee were unable to compete in international markets. The profitability of coffee relative to alternative crops resulted in excessive coffee plantings in the newly opened lands in Parana so that by 1963 almost 10 percent of total cultivated land and some of the most fertile land was devoted to cultivation of coffee. Meanwhile, domestic production of many other foodstuffs did not keep up with the rising domestic population and income.

The final and most obvious impact of the coffee policy of the 1950s was the over-production and stockpiling of coffee. A 100 percent increase in the nominal price of coffee from 1950-52 to 1953-55 and a record world price for coffee resulted in huge investments in new trees and plantations in the immediately following years. The output of these new investments (given the normal five- to six-year maturation period) resulted in a 75 percent increase in coffee production by the first years of the 1960s, from an average of 16 million bags in the early 1950s to an average of 28 million bags in the early 1960s (see table X-1). In 1958 Brazil purchased for stockpiling 9 million bags, one-third of its registered production in that year. By the end of 1963 the stockpile had grown to an estimated 58 million bags. If we consider that the cost of this stockpiling is "a subsidy paid by the population in the form of inflation, we arrive at the conclusion that society paid for not growing."[6]

Coffee Defense Fund—1961 to 1964

An overvalued exchange rate ceased to be an instrument of coffee policy following the exchange crisis and devaluation of 1961. Stagnant exports, growing foreign debt repayments and rising imports forced a reassessment of exchange and coffee policies. The result was the separation of exchange rate policy from coffee pricing policy. To make this separation, Quadros's experts established a minimum coffee registration price for both producers and exporters. The exporters were permitted to retain only a fixed amount, with any excess from the foreign sales of coffee to be deposited in the Coffee Defense Fund.[7] Previously the exporter had retained the full cruzeiro amount

---

[6] Antônio Delfim Netto, *O Problema do Café no Brasil*, p. 249.

[7] The Coffee Defense Fund is a deposit account with the Bank of Brazil which is fed by receipts of the contribution quota (the difference between the cruzeiro value of coffee exports and the amount retained by the exporter as fixed by the authorities) and proceeds from the sale of official stocks for domestic consumption or for export. Expenses charged to the fund are purchases of coffee by the Brazilian Coffee Institute, which manages the fund, its administrative expenses, and the expenses of the eradication or rehabilitation programs.

of the foreign sale. His returns were limited by the overvalued exchange rate which gave him only 90 cruzeiros in return for a dollar export earnings, and paid 229 cruzeiros for a dollar of imports. The difference was retained by the monetary authorities, and much of it was used to finance the purchase of coffee for the stockpile. The regulations concerning coffee had stipulated that the surplus be distributed to the planters through a Fund for the Modernization of Agriculture, but the net result was an effective tax on coffee exports ranging from 23 percent of the total value of coffee exports in 1954 to 48 percent in 1958.[8]

With the establishment in 1961 of a separate pricing policy for coffee, the difference between the export receipts and the amount retained by the coffee exporter was deposited in a Coffee Defense Fund in the Bank of Brazil for use by the coffee sector. The rapid increase in coffee stockpile in 1961 and 1962 meant that much of the Coffee Defense Fund was used for this purpose. The advantage in separating coffee pricing policy from exchange rate policy was that it offered the Brazilian authorities an additional policy instrument. The exchange rate became a more flexible instrument once it was freed of its direct impact on coffee export prices. Domestic production of coffee and income of the coffee growers was more directly influenced by the domestic support prices fixed annually by the authorities. With the addition of a policy instrument there also came a change in policy objectives from maximizing foreign exchange earnings to one of maintaining the income of the coffee sector. By raising the support price when the coffee crop was low and maintaining the price when it was high, the authorities hoped to stabilize coffee sector income and eventually to have some influence on the level of production. Professor Delfim Netto described this as the first time Brazil preoccupied itself with elimination of excess production.[9]

Following a bumper coffee crop in 1961, a year in which almost 36 million bags were registered with the Brazilian Coffee Institute, the price to the producer was raised only 18 percent. Table 2 traces the trend of coffee prices in current and constant prices from 1946 to 1969. With general price increases running in excess of 50 percent this meant a decline in the real price to the producer which, added to the decline in the 1962 output to 28 million bags, contributed to the sharp decline in the real income of the coffee sector. Coffee sector income continued at a low level in 1963 and 1964 despite nominal price increases exceeding 100 percent in each year as poor weather, a combi-

[8]Leff, *Economic Policy-Making and Development*, Table 3, pp. 24-26.

[9]Antônio Delfim Netto and Carlos Alberto de Andrade Pinto, *O Café do Brasil*, p. 32.

Table X-2
COFFEE GUARANTY PRICES, 1946–1970

Coffee Crop Year[a]	Guaranty Price to Producer (Cr$ 1 bag)	
	Current prices	Constant prices (1949 Cr$)
1946/47	.421	—
1947/48	.438	5.32
1948/49	.455	5.05
1949/50	.655	6.55
1950/51	1.047	9.40
1951/52	1.049	8.45
1952/53	1.076	7.60
1953/54	1.516	9.35
1954/55	2.186	11.10
1955/56	1.896	8.20
1956/57	1.894	6.67
1957/58	1.983	6.20
1958/59	1.983	5.55
1959/60	2.716	5.90
1960/61	2.716	4.68
1961/62	4.857	6.25
1962/63	5.760	4.78
1963/64	14.624	6.82
1964/65	37.440	9.35
1965/66	31.610	5.05
1966/67	35.624	4.12
1967/68	52.630	4.77
1968/69	69.000	4.90
1969/70	94.000	5.48

[a]1 October to 30 September.
Source: *Relatório do Banco Central do Brasil*, 1968; *Conjuntura Econômica*, June 1970

nation of frosts and droughts, reduced coffee output to 18 million bags in 1964, and coffee income remained relatively depressed.

Consequences of Coffee Policy—1953 to 1964

Coffee policy during the postwar years had as its basic objective to maximize Brazil's foreign exchange earnings, which was consistent with the general assessment that the limiting factor in Brazil's eco-

nomic growth was the import constraint. This objective was achieved
in the sense that coffee receipts remained at the relatively high level
of $700 to $800 million per year (see table X-3).

Table X-3
COFFEE EXPORTS, 1946–1970
(millions of US$)

Calendar Year	Coffee Exports (millions bags)	Average Value of Coffee Exports[a]	Foreign Exchange Earnings from Coffee Beans	Soluble Coffee Exports
1946	15.6	$22.41	$ 350	—
1947	14.7	28.18	414	—
1948	17.5	28.05	491	—
1949	19.3	32.61	632	—
1950	14.8	58.34	865	—
1951	16.4	64.71	1,059	—
1952	15.8	66.07	1,045	—
1953	15.6	70.05	1,090	—
1954	10.9	86.84	948	—
1955	13.7	61.62	844	—
1956	16.8	61.28	1,030	—
1957	14.3	59.05	846	—
1958	12.9	53.36	688	—
1959	17.7	41.98	744	—
1960	16.8	42.38	713	—
1961	17.0	41.86	710	—
1962	16.4	39.24	643	—
1963	19.5	38.28	747	$ 0.2
1964	14.9	50.84	760	0.2
1965	13.5	52.41	706	0.8
1966	17.0	45.42	764	9.5
1967	17.3	42.29	705	28.3
1968	19.0	41.88	774	22.8
1969	19.6	43.13	813	32.8
1970	16.0	55.88	939	42.5
1971	17.2	44.81	773	49.7
1972	N.A.	N.A.	1,029[b]	65.0[b]

[a]US$ per bag.
[b]Estimated.
Source: *Relatório do Banco Central do Brasil*, 1965, 1969, 1971.

At the risk of only slight exaggeration, we conclude from this analysis that coffee policy carried huge social and economic costs in terms of (a) opportunities foregone in exporting of alternative crops; (b) opportunities foregone in producing alternative foodstuffs for domestic consumption; (c) the cost of maintaining a 60-million bag stockpile; (d) intensification of the regional and perhaps, personal, income distribution in Brazil; and (e) its contribution to inflationary pressures.

Coffee Policy—1964 and 1965

The Castello Branco government did not alter coffee pricing policy during the first year after the revolution. The decline in coffee output during 1963 and 1964 due to poor weather tended to conceal the potential productive capacity of the coffee sector and as part of an effort to restore coffee sector incomes, the coffee support price to the producers for the 1964-65 crop (June 1964) was doubled in nominal terms (see table X-2), resulting in the highest level in real terms since 1954.

The Action Program of the Revolutionary Government did not provide a specific diagnosis of the coffee problem nor did it offer a clear statement of coffee pricing policy; but it did point out that coffee production and productivity increased during the previous decade relative to alternative agricultural crops. The average yield of coffee per hectare (1000 square meters), it was noted, increased from 410 kilograms in 1947-51 to an average of 750 kilograms in 1957-61, while the average yield of most alternative crops remained stagnant or actually declined. The policy called for in the Action Program was a reduction in the cultivated area devoted to coffee from 4.5 million hectares in 1962 to about one-third of that, or 1.2 million hectares in 1965, but there was no indication of how this reduction was to be implemented.[10]

Coffee Eradication Program—1966 to 1967

The Coffee Eradication Program became in 1966 part of the Castello Branco government's two-pronged attack on the problem of excess coffee production with the immediate objective of reducing coffee productive capacity and diversifying production into alternative crops, such as corn, rice, soybeans, beans, and cotton. The first prong, initiated in 1964, was an increase in price incentives for agro-

[10]Ministério do Planejamento e Coordenação Econômica, *Programa de Ação Econômica do Govêrno, 1964-1966*, Table 22, p. 100.

nomically alternative crops through elimination of price controls, establishment of a more realistic exchange rate, and improved farm credit and minimum price programs. The second prong of the coffee program was directed at reducing the profitability of coffee by cutting prices (in real terms) to coffee producers. This reduction in producer prices came somewhat belatedly, however, as the huge 1965 output more than offset the lower prices. But this phase of the program became more effective in 1966.

The Coffee Eradication Program contributed to both prongs of the attack on excess coffee production. The coffee grower was paid a fixed inducement for each uprooted tree, if he eliminated at least 15 percent of his trees. This was followed by another payment when an alternative crop was planted in the area of the uprooted tree. The Eradication Program was relatively successful as an estimated 625 million trees or 20 percent of the existing trees were uprooted between October 1966 and April 1967. (By the latter date the number of coffee trees in production in Brazil was estimated by the U.S. Department of Agriculture at 2.5 billion.) The original eradication program, scheduled for two years, was cut short for several reasons. First, the rather sizable number of trees uprooted in the initial six months. Second, the low estimates of the forthcoming 1967 crops, combined with a desire to stimulate a sluggish economy through restoring the coffee sector. Finally, the belief that other coffee-producing countries were not matching the Brazilian effort and that Brazil was bearing the full burden of removing the excess world output of coffee. This was combined with the aim, on the part of the new finance minister, Professor Delfim Netto, to initiate a more active coffee export policy.

Coffee Policy—1967 to 1970—and Domestic Outlook

There can be no doubt about the success of Brazilian coffee policy after the initial unfortunate experiences with a coffee crop of 38 million bags in 1965. Coffee production, as measured by registrations with the Brazilian Coffee Institute (IBC), averaged 18 million bags during the succeeding five years, 1966 to 1970, ranging from a high of 23.4 million bags in 1967 to 13 million in 1970. With the total domestic plus export demand averaging 24-25 million bags, the coffee stockpile was reduced from an estimated 70 million bags at the end of 1965 to an estimated 29 million bags at the end of 1970 (see table X-1). Coffee exports recovered in 1966 to 17 million bags and increased steadily to 19.6 million bags in 1969 (see table X-3). And Brazil has managed to retain its share of the world coffee market.[11] The drawdown of stocks and the favorable export performance has also meant a sizable monetary contractionary impact from coffee operations. Table X-4 shows the growth in the size of the Coffee Defense Fund, rising from $282 billion in 1966 to Cr$ 1408 billion in 1969. The significance of these figures is indicated by the fact that in 1968 the net contractive impact of coffee operations offset two-thirds of the federal government deficit. Finally, the success of coffee policy can be viewed in the more rapid growth of production and exportation of alternative crops. Exports of noncoffee agricultural commodities increased by 45 percent from the three-year average of 1961-63 to 1966-69. This compares with only an 18 percent increase from 1956-58 to 1961-63.

Doubts remain, however, about the long-term developments in coffee production and whether a viable equilibrium has been reached between supply and demand. Much of the success of the 1966 to 1970 coffee policies was due to poor weather (frosts and drought). There is also much evidence that Brazilian coffee policies are being reversed and that the profitability of coffee is once again increasing relative to alternative crops, with a potential overproduction of coffee in the coming years. On the policy side, it was noted that the Eradication Program was cut short in April 1967 shortly after the Costa e Silva government took office (15 February 1967). The tight coffee pricing policy of the Castello Branco government, that is, to maintain a stable nominal price, was also relaxed to permit nominal price increases comparable with increases in the general price index. In June 1967 the average nominal coffee price to the producer was increased by about 48 percent, after being held relatively constant for three years. Additional increases brought the real price to the producer above the 1965 price, yet it remained only 80 percent of the 1963 price (see table X-2).

Some studies have concluded that the price of coffee had risen in recent years relative to the prices of some alternative crops. One such study concluded that only rice could compete with new coffee plantings in the state of São Paulo and that "price and productivity conditions are such that an expansion of coffee production should be expected in coming years."[12] The 23 percent increase in cotton production and the 20 percent increase in soybean production in São

[11]Changes in the ICA in March 1965 released Brazil in part from its role of residual supplier in the international market. The policy is to adjust quotas automatically when prices move beyond a specified range. The quota increases have also been small. These measures and Brazil's more flexible price policy for coffee enabled Brazil to sell its entire quota during recent years.

[12]Stahis Panagides, "Erradicação do Café e Diversificação da Agricultura Brasileira," p. 41.

Table X-4

NET MONETARY IMPACT OF COFFEE OPERATIONS, 1961–1969
(millions of Cr$)

Year	Total Receipts[a]	Contribution Quota	Sales of Stocks	Total Expenditures[b]	Purchases of Stocks	Net Defense Fund	Total Loans & Rediscounts	Net Coffee Operations[c]
1961	49	42	—	5	3	44	+33	11
1962	128	128	—	119	110	9	+26	−17
1963	214	214	—	108	87	106	+66	40
1964	382	382	—	153	80	229	+100	128
1965	703	703	—	805	736	−102	+29	−131
1966	1,051	815	236	769	585	282	−69	352
1967	1,110	928	132	959	483	151	199	−48
1968	1,411	1,064	346	498	168	913	305	597
1969	2,235	1,651	548	827	119	1,408	756	641

[a] Other miscellaneous receipts are not itemized.

[b] IBC budget and other miscellaneous expenses are not itemized.

[c] Net defense fund minus total loans and rediscounts. Differences between these figures and the monetary budget figures are due to items in transit. Since net coffee operations reflect changes in nonmonetary liabilities of the monetary authorities, a reduction has an expansive monetary impact, and vice versa.

Source: *Relatório do Banco Central do Brasil*, various issues.

Paulo during 1969 indicates that these crops may also be reasonable alternatives to coffee.

Another factor entering the coffee profitability equation is the planting of new coffee trees with a higher productivity than the previous trees, especially in the state of Parana which produces about half of Brazil's coffee output.[13] Since the 1967 and 1968 plantings will not start producing before 1972 and 1973, it is too early to tell whether or not Brazil's coffee productive capacity will once again exceed the demand.[14]

While coffee prices appear to have increased relative to alternative crops from 1966 to 1969, other factors weigh in the balance on the side of alternative crops. The new adjustable pegged exchange rate system initiated in August 1968, the expansion and improvement in the agricultural credit program in 1967 and 1968, and the improvements in the minimum price program and subsidies for farm inputs such as fertilizers have all had a more favorable impact on alternative crops. As a result of these measures affecting both coffee and alternative crops, the role of coffee in the Brazilian economy has fallen significantly both in the export sector, from 53 percent of total exports in 1964 to 35 percent in 1970, and in the domestic sector (value added in the coffee sector as a percentage of GNP has declined from 2.9 percent in 1964 to 1.2 in 1968).

An innovation in coffee pricing policy initiated in 1967 which has significant implications for monetary and credit policy is the more frequent adjustments in prices. Prior to 1967 the price to the producer and exporter of coffee was set annually. In June 1967 the National Monetary Council announced a 40 percent increase effective in July and an additional 11 percent on 1 January 1968. The aim of this more flexible pricing policy was to encourage growers to hold their coffee longer and thereby moderate the expansive impact of the second semester of the year. This policy was continued in 1968 when the price was again raised 15 percent on 1 July; another 12 percent increase was granted on 1 November 1968, and yet another increase of 8-10 percent on 1 April 1969. The more frequent price changes induced growers and exporters to hold coffee longer and to even out the flow of coffee funds, which, in turn, facilitated monetary management in

---

[13]Robert Johnson, "Coffee Policy Considerations in Brazil," p. 2, notes that the new varieties under experimental conditions have produced several times as much as older varieties. Under field conditions these new varieties are expected to produce four times as much as the older varieties.

[14]The Brazilian coffee authorities estimate that existing capacity will produce about 26 million bags per year. Existing demand is estimated at 26 million bags, 18 million bags for exports, and 8 million for domestic use. Demand is estimated to be rising at a rate of about one million bags per year.

in the same manner as the new flexible exchange rate system. Another innovation initiated on February 24, 1971, was the abandonment of the unilateral price fixing and the adoption of a system of flexible coffee prices. The objective of this new policy was to maintain the competitiveness of Brazilian coffee, permitting the IBC to establish supply ceilings and export control mechanism.

A major unresolved policy issue confronting the Brazilian authorities is the use of the proceeds of the Coffee Defense Fund. While many tend to describe the receipts from the difference between the prices received by exporters and the cruzeiro return from exports as an export tax, these receipts do not go into the general funds of the Treasury, but are used almost entirely on behalf of the coffee sector. As late as 1965 the Defense Fund had a negative balance. Starting in 1966 and accelerating in 1968 the Defense Fund has produced a large deposit balance, reaching more than NCr$ 1.4 billion at the end of 1969. To the extent that these deposit balances are sterilized in the Bank of Brazil, they serve a monetary contractive purpose as an offset to other expansionary operations, credit to the private sector or an export surplus, for example. But the availability of these funds tends to create pressure to use them for the coffee sector. This increase in incentives to coffee will tend toward a new surge of investment. An offsetting gesture, however, was the establishment of an Agricultural Development Fund with the proceeds of the increase in the domestic consumption price in March 1970. The difference between the 32 and 50 cruzeiros per bag will go to this fund instead of to the Coffee Defense Fund. However, the issue of the disposition of the more than NCr$ 1.4 billion in the Defense Fund and future contribution quotas to this fund has not been resolved. The most direct solution would be an export tax on coffee with the proceeds deposited to the general funds of the Treasury. Neither the Castello Branco nor the Costa e Silva governments were able to overcome the political opposition of coffee growers to this move. Such a tax would contribute toward reducing the possibility that excess coffee production would again be a fact of Brazilian life.

International Outlook for Coffee

The decline in Brazil's coffee production during the five-year period 1966-70 has also altered the outlook for coffee in the world market to the point where economists in the U.S. Department of Agriculture were writing of "increasing evidence that the corner has been turned and that we are, in fact, moving from a period of glut and depressed prices to one of tight supplies and higher price levels."[15]

My assessment of the prospects for Brazilian coffee investment and production does not lead to the same firm conclusion. New investments since 1967 will increase the Brazilian coffee productive capacity in 1972 or 1973, depending upon the weather. On the other hand, Brazil will no longer have the large stocks of coffee to underwrite the coffee market as has been the case in the past decade. The large Brazilian stockpile and its volunteered position as residual supplier in the market contributed greatly to the stability of coffee supply and prices during the 1960s.[16] This period of stability stands out in stark contrast with the chaotic coffee marketing conditions, with alternating periods of booming and depressed prices, with the unstable coffee export earnings, and with the revenue uncertainties prevailing prior to the 1960s. The International Coffee Agreement, established in 1962, contributed to the stability in coffee prices and in foreign exchange earnings during this period, but it would not have been possible without the Brazilian stockpile. Brazilian coffee stocks have comprised over 80 percent of total world coffee stocks and even with the recent decline in ite stocks, Brazilian stocks still comprise over 70 percent of the total. But the development and maintenance of these stocks was costly to Brazil, in terms both of domestic costs and foreign exchange losses. Looking ahead, the question might be raised as to who will bear the future costs of stabilizing the supply of coffee for the world consumers. Should the primary producing countries, whose production of a given commodity accounts for a major share of total world output, accept the costs of stabilizing the supply? Brazil's experience indicates that the country which takes the lead in stabilizing supply and prices must also accept a major share of the costs. Brazil is still counting the economic, political, and social costs of its coffee policies of the 1950s. Unless the Brazilian authorities have extremely short memories, they are unlikely to make the same mistakes in the near future. Thus, unless another formula is developed for financing the world's stockpile of coffee, we are likely to experience once again the alternating periods of shortages and gluts of an earlier decade.

---

[15]John I. Kress and J. Phillip Rourk, "Story of the 1960's: Coffee in World Trade," p. 6.

[16]Ibid., p. 8. Kress and Rourk note that U.S. dollar prices for coffee were not significantly different in 1968 from those in 1959.

CHAPTER XI

Mobilization of Resources for Investment and Growth: Capital Market Policies— 1964 to 1972

> The economic growth process is characterized by a market economy that uses the price mechanism for resource allocation during which there is an increase in the number and variety of financial institutions, and a substantial rise in the proportion not only of money, but also of total financial assets with respect to GDP and to wealth.
>
> Hugh T. Patrick
> *Financial Development and Economic Growth in Underdeveloped Countries*

In altering relative prices in the economy, the set of market-oriented economic policies pursued by the Brazilian economic authorities since 1964 stimulated changes in the structure of investment and production; but they did not offer a sufficient condition for rapid and sustained growth. The Brazilian economic boom began only in mid-1967 with the effective implementation of a number of new programs and the establishment of new institutions which had as their purpose the mobilization of domestic savings and the channeling of these savings into productive investments.

The post-1964 development strategy emphasized the need to mobilize both domestic and foreign savings, and the efforts to achieve domestic savings proved as difficult as those to expand foreign savings. Sharp exchange rate devaluations, combined with restrictive

tariff policies, provided the current account surpluses needed to reduce the foreign indebtedness and to restore Brazil's international
creditworthiness; but current account surpluses during the years 1964
to 1966 meant dissaving at a time when Brazil desperately needed an
expansion of savings to stem the inflationary pressures. Only after
three years of concerted effort to expand exports, to reduce tariffs
and other restrictions to imports, and to restructure the foreign debt
was it possible for Brazil to achieve a modest level of foreign savings.[1] The measures taken to achieve the targeted foreign savings
were described in Chapter VIII. This chapter examines the programs
and institutions aimed at stimulating domestic savings.

A full rendering of the measures to increase compulsory domestic savings would include fiscal savings (that is, the current account surplus of the federal government), savings generated by the
autonomous and semi-autonomous agencies whose operations do not
fall within the budget, and savings generated by earmarked revenues
which are channeled directly to specific investment purposes. The
trends of these public sector savings and investments are examined in
Chapter VI. Described here are the several programs which have
generated private sector savings and investments: the National
Housing Program, the Northeast Development Program, the Agricultural Credit Program, the Capital Market Development Program, and
the Program for Social Integration.

National Housing Program

Perhaps the most effective of all the economic programs and policies
initiated by the Castello Branco government has been the revolutionary new National Housing Program. This program has served not
only to meet the burgeoning housing deficit, but, given the importance of the construction industry in the economy, as the key source
for generating new investments and expanding employment.

At the time of the 1964 revolution, housing construction had
virtually ceased. The Brazilian home financing institutions had long
since gone out of existence as their deposits dried up in the face of
hyper-inflation and controlled deposit rates. At the same time, controls on rents undermined incentives to invest in housing. The resulting stagnation in home construction intensified the traditional

---

[1] Foreign savings are equated with a deficit in the current account of the balance of
payments. A sustained level of foreign savings requires, assuming no reserve changes,
a corresponding inflow of foreign capital. To be sustained over time, foreign capital
flows are dependent upon maintaining a sound debt service capacity which, in turn, is
primarily a function of the rate of growth of export earnings and the level of service on
outstanding debts.

housing deficit. The Brazilian authorities estimated that, in 1964, eight million families, more than a quarter of the population, lived in sub-standard housing, and that the rapidly growing population added new housing requirements of 400,000 units per year. In the conditions prevailing in Brazil in 1964, a high priority had to be given to housing, not solely for social purposes, although the desperate housing shortage proclaimed this as reason enough, but for the health of the economy itself. No other industry could have a greater impact in terms of expanding effective demand, so necessary for the stimulation of new investments and output in the industrial sector. But how to generate additional savings in an inflationary environment and how to channel these savings into housing?

The housing sector received immediate attention from the Castello Branco economists with the establishment of the National Housing Bank in August 1964.[2] Unfortunately, neither the management nor the resources of the bank proved sufficiently effective to have any significant impact during the first two years of its existence. Nevertheless, during this period much was done to establish the necessary conditions and incentives for effective operation of the national housing program in later years. But some of the new incentives tended to conflict with other economic and social objectives of the government. For example, the gradual reduction of rent controls, an essential incentive for investment in housing, conflicted with the price stabilization effort, as rents inevitably rose more rapidly than the general price level, thus intensifying the economic difficulties of the urban working class whose rents rose faster than their salaries.

Despite the conflicting objectives and institutional complications, the Brazilian authorities managed by the end of 1966 to piece together the three essential conditions for an effective national housing program: a well-managed National Housing Bank with affiliated institutions throughout the country, monetary correction applied to all the assets and liabilities of these institutions, and the Workers' Tenure Guarantee Fund as the major source of funding.

The National Housing Bank itself served primarily as an intermediary to channel funds received from its various sources to secondary financial institutions which dealt directly with the investing public. Initially, the Housing Bank relied on existing intermediaries such as the commercial banks, private and official development banks, and other existing credit and finance companies. But the same law which created the Housing Bank also authorized the creation of Real Estate Credit Societies, a form of joint-stock savings and loan association, as

---

[2]Law 4380; 21 August 1964.

an additional form of intermediary. These savings and loan institutions were also authorized to sell mortgage paper (*letras imobiliárias*) to the public as a means of augmenting the resources available from the Housing Bank. In 1966 savings banks (*caixas econômicas*) and in 1970 mutual savings and loan associations became authorized intermediaries of the National Housing Program. By the end of 1970 the National Housing Program comprised a large variety of institutions throughout the country, including eight regional offices of the Housing Bank, thirty-nine mutual savings and loan associations, forty-three real estate credit institutions, and twenty-six savings banks (twenty-two federal- and four state-chartered) with 1,500 branches.

The monetary correction mechanism constituted the second essential element of the housing program. It provided the answer to the question of how to maintain the real value of financial assets in an inflationary environment. The application of monetary correction to both the assets and liabilities of the institutions comprising the National Housing Program ensured both the maintenance of value of the workers' pensions and the continued economic viability of the housing institutions and the housing program. But monetary correction also provided a necessary incentive for attracting voluntary deposits into the Housing Bank and the newly formed house financing institutions throughout the country, by assuring the private sector a return on letras imobiliárias comparable to the rate of inflation in the economy plus a deposit rate of 8 to 12 percent. Monetary correction for the assets and liabilities of these institutions is calculated in the same manner as in the case of government bonds and other financial instruments described in Chapter IV.

The first two years of experience with the housing program revealed that it could not be effective without additional sources of funds. The extensive institutional framework and the monetary correction mechanism did not attract sufficient voluntary savings to make a significant dent in the housing deficit. Recognizing this shortcoming of the program, the Brazilian authorities initiated in October 1966 a new major source of funding, the Workers' Tenure Guarantee Fund (*O Fundo de Guarantia do Tempo de Servico*).[3] With the establishment of this Fund under the management of the National Housing Bank, the authorities added the third essential element of the housing program.

---

[3]Law 5, 107. 13 September 1966, and Decree Law 20, 14 September 1966 created the Fundo de Guarantia do Tempo de Servico; Central Bank Resolution 46, 12 January 1967, set forth the financial criteria for the collection, deposit, and application of the fund.

The Workers' Tenure Guarantee Fund, similar to the social security pension fund in the United States, is comprised of monthly compulsory deposits amounting to 8 percent of the wages of each employee, with deposits made by the employer in the name of the employee. The significance of this Fund for the operations of the Housing Bank is indicated in Table XI-1; inflows from this source in 1967 alone amounted to almost six times the total resources of the Housing Bank at the end of 1966. With this new major source of financing the Housing Bank began to have a significant impact, not only on housing construction, but also on the level of investment, output, and employment in the Brazilian economy (see Table XI-5).

Northeast Development Program

Another program for resource mobilization—both for the generation of financial savings and for the channeling of these savings into investments—had as its primary purpose the development of the northeast region. But the Northeast Development Program, as it evolved with both compulsory and induced savings elements, also played a significant role in the recuperation of investment demand in

Table XI-1
NATIONAL HOUSING PROGRAM, 1965–1972[a]
(millions of Cr$, current prices)

Year	Workers' Tenure Guarantee Fund	Housing Bonds Sold to Public	Savings Generated	Loans	Investment Demand[b]
1965	—	—	—	19	28
1966	—	7	7	80	120
1967	629	133	762	362	540
1968	1,272	321	1,593	1,422	2,140
1969	1,710	461	2,171	1,709	2,560
1970	2,429	802	3,231	2,649	3,980
1971	3,773	1,038	4,811	3,696	5,550
1972 (Sept.)	3,785	942	4,727	2,970	4,460

[a]The National Housing Program includes the National Housing Bank, savings banks, housing cooperatives, real estate credit societies, savings and loan associations, and other affiliated financial institutions.

[b]Estimated on basis of average down-payment on housing loans of 33 percent.

Source: *Boletim do Banco Central do Brasil*, December 1972, Tables 1.17 and 1.19, pp. 36-39.

Brazil starting in 1967 and continuing through 1972. When established in 1959, the Northeast Development Program, implemented by the Superintendent for Development of the Northeast (SUDENE), received its funds primarily from earmarked taxes. These monies were applied entirely to infrastructure projects, largely hydro-electric power plants. In 1961 the Brazilian government introduced a new aspect of the program with the authorization of fiscal incentives to the private sector to invest in the northeast states.[4] This new induced savings program, which continues to be known as the Article 34-18 fiscal incentives, permitted all legal persons from any part of the country to deduct 50 percent of their income tax liability by investing this amount in the Northeast, with initial deposits to be made in the Bank of the Northeast (BNB). In order to use these funds, however, the taxpayer-depositer had to invest them, together with a matching amount, in a project in the Northeast region approved by the SUDENE. While the law initially required that the fiscal incentive funds be matched by new equity money, SUDENE later modified these requirements, in order to make investments in the Northeast more attractive, by varying the amount of new money required with the priority of the project for the region. For high priority projects, the Northeast Bank also extended loan capital, so that the leverage from a given deposit of tax funds varied from two to one to ten to one, depending on the priority of the project.

With the gradual improvement in the Article 34-18 investment incentives and the intensified tax enforcement program of the Castello Branco government, more and more individuals and corporations began to make use of the 34-18 tax incentive. Deposits in the Bank of the Northeast jumped from Cr$ 37.3 million in 1964 to Cr$ 149.4 million in 1965, as shown in Table XI-2. For the first several years, however, the program resulted in large net flows into the Bank of the Northeast, draining these financial resources from the south-central states (from which an estimated 80 percent of the resources were derived) without an accompanying increase in effective investment demand. Disbursements from the Northeast Bank remained minimal in these years, as investment opportunities in the region required extensive feasibility studies on the part of the depositors who, in the main, resided in the south-central states and had little knowledge of the region. But as the two-year deadline for use of the funds approached, the depositors began increasingly to seek out investment opportunities, and an innovative group of entrepreneurs

[4]The Northeast Development Program was initiated by Law No. 3692, 15 December 1959; later revised by Law 3995, 14 December 1961; and regulated by Articles 34 and 18 of the SUMOC and by Decree Law 5534, 12 December 1964.

Table XI-2

NORTHEAST DEVELOPMENT PROGRAM, 1962–1972

(millions of Cr$, current prices)

Year	34-18 Deposits in Bank of Northeast	Disbursements	Estimated Investment Demand[a]
1962	5.7	—	—
1963	7.7	0.3	0.9
1964	37.3	5.2	14.8
1965	149.4	8.7	24.8
1966	226.6	43.3	123.0
1967	351.1	178.7	513.0
1968	456.7	326.2	1,030.0
1969	680.8	490.0	1,400.0
1970	859.3	732.4	2,080.0
1971	777.6	854.2	2,440.0

[a]Estimated on the basis that the average contribution of 34-18 funds in total investment is 35 percent.

Source: *Relatório Annual*, Banco do Nordeste do Brasil, various annual reports of the Bank of the Northeast Brazil.

found profit in encouraging groups of individuals and corporations to place their 34-18 deposits into joint investment ventures.[5] As a result disbursements from the Bank of the Northeast began to rise sharply in 1967 and have continued upward in each year through 1972.

In 1970, in recognition of the capital intensive nature of the private sector investment in the Northeast, President Medici revised the 34-18 fiscal incentive, earmarking half of these funds for more labor intensive investments in agriculture and related infrastructure. The effect of this action was to reduce the induced savings aspect of the program in favor of a larger compulsory savings.

Agricultural Investments

The market-oriented measures implemented by the Castello Branco government in 1964 and 1965 offered an important stimulant to agricultural output and investments. The more realistic exchange rates increased the cruzeiro return for agricultural exports and the liberation of farm products from price controls improved the return on

---

[5]The article 34-18 required that funds be transferred to the federal taxes if not used by 31 December of the second year following the initial deposit.

domestic sales of farm produce. Nevertheless, limited access to medium- and long-term credit continued to constrain investments in the agricultural sector. (See Chapter IX for greater detail on agricultural credit.) While the provision of official credit for agriculture had long been a principal policy of Brazilian governments, prior to 1962 Brazilian agriculture had received relatively little credit for production and investment purposes. According to a 1962 study by the Brazilian Planning Ministry, the great majority of the farm credit was of a short-term nature to finance marketing.[6]

Recognizing the shortage of medium- and long-term credit for agriculture, the Castello Branco team ranked improvements in agricultural credit high on the list of priority measures. The Rural Credit Law of 14 July 1964 was one of the first major measures authorized by the Castello Branco government; the implementing regulations, however, were not issued until September 1967 and further revisions were necessary in May 1969. The agricultural credit program contained two elements. First, the official credit institutions, especially the Bank of Brazil and the Bank of the Northeast, received larger agricultural credit allocations in the monetary budget. The Bank of Brazil had traditionally provided an estimated two-thirds of total rural credit. The second, and new, element of the program aimed at involving the commercial banks, with their 14,000 branches throughout the country, in lending to the agricultural sector, particularly in the production and investment type credits. To expand commercial bank operations in the rural zones, the Central Bank issued instructions, under the authority of the Rural Credit Law, that 10 percent of the assets of each commercial bank be devoted to agricultural purposes. Another Central Bank regulation offered a financial inducement for the same purpose by permitting the commercial banks to satisfy a portion of their compulsory reserve requirements with agricultural paper. Since the alternative to agricultural credit was non-earning deposits at the Central Bank, the banks found some inducement to expanding their rural credit, even at subsidized rates. The regulations required that all agricultural credit, from both the offical and private institutions, be extended at rates of interest fixed well below the going loan rates. Table XI-5 traces the growth of the Bank of Brazil credit for agricultural investment with the biggest increases in 1968 (30 percent over 1967) and 1971 (47 percent over 1970).

Use of the commercial banking system, both the official and private banks, to finance investments in agriculture constituted, in part, a forced savings mechanism. Just as the credit allocative process

---

[6]Estados Unidos do Brasil, *Three-Year Plan for Economic and Social Development, 1963-1965*, p. 28.

in the industrialization strategy period had served as a mechanism to transfer savings of the agricultural sector into industry, the rural credit program of recent years has tended to reverse the process. As a consequence, total credit to agriculture has grown more rapidly than the output of that sector.

Capital Markets Development Program

The major domestic source for financing industrial investments, exclusive of reinvested earnings, during the decade prior to 1964 had been the National Economic Development Bank (BNDE). Initiated in 1952 with Roberto Campos as its first president, the BNDE functioned largely as a channel of funds from international institutions and domestic fiscal sources, such as earmarked taxes and direct budgetary allocation. Over the decade prior to 1964 the BNDE derived about one-third of its resources from foreign and two-thirds from domestic sources. Aside from the BNDE the only domestic institution which extended any significant amount of financing for investment was the Bank of Brazil.

As an integral part of the development strategy to stimulate long-term savings for investments in private industry, Planning Minister Roberto Campos and Finance Minister Bulhões introduced in 1964 a new Capital Markets Law.[7] This law aimed at reorganizing the existing Brazilian markets and institutions and laying the foundation for development of a capital market. A vital stock market comprises a part of the capital markets development program, but as a means of attracting new savings, it remains a relatively insignificant, albeit growing, market. More important has been the development of new mechanisms and institutions for mobilizing long-term capital. By Decree Law 157 in February 1966 Ministers Campos and Bulhões initiated another tax credit, similar to the Article 34-18 incentive for the Northeast, which permits individuals to meet 12 percent of their personal income tax liabilities by the purchase of shares of new investment funds (*certificados de compras de acões*). The law requires that these DL-157 funds, the name by which they are popularly known, be retained on deposit for a minimum of two years and that the major part of the portfolio in which these funds are invested be in new issues.[8]

---

[7]Law 4728, 14 July 1965.

[8]The regulation initially permitted only 10 percent for individuals and 5 percent for firms, but was later changed to 12 percent for individuals and eliminated the credit for firms.

The institutions authorized to handle these fiscal funds included selected banks, finance companies, and brokers, but a new group of institutions, private investment and development banks, was intended to be the main recipient and manager of the funds.[9] In addition to managing the DL-157 funds, the new investment banks were authorized to serve as intermediaries for resources from FINAME,[10] Resolution 63 funds from foreign sources,[11] sales of acceptances in the market, time deposits, and their own capital resources. They are required to apply these resources on a medium- and long-term basis through purchase of debt instruments, by underwriting stock issues, and by serving as an intermediary in the market for medium-term commercial acceptances.

The dramatic growth and expanded role of the institutions dealing in the medium- and long-term capital market through the following years are traced in Table XI-3. By the end of 1969 the number of institutions authorized to handle DL-157 funds had grown to 24 investment banks; 125 credit, finance, and. investment institutions; and 45 brokerage firms. By 1969 the volume of funds flowing through investment banks and other authorized institutions into the capital market was already greater than the availability of new issues, with the consequence that prices of existing issues rose to excessively high levels, forcing the authorities to focus on measures to increase the number of new security issues in the market.

Program for Social Integration

By 1969 it had become evident that both foreign and domestic resource mobilization measures of the previous five years had been effective. Foreign capital was moving into Brazil at an ever-increasing rate and domestic savings were rising rapidly. Projections of these trends, however, indicated an excessive reliance on foreign savings, with two unacceptable consequences. First, it meant a sharply rising foreign debt service burden requiring an equally sharp increase in export earnings, and a growth in Brazil's dependence on foreign markets. Secondly, it meant a disproportionate expansion in foreign ownership of Brazilian industry.

The options open to the Brazilian government were (a) to reduce foreign savings and, therefore, the role of foreign capital, or (b) to

---

[9] Central Bank Resolution 18 of 18 February 1966.

[10] FINAME, a special agency for industrial financing, was established in 1964 as a fund within the BNDE, and in 1966 was given its own staff but remained under the BNDE president. It operates solely as an intermediary to channel funds from foreign sources.

[11] See Chapter V; p. 208.

Table XI-3

CAPITAL MARKET DEVELOPMENT PROGRAM, 1965–1972

(millions of Cr$, current prices)

Year	OL-157 Funds Administered by Investment Banks	FINAME Funds (gov't & foreign)	Resolution 63 Funds (foreign sources)	Sales of Acceptances	Time Deposits	Total Savings	Total Investment Loans
1965	—	—	—	—	—	—	—
1966	—	13	—	99	2	114	149
1967	28	31	11	461	83	614	681
1968	87	53	193	363	324	1,020	1,049
1969	269	81	155	705	690	1,900	2,070
1970	153	197	311	146	1,709	2,516	2,633
1971	483	337	563	339	1,538	3,260	5,086
1972 (June)	-119	178	2,668	804	3,328	6,859	3,230

Source: *Boletim do Banco Central do Brasil* October 1972, Table 1.13.

stimulate a faster growth in domestic savings. Preferring the latter course, President Garrastazu Medici initiated in September 1970 yet another nationwide compulsory savings-investment program, the Program for Social Integration. This program served two purposes: first, to supplement the capital market development measures in providing medium- and long-term financing for Brazilian business; second, to integrate Brazilian workers into the economic system by providing them with some of the benefits of economic growth and giving them a vested interest in the system itself. As part of his effort to mobilize public opinion for the development effort, President Medici announced this new program on 7 September 1970, shortly after his announcement of the Transamazonic Highway project.

The funds for the Program for Social Integration are derived from two sources, a percentage of the existing income tax on business and a small increase in the value-added tax.[12] These earmarked tax revenues are deposited in the Federal Savings Bank (*Caixa Econômica Federal*) and several affiliated banks for relending to Brazilian business in the form of convertible debenture bonds, stocks, and mortgage shares. The Brazilian workers participate in the program in two ways: first, each worker is credited with an amount in the Fund for Social Integration based on the contributions of his employer to the fund. He cannot use this initial contribution, however, except for specific purposes, such as retirement, marriage, disability, and the purchase of a home. The annual earnings of the fund, on the other hand, are available to the worker, including the annual monetary correction and a 3 percent interest rate on his share, plus his share of the net profits of the fund after deduction for administrative expenses and reserves.

Finance Minister Delfim Netto initially estimated the resource mobilization from this source at Cr$237 million by the end of 1971 and Cr$2821 million by the end of 1974. By the end of 1971 the Program for Social Integration had actually received contributions of Cr$279 million; by the end of its first year in operation, June 1972, had received Cr$643 million; and was accumulating additional resources at a rate of Cr$1 billion per year. Also by June 1972, the Federal Savings Bank, which administers the funds, had lent out Cr$592 million, the major part, about 70 percent, for production purposes.[13]

---

[12]The first contribution was to be made to the fund in July 1971 with graduated increases in the tax rates, the business income tax deduction of 2 percent in 1971 rising to 5 percent in 1973 and thereafter, and the tax on gross sales rising from ½ of 1 percent in 1971 to 1 percent in 1974.

[13]*Boletim do Banco Central do Brasil*, December 1972, Table I.21, pp. 44-45.

Domestic Savings

The significance of the National Housing Program, the Northeast Development Program, and the Capital Market Development Program for the recuperation of the Brazilian economy in 1967 cannot be overstated. These three programs accounted for the major part of the growth in financial savings and, by providing the necessary inducements for investment, also generated the largest part of the increase in Brazilian investments in 1967 and ensuing years.

Table XI-4 compares the financial savings mobilized under these programs with total domestic savings (based on national accounts data). In 1964 and 1965, only the Northeast Development Program had any significant effect, amounting to less than 1 percent of domestic savings. In 1967 the National Housing and Capital Market Programs were effectively set afoot; in that year the three programs generated financial savings equivalent to almost 17 percent of total domestic savings, and by 1970 they accounted for about 21 percent of domestic savings. The Program for Social Integration, which began in 1971, exceeded the importance of the Northeast Development Program even by the end of its first year in operation, and will provide another major source of domestic savings to finance Brazilian investments in future years.

Investment Demand

The three domestic savings programs, summarized above, also played a crucial role, beginning in 1967 and continuing in the ensuing years, in the inducement and financing of new investments in Brazil. Table XI-5 traces the trend of investments (in constant prices) generated by each of these three programs. The Housing Program got underway in 1967, expanded rapidly in 1968 and then, after a year of pause to permit the construction industry to catch up on the supply side, rose steadily in the following years. The Northeast Development Program picked up activity sharply in 1967 and increased steadily through 1970, but experienced a decline in 1971 following the cutback in the use of 34-18 funds. The Capital Market Development Program also added significantly to the rapid growth in investment demand in 1967 and became second only to the Housing Program as a source of investment financing.

These three programs and two additional investment financing sources, the Agricultural Credit Program and the National Economic Development Bank, explain the major part of the rejuvena-

Table XI-4

PROGRAMS TO MOBILIZE FINANCIAL SAVINGS, 1964–1972

(millions of Cr$, current prices)

Item	1964	1965	1966	1967	1968	1969	1970	1971	1972[a]
1. National Housing Program	—	—	7	762	1,593	2,171	3,231	4,811	4,727
2. Northeast Development Program (34-18 fiscal funds)	37	149	227	351	457	681	859	778	800
3. Capital Market Development (Excluding FINAME and Resolution 63 sources)	—	—	99	572	774	1,664	2,008	2,360	4,013
4. Program for Social Integration	—	—	—	—	—	—	—	279	875
5. Total domestic financial savings under these programs	37	149	333	1,685	2,824	4,516	6,098	8,228	10,415
6. Total domestic savings (National Accounts Data)	4,388	7,311	8,128	10,013	15,628	21,747	27,942	37,051	N.A.
7. Total savings under programs as percentage of total domestic savings	.8	2.0	4.1	16.8	18.1	20.8	21.8	22.2	N.A.

[a]Estimated.

Source: Data for the first three items from Chapter 11, Tables 1, 2, and 3 respectively; item 4 data from *Boletim do Banco Central do Brasil*, December 1972, Table I.21; and item 6 data from Chapter 3, Table 1.

Table XI-5

TREND OF INVESTMENT DEMAND, 1964–1972
(constant prices)[a]

Item	1964	1965	1966	1967	1968	1969	1970	1971	1972
1. National Housing Program	—	39	120	421	1,346	1,333	1,730	1,986	1,429 (June)
2. Northeast Development Program	32	34	123	401	648	729	904	881	N.A.
3. Capital Market Development Program	—	—	149	532	659	1,078	1,145	1,836	1,035 (June)
4. Agricultural Credit Program of Bank of Brazil	115	72	147	147	205	230	244	380	N.A.
5. National Economic Development Bank	106	80	59	103	351	662	681	542	N.A.
6. Program for Social Integration	—	—	—	—	—	—	—	22	259 (Aug.)
7. Total investments induced by above programs and institutions	253	225	598	1,604	3,209	4,072	4,704	5,647	N.A.
8. Total investments/savings (gross capital formation)	9,335	9,355	8,212	8,475	10,832	11,920	13,478	15,884	N.A.
9. Investments induced by above programs as percentage of total investments/savings	2.7	2.4	7.3	18.9	29.6	34.2	34.9	35.6	N.A.

Note: The above data, while based on the best sources available, can only be considered as estimates of the investments financed and induced under each of these programs.

[a] Deflated by general price index, 1965-67 = 100.

Source: Item 1 data from Chapter 11, Table 1 (investment demand); item 2—Chapter 11, Table 2 (estimated investment demand); items 3 and 5—Chapter 11, Table 3 (total investment loans); item 4—*Relatório do Banco Central do Brasil*, various years.

tion of Brazilian investments in 1967 and 1968.[14] Moreover, they continue to explain the stability at high growth rates of Brazilian investments since that time. As shown in Table XI-5, these five sources have generated about one-third of total investments since 1968. Projections of these sources for the years ahead are for a continuation of the same high growth rate. The Program for Social Integration, which began to extend long-term loans and to purchase investment securities in 1972, should add another Cr$ 1 billion per year (in 1971 prices) or about 5 percent of total investments for the years ahead.

Assessment of Resource Mobilization Programs

The prospects for the stability and growth of the economy in the years ahead will depend in a large part on the continued effectiveness of these programs in mobilizing domestic resources for development, particularly the Brazilian private sector.

First, with these programs, an estimated 65 to 70 percent of total investments in Brazil are subject to direct governmental control.[15] This high degree of control ensures a greater degree of stability of savings and investments, and allocation of private as well as public investments to priority regions, sectors, and industries.

Second, they helped to restore and to maintain the vitality of the Brazilian private sector. All of the investments financed by these sources, except a portion of the BNDE credits, are private sector investments. Although the savings decision in each case may be compulsory, forced (through inflation), or voluntary, the investment decision is entirely voluntary, based upon the price and market motivations of the private investor but acting within the scope of the respective program requirements. Comprising an estimated 35 percent of total investments, these financial sources provide the private sector with a firm share of total investments. The Program for Social Integration adds a new source, to comprise an estimated 5 percent of total investments. These several sources of investment funds, to-

---

[14]The Agricultural Credit Program and the BNDE operations are excluded from the savings table (see table XI-4) because both serve as channels for official foreign loans and credits, which are distinguished from domestic sources only with difficulty. The BNDE receives an estimated one-third of its resources from foreign credits; the Agricultural Credit Programs of the Bank of Brazil and the commercial banks derive a portion of their resources from the PL 480 program and credits from other international financial institutions. Also, the agricultural credit is in part based upon forced savings through inflation.

[15]1967 national account data estimate public sector investments at 31 percent of total investments.

gether with credit policies, are protecting the relative investment shares of the Brazilian private sector from the encroachment of both the Brazilian public sector and the foreign sector.

Third, the converse of points one and two above is that the interest rate and profit motives play a more circumscribed role in the decision to save and to invest. These resource mobilization programs have compartmentalized available savings-investments for those regions, sectors, and industries which are considered to be priority by the economic authorities. This segregation of available savings for specific purposes limits the access of other sectors and industries to savings for investment. It remains to be seen whether the authorities can make better decisions on this score than the market mechanism.

Fourth, and finally, these domestic resource mobilization programs have reduced the reliance of the Brazilian economy on foreign savings, with all the political and economic consequences which this might mean. The ability of a country to mobilize its own domestic savings is a fundamental prerequisite for economic growth. Foreign savings can be helpful for a time, and under favorable circumstances they can be sustained over a longer period of time, as U.S. historical experience has shown. But foreign savings cannot cover more than a marginal portion of a country's investment requirements, especially a country the size of Brazil; and excessive reliance on foreign savings can lead to serious difficulties. During the 1950s Brazil's excessive reliance on foreign savings to finance its development efforts resulted in an unsustainable growth of foreign indebtedness, enlarged the foreign ownership of Brazilian industry to an unacceptable level, and contributed to the domestic crisis. Is Brazil once again relying too heavily on foreign savings? After three years of dissaving, 1964 to 1966, Brazil began to import capital at an increasing rate. By 1971 foreign savings comprised 16 percent of total savings. The trend of domestic and foreign savings as a percentage of total savings can be seen in Table XI-6. Whether this trend can be sustained depends very much on the dynamics of the rate of growth of exports, the level and conditions of capital inflows, and the continued confidence in the Brazilian economy.

Many developing nations have over-emphasized the foreign savings element in their development programs, and the economic literature has not been very helpful to them on this score. The emphasis of the academic economists on foreign assistance and absorptive capacity have tended to focus the attention of economic policy makers in the developing nations on maximizing

Table XI-6
DOMESTIC AND FOREIGN SAVINGS
AS PERCENTAGE OF TOTAL SAVINGS, 1946–1971

Year	Domestic Savings	Foreign Savings[a]	Year	Domestic Savings	Foreign Savings[a]
1962	87	13	1967	92	8
1963	95	5	1968	91	9
1964	102	−2	1969	95	5
1965	108	−8	1970	90	10
1966	99	1	1971	84	16

[a]Current account surplus.

Source: *Boletim do Banco Central do Brasil*, various issues; *Conjuntura Econômica*, June 1970.

foreign capital flows and foreign savings rather than on domestic resource mobilization.[16]

Lessons in the Brazilian Experience

This assessment of the economic policies and performance of the Brazilian economy during the past two decades offers some important lessons for both the industrial nations and for other developing nations, including future Brazilian governments. Brazil's experiences of the 1950s present clear evidence of the effectiveness of the industrialization policies in achieving a high rate of economic growth; but the costs in social, economic, and political terms cannot be overlooked. If it were possible to say that there was no alternative path to economic development, one might well conclude that the accomplishments were worthy of the sacrifices. This is not the conclusion of this study. Brazil could have achieved a higher rate of sustainable growth and over a longer time with lower social and political costs if the policy makers had had the will and capacity to change their policies with the changing times.

Those who have studied the political decision-making process during the Kubitschek, Quadros, and Goulart regimes conclude that the failure to revise the course of economic policies was as much due to the inability of their economic advisers to agree on the proper

[16]The "two gap" concept is said to have contributed to this erroneous focus by offering the policy makers in the developing nations a model "better suited to reveal the payoffs from more assistance, than to explore what can be done without more assistance." Richard R. Nelson, "The Effective Exchange Rate: Employment and Growth in a Foreign Exchange—Constrained Economy," p. 547.

course of action as it was to the unwillingness of the politicians to accept the political risks of unpopular measures. Thus, stabilization efforts were repeatedly halted in mid-course by presidents seemingly unwilling to risk their political futures; at the same time, behind each president stood an economist with a theoretical rational for his actions. And while the academic economists bickered among themselves over the tradeoff between growth and stability or the structuralist versus the monetarist approach to stability, the international financial institutions pursued an inflexible line of denying assistance without stabilization. Confused by it all, the politicians understandably adopted the politically popular course of action.

The Brazilian experiences thus highlight the gaps between the evolving realities and the recognition of these realities by the economic and political leaders, and between the empirical economists studying the realities and the theorists who reject the realities until they can be neatly programmed into a body of doctrine. These experiences also reveal the complications arising from such gaps, for the longer the delay in correcting structural imbalances and financial distortions, the greater the political difficulty in making the necessary changes in policy. The lesson is that policy changes should be initiated as soon as the need arises; the longer the delay, the greater the change necessary and the greater the economic, social, and political consequences, and, therefore, the greater the opposition from vested interests to such changes. Just as the industrialization policies of pre-1964 had their own built-in self-perpetuating mechanism, which changed only after a complete economic breakdown and political revolution, the structural and institutional changes of the past eight years have developed vested interests and a growing momentum of their own which may also tend to be self-perpetuating until they, too, prove to be inadequate to the task.

Development requires a will to develop and a belief that improvement in the economic welfare of the country is attainable. There has been a great deal of defeatism in the developing world. In the past this defeatism has been based upon economic realities, such as limited energy, transportation, and communications infrastructure, illiterate populations, inadequate technology, poor resource base, and population pressures. More recently this defeatism has been based upon outworn traditions and not infrequently upon imported ideologies.

"Our destiny is of our own making," reflects the attitude not only of Finance Minister Delfim Netto but also of today's military rulers and economic leaders of Brazil. This attitude is new. The economic history of Brazil strongly reflects foreign influences, both real and ideological. For centuries Brazilian economic prosperity rose and fell with the changing foreign demands for Brazilwood, sugar, rubber, and, more recently, coffee. Imported ideologies also determined the diagnoses and policy responses to Brazilian problems. While foreign influences, both real and ideological, remain, the Brazilian economic policy makers have today molded them to fit the realities of Brazilian traditions, institutions, and resources. While striving to reduce inflation, the Brazilians have cleverly exploited the residual amount as an instrument for allocating resources. They are also pursuing a pragmatic, eclectic course between liberal laissez-faire capitalism and doctrinaire communism. They have developed mechanisms to adjust promptly the major prices, that is, exchange rates, interest rates, and wage rates to reflect their respective markets; yet, they have not relied solely on the markets, but have developed planned programs for generating savings and inducing investments in priority sectors and regions. They have been successful in attracting huge inflows of private foreign investment while, at the same time, controlling and channeling these investments to meet Brazilian priorities. And, after a tragic experience with a one-sided emphasis on import substitution industrialization policies, the economic policy makers of Brazil have put protectionist and liberal trade policies each in its time and place, recognizing that excessive reliance on either may not be in the best interests of their country.

The Brazilian experience shows that a country can overcome defeatist traditions and ideologies and can develop if it applies sound economic policies to that end. It also teaches that each nation must find its own way to development, based on its own traditions, institutions, and resource base. Since all economies are not similar in these respects, there is no single grand development strategy which applies to all.

BIBLIOGRAPHY

Baer, Werner. *Industrialization and Economic Development in Brazil.* Homewood,Ill.: Richard D. Irwin, Inc., 1965.

Bergsman, Joel. *Brazil's Industrialization and Trade Policies.* New York: Oxford University Press, 1970.

_____. "Foreign Trade Policy in Brazil." Mimeographed. Washington, D.C.: Agency for International Development, February 1971.

Bittermann, Henry J. *Refunding of International Debt.* Durham, N.C.: Duke University Press, 1973.

Brothers, Dwight S., and Solis, Leopoldo M. *Mexican Financial Development.* Austin: University of Texas Press, 1966.

Campos, Roberto. *Do Outro Lado da Cerca.* Rio de Janeiro: APEC Editôra S.A., 1968.

Chenery, H.B., and Strout, A. M. "Foreign Assistance and Economic Development." *American Economic Review* 61 (1966): 679-733.

Cipollari, Pedro. "O Problema Ferroviário no Brasil." Boletim No. 52, Universidade de São Paulo, 1968.

Clark, Paul. "Brazilian Import Liberalization." Mimeographed. Williamstown, Mass.: Williams College, Center for Development Economics, 1967.

Clark, Paul, and Weisskoff, Richard. "Import Demands and Import Policies in Brazil," Mimeographed. Rio de Janeiro: Agency for International Development, 1966.

Cohen, Benjamin I., and Leff, Nathaniel. "Employment and Industrialization: Comment." *The Quarterly Journal of Economics* 81 (1967): 162-164.

Coutinho, Antônio de Abreu. "A Taxa de Juros e Mercado Financeiro." *Estudos Econômicas Brasileiros* 2 (1968).

Delfim Netto, Antônio, and Pinto, Carlos Alberto de Andrade. *O Cafe do Brasil.* São Paulo: Associação Nacional de Programação Econômica e Social, 1967.

Delfim Netto, Antônio. "Sugestôes para uma Política Cafeeira." *Revista de Ciencias Econômicas,* No.1 (March 1962): 3-56.

Delfim Netto, Antônio."O Problema do Café no Brasil." Boletim No. 5, Universidade de São Paulo, Faculdade de Ciencias Econômicas e Administrativas, 1959.

Delfim Netto, Antônio. *Planejamieto para o Desenvolvimento Econ-ômico*. São Paulo: Editôra da Universidade de São Paulo, 1966.

Donges, Juergen B. *Brazil's Trotting Peg: A New Approach to Greater Exchange Rate Flexibility in Less Developed Countries.* Washington, D.C.: American Enterprise Institute, 1971.

Economic Commission for Latin America. "Fifteen Years of Economic Policy in Brazil." *Economic Bulletin for Latin America* 9 (November 1964): 153-214.

——————. "Inflation and Growth: A Summary of Experience in Latin America." *Economic Bulletin for Latin America* 7 (February 1962).

Ellis, Howard S. "The Applicability of Certain Theories of Economic Development to Brazil." Milwaukee: University of Wisconsin, Latin American Center Essay Series, 1968.

Ellis, Howard S., ed. *The Economy of Brazil*. Berkeley: University of California Press, 1969.

Enke, Stephen, and Salera, Virgil. *International Economics*. Englewood Cliffs: Prentice-Hall, 1947.

Estados Unidos do Brasil. *Three-Year Plan for Economic and Social Development, 1963-1965*. Estado da Guanabara: Lucas, 1962.

Fishlow, Albert. "Brazilian Size Distribution of Income." *American Economic Review* 62 (May 1972): 391-402.

Furtado, Celso. *Diagnosis of the Brazilian Crisis*. Berkeley: University of California Press, 1965.

——————. *The Economic Growth of Brazil*. Berkeley: University of California Press, 1963

——————. *Development and Underdevelopment*. Berkeley: University of California Press, 1964.

Fundação Getúlio Vargas. *Conjuntura Econômica*. Rio de Janeiro, December 1964.

Gordon, Lincoln, and Grommers, Engelbert L. *United States Manufacturing Investment in Brazil: The Impact of Brazilian Government Policies, 1946-1960*. Cambridge: Harvard University Press, 1962.

Gregory, Peter. "Evolution of Industrial Wages and Wage Policy in Brazil, 1959-1967." Mimeographed. Washington, D.C.: Agency for International Development, September 1968.

Gudin, Eugenio. *Análise de Problemas Brasileiros, 1958-1964*. Rio de Janeiro: Livraria AGIR Editôra, 1965.

Herman, Louis F. "Brazil: Room to Grow." *Economic Progress of Agriculture in Developing Nations, 1950-1968*. Washington, D.C.: Department of Agriculture, Foreign Agriculture Economic Report No. 59, 1970.

Higgins, Benjamin. "The 1964-1966 Action Program of the Brazilian Government." Analytical summary prepared for the Ministry of Planning, Rio de Janeiro, 1964.

Hirschman, Albert O. *The Strategy of Economic Development.* Binghamton, N.Y.: Yale University Press, 1958.

Huddle, Donald. "Furtado on Exchange Control and Economic Development: An Evaluation and Reinterpretation of the Brazilian Case." *Economic Development and Cultural Change* 15 (April 1967): 269-285.

_____. "Notes on the Brazilian Industrialization: Sources of Growth and Structural Change, 1947-1963." Yale University, Economic Growth Center Discussion Paper No. 30, 1967.

International Monetary Fund. *International Financial Statistics.* Published monthly by International Monetary Fund, Washington, D.C.

Johnson, Robert. "Coffee Policy Considerations in Brazil." Manuscript prepared for U.S. Department of Agriculture, 1969.

Joint Brazil-United States Economic Development Commission. *The Development of Brazil.* Washington, D.C.: Institute of Inter-American Affairs, 1953.

Kafka, Alexandre. "The Brazilian Exchange Auction System." *Review of Economics and Statistics* 38 (August 1956): 308-322.

_____. "The Brazilian Stabilization Program, 1964-1966." *Journal of Political Economy* 75 (August 1967): 166-200.

_____. "The Theoretical Interpretation of Latin American Economic Development." *Economic Development for Latin America.* Edited By Howard Ellis. London: MacMillan & Co., 1967.

Kahn, Herman, and Wiener, Anthony J. *The Year 2000.* New York: Macmillan Co., 1967.

Knight, Peter. *Brazilian Agricultural Technology and Trade.* New York: Praeger, 1971.

_____. "Export Expansion, Import Substitution, and Technological Change in Brazilian Agriculture: The Case of Rio Grande do Sul." Ph.D. dissertation, Stanford University, 1970.

Kress, John I., and Rourk, Phillip J. "Story of the 1960's: Coffee in World Trade." *Economic Progress of Agriculture in Developing Nations; 1950-1968.* Washington, D.C.: Department of Agriculture, Foreign Agriculture Economic Report No. 59, 1970.

Langoni, Carlos Geraldo. "Distribuição da Renda e Desenvolvimento Econômico do Brasil." *Estudos Econômicos* 2 (1972): 5-88.

Leff, Nathaniel H. *Economic Policy-Making and Development in Brazil, 1947-1964.* New York: John Wiley & Sons, 1968.

——————. "Import Constraints and Development: Causes of the Recent Decline of Brazilian Economic Growth." *Review of Economics and Statistics* 49 (November 1967): 494-501.

Leff, Nathaniel, and Delfim Netto, Antônio. "Import Substitution, Foreign Investment, and International Disequilibrium in Brazil." *Journal of Development Studies* 2 (April 1966): 218-233.

Leite, Antônio Dias. *Caminhos do Desenvolvimento: Contribuição para um Projeto Brasileiro.* Rio de Janeiro: Zahar Editores, 1966.

Melo Filho, Murilo. *O Desafio Brasileiro.* Rio de Janeiro: Edicões Bloch, 1970.

Ministeŕrio do Planejamento e Coordena,ção Economica, *Programa de A,ção Econômica do Govêrno, 1964-1966.* Rio De Janeiro: Documentos EPEA, 1964.

Morley, Samuel A. "Inflation and Stagnation in Brazil." *Economic Development and Cultural Change* 19 (January 1971): 184-203.

Melo Filho, Murilo. *O Desafio Brasileiro.* Rio de Janeiro: Edicões Bloch, 1970.

Nelson, Richard R. "The Effective Exchange Rate: Employment and Growth in a Foreign Exchange Constrained Economy." *Journal of Political Economy* 78 (May-June 1970): 546-564.

Panagides, Stahis. "Erradicação do Café e Diversificação da Agricultura Brasileira." *Revista Brasileira Econômica* 23 (March 1969).

Patrick, Hugh T. *Financial Development and Economic Growth in Underdeveloped Countries.* New Haven: Yale University Economic Growth Center, 1966.

Robock, Stefan. "We Can Live with Inflation." *Harvard Business Review* 50 (November-December 1972): 20-44.

Schaub, John R. "Agriculture's Performance in the Developing Countries." *Economic Progress of Agriculture in Developing Nations, 1950-1958.* Washington, D.C.: Department of Agriculture, Foreign Agriculture Economic Report No. 59, 1970.

Schuh, George Edward. *The Agricultural Development of Brazil.* New York: Praeger, 1970.

Schultz. T. W. *Transforming Traditional Agriculture.* New Haven: Yale University Press, 1964.

Simonsen, Mário Henrique. *Brasil 2001.* Rio de Janeiro: APEC Editôra S.A., 1969.

——————. *Inflação: Gradualismo & Tratamento de Choque.* Rio de Janeiro: APEC Editôra S.A., 1970.

——————. "O Crecimento do Sector Publico na Economia Brasileira." *Journal do Brasil* (Rio de Janeiro), March 15, 1968.

Sirkin, Irving. "Fighting Inflation in Brazil: Some Tentative Lessons." *Finance and Development* 5 (September 1968): 38.

Skidmore, Thomas E. *Politics in Brazil, 1930-1964: An Experiment in Democracy*. New York: Oxford University Press, 1967.

Smithies, Arthur. "Economic Welfare and Policy." *Economics and Public Policy*. Washington, D.C.: The Brookings Institution, 1955.

_____. "Inflation and Development in Latin America." *Public Policy*. Washington, D.C.: The Brookings Institution, 1964.

Syvrud, Donald E. "Estructura e Politica de Juros No Brasil 1960/70." *Revista Brasileira de Economia* 26 (January-March 1972): 117-139.

Tendler, Judith. "Agricultural Credit in Brazil." Mimeographed. Washington, D.C.: Agency for International Development, 1969.

Urquidi, Victor L. *Fiscal Policy for Economic Growth in Latin America*. Baltimore: The Johns Hopkins Press, 1965.

INDEX

Abreu Coutinho, Antônio de, 95
Accounts Data, National, 269
aceites cambiais, 112
Action Program, 28-29, 38-51, 73-74, 81, 128, 131, 140, 205; Law 4131,
    115, 187n, 190, 193, 203-4, 211; wages and, 155-56; foreign trade and,
    187-88, 199; and agriculture, 229, 249
Act of Paris, 187
Agrarian Reform Law, 230
Agricultural Credit Law, 143
agricultural credit program, 143, 253, 257, 262-64, 268, 270, 271n
Agricultural Development Fund, 254
agriculture, 216-39; pricing for, 7, 11, 20, 21, 65, 190; credit policies for, 7,
    11, 20, 48, 60, 65, 79-80, 92, 97, 107, 111, 115; investment in, 9, 11,
    41, 48, 49, 57, 126, 131, 178-79, 262-64, reform in, 9, 22, 25, 41, 217-18,
    225, 229, 230; in industrialization, 13, 15, 16, 24, 30, 37; output of,
    16-17, 24-25, 31, 32, 39-41, 216-31 *passim*, 238-39, 262; imbalance with
    industry, 21, 28, 30, 50, 120-21, 216-19, 224-25; income distribution
    and, 24-25, 37, 38, 41, 55; minimum price programs, 48, 61-65, 76-80,
    143, 155, 217, 219, 229-32, 236, 238-39, 250, 253; and fiscal policies,
    118, 142; wages and, 150, 154-55, 159, 163-64; exports from, 177, 198,
    206, 223; subsidies to, 217, 229, 231, 235-39, 245, 253, 263; mentioned,
    39, 52
—noncoffee: prices for, 20, 21, 229-32; exports of, 174-75, 177, 180, 196,
    198, 214, 223, 228, 237-38, 241, 244-45, 249, 251; output of, 221-22,
    224, 237, 243, 244, 251-53; incentives for, 240, 241, 249-50. *See also*
    by crop
Agriculture, Fund for the Modernization of, 246
AID, 73, 187, 205, 206, 207, 214
Alliance for Progress, 206
Amazon, the, 137
Amazonas, Brazil, 23, 24
Argentina, 221n, 222, 223
army, *see* military, the
Article 34-18 incentives, 261-62, 264, 268, 269
austerity measures, 5, 7, 29, 34, 58

Baer, Werner, 28n
balanced growth strategy, 10, 11, 37-38, 46-50, 53, 55-58, 119, 128, 132
balance of payments, 9-10, 105, 118, 185-87, 189, 213, 215, 244;
    exchange rate and, 14, 196; in disequilibrium system, 16, 22, 28-30, 37,
    167-68, 179-81; deficit in, 34, 39, 46, 82, 180-85; surplus in, 52-53,
    57, 78, 79, 196, 211; import policy and, 170-71, 201; and foreign
    investment, 179, 206. *See also* current accounts; foreign debt

Banking Law of 1964, 63, 74

Bank of Brazil, 33, 35, 60-63, 66, 134, 141-44, 264; foreign exchange department, 61-62, 75, 197; private credit and, 68-86 *passim*, 90, 91; interest rates of, 96-101, 103, 107; and federal spending, 119, 129, 134, 135; foreign trade and, 184n, 197; agricultural credit from, 231-33, 235-36, 263, 270, 271n; Coffee Defense Fund and, 245n, 246, 254

Bank of the Northeast, 36, 48, 61, 73, 141-42, 219, 261-62, 263

bankruptcy: of Brazil, 12, 21, 29-30, 182, 216; of businesses, 34, 43, 57, 92, 103, 109; of banks, 135-36

banks, 42-43, 60-61, 102, 259; central, 63, 74-76; commercial, 63, 82-103 *passim*, 107-17, 183-84, 192, 232-36, 258, 263, 271n; state, 69, 135-36, 138, 142; investment, 110, 112, 114, 192, 265. *See also* reserves *and banks by name*

beef, 221n, 222n, 224, 229, 243

Beltrão, Helio, 35

Bergsman, Joel, 173, 176-77, 201

Bernstein, Edward, 165-66

Bilateral Consolidation Agreement, 187

Biolchini, Luiz, 33, 75

black market, 114, 179

BNB, *see* Bank of the Northeast

BNDE, *see* National Economic Development Bank

Branco, Castello, 4-7, 10, 27-59, 90-92, 144, 257-58, 261; monetary policies of, 72-79, 109; fiscal policy of, 126, 128-31, 140, 142; wage policy of, 147, 155, 157, 160-61; foreign trade under, 168, 187-89, 197, 201, 206, 214; and agriculture, 217, 230, 233, 236, 238, 262-63; on coffee, 241, 249, 251, 254

Brasilia, Brazil, 2, 7, 14, 121n; District of, 24

Brazil-United States commissions, joint, 14, 29, 34

Brazilian Coffee Institute, 61, 75, 77, 85-86, 142, 242, 245n, 246, 250, 254

Bretton Woods institutions, 74

Brito Lyra, Germano de, 35

Bulhões, Octavio, 4-6, 31, 33, 37, 55, 106-7, 129n, 135-36, 144-45, 264; monetary policies of, 62, 63, 72, 75, 82; foreign trade and, 185, 200

Burger, Ary, 36, 234

caixas econômicas, 259

Campos, Roberto, 4-6, 18, 29-38 *passim*, 55, 144-45, 156, 230, 264; monetary policies of, 75, 82, 109, 114; foreign trade under, 185, 200

Candal, Arthur, 176

capital market: development program, 11, 257, 264-70; investment incentives, 126, 131, 142, 143

Capital Markets Law, 106n, 142, 264

Castro Magalhães, Rui de, 75

Central Bank, 33, 35-36, 60-61, 63, 68, 69, 73-75, 136; Board of, 75; foreign trade and, 78, 87-88, 142, 191, 210, 211n; Resolution 63, 99, 101, 110-12, 115, 190, 192-93, 204-11 *passim*, 265-66, 269; other resolutions, 106n, 108n, 110n, 111, 112, 116, 136n, 200, 233n, 234,

259n; interest rates and, 113; and agriculture, 234, 263
centralized planning, 6, 37, 139
Chagas Nogueira, Denio, 33
Cibrazem, 142
Cipollari, Pédro, 153
clubs, private, 104-5
cocoa, 60, 69, 142, 174, 188, 228
coffee, 1, 2, 214, 226, 240-55, 275; production of, 20, 21, 30, 31, 240-51
    passim; stockpile of, 30, 33, 77, 155, 180, 240-41, 245-46, 249-50, 255;
    credit policy and, 61, 63-65, 69, 76-77, 79-80, 82-86, 90-91; exports of,
    77, 172-76, 180, 185-87, 190, 198, 228, 240-54 *passim*; income from,
    77, 246-47; and noncoffee agriculture, 218, 219, 232, 237, 240;
    eradication of, 245n, 249-50, 251
Coffee Defense Fund, 64, 77, 245-47, 251, 254
Coffee Eradication Program, 249-50, 251
coffee pricing, 11, 20, 52, 56, 60, 142, 246, 253; under Quadros, 15, 246;
    under Costa e Silva, 46, 86; support of, 77, 244-54 *passim*; foreign trade
    and, 173-76, 180, 185-87, 190, 198, 245-46; under Branco, 249, 251
Cohen, Benjamin I., 163-64
Colombia, 221n
commercial arrears, 183-84, 186, 205
commodity purchase program, 80, 83
compensatory financing, 205, 206, 208, 210, 211
Congress (national), 152, 153, 200
Constitution (1945), 125, 136, 137; (1967), 106, 136n, 197
construction industry, 54, 83, 105,'257, 268; housing, 7, 118, 143, 260;
    highway, 15, 219, 227, 238
consumer goods, 43, 52, 56, 57, 102, 109, 114, 169n, 199
Costa e Silva, Marshall, 5, 35-36, 44-45, 75, 111, 158; monetary policies of,
    81-83, 90; foreign trade under, 188, 192, 201; coffee and, 251, 254
cost-push inflation factors, 45-46, 71, 81, 89-90, 152, 154; interest rates
    and, 96, 111, 113, 114
cotton, 69, 228, 230, 231, 249, 251
credit policy, 7, 21, 34-35, 44, 46, 73, 231; for agriculture, 48, 61, 219,
    231-36, 238, 250, 263-64, 271n; stabilization and, 45, 51, 56; for private
    sector, 55-58, 61, 65-85, 90-95; rationing, 59-60, 92, 94; nationalization of, 71
crops, alternative, *see* agriculture, noncoffee
current accounts, 13, 105, 181, 199, 201, 202, 215, 257n; deficit in, 21-22,
    49, 167-68, 214n; surplus in, 79, 85, 199-201, 210, 214, 257. *See also*
    foreign savings
CVRD, 60

Dantas, San Tiago, 18, 185, 224-25
debt rescheduling, 22, 118, 167, 173, 179, 182, 184-85, 187, 205
Decree Laws, 134, 264
deficit, 52, 76, 78, 111, 119-20, 133-35, 184n, 251; financing of, 33, 59,
    76, 78, 119, 133-35; fiscal policy and, 128-38 *passim*, 144. *See also*
    balance of payments

Delfim Netto, Antônio, 1, 5, 10, 31, 35-36, 44-45, 55, 92, 240, 267, 274;
    monetary policies of, 59, 72, 79-83, 85-86; interest rates under, 111,
    114, 117; fiscal policies of, 136, 137; wages under, 158; foreign trade
    under, 170, 193-94; coffee and, 246, 250
demand deposits, 65, 70
Development Bank of the Northeast, 144
"disequilibrium system," 16, 168-86, 213
DL-157 funds, 264-65, 266
dualism: of economy, 13, 16, 30, 54; of agriculture, 239

Economic Commission for Latin America, United Nations, 6, 12, 14, 18,
    27, 40, 184n
economic efficiency, 13, 38, 42, 118, 128
educational opportunities, 8-9, 13, 31
Elektrobras, 60
Emergency Tax Reform Law, 106n
Enke, Stephen, 189
equilibrium strategy, 52-54, 187-98, 213, 215
Espirito Santos, Brazil, 23, 24
"Estado Novo" period, 147
Europe, 2, 41, 141, 185, 187, 212, 213
exchange auction system, 169-70, 173, 180, 218
exchange rates: pre-revolution, 7, 15, 22, 172, 174; guarantee, 22, 78, 110,
    142, 182, 184n, 188, 190, 193, 197; under Costa e Silva, 46; trotting
    peg, 46, 56, 86, 110, 168, 193-96, 215, 253; under Branco, 47, 48, 56,
    168, 187-98; correction option, 108, 134; agriculture and, 217, 229, 235,
    238, 243-46, 250, 262; mentioned, 42, 51, 213, 215, 275
—overvalued, 14, 15, 20, 21, 25, 118, 180, 214, 226; as crisis cause, 29, 178;
    foreign savings and, 167; and trade policies, 169, 172-73, 174; agriculture
    and, 218, 219n, 223, 243-46
—devaluation of, 45, 52, 110, 115, 168, 174, 214-15, 256; annual, 86,
    189-92, 196, 203n; agriculture and, 235, 243, 245
Exchange Stabilization Fund, 187
expenditure policy, federal, 4, 6, 27, 31, 47-48, 119-31 passim, 140-41, 227.
    See also subsidies
Export Import Bank (Eximbank), 183-84, 187, 205-6, 207, 210, 214
exports, 7, 38, 115, 126, 138, 142, 186, 211, 213; promotion of, 5, 41, 47,
    48, 53-54, 168, 210, 214-15; expansion of, 9, 187, 196-99, 213-15, 257;
    industrialization and, 13, 16, 37; and exchange rate, 20, 21, 196; credit
    for, 60, 73, 92; taxes on, 132, 138; agricultural restrictions, 154-55,
    206, 217, 219n, 220, 223, 229, 238; stagnant, 154, 173-79, 186, 218;
    foreign savings and, 167, 257; noncoffee, 174, 175, 177, 180, 196, 198,
    214, 223, 228, 237-38, 245, 249, 251. See also under coffee

Faraco, Daniel, 75
Federal Electricity Fund, 125
Federal Public Service, 155

Federal Savings Bank, 267
Federal Savings Institutions, 141-42
fertilizer, 217, 220, 229, 235-38, 253
Filho, Café, 147
FINAME, 265, 266, 269
finance companies, 42-43, 98-100, 102, 109-16, 258, 265
Finance Ministry, 60, 73, 74, 129, 134
financial intermediation, 42-43, 71-72, 100, 102, 113, 258-59
fiscal incentives, 6, 125, 187, 203, 237, 261-62; for industry, 118, 124-26,
     128, 131, 132, 142-43
fiscal policies, 11, 128-39, 143-45; defined, 60
Fishlow, Albert, 26
food: prices, 43, 52, 83, 217; export, 154-55, 206, 217, 219n; supply,
     225-32 *passim*, 238, 245, 249
foreign debts, 3, 16, 21-22, 29, 41, 142, 182-87, 206-11, 245, 257, 272;
     rescheduling of, 22, 118, 167, 173, 179, 182, 184-85, 187, 205;
     restructuring of, 53-54, 168; service burden, 167, 182-83, 185, 209-12,
     214, 226, 257n, 265
foreign exchange: policies, 11, 14, 22, 61-62, 65, 167-215; reserves, 47, 52-53,
     59, 63, 83, 168, 182, 191-92, 196, 200, 209, 211-13; primary reserve
     money and, 76, 78, 84-87, 90, 91; inflows, 83, 104, 105, 155
foreign investment, 1-2, 21, 85, 92, 142, 178-80, 196, 201-5, 213, 275;
     nationalism and, 5-6, 16, 92, 192, 201; industrialization and, 16, 167,
     170-71, 176, 226; under Action Program, 41, 48, 53-54, 57, 187, 193;
     credit for, 72, 110, 115-16, 176
foreign savings, 11, 167-68, 200, 201, 213-15, 257, 265, 272-73; reliance on,
     21, 29, 265, 272; under Branco, 48, 49
foreign trade, 21, 28, 32-33, 45, 91, 142, 180; protectionism, 5-6, 10, 14,
     21, 27, 37-38, 168-70, 187, 201, 275; policies, 9-11, 14, 167-215.
     See also balance of payments; exchange rates; exports; imports
France, 187, 213
Franco, Aldo, 75
Freyre, Gilberto, 165
fringe benefits, 151-52, 153, 159, 160, 164
FUNAGRI, 234
Fund for the Financial Promotion of the Use of Fertilizers and Mineral
     Supplements (FUNFERTIL), 236
Furtado, Celso, 12, 18, 27-28, 33, 167, 218, 224-25, 244

Galveas, Ernani, 35, 87
Garrido Torres, José, 33, 75
GECRI, 234n
General Agreement on Tariffs and Trade (GATT), 213
Germany, 2, 187
Getúlio Vargas Foundation, 33, 220n
gold clause law, 96n

Gordon-Grommers study, 150, 176n
Goulart, João, 3, 22, 27, 30, 40-41, 57, 129n, 273-74; wages under, 146,
    147n, 151, 155; foreign trade under, 163, 173, 176, 179, 185, 187, 201;
    and agriculture, 217, 218, 230
government bonds, 79, 80, 83, 107, 116-17, 132, 233; ORTN, 87-88, 101,
    103, 106-8, 111, 133-36
gradualism, 42-44, 45, 47, 55-56, 106, 156
Greece, 141
Gregory, Peter, 150-52, 154n, 159, 161, 164, 166
gross national product, 16, 17, 50, 80, 83, 85, 90-91, 131
growth rate, 2-3, 8-10, 12, 16, 19, 37, 94, 144; import substitution program
    and, 29-30; under Branco, 39, 49, 50; wages and, 163
Guanabara, 19, 23, 24, 138; state bank of, 135. See also Rio de Janeiro (city)
Gudin, Eugenio, 146, 152-53, 178

Hague Club, the, 185, 187
Higgings, Benjamin, 173
highway construction, 15, 219, 227, 238
Highway Construction Fund, 125
Highways Department, National, 120
Highway System, National, 60
housing, 9, 107, 162, 227, 257-58; construction, 7, 118, 143, 260; programs,
    11, 34, 38, 47-48, 57, 165, 257-60; inflation and, 13, 16, 20, 21, 31,
    32; and industrialization 13, 26, 27; under Branco, 34, 38, 40, 41, 49,
    52; interest rates and, 105, 107
Housing Bank, 36, 47

IBC, 61, 75, 77, 85-86, 142, 242, 245n, 246, 250, 254
IBRD, 73, 205, 214
ICM, 197
IDB, 206, 207, 210, 214
IFC, 205, 207
Ilheus, Brazil, 154
IMF, see International Monetary Fund
imports, 167-72, 180, 188, 192, 226, 228, 247-48; restrictions on, 14, 15,
    29, 142, 168-70, 172-73, 180, 189; licensing system for, 169, 180;
    liberalization of, 199-214. See also tariffs
import substitution industrialization, 3, 8-31 passim, 37, 38, 40, 275; foreign
    trade and, 170-71, 177, 180, 197; agriculture and, 219n
income, per capita, 1, 3, 23-26, 220, 226n
income distribution, 4, 12, 13, 16, 28, 138, 225, 229; economic growth and,
    8-9, 37, 58; import substitution industrialization and, 8, 22-27, 30; under
    Branco, 34, 37-40, 54-55, 58, 128; fiscal policy and, 118, 132; and wage
    policy, 162, 166; coffee policy and, 241, 243, 249
index bond, 133
India, 2, 221n
industrialization, 12-16, 31, 34, 104, 163, 225-28; effects of, 13, 21-30

passim, 37, 273, 274; foreign trade and, 168-72, 176, 178, 200-201.
    See also import substitution industrialization
industry: investment in, 7, 9, 15, 32, 143, 167, 170, 201, 226; wages for,
    9, 150-51, 159-61, 163-64; growth of, 12-13, 81, 92, 118; output from,
    16-18, 24-25, 28, 30, 51-52, 56, 102, 109, 258; recession in, 17-18, 49,
    52, 79-82; agriculture and, 21, 28, 30, 50, 120-21, 216-19, 224-25;
    subsidy for, 115, 172; mentioned, 20, 27-28, 55, 72, 104
inflation, 2-16 *passim*, 18-21, 51, 82-83, 88-94, 100, 105; hyper-, 12, 16,
    18, 21, 28, 134, 144, 155, 216, 257; under Branco, 36-37, 42-44, 79-80;
    cost-push factors in, 45-46, 71, 81, 89-90, 96, 111, 113-14, 152, 154;
    corrective, 51-53, 89, 94; fiscal policy for, 118-45; wages and, 152, 155,
    163, 165; agriculture and, 190, 215, 217, 219, 240-55
Institutional Act No. 5, 137
Instruction 289 transactions, 110, 142, 190-93, 203-4, 208, 211. *See also*
    SUMOC
Inter-American Development Bank (IDB), 206, 207, 210, 214
interest rates, 11, 15-16, 20, 80, 95-117, 136, 191, 272, 275; negative, 20,
    62, 96, 100, 107, 114-15, 134, 231n; stabilization and, 42-43, 45-46,
    51, 56; ceilings on, 46, 52, 87, 107, 108, 111-16, 235; credit policy and,
    68-69, 72, 86, 88, 95-117; for agriculture, 233-36, 263
interior: thrust to, 14, 31, 219, 230, 238; migration to, 24, 224; minister
    of, 60-61, 143
Interministerial Price Commission, 46
International Coffee Agreement, 251n, 255
International Finance Corp. (IFC), 205, 207
International Monetary Fund (IMF), 18, 19, 36, 41-42, 51, 73, 136; foreign
    trade and, 182, 184-87, 206, 208, 211n, 212, 213
investment, 9-11, 27-29, 125, 163, 196, 201, 275; government and, 7, 121-22,
    140, 141, 271; in priority sectors, 11, 115, 126, 128, 143, 145, 215,
    237-38, 254-64 *passim*, 271; under Branco, 35, 39-41, 48-49, 56, 57;
    credit policy and, 72, 80, 94; taxes and, 119, 123, 127-28, 137, 264;
    private, 128, 257, 264; in industry, 118, 226, 258, 264; in coffee, 241,
    245, 254; domestic savings and, 268-71. *See also* foreign investments
Investment Guarantee Agreement, 142, 203
IPI, 197
iron, 1, 60, 141, 142, 143
Italy, 2, 187

Japan, 2, 185, 187, 220, 221, 222, 223
Jost, Nestor, 35

Kahn, Herman, 8
Keynesian economics, 31, 144
Knight, Peter, 221-22, 236
Korean War boom, 175-76, 179-80, 228
Kubitschek government, 3, 14, 18, 22, 29-30, 33, 91, 147, 273-74; interior
    thrust of, 7, 8, 227; foreign trade under, 78, 131, 179

labor, 142, 158-59; productivity, 9, 15, 20, 154-56, 161-63, 166; unions,
    142, 147; wages, 146-66; courts, 147, 152, 154; supply, 151, 225-27, 229
laissez-faire school of economics, 4, 275
land reform, 9, 25, 41, 217-18, 225, 229, 230
Latin America, 1, 2, 176-78, 197, 221, 223, 224. *See also by country*
Law 4131, 115, 187n, 190, 193, 203-4, 211
Law of similars, 170
"Law of Two-thirds," 161
Leff, Nathaniel H., 163-64, 170, 172n, 177
Leme, Ruy Aguiar da Silva, 35, 87
letras de cambio, 67, 72, 97, 99, 101-4, 108-16 *passim*
letras imobiliárias, 103, 259
Linder, Harold, 205
livestock, 221, 228. *See also* meat

Mannesman case, 109, 114
Maranhão, Brazil, 24, 137
Marques Vianna, Helio, 35
Mato Grosso, Brazil, 7, 24
meat, 220, 221, 222n, 224, 228, 229, 243
Médici, Emílio Garrastazv, 8, 36, 262, 267
Melo Filho, Murilo, 8
Merchant Marine, 120
Mexico, 119n, 141, 220-23
migration: to cities, 23-24, 55, 121, 218, 226-27; to interior, 24, 224, 227
military, the: in government, 3, 4, 34; salaries of, 42, 44, 129, 155
Minas Gerais, Brazil, 23, 24, 238; state bank of, 135
minimum price programs, 48, 61-65, 76-80, 143, 155, 217, 219, 229-32,
    236, 238-39, 250, 253
minimum wage, 146-52, 154-56, 159, 160, 163
monetarism, 5-6, 42, 44, 274
monetary correction, 105-10, 113, 116-17, 133-34, 136, 267; in agricultural
    pricing, 230, 233; in housing program, 258, 259
monetary policies, 11, 44, 59-94, 142; defined, 60
money: creation of, 19-20, 47; income velocity of, 65, 79, 82, 83, 89;
    supply, 65-67, 73-74, 76, 80, 83-85, 89-91, 119, 170
Money and Credit, Superintendency of, *see* SUMOC
Moraes, Marcus Vinicius Pratini de, 36
Moraes Barros, Luiz de, 33, 75

National Economic Council, 147n
National Economic Development Bank, 7, 33, 60-62, 73, 141-44, 219, 264,
    268, 270, 271n; interest rates of, 96, 98, 115; tax use by, 125; FINAME,
    265n
National Housing Bank, 7, 47, 98, 141-42, 143, 161, 258-60
National Housing Program, 7, 11, 47-48, 73, 107, 143, 257-60, 268-70

nationalism, 5-6, 16, 92, 192, 201
nationalization, 72, 92, 129, 140, 142, 193
National Monetary Budget, 63-64
National Monetary Council, 7, 60-63, 73, 74-75, 108, 156-57, 234, 253
National Readjustable Treasure Bonds, *see* ORTN
Naval Fund, 125
Netherlands, the, 187
newsprint, 169, 172, 188
Nogueira, Denio, 75, 87, 114
Northeast, 29, 137-38, 143, 148, 230, 237; under Kubitschek, 22-24;
    under Action Program, 41, 46-49, 54-55, 57; tax incentives for,
    126, 131, 261
Northeast, Superintendent for Development of the, *see* SUDENE
Northeast Development Agency, 120
Northeast Development Program, 7, 11, 33-34, 37, 48, 49, 52, 73, 257,
    260-62, 268-70

oil, 15, 60, 61, 141, 142, 143, 169; Petrobrás, 35, 60, 125, 142
open market operations, 68, 87, 91, 192
Operation Tupiquiniquin, 87
ORTN, 87-88, 101, 103, 106-8, 111, 133-36
output, per capita, 39, 127-28, 144; credit policy and, 72, 85, 91; agricultural,
    221, 229, 237

Para, Brazil, 23, 24
parallel market, 114, 179
Parana, Brazil, 24, 224, 245, 253
Participation Fund for States and Municipalities, 83, 136-39. *See also*
    revenue sharing plan
paternalism, 37, 165, 227
Patrick, Hugh T., 256
Paulo Velloso, João, 8
Pereira Lira, Paulo, 36, 210-11
personnel expenditures, 120, 121, 129, 131, 132, 161, 163. *See also* wage
    policies
Petrobrás, 35, 60, 125, 142
petroleum products, 21, 60, 172, 188. *See also* oil
Piauí, Brazil, 24, 137
Planning Institute, 8
Planning Ministry, 18, 61
population, 1, 2-3, 17, 137
Portaria, 71, 126
Port Fund, National, 125
Port of Santos, Brazil, 153, 154
Portugal, 141
power supply, 1, 14, 15, 29, 60, 141, 143, 261

Prebisch, Raul, 14; doctrine of, 197, 243
price control, 6-7, 15, 20-21, 33, 37-38, 42-43, 46, 60, 75, 95; for agriculture,
    20, 154-55, 219-20, 228-29, 238, 250, 262; under Branco, 41, 48, 79,
    122, 262; interest rates and, 113-15. *See also* coffee pricing; minimum
    price programs
price stability, 13, 20-21, 30-31, 33, 51, 88, 258; general price index, 19,
    79, 82-85, 107-8, 126, 131, 134, 196; under Action Program, 39, 41-51
    passim, 56, 79, 128; under Costa e Silva, 44-46, 85; fiscal policy and,
    118, 129, 144; of coffee, 255
primary reserve money, 63, 64, 74-94 *passim*
private sector, 5, 6, 14, 21, 38, 45, 125, 142; credit, 20, 44, 55-61, 65-72,
    74, 78-82, 84-85, 90-95, 142-44, 154, 165; investments and, 40, 41, 49,
    50, 142, 257, 261-62, 271-72; under Branco, 42, 44, 65-72, 74, 78-80,
    90-95, 140, 142; wages for, 44, 148-53, 155-61, 165; savings, 80, 257
Profit Remittance Law, 57, 176, 179, 187, 201, 203
protectionism, 5, 10, 14, 21, 27, 37, 168-70, 187, 201, 275. *See also* tariffs
Public Debt, Office of the, 87n
public sector, 5, 11, 14, 21, 37, 45, 59, 127; expenditures by, 4, 6, 27, 31,
    47-48, 119-31 *passim,* 140-41, 227; investments, 14, 40, 41, 49, 50, 56,
    121-22, 128, 271; under Branco, 42-44, 57, 90, 142; wages for, 42, 44,
    129, 152-55, 157, 161, 163; credit policy for, 55, 65-67, 74-78; under
    Costa e Silva, 81-84, 90; fiscal policy for, 119, 139-43. *See also* subsidies
public utilities, 20, 31, 42-43, 75, 83, 89, 121, 129, 141
purchasing power parity concept, 189, 215

Quadros government, 3, 15, 22, 30, 34, 184-85, 245, 273-74; foreign trade
    under, 169, 173
Queiroz, José Vilar de, 200
Queiroz Committee, 200

railroads, state, 120
real estate, 103, 104
Real Estate Credit Societies, 258-59
recession, 13, 27; in industrial sector, 49, 52, 79-82
rediscount, 62, 74, 83, 86, 135; rates, 68-69; for agriculture, 231, 234
rental controls, 20, 43, 52, 56, 83, 94, 154, 257-58
reserves: foreign exchange, 47, 52-53, 59, 63, 83, 168, 182, 191-92, 196,
    200, 209, 211-13; of commercial banks, 62-63, 68-74 *passim,* 78-82,
    86-87, 111, 116, 134, 154, 232-33, 263; primary, 63, 64, 74-94 *passim*;
    secondary, 88, 116
Resolution 63 transaction, 99, 101, 110-11, 192-93
revenue sharing program, 7, 82, 125, 132, 136-39, 143
revenue system, *see* tax structure
revolution of 1964, 3, 8-9, 22, 31, 62, 207
Ribeiro, Casimiro, 33, 75, 109
rice, 52, 77-78, 79, 222, 224, 230, 231, 249, 251
Rio de Janeiro: city, 19, 23-24, 26, 29, 55, 104, 148-49, 227n; federal
    district, 23, 138; state, 23, 24

Rio Grande do Sul, Brazil, 221-22, 224, 236, 238
road building program, 15, 219, 227, 238
Robertson, Sir Dennis, 152
rubber, 2, 61, 275
Rural and Industrial Credit, Office of Coordination of, 234n
Rural Credit, National Coordination Commission for, 234
Rural Credit Law, 73, 233-34, 263
rural credit program, 48, 217, 219, 231-35, 236, 239, 263-64

salaries, *see* wage policies
Salera, Virgil, 189
São Paulo, Brazil, 5, 29, 48, 163, 226, 243n; state, 22-24, 35, 55, 138, 238,
    251-53; state bank of, 135
São Paulo, University of, 5
savings, 7, 80, 103, 104, 164, 256-75; inflation and, 9, 19, 20, 27, 28, 40;
    for priority investment, 11, 41, 94, 256, 260; real, 15, 18, 161-62; for
    industrial growth, 20, 219, 226; under Branco, 40, 41, 47-49, 53, 128;
    compulsory, 49, 161-63, 257, 260, 262, 267, 271; induced, 49, 260,
    261-62; private sector, 80, 257; interest rates and, 100, 101, 105; forced,
    128, 263, 271; fiscal policy and, 143; wages and, 147, 161-62; and foreign
    trade, 167, 171, 210, 267; agriculture and, 219, 262-64. *See also*
    foreign savings
savings and loan institutions, 258-59
Schultz, T. W., 216
service sector, 16, 17, 25, 52, 55, 150, 159, 163, 219, 225-27
shipping rates, 121
Simonsen, Mário, 8, 82-83, 96n, 100, 102n, 113
Smithies, Arthur, 163
Social Fund, 125
Social Integration, Fund for, 165
social integration program, 257, 265-71
social objectives, 6, 8-9, 13, 26-27, 34, 37-40, 45, 51
social security system, 60, 75, 120-28 *passim*, 146, 165
south-central industrial region, 22-23, 26, 118, 137-38, 239, 243, 261
Spain, 141
Special Fund, 137, 138, 139
stabilization, 5, 29, 88-89, 126, 133, 217, 225, 274; monetarism *vs.*
    structuralism, 5-6, 42, 44, 274; under Branco, 7, 41-59, 73, 91-92; under
    Kubitschek, 18-22; under Quadros, 34, 184n; under Costa e Silva, 44-46,
    55, 81; interest rates and, 95, 102, 104, 114
stabilizers, automatic, 118, 123, 126-27
stagnation, 3, 20, 21, 80, 91, 126; stabilization and, 5, 34, 45; industrialization
    and, 13, 16, 17, 29; interest rates and, 105; and wages, 155; foreign trade
    and, 167, 199; in agriculture, 216, 220-24
state bonds, 136, 138
states, 22-24, 28, 153, 224. *See also by name*
steel, 15, 60, 120, 141, 143

stockpiling, 231; of coffee, 30, 33, 77, 155, 180, 240-41, 245-46, 249-50, 255
structuralism, 5-6, 42, 44, 274
subsidies, 46, 92, 110-15, 120-22, 140, 169, 178, 188; industrial, 13, 172, 226;
    to transportation, 44, 120, 121, 129-31; input subsidy program, 217, 229,
    239; agricultural, 231, 235-36, 238, 245, 253, 263
SUDENE, 261
sugar, 1, 2, 60, 61, 64, 142, 188, 228, 275
SUMOC, 33, 62, 63, 74, 169, 173, 261; Council of, 60, 62, 63; Instructions,
    110, 142, 178-79, 188n, 190-93, 197, 203-4, 208, 211
swap transactions, 22, 78, 167, 179, 182, 184, 186, 191, 203-4
Switzerland, 187

Target Plan, 14, 18
Target Program, 14, 29, 34, 91
Tariff Law (1957), 173
Tariff Reform (1957), 179
tariffs, 75, 169, 199-201, 213-15, 235, 237, 256-57; protective, 7, 15, 32,
    118, 131, 142, 143, 168-70, 187
tax structure, 4, 6, 43, 87, 119, 123-28, 131, 261, 264; policy of, 15, 56,
    82, 131-33, 142, 143, revenues from, 19-20, 37, 45, 118, 123-24, 126,
    130-33, 136-38; enforcement of, 44, 126, 131, 261; delayed payment,
    72, 82, 106, 127, 133; value-added, 82, 124, 133, 136, 137, 197, 237,
    267; income, 119, 124, 131, 197, 267
Three-Year Plan, 1963-1965, 18, 27, 149, 216
time deposits, 67, 70, 72, 84, 103, 265, 266
Transamazonica Highway Project, 8, 267
transportation, 29, 141, 227, 238; subsidies to, 44, 120, 121, 129-31, 132;
    salaries in, 152-54, 163; agriculture and, 219, 224
Treasury, 60, 69, 75-80 passim, 85, 106, 138, 254; loans to, 61-69 passim,
    79, 83, 134; bills, 88, 115, 116
Trinidade, Mário, 36, 47
Turkey, 141

unemployment, 3, 8, 28, 31, 105, 165, 227, 257; industrialization and, 8,
    13, 15, 26-27; in stabilization, 18, 43, 54; under Action Program, 34, 39,
    40, 43, 54; under Costa e Silva, 45, 85; fiscal policy and, 118, 120-21,
    129, 132, 144; and wages, 151, 162; agriculture and, 225-27, 243
United Kingdom, 187, 213
United States, 68, 87n, 108, 142, 176, 194-95, 212, 222, 228; joint
    commissions, 14, 29, 34; AID, 73, 187, 205, 206, 207, 214; taxes
    compared, 124, 127; Eximbank, 183-84, 187, 205-7, 210, 214; trade
    with Brazil, 185, 187, 189, 203, 213, 272; USDA, 220, 221, 254-55
urbanization, 23-24, 26, 55, 121, 218, 226-28
usury law, 20, 68, 96, 99-100, 104-9 passim, 116, 133-34
utility rates, see public utilities

Vale do Rio Doce, 142

Vargas, Getúlio, 146, 147, 165, 244
Velloso, João Paulo dos Reis, 36
Vidigal, Gastão, 75

Wage Policy Council, National, 155, 162
wage policies, 11, 20, 42, 146-66, 190, 243n, 275; military and, 42, 44, 129, 155; of Action Program, 42, 44, 155-59, 162, 165; and stabilization, 45, 51, 54; interest rates and, 113, 114-15; government expenditures and, 120, 121, 129-32, 161, 163; minimum, 146-52, 154-56, 159, 160, 163; real, 162-66
wheat, 21, 60-61, 64, 142, 169, 172-73, 188, 220n, 222-28 *passim*
Woods, George, 1
workers' funds, 47, 49, 132, 143, 161, 258-60
work incentives, 146, 164
World Bank, 1, 183, 205, 207, 210
World War II, 179-80, 182

Year 2000, The, 8